War under Heaven

War under Heaven

Pontiac, the Indian Nations, & the British Empire

GREGORY EVANS DOWD

WITHDRAWN

The Johns Hopkins University Press
Baltimore & London

© 2002 The Johns Hopkins University Press
All rights reserved. Published 2002
Printed in the United States of America on acid-free paper
2 4 6 8 9 7 5 3 1

The Johns Hopkins University Press
2715 North Charles Street
Baltimore, Maryland 21218-4363
www.press.jhu.edu

Library of Congress Cataloging-in-Publication Data
Dowd, Gregory Evans, 1956–
War under heaven : Pontiac, the Indian Nations, and the British Empire /
Gregory Evans Dowd.
p. cm.
Includes bibliographical references and index.
ISBN 0-8018-7079-8 (hard : alk. paper)
1. Pontiac's Conspiracy, 1763–1765. 2. Pontiac, Ottawa Chief, d. 1769.
3. Indians of North America—Wars—1750–1815. 4. Indians of North America—
Ethnic identity. 5. Nativistic movements—United States—History—18th century.
6. United States—History—Colonial period, ca. 1600–1775.
7. Great Britain—Colonies—America. I. Title.
E83.76 .D69 2002
973.2′7—dc21
2002000596

A catalog record for this book is available from the British Library.

*For Ada
and Catrin*

"The Romans were triflers to us."

—HORACE WALPOLE, 1763

*"Cultivate peace between your different Tribes,
that they may become one great people."*

—THE TROUT (OTTAWA), 1807

Contents

Illustrations

Figures

Maps

Acknowledgments

Somewhere there must be historians who "write up their research" in the relative isolation of a study, with long days to dwell on their work. Leading the contemplative life of the scholar, they work alone. Perhaps they have butlers and oak panels; some might even have clean desks, with tea on the tray. I am not one of these historians, nor would I want to be. I have worked with higher privileges. To be sure, I have a study of sorts, an office at work (with an open door, interminable e-mail, and a pesky telephone), and a teapot. I may not always welcome the intrusions of others, but I have learned that I need them. This work is the result of the privilege and the luck—perhaps these are really the same thing—of having family, friends, supporters, and colleagues.

This book was written in quiet, but it was often the quiet of the early morning kitchen or front stoop, the quiet of the professor and dean's office—after hours. I have stolen time for this book in trains, airport lounges, airplanes, libraries, museums, hotel rooms, bookstores, computer clusters, archives, automobiles (parked—I am not dangerous), and even the bleachers at swim meets, living here and there on three continents. In my travels and at home in the American Midwest I have depended on many, many people. I must acknowledge a few who have been most connected with this work.

First of all, I thank my father, Victor Eugene Dowd, for his help with the maps. We drew on a variety of sources but most heavily on Helen Tanner Miklos Pinther, et al., *Atlas of Great Lakes Indian History* (Norman, 1987), and Lester J. Cappon, et al., *Atlas of Early American History: The Revolutionary Era, 1760–1790* (Princeton, 1976). The University of Notre Dame, my professional home for fifteen years, provided excellent support to this teacher-scholar-administrator. The Hesburgh Library and its faculty and staff deserve my thanks, as do many of my colleagues and students. David Waldstreicher and Nicole Gothelf, for example, each read a bloated version of the manuscript from cover to cover. Most members of the History Department turned out for a talk on what evolved into Chapter 6, and many of the university's fine scholars of religion shared their thoughts with me on what has become Chapter 3. In particular, I thank historian Gail Bederman and anthropologist Patrick Gaffney, C.S.C., for their comments on that piece. While I was finishing the book, Jeanette Torok helped me secure permissions for the artwork.

Two other universities hosted me while I wrote this book. I am grateful to the Fulbright Foundation for providing me with a fellowship at the University of the Witwatersrand in Johannesburg, South Africa. Professor Bruce Murray, chairman of the Department of History at "Wits," extended every possible courtesy and effort to make my teaching and research productive that year, which saw that nation's transition to democracy from white minority rule. The year 1994 was a time of rumor and constitutional debate, and those characteristics, along with my exposure to South Africa's own imperial past, must somehow have shaped my thinking as I there drafted portions of the chapters that follow. During that year of great memories, Catrin Verloren van Themaat literally gave up her home to her sister, niece, and me, her brother-in-law.

I visited my alma mater, the University of Connecticut, for the academic year 1996–97. I thank Altina Waller and Richard D. Brown for arranging that stay and Guanhua Wang, Lawrence Langer, and Robert Asher for their friendship and support. UConn's faculty twice gathered to hear papers related to this work, and I am thankful for having had the company of that superb group of historians. While at UConn, I relished the chance to teach in classrooms where once my own interest in history was sharpened by such professors as R. Kent Newmeyer and Karen O. Kupperman. Teaching a full load at UConn, I was nonetheless free of service obligations. Those who have worked in ambitious universities will understand what such freedom can mean.

This book was written on several computers, but the computer has not yet overtaken the library or the archive as the historian's best technology for gathering information. Particular thanks go to John Dann, Brian Leigh Dunnigan, Barbara De Wolfe, John Harriman, and Robert S. Cox at the William Clements Library of the University of Michigan, Ann Arbor, and to David Poremba at the Burton Historical Collection of the Detroit Public Library. I do not know the names of the many professionals who helped me find materials at the remarkably efficient British Public Record Office in Kew, England, but I thank them and their institution for their wonderful service.

A National Endowment for the Humanities/Lloyd Lewis Fellowship at Chicago's Newberry Library in 1999–2000 pushed this book through to a foreseeable conclusion. The Newberry provides no butler and no tea trays, but it does have oaken walls, Diet Coke, and dubious coffee. Working in that hothouse of the humanities—sharing arguments in three separate papers with students of literature, cultural anthropology, and history— was a tremendous and even exhilarating experience. I am very grateful to the many Newberry personnel and fellows who made my stay enjoyable, and in particular to those who read and commented on portions of this book: Alfred Young, Terry Bouton, Amy Froide, Janine Lanza, Frances Dolan, Helen Hornbeck Tanner, James Grossman, Jean M. O'Brien, Charles Cullen, Anne Cruz, John Aubrey, Laurier Turgeon, Adam Stewart, Michael Willrich, LaVonne Ruoff, Harvey Markowitz, and Carla Zecher were particularly helpful.

Receiving grants is also a function of having patrons, on whom scholars depend as much now as did eighteenth-century Britons on the make. Here I acknowledge individuals who helped win me support over the years: Walter T. K. Nugent, Jim Goodman, Raymond D. Fogelson, Wilbur Jacobs, Andrew Cayton, Karen O. Kupperman, Thomas Kselman, and others who are elsewhere acknowledged. No one has written me more letters of support than John M. Murrin, long ago my dissertation adviser at Princeton University; my gratitude to John extends to things well beyond those letters. Norman Risjord first suggested to me the need for a new book on Pontiac; this book is not that exactly, nor is it what either of us then thought it would be, but I do not forget my debt to Professor Risjord for his many helpful comments on early chapters.

I took the opportunity to present segments of this work before the New Jersey Historical Commission, the Georgetown University Law Center and the Georgetown University Center for Australian and New Zealand Studies, Davidson College, Michigan State University, the University of Michigan, the Lawrence Henry Gipson Institute at Lehigh University (which may someday publish a version of Chapter 6), the Southern African-American Studies Association (in Durban, South Africa), and the Omohundro Institute for Early American History and Culture. Thanks here go to David Hancock, Susan Juster, John Carson, John Juricek, Jonathan Berkey, Vivien Dietz, J. Russell Snapp, Eric Hinderaker, Nancy Shoemaker, Daniel Ernst, Mary Murrin, Susan Sleeper-Smith, Jean Soderlund, and Ned Landsman.

This book contains fragments of my article "The French King Wakes Up in Detroit: 'Pontiac's War' in Rumor and History," *Ethnohistory* 37 (1992): 254–78, and essay "The Romans Were Triflers to Us': British and American Myths of Empire (a Comment)," in James Belich, *Empire and Its Myth: Occasional Papers*, ed. Daniel Ernst (Washington, D.C., 2000), 17–23. I tested some of the ideas in "'Insidious Friends': Gift Giving and the Cherokee-British Alliance in the Seven Years' War," in Fredrika Teute and Andrew R. L. Cayton, eds., *Contact Points: American Frontiers from the Mohawk Valley to the Mississippi, 1750–1830* (Chapel Hill, N.C., 1998), 114–50.

At the Johns Hopkins University Press, I have greatly benefited from the sound advice of Henry Tom, the humbling copyediting of Grace Buonocore, and the administrative correspondence of Michael Lonegro and Julie McCarthy. Colin G. Calloway, twice a reader of the manuscript, offered not only expert technical criticism but also sensible suggestions for reframing the work. Kim Johnson helped with the final stages of production, and Alexa Selph compiled the index.

Ada Verloren and Catrin Naudé Dowd have been with this book as long as I have; Catrintjie was born not long before I first turned to it. Ada has given me enormous help—including but by no means limited to keen editorial help. And she has also allowed me to steal from our time's pockets the silence that I have needed to take back the past. I would not want her ever to leave me alone. To Ada and Catrintjie, this historian has been a thief of time in more ways than one, and I am as grateful for their tolerance as I am dependent on their support and love. Baie, baie dankie!

ACKNOWLEDGMENTS

War under Heaven

INTRODUCTION

Heroes of History, Heaven, and Earth

On December 26, 1760, the Ottawa Indians of Detroit saw the flag of the French king, the *drapeau blanc*, flutter above Fort Pontchartrain for the last time. The white banner then dropped below the picketed walls, and the "English colours were hoisted . . . at which about 700 Indians gave a great shout."[1] A white sheet lowered, a largely red sheet raised: no one then knew that the red waved over an empire at the zenith of its power in North America. Within three years, groups of widely scattered Indian peoples who together numbered in the tens of thousands would challenge the might of this "First British Empire" of tens of millions. Shouting and shooting, they forced down British battle flags from Green Bay to the Allegheny River, from the Straits of Mackinac to the Wabash. In some of these places, they raised the *drapeau blanc* and appealed to French officials to support them. In others, they spoke of driving out all white people. At Detroit, the Ottawa Indian called Pontiac launched the first of the sieges, and he later claimed to lead all the Indian forces. The empire would take the claim seriously. The war has since borne his name.

The war named Pontiac's came at a critical juncture in the history of Native American relations with the British Empire—at a critical juncture in the history of that empire itself. Through the Treaty of Paris (1763), Great Britain acquired both a vast European claim to much of North America east of the Mississippi and the vexing task of making the claim good against Indian nations who saw it as nothing short of outrageous. The ensuing struggle involved much more than establishing title to acreage; it meant creating stable relationships between Native Americans and British subjects. The status of the Native American peoples in this part of the realm claimed by the British Crown emerged as the single most important issue in Pontiac's War, far more important than, for example, trade, Indian hating, or even title to the lands themselves.

Throughout the 1760s, Indians and Britons gave creative, passionate, and violently contentious consideration to what we can properly call their social and political relationships. As British officers worked to assert imperial superiority over both woodland Indians and colonial "country people," they demanded tokens of Indian and colonial esteem. To have done less would have meant that they were not the officers and gentlemen they held themselves to be, that they were neglecting their duty to the Crown. Indian leaders, highly conscious of British claims, sought from the officers proper tokens of British "regard" and "notice." Accepting less would have meant surrendering their standing as the protectors of their followers' autonomy and security, giving up their peoples' independence, perhaps even exchanging it for slavery. In Chapter 2, this polarity is introduced as crucial to the outbreak of war.

The war, fought in large part over how Indian peoples and an expansive colonial power related, politically and socially, to each other, did not resolve the issue; nor is it yet fully resolved in either of the two great North American political nations spawned by the British Empire—the United States and Canada. The war did not, as some scholars have hinted, convince British imperial or colonial officials to accept tacitly the Indian terms for the relationship; nor did it reshape the imperial authorities into potential buffers between Indians on the one side and an Indian-hating colonial populace on the other. At its core, the British Empire remained as hostile to fundamental Indian interests as it had ever been and as its successor states would soon come to be. The war did, however, force more open and systematic, if highly contentious and inconclusive, colonial thinking about the Indians' proper political and social place. Chapters 6 and 7 examine various colonial and imperial positions on the Native Americans' status within the British Empire during and after the war.

If Pontiac's War rode on waves stirred by a fight over status, it was also awash in matters of the spirit, explored later in this introduction and in Chapters 1, 3, and 8. Preparing to fight, pleading with others to join them, Indians regularly invoked their deity, the Master of Life. Pontiac himself, though an Ottawa from the western end of Lake Erie, launched the war while reciting the prophecies of Neolin, a Delaware from hundreds of miles away. Neolin urged Indians to consider their standing not only in this world but also in the afterlife, and he warned against grave colonial dangers on the difficult path to the Great Spirit's home. Although Neolin is well known, how it came to pass that Great Lakes Ottawas attended to a Delaware from far to the east has not previously been explored; Chapter 1 will do so. Importantly for the crucial issue of the Indians' standing under heaven, the Great Spirit lay at the basis of their claim to what we can call sovereignty, though *sovereignty* was not a word that fell from Indian lips through the tongues of translators and onto the written page. What Indians did say, in a succinct expression of territorial sovereignty—and they said it often—was that God had made their country for them; God had given it to them. No British official could accept this. None could argue legally that Indians held sovereign rights to territory claimed by George III. British law could not admit that God intended the country for Indians when it held instead that the king, as the embodiment of sovereignty, possessed eastern North America. Nonetheless, in one of the war's most startling legacies to the United States (Canada would recoil from the innovations), British officials would increasingly admit that Indians, though within the king's dominions, were not His Majesty's "subjects." In raising the conundrum that Native Americans were neither subjects nor sovereigns, the British, including British colonists, had described by the 1760s anomalies fundamental to later federal American Indian law.

The British leaders most involved in the war, unlike Pontiac, Neolin, and many other Indians, rarely mentioned God in their wartime writings. Sir William Johnson, Colonel Henry Bouquet, Major Henry Gladwin, Sir Jeffery Amherst, Colonel George Croghan, Major Robert Rogers, and General Thomas Gage were not men best known for their piety. Still, they took their standing as Protestants in the British service very seriously when it came to Catholics, the French, and Indians whom they suspected of being under the "malign" influences of Versailles and Rome. White flags, defecting French speakers, and Indian appeals to France inspired in British colonial offices and settlements powerful conspiracy theories involving Frenchmen, Catholics, and Jesuits. As for the last two, the theories could not have been more wrong. Catholic Indians were the least likely to ally with Pontiac; the Catholic mission repelled the militants' spirited appeals.

Robert Rogers, in an engraving published by Thomas Hart, 1776. Courtesy Clements Library, University of Michigan. The famous colonial soldier-warrior is here portrayed as a man who could lead Indians.

In Chapters 4, 5, and 7, I explore Native American strategy and tactics, demonstrating that Indian deployments were not random but calculated. They included war parties and ambuscades, as well as deception and rumor—powerful weapons for those short on firepower but also weapons sanctioned by traditional Indian faith. Pontiac and his allies initially targeted British garrisons and focused their energies on cutting the communications to them. The Indians attacked settlers, too, destroying entirely several particularly invasive settlements in the Susquehanna, Greenbriar, Jackson, and Monongahela Valleys. But most of the settlers who faced the onslaught lived along crucial British supply lines, an overlooked fact that suggests much about Indian intentions.

This volume attempts to open up a discussion about the issues the war raised and the ways those issues shaped both the course of the war and its unsettling conclusions. Throughout, this work asks of the old sources—some underutilized—new sets of questions. In examining the issues of status, faith, leadership, and power, it assumes that Indian men and women acted as thinking and feeling people, whose thoughts and feelings were conditioned in part by culture and in part by the history of their rapidly changing human relationships.

Pontiac

Since the time of Pontiac, historians have described many Pontiacs. Francis Parkman, while not the author of the first "version" of the man, certainly designed the most enduring monument to him, *The Conspiracy of Pontiac and the Indian War after the Conquest of Canada* (Boston, 1851). Parkman casts Pontiac as the Indians' forlorn hope, the best and brightest of a doomed and inherently benighted race, a man of the savage past valiantly but futilely fighting the civilized future. Admiring Parkman from the present, but critically inverting his argument, is the late Wilbur Jacobs, who most pointedly calls Pontiac the leader of a "War of Independence." The late Francis Jennings, Parkman's severest modern critic, agrees that the war was for "liberation," but he dismisses Pontiac's importance, while Howard Peckham, in the most detailed and scholarly biography to date, busts Pontiac from great chief to local commander. Most recently, William R. Nester has thrown Pontiac out of the title of the war altogether and has renamed it for General Jeffery Amherst, to whom he assigns responsibility for the disaster. Anthony F. C. Wallace has emphasized the religious aspects of the movement to which Pontiac's name has for so long been attached, while Richard White and Michael McConnell have, in very different language, shaped another interpretation, insisting that we take very seriously Pontiac's appeals to France and to the legacy of French practices in his homeland.[2]

So we have in Pontiac a secular militant and a zealous devotee (in one recent historian's phrase, "a murderous cult leader"), a great chief and a commoner mistaken for a great chief, an enemy of empire and an advocate of a restored New France.[3] We have so many Pontiacs and counter-Pontiacs because, in part, we have so little evidence for the man. No contemporary portrait exists. Nor do the documents give us a full picture of him or of his role. Not only is the evidence sketchy, but it is flawed. None of our sources, for one thing, comes from the pens of Ottawas who knew Pontiac best. Moreover, a troublesome uncertainty surrounds the most important sources. Our most informative document is the "Journal of a Conspiracy" at the Detroit Public Library, a very thorough account of several months of Pontiac's siege of Detroit in 1763, written in the form of a journal or, perhaps better, a chronicle. Since 1912, scholars who use it have generally and fairly convincingly attributed it to Robert Navarre, notary at Detroit during the war, but we are not certain even of that. And though it has the shape of a journal, any serious reading reveals that portions of it were written after the fact. The ink and the penmanship on the actual manuscript have a consistent quality until pages 63 and 65, around the entry for July 9, 1763. This suggests that the entries for at least the first two months, which lead up to that date, were recorded later. Perhaps the writer began to record events on that date. In any case, much of the action recorded in the journal comes to us secondhand, for it could not possibly have been witnessed by any single person, not even by Navarre, who had good access to what was happening on both sides of the war. Assuming, then, that Navarre wrote the document, it is at best, like many of the other documents, close memoir and close hearsay: valuable to be sure, but far less immediate than we would desire.[4]

Apart from the "Journal of a Conspiracy," there are the administrative, descriptive, and often accusatory documents left by such men as George Croghan and Robert Rogers. Croghan, a trader and member of the British Indian department with good connections among Indians, was widely known in the British colonies as an artful liar and a determined smuggler.

WAR UNDER HEAVEN

His sometime political ally, Thomas Penn, called him "by no means a person to be depended upon," while an admiring but honest biographer called his dealings characteristically "devious and dangerously speculative." Similarly, Robert Rogers, a skilled irregular soldier who provided our most complete description of Pontiac's appearance—complete with nose ring and imperious bearing—knowingly passed counterfeit bills and escaped conviction for the crime of forgery only by the timely arrival of the Seven Years' War, in which he made his name. As Pontiac's War drew to a close, moreover, Rogers was arrested and imprisoned for conspiracy and illegal trade. Few among his fellow British officers trusted him, which puts a question mark over his writings.[5] Facing such flawed data, one might reasonably conclude that it is time to give up the serious inquiry into Pontiac's War as hopelessly fraught with the dangers of poor documentation from the eighteenth century and politicized interpretation (pro-imperial, anti-imperial, or postcolonial) from our own time.

This would be a mistake. There is an abundance of good information on the events surrounding the war, and from Parkman to the present there has been a great amount of excellent, if contradictory and contentious, research and analysis. Parkman's touchstone work and his other writings have been so heavily criticized by modern scholars for their Anglo-Saxonism and racism that one turns to the Homeric Bostonian, riding crop in hand, as one turns to a dead horse. But Parkman's work, valuable for its many keen insights as well as for its famous prose, is still in print. Moreover, since Parkman made Pontiac's leadership famous, and since it is Pontiac's role as a leader that has drawn much of the historical debate, we, too, must turn briefly to Parkman.

Few men have believed as fervently in a people's need for leadership as Parkman, elitist par excellence and critic of popular democracy. When the Civil War erupted, he searched for a true leader to turn back the unreasoning throng: "Our ship is among the breakers, and we look about us for a pilot.... America ... is strong in multitudes, swarming with brave men, instinct with eager patriotism. But she fails in that which multitudes cannot supply, those master minds, the lack of which the vastest aggregate of mediocrity can never fill." Dismissing Abraham Lincoln as the "feeble and ungainly mouthpiece of the North," Parkman scorned such "men of the people." His obsession with leadership and his faith in the power of "master minds" breathed life into his history of Pontiac's War. Within the confines that Parkman's lofty racism allowed, Pontiac, "a thorough savage," was a true genius, possessing "a commanding energy and force of mind" and engaging "a wider range of intellect than those around him." If Parkman's Pontiac could not elevate his people, he could nonetheless lead them: "It would be idle to suppose that the great mass of the Indians understood, in its full extent, the danger which threatened their race. . . . But the mind of Pontiac could embrace a wider and deeper view."[6]

Parkman's history was not idiosyncratic; it grew out of and was informed by an intellectual tradition that was already flourishing among the British officers who recorded most of the details of Pontiac's War. Eighteenth-century Britons increasingly believed that individuals, not God, controlled the levers of history. David Hume argued confidently that "the revolution of states and empires depends upon the smallest caprice or passion of single men." Gordon Wood has most sympathetically explained the view: "In this face-to-face society, particular individuals—specific gentlemen or great men—loomed large, and people naturally explained human events as caused by the motives and wills of those who seemed to be in charge, headed the chains of interest, and made decisions. No one as yet could perceive of the massive and impersonal social processes—industrialization, urbanization, modernization—that we invoke to blithely describe large-scale social developments."[7] Small wonder, then, that British officials, confronting the Indian assaults, searched for their singular leader and stumbled in the end upon Pontiac as the "great chief" at the origin of the war. When the war was not yet a year old, General Thomas Gage described the Ottawa "not only as a savage possessed of the most refined cunning and treachery natural to Indians, but as a person of extraordinary abilities." Gage, himself the son of a noble, later wrote, "This Fellow should be gained to our Interest, or knocked in the head. He has great abilities, but his savage cruelty destroys the regard we should otherwise have for him." Parkman rallied Gage's rhetoric to describe Pontiac as a genius flawed by race. From Gage's time to the twentieth century, this view held sway: "The American forest never produced a man more shrewd, politic, and ambitious."[8]

Notwithstanding the past two generations' efforts to downgrade Pontiac, he did display those three characteristics, and he also imagined a united Indian effort to throw back the redcoats, but if that qualifies him as a "genius leader," then the Indian clearings in the American forest were bathed in brilliance. Indians throughout the Eastern Woodlands had long appreciated both the potential of intertribal cooperation and the dangers of British expansion. Ottawas had valued their intertribal connections for well over a century. The Delawares with whom Pontiac communicated had long felt, far more strongly than Ottawas, the dangers posed by Great Britain. In 1763, Pontiac, capable as he was, was not alone.

Nor did Pontiac, as some "great chief" of the Ottawas, Ojibwas, and Potawatomis, command "with almost despotic sway." Peckham challenged Parkman along these lines more than half a century ago, charging that there simply was no "principal chief" of these three peoples.[9] It is true that the three Algonquian-speaking peoples recognized, and continue to recognize, a fellowship, trading regularly, intermarrying easily. They called themselves collectively Anishinabeg (that is the plural form; the singular is Anishinabe). Linguistically, there was little difference among them, and they were particularly loathe to fight one another in war. But they had no united authority; they were not a confederacy, not even a league. When speaking of the Ojibwas (including Mississaugas), Ottawas, Potawatomis, or even the "Anishinabeg" as a people, one implies strong senses of commonality and identity, not of political and social unity.

Not even the Ottawas had a singular "chief." As Richard White has written, "There was no more an office of chief in Algonquian societies than there was in French society."[10] To call leadership decentralized in these societies is almost to miss the point, because centralization was not an issue. Even the local civil and military leaders had very little political power. Certainly they could not simply command. Since neither the Anishinabeg nor their Ottawa constituents had a single chief, and since Indian leadership was not authoritarian, Pontiac could not have been the "almost despotic" figure that Parkman found in the historical sources. Yet if Parkman promotes Pontiac to a status he could not have held, Jennings, Peckham, and Nester demote Pontiac too far. The Ottawa may not have commanded many obedient men, but for three years, beginning in 1763, he commanded much respect from Detroit to southern Illinois to Michilimackinac, as we shall see. Indeed, it was in the Illinois Country, the hitherto least-studied theater of Pontiac's War, that Pontiac's skills became most apparent to European officers, even though it must also be said that it was in the Illinois Country that Pontiac's actions as a leader would lead to an early grave.

Ottawa Leadership

When Europeans first met them, the Ottawas, while sharing a larger Anishinabe identity, were themselves subdivided into at least three, and perhaps four, smaller networks of extended families and villages variously referred to in the record as "tribes" or "nations," though anthropologists might more readily call them bands. Each of these groups had enough of a sense of unity that they could on rare occasions defer to a single spokesman for diplomatic purposes, but such spokesmen held ad hoc appointments (often dubious self-appointments). They were not regular governors.[11] In the Great Lakes region, Indian tribes existed in the sense that various villages of Indians might recognize commonality, be linked by broad kinship lines, agree on the use of lands, and be particularly quick to resolve disputes among one another or to unite militarily in opposition to an enemy.

Early French sources generally employed the name "Ottawa" to designate, at the most basic level, several groups of people who acknowledged such a commonality, but a few sources have troubled historians. The very term *Ottawá* is related in the Ojibwa language to the word for commerce, *atawewin*. In the *Jesuit Relations*, Father Claude Jean Allouez wrote, "All who go to trade with the French, although of widely different nations, bear the general name Outaouacs, under whose auspices they make the journey." This quotation stands as a warning that not all those called Ottawas in the record were ethnically "Ottawa," but Allouez should not be taken too far toward obliterating the term as the name of a distinct people, a people whom he knew well. The quotation itself acknowledges that there was an Ottawa people who sponsored the trade of others, a people known by its neighbors for a special role in trade and diplomacy. As Ottawas sought strength through good trading relations with their neighbors, they were willing to allow others to ply their routes. Their diplomatic character, exemplified by their concern for relations of exchange with others, strongly marked Ottawa history, and it left a legacy to Pontiac. It takes us from what Indian leadership was not (unitary and authoritarian) to what it was. It brings us to the positive foundations of Indian leadership.[12]

The Ottawas knew that their control of trade routes in the northern Lake Huron region was an exercise more of diplomatic reciprocity than

WAR UNDER HEAVEN

of military muscle or economic might. Ottawa leaders likewise knew that their status as headmen depended on their abilities to mediate and to bring about fruitful exchanges.[13] For the Anishinabeg, the attributes of leadership, greatness, and heroism arose more from the power to give—a power that grew from good relationships with others—than from the authority to discipline. As in British North America, the path to leadership among Ottawas could be through "trade," but in a different sense and for different reasons. Pontiac's contemporary, the prototypically successful British North American Benjamin Franklin, made a fortune and retired from business to a life of gentlemanly authority, collecting his rents, profiting from investments, drawing on his savings, staking his claim to leadership on his freedom from work—that is, on his complete independence. A successful Ottawa trader, conversely, amassed no fortune and sought no propertied independence; instead, he carefully gave away his goods to acquire both socially indebted followers and personal prestige. He forged alliances, personal, familial, and diplomatic. The system worked because trade, rather than being a way to wealth, was an avenue to the authority achieved through the generous distribution of goods and services. Trade was a way to forge bonds, to seal human relationships as a hedge against the perils of hunger and strife. Trade relations were, then, a way to power. They could put a man on the path to civil leadership. Trade was diplomacy, and diplomacy was an Ottawa way of life.

The Ottawa term for the civil leader is *ogema*. The *ogema*, a "most respected man," headed a network of extended families. Several *ogemas* together might form a council to deal with affairs in a village or cluster of villages. These *ogemas* were to be respected, but as anthropologist James McClurken has written, they had "no authority to impose opinions on their constituents." In the 1670s, Nicolas Perrot noted that war leaders, like civil leaders, similarly cultivated their relations with others through gift exchanges.[14] This careful forging of relationships with others through a variety of exchanges—material, marital, and martial—characterized the rise of Ottawas to leadership. The ideal Ottawa leader forged alliances through displays of generosity. He was composed, dependable, and willing to withstand long hours of negotiation. He mediated disputes among his followers and between his followers and others. He received gifts and redistributed them to his people; likewise, he gathered gifts from his people and gave these, in exchanges, to others.

Anishinabe Heroism

These others who were recipients of gifts were not always human. In a belief still shared by Ottawas and other Anishinabeg, the greatest of all heroes is no mere human but a human, a rabbit, a giant, and a sacred power all rolled into one. Uncertain early European writers recorded many names for him, including variations of the name most common in Ojibwa today, "Nanabush." In this anything-but-stoical person we begin to sense that heroism, in an Ottawa sense, is far from Parkmanesque. For Nanabush there is no Judeo-Christian equivalent. Not even the ancient mythologies of Greece or Rome supply a fully congruent type, though the Hermes/Mercury figure at times comes close. European folklorists of a structuralist turn no doubt could find popular equivalents enduring in areas less dominated by orthodox Christianity—in the leprechaunlike survivals of Europe's great islands, in the bawdy carnivalesque Saint Blaise of sixteenth-century southeastern France, in Shakespeare's Puck— but any such comparison would only underscore the fact that these beings are too remote from the central issues of life to approximate the great Nanabush of the upper Great Lakes.[15]

Nanabush is, according to the nineteenth-century Ottawa historian Andrew J. Blackbird (or Mackawdebenessy), the "most remarkable, wonderful, and supernatural being that ever trod upon the earth." In the seventeenth century, Nicolas Perrot, calling the figure "the Great Hare," observed, "[The Ottawas] revere and adore him as the creator of the world." Alexander Henry, publishing in 1809 his memoirs of life among the Ottawas and Ojibwas from 1761 to 1776, wrote of "Nanibojou, a person of the most sacred memory . . . , *The Great Hare.*" This figure is at the center of Anishinabe religion, and he has his counterpart among many other peoples of the upper Great Lakes region. By Anishinabe standards of leadership he was at first deeply flawed, being capable of great selfishness and deceit. But he outgrew some of these flaws to become highly creative, and he could be both selflessly generous and bravely loyal. In his greatest act, he transformed the entire universe, giving the best things—life, meaning, and ritual—to humanity. "He has done much mischief," yet he has also given "many benefits to the inhabitants of the earth," says Blackbird, and "he shaped almost everything." Paul Radin, in an anthropological classic, *The Trickster* (1956), describes this type of sacred Native American being as "a hero who is always wandering, who is always hungry, who is not guided by normal [that is, Euro-American?] conceptions of good and evil, who is either playing tricks on people or having them played on him." In the basic plot Nanabush is a gluttonous and crafty wanderer: a cosmic con man whose immense powers of persuasion bring others into his trap, his belly, or his bed. At one level, he is an antihero; he is what one should not be—and he often suffers from his own misadventures. Yet he also, as Blackbird and Henry noted, has overriding positive aspects. As his tales are told, he is well liked by the listeners, who laugh at his misdeeds and misfortunes, for "in the end" it is Nanabush who brings the current world into being—"he produced a new earth"—and who looks fondly upon the Anishinabeg. Admonishing with laughter his unbridled cravings and emotions, they praise in return his transforming attributes. Mere humans may correct; Nanabush, the Great Hare, destroys and renews.[16]

The Nanabush stories, told by a good teller, unfold in words and gestures, in sound effects and pantomimes, which might be imagined in the following tale. "Big Skunk," the sacred leader of all skunks, once gave Nanabush, ravenous from his travels, the gift of the power to kill many moose. Big Skunk taught Nanabush how to play a sacred flute, which could call the racked giants into a sacred lodge, where Nanabush could kill them by powerfully breaking wind. Characteristically, the over-curious Nanabush blundered, and he abused his new flatulent powers, passing useless gas while propelling himself joyfully through the air. Told with mimicry ("do it so"), the tales convey a boisterous slapstick performed in faith, and we can well imagine parents and children giggling together at the foibles of their favorite sacred hero. Although it is easy to see how serious parents might tell such stories in order to teach children precisely how *not* to behave, Radin and Sam Gill see much more to the trickster's antics than that. Writes Gill: "The incongruence, even the broaching of the unthinkable that the stories often dallied with, raised for people the question of meaning itself. That is, in their way, they showed that order and rules were in some sense linked with the creation of meaning, in contrast with the shock of chaos experienced through the sometimes unrestrained violation of order by these characters. Laughter and religion were at one in these stories."[17]

At a less interpretive level, Nanabush's chaotic life of loss, killing, hunger, and eroticism dealt more with the meaning of creation than with the creation of meaning. For those who believed in him, it was Nanabush who had brought this world into being, the world of the Anishinabeg, the world sustained by ritual exchange, death, and transformation. The Nanbush stories get at the heart of Ottawa and other Anishinabe understandings of life, of how the world works—and, critically for students of history, understandings of how the world may be changed.

Nanabush had once lived with his brother, who hunted in the form of a wolf. Loping across a frozen lake, the wolf broke through the ice, fell into the cold underworld, and was destroyed by its chaotic, devouring spirits: the submarine panthers and great serpents of the deep. Against these, a furious Nanabush plotted his revenge. Disguising himself as a tree stump, he sank roots into the sand beside the lake and awaited the spring thaw. As he had foreseen, the spirits of the underworld rose from the depths to sun themselves on the warming beach, carefully checking that no enemies were about. The serpents, suspicious of the stump, coiled about it, while the panthers scratched it with their claws. Convinced that all was safe, they called upon their headman to come ashore and relax.

As the water monsters slept on the beach, Nanabush resumed his shape, fixed his straightest arrow, and shot it into the chief spirit's heart, killing him instantly but arousing and enraging his monstrous fellows. The Great Hare fled as monsters pursued, bringing with them angry seas and waters, consuming the world in flood as they gained on the fleet Nanabush. Upward and upward he raced. In some versions he climbed lofty trees atop high mountains; in others he found a floating canoe and so escaped the depths. Once high and dry, atop his tree or afloat in his canoe but with no land in sight, he asked other creatures to dive into the deep in an effort to retrieve some of the lost earth from the bottom. Several attempted the task, but all failed until a lowly muskrat barely scraped the bottom and floated upward, dying in the return ascent. Nanabush cradled the muskrat in his arms, found a bit of mud in the claw, and breathed life back into drenched creature. Placing the mud in a pouch and tying that to the neck of a raven, Nanabush had the bird fly about, and wherever the bird flew, the waters ebbed, and there formed a new earth, the current world.[18]

Nanabush, though a Great Hare, is a sacred being who is also very much in the image of a human. Even though in some myths he becomes a tree in order to hide, a bird in order to fly, a carcass in order to capture a buzzard, and even though his body in some versions is other than human in more extreme ways, he is the most human of the sacred beings and the most closely identified with the people.[19] But Nanabush is no ordinary person. Although Nanabush stands as the central mythical heroic figure, he can provide no exact model for an Ottawa seeking greatness, and he certainly is no model leader.

Except for this: He raises possibilities for victory over powerful under-worldly, watery beings who cause great offense; he raises possibilities for a revolutionized world. Though the archetypal loner, Nanabush does not act alone. Even after the flood, he relies upon muskrats and ravens to help him reform the land. As Joel W. Martin has written in another context of such powerful "earth-diver" stories, the "world had been barely extracted from chaos through the agency of powerful spirits."[20] If it had happened before, it could and would happen again; there were other forms of chaos, other malevolent powers closing in on the Anishinabe world, and also other powerful, if fickle, beings to whom one could appeal for assistance. This lesson would not be lost on Pontiac and his allies.

Transformation

Pontiac's society produced seekers, if at more modest levels, of Nana-bush's awesome abilities to prevail over his own obvious limitations and to transform not only his own shape but a chaotic universe. Religious specialists known as *mides* (also *mites*), like other, lesser shamans, gained the power to converse with spirits through ceremonial rites of passage that utterly transformed their natures. The ceremonies were said to be gifts from Nanabush himself. The *mides*, in turn, attended and presided over the Midewiwin ceremonies at which they were said to shoot sacred shells into the initiate's body, transforming him or her into a power altogether new.[21]

Mides could be men or women, and their celebrations were public enough that the term *Midewiwin* was translated in the early nineteenth century to mean "ceremony" and "religion." But they were not the only religious specialists among the Anishinabeg to perform special public rituals. *Jaasakids*, seers, widely celebrated "shaking tent" ceremonies, as they have come to be called in English. Here, the male or female *jaasakid* entered a small lodge or tent and waited for the sacred winds to carry prophecies. Onlookers, outside the structure, heard the winds rise and voices cry out and saw the shelter convulse. The winds delivered prophecies and wisdom, which the *jaasakid* shared with the people. So convincing were the *jaasakids* that a leading nineteenth-century authority on the Anishinabeg, Henry Rowe Schoolcraft, wrote a paper asserting the *jaasakids'* genuine access to what he was certain were satanic influences.[22]

Regeneration was a key ceremonial feature all around seventeenth-century Lake Huron, home of the Ottawas. As early as the winter of 1623–24, Father Gabriel Sagard found that Hurons (or Wendots), Iroquoian-speaking trading partners of the Ottawas, enacted ceremonial "resurrections of the dead, chiefly of those who [had] deserved well of their country by remarkable services, to the end that the memory of illustrious and valorous men [might] in some manner come to life again in the persons of others." Miamis, to the south of the Ottawas, followed the practice into the nineteenth century. A dead person's child adopted a successor to the deceased, an event that was attended "with a considerable ceremony." The missionary to the Ottawas Louys André, who witnessed in the early 1670s an intertribal celebration on an island in northern Lake Huron, recorded that, three years after the death of a leading Ottawa warrior, the eldest son held an intertribal gathering "in his father's honor." There he was able to "resuscitate [his father], as they say, by taking his name." André continued, "It is customary to recall the illustrious dead to life at this Festival, by conferring the name of the deceased upon one of the most important men, who is considered his successor and takes his place." Nicolas Perrot discovered the same pattern among all the upper Great Lakes Indians in the late seventeenth century: "If it is a chief who has died . . . [mourning] lasts a whole year, at the end of which time the relatives assemble to adopt a person who is qualified to assume the office of the dead chief, and who must be of the same rank." Even captives of war might be adopted to replace an admired individual, as Pierre François Xavier de Charlevoix found among Hurons at Lake Erie in 1721.[23]

In these adoption ceremonies and feasts of the dead the Ottawas and their neighbors understood that they had the power, through ceremony, to influence even departed souls. Once more, tantalizing but bad evidence confronts us with possibilities, for we have one contemporary report that Pontiac had been a Catawba Indian, captured and adopted by the Ottawas.[24] It is unlikely that Pontiac had been ritually remade in that fashion, but it is not impossible, given the persistent eighteenth-century wars between Lakes peoples and the Southeastern Indians. Whatever the truth of that particular report, the ceremonial power to restore lost souls to life, to transform the fundamental condition of death, was familiar to Pontiac and his allies. A central feature of the Anishinabe Feast of the Dead was the game of *baggataway*, or lacrosse, a game that would be used with deadly effect against the British at Michilimackinac in 1763. During that war of 1763, and for some time after, many Anishinabeg would seek to resurrect their powerful French "father," the metaphorical leader of the French-Anishinabe alliance. Feasts of the Dead, often celebrated as peoples seasonally gathered for rich fishing runs, provided a sacred dimension to intertribal diplomacy around Lake Huron.[25]

Parkman claims that an Ojibwa once told him that Pontiac had been a *mide*, a powerful shaman, therefore, conversant with Nanabush or perhaps with the otters, muskrats, and turtles whom Nanabush enlisted as allies. There is no evidence to that effect from Pontiac's day, though there is evidence both for regenerative rites being celebrated at Detroit in the 1760s and for Pontiac's spiritual attentiveness.[26] This claim, although it cannot be verified, nonetheless has its lessons. At very least, it provides a useful foil to the Euro-American depiction, which oddly enough found its fullest form in Parkman, of Pontiac as a "great chief." At its most obvious level, the claim underscores the possibility that Pontiac was as much a religious as a political, diplomatic, or military leader. Many Anishinabe political leaders from a later period, about whom we know much more, were also powerful *mides*. We do know that, like Anishinabe *mides*, Pontiac and his allies sought a powerful transformation in their world. We also know with certainty that in seeking such great change they appealed to great powers.[27]

Imminence

Father Claude Jean Allouez, a French Jesuit visiting the Ottawas a century before Pontiac's War, wrote of them, "[They] recognize no sovereign master of heaven and earth, but believe there are many spirits— some of whom are beneficent, as the sun, the moon, the lake, rivers, and woods; others malevolent, as the adder, the dragon, cold and storms. And, in general, whatever seems to them either helpful or hurtful, they call a manitou and pay it the worship and veneration which we render only to the true God."[28] Allouez hinted at several of the most powerful beings in the Ottawa cosmology, but he failed to see the meaning in what to him was disorderly and possibly satanic. Indeed, Ottawas did recognize a multitude of powers, or manitous. The sun, the moon, and the thunder beings were beneficent; underworldly panthers, serpents, and icy northern monsters were highly malevolent. Hardly omnipresent, these beings were nonetheless immediate and accessible, unlike the Great Spirit, who was more remote and visited only by the most exceptional of men and women. The manitous emerge most clearly in stories, often those set in the past, but what is most striking about the stories is the imminence of the past they describe.

Eastern Woodland Indian myths recall a primordial age, a time in which lived the prototypes of all those beings that inhabit our epoch. In 1764, Ottawas told Alexander Henry that beavers, for example, "were formerly a people endowed with speech, not less than with the other noble faculties they possess; but, the Great Spirit has taken this away from them." The animals' loss of language accompanied the great transformation from the ancient world to this world.[29] These primordial beings sacredly persisted in a separate but nearby and religiously accessible dimension, and they offered important lessons for and powers to the living.

Indian hunters did not simply surprise and kill beasts. Rather, as Henry Rowe Schoolcraft wrote of the Anishinabeg, they invoked spirits through rituals, which were "supposed to operate in such manner on the animal sought for, that he voluntarily enter[ed] the hunter's path." John Tanner, captured at nine years of age in Kentucky in 1789, lived among Ojibwas in both Michigan and western Ontario well into adulthood. He matured as a young hunter according to Anishinabe ways. He carried a sacred bundle, filled with ritual items to help him secure game. His adoptive Indian mother, Net-no-kwa, was careful to prepare ceremonial feasts whenever Tanner killed a particular species, whether elk or sturgeon, for the first time.[30] Net-no-kwa was a powerful dreamer, and she also sought to induce her own dreaming: "Nearly all night I prayed and sung, and when I fell asleep near morning, the spirit came to me, and gave me a bear to feed my hungry children." Other sources indicate that the dreams of older Indian women were much attended to by Ottawas. This is not the only time that Tanner reports Net-no-kwa dreaming deliberately about the hunt. The "spirit" that gave her the bear was likely the owner of the bears, the animal guardian that controlled the supply of bears. But other powers could also play a role. Allouez reported a man honoring the sun in a ceremony, thanking it "for having lighted him so that he could successfully kill some animal."[31]

"The more deeply we penetrate the world view of the Ojibwa," wrote A. Irving Hallowell of the Ottawas' near neighbors, "the more apparent it is that 'social relations' between human beings . . . and other-than-human 'persons' are of cardinal significance." Successful hunting in Pontiac's day therefore had as much to do with good spiritual relations with the targeted animals' spiritual guardians as it did with acquired skill, physical prowess, agility, technology, observation, and determination. Like many of the fundamental activities of Indian men and women, hunting, as a relationship between "our people" on the one hand and the four-footed animals and their spiritual guardians on the other, involved communication, a kind of ritual diplomacy accompanied by gifts that smoothed the exchanges among the people, the spirits, and the beasts. Christopher Vescey, modern student of Ojibwa religion, points out that "almost all persons, including animals, went to the same afterworld, ruled by Nanabozho [Nanabush]."[32]

Death, a fact of the hunters' task, was less a final moment than a transforming event. Out of such events came Anishinabe life. Eastern Woodlands peoples of the colonial era believed, on one level, that the universe inclined toward decay, degeneration, and disorder. Indeed, death —the ultimate disorder—was not only inevitable but essential. Great Lakes Indian peoples gave death a critical role in life: as Vescey has written, a basic theme of Anishinabe religion was "the necessity of death for the continuation and strengthening of life." Thus, Nanabush's muskrat died in its successful efforts to help restore the earth. Similarly, Nanabush secured the people's right to hunt, in another tale, in a deadly contest with spirits of the underworld. As early as the winter of 1709–10, Antoine Denis Raudot found that shamans among the Ojibwas of the Sault Ste. Marie symbolically killed and revived one or more people in displays of their sacred power. Without death there could be no transforming rebirth.[33]

Catholicism

Into this religious New World of transforming death, farting spirits, cosmic grief, pride, vengeance, gifts, reciprocity, loyalty, generosity, creativity, and laughter came the vanguard of Rome: first the Recollect missionaries, the most notable of whom was the tough Father Gabriel Sagard, missionary to the Hurons; and later the elite corps of the Catholic

Reformation, the missionaries of the Society of Jesus, whose impact would be more significant. These highly educated men came from Europe's best universities to the North American Indian interior.[34] They came with a religion of gravity and solemnity, a religion for which ultimate love meant ultimate sacrifice, for which grace meant salvation.

They were not, however, the kind to experience pious shock at Indian practices or at much else. The best of them were too confident, too curious, too worldly, and too faithful to be easily surprised. Their writings reveal men of wry humor as well as earnest zeal. They came, moreover, from an order experienced in confronting riotous, rough, and unorthodox popular rituals, even in France, notably the frolicking French carnival, which the church had long striven to suppress; Allouez himself saw Ottawa rites as North American versions of such practices. He also compared Ottawa faith to "the beliefs of some of the ancient Pagans," which was, in his mind, at least faint praise.[35] One way or another, Jesuits assimilated Indian religion into their own understandings, however intolerant those inevitably were.

Determined to work with the materials at hand, Jesuits hoped to identify analogous features of Indian belief (for them not a faith but, at best, a bizarre assortment of misunderstandings held by very human but highly vulnerable souls). They emphasized these features at the expense of other aspects. They adopted a self-conscious and careful pose, deliberately quieting their enthusiasm. Father Paul Le Jeune, who worked far to the east among the Montagnais, put it well: "The four Elements of an Apostolic man in New France are Affability, Humility, Patience and a generous Charity." Le Jeune had clearly grasped patterns of Indian leadership. "Too ardent zeal," he continued, "scorches more than it warms, and ruins everything."[36]

Jesuits found congruence in Ottawa beliefs, for Catholic missionaries and Ottawas alike, though in different ways, deplored greed, bridled sexuality, and frowned on dishonesty. But Ottawa and Jesuit paths could part as easily as unite. When Jesuits caught themselves or their converts involved with what they deemed to be sin, they made things right with acts of penance, sometimes a corporal matter. Mortification of the flesh could bring to the traditionally minded Ottawa not so much the forgiving of sins as the sympathy of the sacred powers. Although Ottawa worship could be as solemn as the Jesuits' Mass, it could also be deliberately humorous. Whereas for Jesuits sacred love meant sacrifice, for Ottawas it meant gift. Ritual exchange brought grace and salvation for Jesuits, but it brought power and life for Ottawas. Jesuits insisted on matters that made no sense to Ottawas, such as the prohibition of polygamy or of divorce. The divergences between the faiths were as powerful as the similarities. As they won some converts among the Ottawas, the Jesuits came, like Father Jacques Marquette in 1669, to denounce others as "far from the Kingdom of God" both because of "indecencies, sacrifices, and jugglery" and because, as Allouez put it a few years earlier, of "libertinism; and all these various sacrifices [that] end[ed] ordinarily in debauches, indecent dances, and shameful acts of concubinage."[37]

Although we cannot quantify Jesuit success, we know that seventeenth-century Jesuits converted some Ottawa families and villages and that conversions could endure. Allouez was particularly successful among the Kiskagon band of Ottawas, refugees in 1665 in what is now northern Wisconsin on Lake Superior. But by Pontiac's time, a century later, the "heroic age" of the Jesuits had passed long ago, and most of the Indian Catholics had either moved to mission villages on the St. Lawrence River or had small communities, often without clergy and run by lay workers and catechists, thinly scattered about the Great Lakes and Illinois. Among Ottawas, the most devout group resided at L'Arbre Croche, in the north-western part of the Lower Peninsula of Michigan. Few of the Ottawas near Pontiac's Detroit were Christian in 1760, although there was an active parish of Wyandots (former Hurons or Wendots) led by a French priest. Widespread Ottawa Catholicism would come much later, in the nineteenth century.[38]

Jesuit influence went beyond the converted, however, for Anishinabe religion came, in the manner of Nanabush, to embrace and transform elements of the Catholicism it encountered even as Catholics gave new shape to the Anishinabe world. The Midewiwin itself, with its priesthood, may have arisen from Anishinabe traditions to meet the Jesuit challenge successfully, though this is a point that Anishinabe traditionalists, supported by a growing body of scholars and by documentary evidence, dispute.[39] More critically, such Christian notions as heavenly salvation, hellish punishment, and life as a "road" became elements of Pontiac's faith. These elements, like the Nanabush stories, contained enormously transforming properties that thousands of Indians would put to the test in 1763.

CHAPTER ONE

Ottawas, Delawares, and
the Colonial World, 1615–1760

When Pontiac called for a renewed world in 1763, he appealed directly to neither Nanabush nor Jesus; he celebrated neither the traditional shaking tent ceremony nor the Mass (though both were well known to him). He spoke instead, and at length, of a prophet from the east, a Delaware who had visited the Master of Life. How it came to be that a Delaware prophet inspired an Ottawa *ogema* is the subject of this chapter. One hundred and fifty years earlier, it would not have happened. The peoples had then lived too far apart to be well acquainted. When Ottawas came into sustained contact with Europeans in 1615, their homeland lay around northern Lake Huron, with strong cultural hearths on Ontario's Bruce Peninsula and Manitoulin Island, and they probably had camps on many of the islands that freckle the icy Georgian Bay and Lake Huron. It is likely, too, that they inhabited the northwestern portion of Michigan's Lower Peninsula, and scholars have controversially placed them as far south as the straits at Detroit.[1] By contrast, the Delawares' Middle Atlantic homeland lay four hundred miles away, between the lower Hudson and Delaware Valleys.

Ottawas had several means of subsistence, probably the most basic of which were fishing, hunting, and farming, likely in that order. Together these activities were efficient enough in good seasons to leave ample time for trade, an important supplementary activity that provided a critical hedge against crop failure in their far northern homeland. Rivers and the sheltered areas of the Georgian Bay made for good travel deep into the interior of what is now northern Ontario. Abundant cedar and white birch—resources many tribes lacked—allowed Ottawas to fashion their highly decorated and easily transportable bark canoes, among the best in North America. No Great Lakes Indian people were more at home in deep water than the Ottawas, who commonly ventured over lake water, out of sight of land. Well before contact with the French, the Ottawas had been in a good position to trade. Their location between the subarctic hunters north of the lakes and the more southerly Tionnontatés (Petuns) and Wendots (Hurons), whom archaeologist Bruce Trigger has called the "Farmers of the North," provided them with ideal opportunities for trade in meat, fish, pelts, and agricultural foodstuffs.[2]

Although Ottawas had both good neighbors and certain geographic advantages, they hardly inhabited a paradise. Brutally cold winters—far worse in the seventeenth century than they are today—often exhausted food supplies, leaving them to face starving times in the spring. That season brought clouds of mosquitoes and blackflies, against which the only protections were bear grease, rapid movement, or smoke.[3] The Ottawas had human enemies, too, particularly the Five Nations Iroquois, though the great distance to Five Nations towns probably minimized casualties. Whatever the difficulties of life at the turn of the seventeenth century, worse was to come. Sickness, war, and hunger took a heavy toll in the years after the arrival of the French, and many Ottawas abandoned their homeland.

Great, invisible forces descended like evil spirits upon the Great Lakes in the first half of the seventeenth century. Smallpox, the most infectious of all known diseases, has received the most attention, but also devastating were the plagues of flu, measles, and even mumps—highly dangerous to adults—that crushed the life out of thousands. The Wendot population fell to nine or ten thousand by 1638, half of what it had been in 1615. The Five Nations of Iroquois—known as the Iroquois League or the Longhouse—who lived south of Lake Ontario, suffered equally. Their suffering, indeed, contributed to the second great disaster.[4] The Five Nations had been at periodic war with New France and its Wendot and Algonquian Indian allies almost since the founding of the colony. As families grieved over their losses to the new epidemics, they sought to correct great spiritual imbalances and to replace their dead by intensifying a

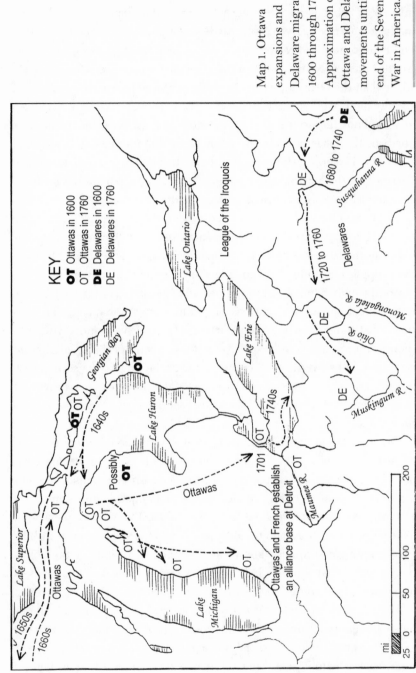

KEY

OT Ottawas in 1600
OT Ottawas in 1760
DE Delawares in 1600
DE Delawares in 1760

Map 1. Ottawa expansions and Delaware migrations, 1600 through 1760. Approximation of Ottawa and Delaware movements until the end of the Seven Years' War in America.

pattern scholars have called "mourning war." Previously desultory fighting flared in the 1640s as Five Nations warriors, well armed by the Dutch in what is now New York, raided, scattered, killed, captured, and adopted members of the embattled Neutrals, Eries, Wendots, and Tionnontatés—all of whom spoke Iroquoian languages and could in some measure be more easily incorporated than Algonquian speakers. Within a century, the descendants of those who were not captured had united to form the Wyandots.[5]

Cushioned in the 1630s and early 1640s by the allied Tionnontatés and Wendots, who bore the brunt of the Iroquois League's attacks, the Ottawas nonetheless faced a disaster as the societies of their highly agricultural allies and trading partners collapsed. By the end of the late 1640s, the mainland Ottawas were fleeing westward to dwell among their compatriots on Manitoulin Island and among the closely related Potawatomis and Ojibwas of Michigan's Lower Peninsula, Lake Michigan's Green Bay, and eventually Lake Superior's Chequamegon. The Michigan lands were already familiar fishing and hunting grounds. Clearings among maples, birches, and hemlocks encouraged agriculture. In 1649, Ottawas had villages in the vicinity of the Straits of Mackinac, and within a few years they could be found at Saginaw Bay and at the Thunder Bay River in Michigan's Lower Peninsula. By the 1760s, they dominated the western half of the peninsula southward to the Kalamazoo River, and they wintered as far south as the St. Joseph's River.[6] The Ottawas hung on to the Lower Peninsula, repulsing Iroquois attacks and encouraging others to join them in the early 1660s. This would become the Ottawa homeland.

Within this context of sickness, flight, and war, Ottawas solidified their relationships with other peoples, Indian and French, and reestablished themselves as important participants in trade and diplomacy. The cluster of villages near the mission of St. Ignace, on the southern edge of the tip of Michigan's Upper Peninsula at the Straits of Mackinac, became for a time a hub of the Ottawa territory. About thirteen hundred Ottawas lived there in the 1670s. Hunting, fishing, trading, and farming provided them with what appears to have been, at least in good times, a rich livelihood. From these communities headmen would lead powerful trading convoys to Montreal, Three Rivers, and Quebec. Armed to the teeth, like any merchantman of the day, these convoys brought enormous returns in status to the leading Ottawa traders.[7]

French officers and even ordinary soldiers traded at the posts, and though they clearly sought profit in material terms, they modified their practices according to Indian circumstances, much as Ottawas learned to haggle when dealing with Europeans. Rather than resenting such French participation as new competition, Ottawas saw in it a chance to deepen the alliance. The traders and the French voyageurs who increasingly powered the trade canoes adapted to their Indian surroundings and provided new sources of material wealth for Indians as they purchased provisions with goods. From the Catholic mission station at St. Ignace, the French officer Claude Charles Le Roy, Bacqueville de la Potherie, wrote that the resident Ottawas earned a healthy living, building canoes and cabins for the traders and their men. They sold everything from corn to whitefish to strawberries. They would have been "exceedingly well-to-do," he thought, had it not been for what he saw as an odd propensity to give away food to strangers.[8]

The alliance with France, however, was far from an ideal, enduring marriage. It was instead a turbulent wartime affair, formed as a haven from the horror that often surrounded it, and it needed constant replenishment and quick satisfactions. The French claimed imperial control, but recent scholarship has revealed that in North America the French "empire" was a very odd empire indeed. Instead of commanding Indians in the *pays d'en haut*, the French adopted layer upon layer of Native American roles and protocols—finding it expedient to act the part of generous Indian "fathers," not of authoritarian European patriarchs.[9]

The French maintained influence in the interior not so much because of advantages over the British but rather more because of disadvantages. First, the French North American population remained tiny by British standards. Although French were present in Canada since 1608, as late as the 1670s only 7,832 were recorded on the colony's census. By 1755, owing almost entirely to a truly inspired rate of natural increase, there were 62,000 Europeans in New France—but still too few either to impose their will upon the Great Lakes Indians or to pose any serious threat to Indian lands outside the St. Lawrence or lower Mississippi Valleys.[10]

A second disadvantage was that French women were relatively few in Canada throughout the seventeenth century, as was the case at the fur-trading posts well into the eighteenth century. As a result, French men formed relationships with other nearby women, that is, with Indian women. As the children of French men and Indian women matured, so too did a Métis population, bound by family, religion, and culture to either

French or Anishinabe heritages or both. Family ties could expand broadly, through Catholic baptism, to include godparents and godchildren. Throughout the French colonial period, the Métis could maintain allegiance to both societies, as long as they were at peace.[11]

Finally, relative to the British, the French had a third disadvantage: the British could undersell them, because British manufactured goods were cheaper. Poorer manufacturing and, particularly as the eighteenth century progressed, a less effective merchant marine left the French scrambling for alternatives to trade as the foundation of Indian alliance.[12] France found those alternatives in service and in war. And it is in these areas that the French and Indians together formed a remarkable association, in which France had considerable authority while Indians had considerable voice and power. Although jerry-rigged and in need of constant repair, the alliance struck fear into the British coastal settlements, threatened British western interests, and enabled outnumbered and outmoneyed New France to maintain an aggressive posture on the continent.

It was in diplomatic service to the peoples of the interior, first of all, that the French filled a void, becoming in the course of the Iroquois wars the chief arbiters among upper Great Lakes Indian groups: smoothing over differences, uniting many of the peoples into a powerful alliance. This consumed time, energy, and resources, for regular gifts had to be made to the allies. In 1682, French intendant Jacques Duchesneau observed that Ottawas "never transact[ed] any business without making presents to illustrate and confirm their words . . . ; they entertain[ed] a profound contempt for the selfish."[13] More than any other people in the *pays d'en haut*, the French had both access to good gifts and, because of the growing British threat to Quebec, the need to give them. In 1730 the French captain Pierre-Jacques Payen, Sieur de Noyan, fully understood, while seeking command of the fort at Detroit, that to lead the Anishinabeg one must adopt a distinctly Indian pose: "true, pleasant and firm, and above all, generous."[14]

A major aspect of French diplomacy in the west from the end of the Iroquois wars in 1701 to the outbreak of the Great War for Empire in 1754 would be the effort to prevent defections from the French alliance to the British traders, a problem that became acute after 1748. To counteract the attractiveness of British goods, France found that it had to subsidize its trade, providing extensive gifts and providing good services by resident blacksmiths and gunsmiths at the posts.[15] Nevertheless, some Wyandots, Ottawas, and Miamis continued to defect to the British traders. The danger to France had become apparent even as the eighteenth century opened; the fort at Detroit, Pontiac's future home, had been one French response.

Antoine de La Mothe, Sieur de Cadillac, the French commander of Fort Baude on the Straits of Mackinac in the late 1690s, proposed to build a post at Detroit; it would anchor the western end of a trade route, much of it deepwater and passable by sailing vessels, from Quebec via the St. Lawrence, Lake Ontario, and Lake Erie. The cost of trade would be cut, and the alliance with the Anishinabeg would be better secured. Moreover, Cadillac imagined that a strong post at Detroit, with considerable Indian support, would preempt any movement of Indians toward a trade with the Iroquois League and thus with the English. Here French aspirations neatly dovetailed with those of the Ottawas, who saw control of the straits at Detroit as critical to the control of Lake Huron. Ottawas had established themselves in the region as early as 1670, and at least one Ottawa would later claim it as an ancestral Ottawa homeland. Historians have criticized the move to Detroit as "ill-advised," for by bringing the Anishinabeg closer to the Iroquois League and the British, it advanced the very threat that, from a French perspective, it was intended to forestall. But Cadillac may have had little choice; if he wanted to maintain good relations with the Ottawas, he sometimes had to follow their lead.[16]

In 1701, Cadillac built his post, Fort Pontchartrain, on the Detroit River, the "straits" between the Michigan and Ontario peninsulas through which Lakes Huron and St. Clair drain southward into Lake Erie. It was at first a small affair, a rough acre enclosed with an oaken, bastioned palisade. Its most important feature may have been its storehouses; though partly intended to provision the garrison in the event of a siege, they mainly served to supply allies, for, like all French posts in the west, preserving and serving the Indian alliance were its primary functions. Wyandots and Ottawas already occupied the region. They were now joined not only by the French but also by strong parties of other Wyandots, Anishinabeg, and Miamis from the Michigan Peninsulas and the region just to their south. By 1705, Cadillac had four hundred warriors and perhaps two thousand to twenty-five hundred people at and around Detroit, and they helped to expand the scope of the alliance's influence. At times, six thousand Indians may have lived in the environs of the post.[17]

By the time of Pontiac's birth in the second decade of the eighteenth century, relations with France had irrevocably altered the Ottawas' material life. After half a century of dislocation and migration, many Ottawas were living in a new country to the south. And though Ottawas had always been traders, the nature of the trade with Europeans and the extended alliances with other Indians had profoundly affected all aspects of life. They demanded, and felt a need for, European-manufactured goods. Scholars may debate the speed with which a mere desire for European goods became a desperate dependence on them, and whether by extension that meant a dependence on Europeans, but by Pontiac's day, the dependence on access to goods was very real.[18]

One good was particularly important: gunpowder. Hunting and defense made it absolutely essential that Ottawas obtain guns and ammunition. Though firearms might last many years, powder was easily spent or spoiled. Indians quickly learned to repair firearms, manufacture ball and shot, and shape fine flints for the flintlocks, but none mastered the art of milling gunpowder—even French colonists never erected a powder mill during the colonial period. Although English colonists had opened such works in 1675, they continued to import much black powder throughout the colonial period.[19] Everywhere in eastern North America, when men looked for gunpowder, they looked to the Atlantic. For Ottawas on the Detroit River, the Atlantic was French.

For their part in the alliance, Ottawas repeatedly demonstrated their military value to France throughout Pontiac's youth. In the 1730s they raided the Chickasaws, trading partners of the British, and they struck the Cherokees and Catawbas, British South Carolina's main defense against an attack from the interior. As for direct conflict with Britain, in the 1740s Ottawas served the French during King George's War (the War of the Austrian Succession), occasionally raiding the British colonies and challenging the new inroads of British traders. During the peace interval of 1748–54, Ottawas led efforts to discipline two errant Algonquian-speaking peoples. They proved their military value most notably, however, once war burst out again in 1754: the Ottawas gave critical support to the French, routing British regulars under Edward Braddock in 1755.[20]

As Richard White and W. J. Eccles have demonstrated, the Ottawas and their Indian allies exacted a price from France. The French empire served the Indians by providing goods, a modicum of local intertribal peace, and strong defense against potential eastern foes. As Denys Delâge has emphasized, Indian communities suffered high costs as well. In the Great Lakes, the alliance meant foreign war, and war meant not only death but the long and very grueling absences of Anishinabe men. The alliance brought missionaries to those villages, whose message of peace proved internally divisive. The alliance brought traders and blacksmiths, whose marriages to Indian women firmed up personal ties even as their violation of social norms at times strained imperial bonds. The alliance brought disease, which exacted its own high price, especially in the seventeenth century. And the alliance brought a never-cresting torrent of brandy, which swept many lives and families into a kind of unnatural disaster.[21]

Dependent on European goods, Ottawas were not dependent on fur production alone. The French traders, officers, soldiers, priests, farmers, and allied Indians who resided near and visited Ottawa villages across Michigan gave the Indian villagers other economic opportunities, which had grown over the course of the eighteenth century. Women produced and traded in foodstuffs from corn to maple sugar. They dried meat and fish, provisioning garrisons, warriors, and voyageurs. The Ottawa economy had diversified. Hunting, farming, sugar making, fishing, fighting, and trading itself: all these brought European goods into the villages. A bad season for beaver meant little to a people not wholly dependent on a single export. But if the Ottawas were less subject than others to the uncertainties of hunting, the Ottawa way of life at midcentury had this great weakness: it was as dependent on the French North American empire as that empire was dependent on its Indian allies. Ottawas understood this and were among the staunchest supporters of New France in North America.

As Ottawas expanded southward across lower Michigan in the first half of the eighteenth century, they did so in a spirit of intermarriage and cohabitation with Wyandots, Potawatomis, Ojibwas, Métis, French, and others, rather than in a spirit of conquest. After a minor Ottawa rupture with Miamis in 1705–6, these peoples, too, entered into largely amicable relations, at least until the 1740s, when new tensions arose. Only with the Foxes and the Mascoutens did genuine warfare erupt within Michigan itself, and these peoples were soon driven westward from that region. Ottawas established towns not only in the vicinity of Detroit but also along Michigan's Grand River, at Saginaw, at L'Arbre Croche, at Michilimackinac, and even as far as the St. Joseph River in northern Indiana and the Maumee River in Indiana and Ohio. By the early 1750s, at least one band from this last place would have good relations with the Delawares and, dangerously for France, with the British.[22] By the 1740s, small groups of Ottawas inhabited polyglot communities as far east as the Cuyahoga River in eastern Ohio, well beyond the French orbit; here they rubbed shoulders with Senecas, Cayugas, Oneidas, Onondagas, Mohawks, Shawnees, Delawares, and other groups from east of the Appalachian Mountains, including westering British traders.[23] Most Ottawas, however, continued to find the alliance with France fruitful and would, along with the Potawatomis, stand firm among France's best allies in the New World. The alliance served Ottawas well, bringing them trade, goods, blacksmiths, gunsmiths, and, most important, good allies among French soldiers, Potawatomis, Ojibwas, and Wyandots. Strengthened by these useful relations, Ottawas would enter the uncertain ground of the Upper Ohio Country, where they came to know the Delawares.

Cadillac recorded what may well be the earliest reference to Delaware-Ottawa encounters when he noted the visit of a band of Indians he called the Openango, or Wolves.[24] Later in the eighteenth century, the term *Wolf* generally applied to Delawares, but here it could also have meant another, more northeastern people. By the time of Pontiac's War, the Delawares and Ottawas knew each other well, and the Delawares' own history had lessons for the Ottawas, as we shall see. The term *Delaware*, unlike the term *Ottawa*, is an English denomination, stemming from Lord De La Warr, a governor of Virginia for whom the seventeenth-century English named the Delaware River. The ancestors of the peoples who by the late colonial period were commonly called Delawares lived in small, autonomous villages along the fertile valleys that drained into the lower Hudson River, the Delaware River, and the Atlantic waters in between. They spoke a single "Delawarean" language consisting of at least two dialects, Unami and Munsee. Conveniently, and perhaps significantly, "Delawarean" belongs, like the Anishinabe languages, to the greater Algonquian family of languages.[25] Delawarean-speaking people generally referred to themselves as "Lenape" or "Lenni Lenape," names that seem to have meant, rather simply, "people," "people people," or, less redundantly, "ordinary people." Wrapping one's tongue around the names "Lenni Lenape" and "Anishinabeg" in quick succession can give one a sense of the relatedness of the languages. "Lenni" meant "people," and "Anish" seems to have been a greeting. "Lenape" and "inabeg" signified "people."[26]

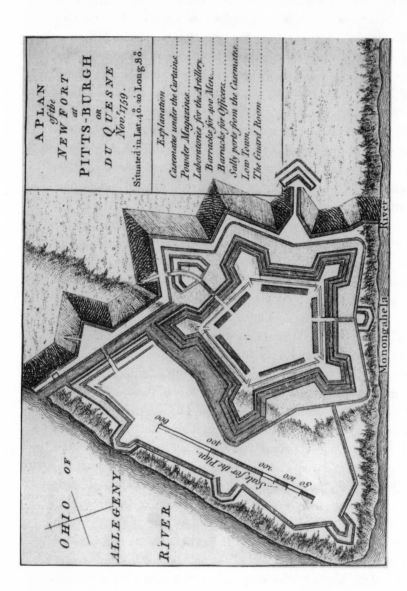

Fort Pitt may never have been as neat as it appears in this plan of 1759, but its large, strong, and elaborate construction sent a clear message that Great Britain intended to dominate the Ohio Country. Courtesy Clements Library, University of Michigan.

As with the Ottawas, there was never a single Delaware polity, never a "chief" or a council that presided over a single, unified nation. Large political and geographic divisions separate the various enduring Delaware groups to this day. But if political disunity marked the Delawares, a sense of commonality as a people had emerged by the mid-eighteenth century. A shared sense of experience, as well as the mutual intelligibility of Lenape dialects, brought about this Lenape identity.[27]

Delawares told the story of their world in idioms that would have been familiar to Pontiac. Their world also formed in troubled waters, through the agency of a sacred person assisted by animals who dove to the sea bottom, resurfacing with the regenerative muck. Like that of the Ottawas, the Delawares' story is less one of creation than of renewal and transformation. The world does not begin out of nothing but out of something else. There are, to be sure, differences between Delaware and Anishinabe cosmologies, for the Delaware hero at the origins of the current world is usually a pregnant woman rather than the "Great Hare."[28] Yet extant sources on Lenape religion in the colonial period do mention a Great Hare. In the 1770s the Moravian missionary David Zeisberger called him Tschimammus, a "great God," who was "one of the twins born to the woman that was thrown from heaven." Zeisberger says that Tschimammus, like Nanabush, "made the land" and then ascended to the sky world, "promising one day to return." Other Lenape manitous also resemble, at times, the Anishinabe trickster. The powerful being known as Mësingw presided over deer and other animals. Delawares represented him with a mask, and his name meant "living solid face." Much as Anishinabeg might appeal to Nanabush when hunting, Delawares might appeal to Mësingw. Delawares, too, respected thunderers, great horned serpents, winter cannibal giants, and much else that a devout Ottawa would recognize, including the very word for sacred power, *manëtu*.[29]

If the Delawares' story of their world's origins and of their relationship to the sacred powers would not have surprised Ottawas, the Delawares' stories of their relations with the British might well have shocked them. The Ottawas had developed close, if difficult, ties with both the neighboring upper Great Lakes Indians and the French. The Delawares had confronted a greater variety of newcomers: Swedes, Finns, Netherlanders, Germans, Africans, and Britons. Moreover, whereas the Anishinabeg played a central part in French imperial expansion into the interior, the Delawares found themselves quickly outclassed in their dealings with Europeans by the Iroquois League. Finally, the French came among the Ottawas to gain their trade, their souls, their hand in marriage, or their comradeship in arms, but the British especially came among the Delawares to gain their lands; they created farms, villages, and even the city of Philadelphia, which was, by Pontiac's adulthood, the largest, most bustling place north of Mexico. This last contrast would profoundly shape the Delaware experience by 1750. Whereas Ottawas had not lost an acre of land to the French but had instead in French company expanded their reach into more fertile country, while still maintaining excellent fisheries and hunting grounds, Delawares had yielded almost all their original holdings to the British.

Delawares and Colonies

In 1664 Charles II, king of England, Scotland, and Ireland, gave his brother James, the duke of York, a generous gift: everything between the Delaware and Connecticut Rivers, including the entire Hudson Valley, plus Long Island, Martha's Vineyard, Nantucket, most of what is now Maine, and a bit of Quebec. Charles, sitting comfortably in England, could easily ignore the Abenakis, Wampanoags, Mahicans, Mohawks, Delawares, and others to whom the regions belonged by birthright; such peoples barely figured in European conceptions of international law. To the Dutch, however, whose colony of New Netherland lay smack in the middle of the grant, Charles and James had to pay attention. Accepting the gift, James sent an armed fleet to take possession, precipitating the Second Anglo-Dutch War (1664–67). New Netherland fell to England without a shot, opening the Hudson and Delaware Valleys to English-sponsored settlement.

Delawares soon found that they had to negotiate with the swelling ranks of new arrivals from colonial New England, Europe, and Africa. These places were to the east: the first of the four cardinal directions orienting Delaware history for nearly the next century. After weathering the devastation of disease brought on by almost a century of sustained contact with Europe, the Delaware population probably stood at around 6,000 by 1700, while in what is now New Jersey alone there were some 14,000 newcomers. New York had some 21,500 colonists, concentrated in the lower Hudson and on Long Island, while Pennsylvania had some 18,000, also concentrated in Delaware environs. By 1750, settler populations in these three colonies had prodigiously swelled to 300,000 by both immigration and natural increase, challenging the Delawares in ways that Ottawas could scarcely have imagined. For well over a century, Ottawas had no reason to associate Europeans with dispossession. As early as 1671 Delawares thought differently: "Where the English come they drive them from their lands."[30]

The second cardinal direction was the west, where the Susquehanna Valley of Pennsylvania beckoned as a refuge. The Susquehannock Indians, battered by wars with the Delawares (to 1634) and with Maryland (1643–52) and devastated by diseases ("purple rash," 1636–37; smallpox, 1661), were dispersed in the 1670s and 1680s in wars with Maryland, Virginia, and the Iroquois League. This was not total extermination. Survivors, for the most part, seemed to have surrendered their tribal identities and merged with the Iroquois and Delawares who now migrated into their valley.[31]

The third point on the Delaware quadrant lay to the south, as ships sailed north up the Delaware River, bringing a truly vast and unusual invasion. The Delaware Valley became the site of Quaker colonization, beginning with the establishment of West New Jersey in 1676 and accelerating in 1682 with the founding of Pennsylvania, William Penn's "Holy Experiment" in religious toleration. Bent on peace, Penn had promised a great deal to the Delawares—primarily a regular, peaceful trade.[32]

Finally, to the north lay the Iroquois League, whose wars with the Great Lakes Indians had done so much to shape the Ottawas' alliance with France. The Delawares' encounters with the British colonies were also influenced by the Iroquois League. The Delawares were not enemies of the league but were the league's junior allies in an arrangement that was increasingly unequal and vague. Delaware power seemed to diminish as Iroquois prestige rose in British North America. Between 1675 and the early eighteenth century the Iroquois and the neighboring English had formed the "Covenant Chain." The partners to this arrangement, which was not quite an alliance, recognized each other's power and authority and agreed to the peaceful resolution of conflict. The most famous event in the history of the Delawares' relations with both Pennsylvania and the Iroquois League was not a war in the wilderness but a hike along a trail. The intricate history of the "Walking Purchase" has often been recounted. It amounted to a great land fraud, in the course of which a faction of Iroquois headmen came to cooperate with members of the proprietary government of Pennsylvania to deprive Delawares of their homes and fields. The fraud had become, by the 1750s, a highly charged political symbol among both Delawares and Pennsylvanians.

The lands, known as the Forks of the Delaware, belonged to a large Delaware group whose most prominent leader was Nutimus. Pennsylvania's proprietors shared an interest in extinguishing Indian claims to the region. Deeply in debt, they had already sold tracts in the region—despite clear Delaware title—to prospective immigrants. In the fall of 1734, the proprietors John and Thomas Penn, supported by their leading agent, James Logan, determined to acquire Nutimus's lands, but Nutimus would not sell. The next year, instead of renewing a probably fruitless effort to buy the land, Logan laid a document on the negotiating table and claimed it to be the copy of a deed from Indians to William Penn, dated 1686. Armed with this dubious paper, Logan maintained that the Delawares had in 1686 sold to Penn the entire western shore of the Delaware River, an area that encompassed much more than the Forks.[33] Nutimus cried fraud, but pacifistic Pennsylvania soon rallied a powerful force against him: the Iroquois League, which had strong influence in the Susquehanna and Delaware Valleys. League spokesmen encouraged the Delawares to negotiate.

This was bad enough, but the exhilarating possibilities of fraud seem to have captured James Logan. Logan met with the overpowered Forks Delawares in August 1737 and persuaded them to sign a document confirming the suspect deed of 1686. As Francis Jennings has shown, the Delawares, who could not read but who knew the local geography well, were shown a map, the cartography of which led them to believe that the lands they now ceded lay downriver from their villages. In fact, the map's writing indicated that the ceded lands lay to the north of Tohiccon Creek and thus included their villages. And, in the most notorious incidence of Logan's fraud, the full extent of the lands to be relinquished were to be determined not by the alleged copy of the 1686 deed or by the new but misleading map but by a one-and-one-half-day "walk."

The direction of the walk on the deed is rendered unclear by blanks in the manuscript. The walk, performed by known colonial athletes on cleared trails, covered 66.5 miles, amounting to 55 linear miles: 12,000 square miles of land. Far beyond anything the Delaware signers of the Walking Purchase deed had imagined, the Walking Purchase took away virtually all their lands. The Delawares did not wait for the walk to be finished before they started protesting, and after it was done, they refused to leave their villages. By 1740, however, Pennsylvania had issued patents on the lands, and settlers moved in. Delawares petitioned the justice of the peace of Bucks County but got nowhere.

Nutimus had one last hope, the Iroquois, but they took Pennsylvania's side. The Onondagas' speaker, Canasatego, claimed that the Delawares had no right to dispose of the lands in the first place, because Delawares had been conquered by the Iroquois. No such conquest is known in the record. Canasatego ordered the Delawares to leave the Forks and to retire to lands that the Six Nations set aside for them in the Susquehanna Valley. As the Delawares migrated westward, the British came to understand that they did so under Iroquois auspices, protection, and, eventually, domination.

The Walking Purchase hardly in itself explains the Delaware hostility toward the British. Not all of Pennsylvania's Delaware Indians once inhabited the Walking Purchase lands. Nor were the Penns and Logan the only Europeans to give the Delawares cause for war. Nutimus and his band, in any case, did not go to war in 1742 as they were being forced from their lands. But as Delawares headed west in the eighteenth century, they carried with them knowledge of the rapid increase in the settlers' population, the rapacious proprietary quest for land, and the irregular workings of the Iroquois-British Covenant Chain. The Delawares had learned a great deal about the empire that was becoming more firmly, and more militantly, established in North America.

To the Susquehanna and Ohio Rivers

Through the diplomacy of the Covenant Chain the Iroquois League had gained sway over the Susquehanna Valley in Pennsylvania and New York in the late seventeenth century. The Iroquois did not seek the region for themselves alone. Rather, they invited a scattering of peoples from east, west, and south to settle the valley in peace under their auspices. One Iroquoian people, the Tuscaroras, migrated to the upper valley from the piedmont of North Carolina to be welcomed as the Sixth Nation of the Iroquois League in the decade before 1722. Though the league did not fully admit other peoples as member nations, it did welcome other nations to the region to form an Indian buffer against English expansion, act as Indian allies in the event of war against any enemy, and work as Indian partners in an extensive trade.[34]

The migrants also made for one of the most ethnically diverse regions on the continent, a fitting counterpart to the Pennsylvania colony. Even as German, Scottish, Scots-Irish, English, Huguenot, and other European settlers—accompanied by African slaves—stood poised to invade the valley, Indians had already foreshadowed the process: western Shawnees, the southern Conoys, Nanticokes, and Tutelos, and the eastern Delawares had learned to live side by side, having migrated to the region in the late seventeenth and early eighteenth centuries. Many Susquehannocks, though thinned in numbers, had also been able to remain there. Delawares soon dominated the valley's Pennsylvanian reaches numerically.[35]

Delawares, Shawnees, and others came to resent the Iroquois League's claim to legitimate authority in the region, particularly as that claim rang louder in the 1740s and after. A good many Delawares and Shawnees left the region for the Ohio as soon as they got the chance in the 1720s and 1730s, independently establishing themselves and underscoring that independence by trading directly with Pennsylvanians and Virginians operating well beyond Iroquoian control. The league's claim to dominate these Ohioans may have elevated league authority, but with it rose Delaware and Shawnee resentments.

These resentments did not add up to ethnic conflict with the Iroquois. The Ohioans did not identify tribalism, in the sense of age-old dislikes between Algonquians and Iroquois, as the source of difficulty. They saw that the league itself was highly divided: riven by pro-French, pro–New York, pro-Pennsylvanian, and pro-neutrality factions who vied for authority and competed diplomatically. From the outside, it sometimes appeared as if the league astutely played one colony or colonial power against the other. But on the inside, the league faced constant bickering, power grabbing, and such serious divisions that civil war appeared likely in the 1750s. The Onondaga people, highly influential in the Susquehanna Valley, tended to support the Covenant Chain with the British colonies, whereas many Senecas, more influential in the Ohio region and more factionalized, took strong anti-British positions.[36]

In fact, as anti-British factions emerged among the Ohio Delawares, they gained allies among the Iroquois. Parties of Senecas and other Iroquois joined the Algonquian migrants in the Ohio region. A large number of these expatriate Six Nations "Mingos" came, like their Seneca cousins, to oppose the Covenant Chain with Great Britain. Anti-British factions of Delawares would have little difficulty cooperating with Iroquoian Mingos during the 1750s and after. In the Susquehanna Valley, as in the Ohio, intertribal associations became the norm, even at the most intimate level of the household. Residents in Delaware villages, even under Delaware roofs, were often ethnically non-Delaware. Various Algonquian peoples formed alliances, and Iroquoian men and women moved, lived, and worked beside Algonquian peoples, sometimes in the same village, even in the same home.

A midcentury description of the Indian towns of Juniata and Wyoming on the Susquehanna reveals the growing importance of such intertribalism in war and religion. The fate of these towns speaks volumes for the causes of the Delawares' war in 1763. Juniata was largely a Conoy Indian town, located on the Great Island at the mouth of the Juniata River, a tributary of the Susquehanna. David Brainerd, the New Light Congregationalist missionary, entered the town one Sunday in 1745. He found the inhabitants "almost universally busy in making preparations for a great sacrifice," and he was entirely unable to preach to them. A huge "sacred dance" dedicated to the "sacrifice" of "ten fat deer" took up the whole night. Two days later, Brainerd was similarly disappointed in his efforts to preach, as the Indians were too busy with another ritual to attend to his Christian teachings. This time six "pow-wows (or conjurers)" endeavored to discover the causes of a diarrhetic fever then sweeping the island. Brainerd, a Bible in hand, watched them and prayed that God would "prevent their receiving any answers from the infernal world." He reckoned his effort a success.[37]

Most striking was his encounter with a Conoy in "pontifical garb," to use Brainerd's anti-Catholic idiom. Beating a rhythm with a tortoiseshell rattle, dancing in remarkable postures, and dressed entirely in bearskin save for a wooden mask painted reddish and black ("the mouth cut very much awry"), the figure danced toward Brainerd, who at first fled a short distance. But when the performance was over and Brainerd spoke with him, the missionary became impressed and visited the man's "house consecrated to religious uses, with divers images cut out upon the several parts of it" and with a dirt floor well pounded by dancers. The Susquehanna Valley Indians were in the midst of a religious revival, with decidedly anti-Christian overtones.[38] Brainerd's younger brother, John, visiting the region six years later, saw more of the revival upriver at the town of Wyoming. Once the southern portion of the Susquehannocks' homeland, Wyoming was by 1750 rich in diversity, hosting Nanticokes, Shawnees, and Delawares; among the last were those defrauded of their lands in the Walking Purchase.[39] Victims of Covenant Chain injustice, these Delawares harbored sentiments that would make it easy to oppose British and Iroquois League authority should an opportunity arise.

At John Brainerd's arrival in Wyoming, the Indians welcomed him warmly, "seeming glad to see [him]." But his timing was unfortunate. When the village council allowed Brainerd to address it, the councillors had other business on their mind, including a local woman's recent vision. This vision called for the destruction of a "poison" that she claimed was secretly kept by the town's "old and principal men," the political leaders of Wyoming, which was still, in the early 1750s, under strong Iroquois League influence. The townspeople, moreover, spoke in a religious idiom that flatly opposed Brainerd's mission. To the evangelist's Christian en-treaties, they replied that "the Great God first made three men and three women, viz: the Indian, the negro, and the white man." Practically accus-ing Brainerd of arrogance, they declared that "the white man was the youngest brother, and therefore the white people ought not to think themselves better than the Indians." Indeed, the Wyoming Indians made it plain to Brainerd that they considered him an enemy: "The white people were contriving a method to deprive them of their country in those parts, as they had done by the sea-side, and to make slaves of them and their children as they did of the negroes; that I was sent on purpose to accomplish that design."[40] Ambivalent toward the league, bitter about past British treatment and fearful of its recurrence, hostile to Christian ministers, nativistic in attitude, critical and even fearful of slavery, the polyglot people of Wyoming were in 1751 on the verge of spurning their standing, as subordinates, in the Covenant Chain.

The Delawares of Wyoming, like other Delawares, had remained at peace with the British colonies for some ninety years. Given their vast losses to disease and to British land hunger, they could be said to have demonstrated remarkable patience. Those ninety years were more than times of suffering at the hands of Britons and Iroquois—though the Dela-wares did suffer and were victimized. They were also times of migration, of adapting to new environments, and of fashioning new landscapes deeper in the American interior. Most important, the times saw the invention of a new Indian identity in the face of the encounter with domineering new peoples. By the time those ninety years ended, Delawares would know well not only the British Empire, the Iroquois League, and the polyglot peoples of the Susquehanna and Ohio Rivers but also the Ottawas of the French alliance.

The two great associations that Indians and Europeans had created together in the second half of the seventeenth century, the Great Lakes Indians' alliance with France and the Iroquois League's Covenant Chain with Great Britain, stood by the 1730s as if they were tall trees with shallow roots, leaning dangerously toward each other amid high winds rising in the Ohio Country. As branches of the two associations brushed, Ottawas and Delawares became acquainted. Their relations would be conditioned by a singular fact: Ottawas, among France's best partners in American empire, bore few of the Delawares' deep historical grievances against their arrangements with Europeans.[41]

Ohioan Rendezvous, 1700–1763

South of Lake Erie lay a land of promise, and many Indian peoples gathered peacefully on it. Shawnees, once expelled by war from the upper Ohio Valley, returned. Mingos, formerly Six Nations Iroquois (especially Senecas), moved in from the east, while Wyandots, formerly Wendots or Tionnontatés, moved in from the north and west. Small groups of Kahnawakes, Abenakis, and others from the French missions on the St. Lawrence became the region's first lapsed Catholics. Delawares and other Algonquians, once familiar with the Atlantic seaboard, moved in to meet Ottawas once familiar with the country north of the Great Lakes. As British traders ventured in to purchase skins, colonial speculators hired them to report on the quality of the lands. We can call the region, broadly, the Upper Ohio Country, bounded to the north by Lake Erie, to the east by the Allegheny Mountains, to the south by the Ohio watershed, and to the west by the Maumee and Miami Rivers.

A well-watered place of woods and plains, knobby hills, strong mountains, and abundant rivers, the Upper Ohio Country would soon be the scene of great conflict. Shawnees, the Iroquois League, the British, the French, and the Wyandots all launched overlapping claims.[42] Converging on the lands, however, the Indian peoples did not fight for them; indeed, their intertribal relations were largely peaceful during the first generation of resettlement. For the first three decades of the century, while the Fox and Chickasaw Wars raged to the west and southwest, the upper Ohio region saw less organized violence: the occasional departure of warriors to raid Catawbas and Cherokees, the occasional eruption of retaliating southeasterners. Hunting grounds in Kentucky were more fiercely contested, but peace generally prevailed in the cornfields and villages of the upper Ohio.

In 1744, King George's War brought to an end a generation of relative peace between Great Britain and France. The war brought no colonial armies into the upper Ohio region, but it did bring colonial attention, as British and French officials sought to secure allies and discipline enemies. British traders such as George Croghan penetrated the Ohio Country, establishing posts as close to Detroit as Sandusky, toward the western end of Lake Erie. There dissident Wyandots in 1747 reinforced French fears by forming a conspiracy to destroy Detroit's Fort Pontchartrain in concert with Miami Indian raids on French posts. The plot did not advance far, but as the European peace of 1748 ended King George's War, Frenchmen and loyal Ottawas united to strengthen the alliance by force of arms. North and south of the lake, joint French-Ottawa expeditions moved to impose discipline on the alliance. In 1749, the first blow hit the Mississaugas, an Ojibwa people north of Lakes Erie and Ontario who had opened a trade with the British. Three years later, well south of the lake, Ottawas allied to France hit the polyglot, Miami-dominated town of Pickawillany. Catching the heavily fortified trading center when most of its men were off hunting, the Ottawas killed several British traders and Indian leaders.[43]

As Ottawas worked to stanch defections to the British trading system, they also supported, in 1749, the most impressive French effort to nail French claims to the Ohio. Captain Pierre-Joseph Céloron de Blainville led 256 French and Canadian mission Indians along with some Ottawas on a circuitous trip through the upper Ohio region. Though he was able to tack plaques proclaiming French dominion to some trees and to bury less brave but more permanent lead plates inscribed to the same effect in the soil, Céloron found many Ohioans barely tolerant of his heavily armed expedition. Céloron saw the French *drapeau blanc* flying its welcome above some villages, but he encountered red British flags above others; tellingly, some villages flew both. In clear terms, the Mingo, Delaware, and Shawnee Indians told Céloron that they would welcome English and French traders alike.[44]

Although the French were determined to gain full sway in the region, they did not seek to gain the land itself, at least not land that lay beyond the walls of their often puny installations. The French officers who, following Céloron, built those places generally had good experience in Indian affairs. Captain Claude-Pierre Pécaudy de Contrecoeur, commander at Fort Niagara among the Senecas, had vast knowledge of the American interior and its Indians. He had served at Fort Saint-Frédéric and had accompanied Céloron on the mission of 1749. In 1754 he moved into the Ohio Country to build and command Fort Duquesne. In his efforts to rally local Ohioans in 1754 and 1755, he had help from Jacques Baby, *dit* Dupéront, and his brothers Antoine and Louis, all three experienced fur traders in the Great Lakes and Ohio Country, all men with excellent Shawnee connections. Captain Daniel-Hyacinthe-Marie Liénard de Beaujeu, who in 1755 would lead the mobile force that smashed General Edward Braddock's army in the most remarkable feat of the entire Seven Years' War, had already fought well beside Indians at Nova Scotia and had also served at Fort Niagara. These were men who knew both the intricacies of Indian diplomacy and the utter military dependence of the French on their Indian allies. More important, when the French came to the Ohio Country, they did so with those allies and with Ottawas in particular. Virginia's agent Christopher Gist learned as much from an Indian trader, who warned him "to keep clear of the Outawais."[45]

Contrecoeur arrived at the confluence of the Monongahela, Allegheny, and Ohio Rivers with some six hundred men, including Ottawas and other Indian allies from the lakes, in April 1754. Without bloodshed, he ordered home a small party of Virginians commanded by Ensign Edward Ward, knocked down the unimpressive, unfinished Virginian stockade, and erected in its place a small but elaborate earthen and picketed structure. Fort Duquesne, as it rose under the profuse sweat of laboring men directed by Captain François Le Mercier, combined the rough elements of a frontier palisade with the principles of fortification developed by French and Dutch engineers in the age of Louis XIV. The floor plan was the standard European star shape; from its pointed corner bastions, studded with fifteen cannon, defenders could easily spray lead into enemies charging its gates. Outside the walls lay a series of elaborate snares.[46]

For all its sophisticated engineering and despite the fact that it was the largest of the French forts in the upper Ohio region, at 154 feet by 160 feet Fort Duquesne was a hoax. Stony Fort de Chartres, in the Illinois Country to the west, dwarfed it by a factor of nine. Fort Saint-Frédéric in the Lake Champlain corridor to the far northeast was commanded by a four-story stone tower, bristling with cannon. It is true that Fort Duquesne looked the part of a citadel, but it did so in miniature. Had it been large enough to accommodate hundreds of men, it could have stood against anything but a well-manned, carefully conducted British siege operation. As it was, it was too small even to accommodate its garrison; the French never expanded it in more than a perfunctory manner, and they had little reason to do so.[47] Fort Duquesne depended on a line of defense not to be found in the great European defensive engineering treatises. This barrier was made of living flesh, not of earth, wood, or stone, and to it France owed its North American empire. Fort Duquesne, medallion of France rather than a genuine military installation, was defended by the very Indians it appeared, at first glance, to dominate.

If, as is possible, Pontiac stood in 1757 among its human defenders, then he must have felt claustrophobic amid the interior jumble of log buildings: barracks, kitchens, and officers' quarters. Still, the magazines, storehouses, prison, and blacksmith shop would have drawn his interest.[48] Ottawas, Ojibwas, Potawatomis, Wyandots, Miamis, Shawnees, Delawares, Mingos, and others, like the French, saw the place as far more than a crammed jumble of buildings or a confusing assortment of terms from a military dictionary. It was primarily a place for organizing the remarkable conglomeration of humanity that slept outside its walls for the purpose of war against the British colonies. In the long run, it was the mixing, the negotiating, the celebrating of victory, and the mourning of losses that would be both of greater historical significance and of more durable legacy than the perishable walls and ditches themselves, for although Fort Duquesne's elaborate defenses and its aggressive claim to the Ohio Valley attracted the approach of three British armies in the 1750s, not one of them would stud its walls with lead.

The first of three British invasions involved some 134 Virginia provincials who would later be backed up by another 200, supported, in the rear, by an independent company of the king's regulars dispatched from South Carolina. It was commanded by twenty-two-year-old George Washington, who would never even lay eyes on the *drapeau blanc* floating above

Duquesne's bastions. When still a four days' march from the fort, Washington was joined by a small, still pro-British party of Mingo Indians under Tanaghrisson, the "Half-King." Together, the British and their allies surprised and killed ten members of a French platoon that had come out to find Washington. Among the dead was Ensign Joseph Coulon de Villiers, Sieur de Jumonville. Back at Fort Duquesne, Contrecoeur, who had already spent a month organizing his troops and appealing to Indians for aid, implored the Indians to support the French father against those who had "murdered" de Villiers and nine other of his "children," sickening his heart: "I unblock your ears so that you will hear well, and unblock your throat so that my words will reach your heart and you will feel the same pain that I feel."[49]

The fort's human shield—a force of almost eight hundred men, mostly French regulars and militia accompanied both by mission Indians from the reserves on the St. Lawrence River and by Mississaugas, Hurons, Nipissings, Ottawas, and others of the Great Lakes-sallied out under the command of the dead ensign's brother, Captain Louis Coulon de Villiers, to swallow up Washington's four hundred effective men. De Villiers carefully "deferred" to Indian judgment on all kinds of matters and promised "not to expose them rashly," a promise he kept. By contrast, Washington had alienated his Mingo allies. As one later reported, "The Colonel was a good-natured man, but had no experience; he took upon him to command the Indians as his slaves, . . . [and he] would by no means take advice from the Indians." Tanaghrisson abandoned him before the French struck. Washington, lacking the protection of living Indians, retreated to the site of a mound, built centuries before by Indian laborers. There he set up a crude stockade aptly named Fort Necessity. He surrendered after a one-day siege on July 4, 1754.[50]

The pattern of French reliance on Indians and British neglect of them intensified when, a year later, General Edward Braddock marched on Fort Duquesne with the second of the three invading British armies. After expertly commanding his forces, many straining at ponderous siege guns, across the high, deep, wooded Alleghenies, and after carefully establishing supply depots along the way, he still had almost fifteen hundred well-armed and, for the most part, well-trained regulars, provincials, wagoners, and sutlers when, on July 9, 1755, he came within reach of his objective. But he had only eight Indians. Even these had become highly wary of their British allies.[51]

A few days before, on July 6, a bold Indian commando from Fort Duquesne had briefly harassed Braddock's line, first firing into its rear, then into its flank, before fleeing. Braddock's few Indian allies attempted to pursue the warriors, only to find themselves under edgy British fire as they returned to the army. The incident cost more than the life of one man, the son of the Oneida headman who had commanded the small party. It also deepened a dislike that these Oneidas had already formed for this British venture.[52] Three days later the dislike became disgust.

At Fort Duquesne, the French dreaded the British approach. Allied Indians could not be expected to fight from the cramped ramparts, yet if the Indians abandoned Duquesne, the British would easily have the three-to-one advantage that most theorists considered necessary to take a fortified position by storm. Braddock's big guns could, moreover, easily destroy the earthen and timbered walls, eliminating the need for such a costly frontal assault. Undermanned and underfortified, Contrecoeur was not even confident in his supply of ammunition. In creative desperation, he had already at one point encouraged warriors to try to slow Braddock's march by killing his horses, at night, with spears.[53]

In the humid midafternoon of a sweltering July 9, the forward columns of the formidable British army collided with the motley force of roughly 250 French regulars and militia under a captain and 640 allied Indian warriors: Ottawas, Ojibwas, Potawatomis, Shawnees, Mingos, and a few Delawares. The Ottawas were "led," if they had such leadership, by Charles Langlade, an Ottawa Métis who had commanded at the Ottawa attacks on the Mississaugas in 1749 and the Miamis at Pickawillany in 1752. The collision began the well-known battle of the Monongahela, the worst British defeat yet suffered in North America. British troops, rapidly encircled by enemy fire, performed so badly that their reputation would remain long tarnished in the folk memory of North America. Fort Duquesne's walls never came under fire as its human defenders, overwhelmingly Indians from the *pays d'en haut*, shredded its professional attackers. Indians from the Ohio Country took note of the British defeat and allied themselves with France.[54] Not for three years would another army threaten the post.

Fort Duquesne became the Ohioan hub of the growing alliance with France. It brought Indians together, hosting meetings to resolve disputes that arose both among the tribes and between the tribes and the French. Fort Duquesne stood most securely when it had strong Indian encampments surrounding it, but keeping these took work. In 1756, a British colonial prisoner at Duquesne observed that "there was about 250 Frenchmen in this Fort, besides Indians, which at one time amounted to 500; but the Indians were very uncertain."[55] Armed from Fort Duquesne, Great Lakes and Ohio Indians terrorized the backcountry of Pennsylvania, Maryland, and Virginia. Many of their cousins east of the Alleghenies, along the Susquehanna River, joined them, severely punishing Pennsylvanians who had settled their valley. Even to the east, on November 24, 1755, the Susquehanna Delawares struck Gnadenhütten, a Moravian Christian mission on the Lehigh River. Ten of the German-speaking men, women, and children were killed. In a weirdly symbolic act, the killers left behind a hat and a blanket, pinned to a stump with a knife. Hats in the Northeast were widely used to symbolize Europeans in native iconography. In Delaware religious symbolism, hats were coming to represent not only Europeans but also greed. Gnadenhütten lay in the Walking Purchase.[56]

Indians of the Susquehanna River area had more immediate grievances. In 1753, Connecticut Yankees of the Susquehanna Company had made "draughts of the lands and rivers" along the Wyoming stretch of the Susquehanna River. In 1754, in the shadow of the Albany Congress, company man John Lydius had encouraged several prominent Six Nations representatives to affix their names to a deed releasing some five million acres of land around Wyoming, "tempting the Indians he could prevail upon with Plenty of Dollars . . . when they were drunk." Pennsylvania Indian agent Conrad Weiser doubted that the Susquehanna Indians would "suffer the New England men, nor anybody else to settle on Wayomack Land." Meanwhile, Pennsylvanians, many without any deed, occupied lands as far up the Susquehanna as the mouth of the Juniata. Delawares, Conoys, and others notified Pennsylvania that they were "much offended" at these intrusions.[57]

One Susquehanna Delaware leader to emerge during the war would best represent the anger of Delawares who for so long had kept peace with both Great Britain and the Six Nations. Teedyuscung, a powerful orator about fifty-five years old, had seen his people suffer at the hand of the Covenant Chain. A direct witness to the Walking Purchase fraud, Teedyuscung had himself for a few years joined the Moravian community at Gnadenhütten, changing his name to Gideon. By 1754 he had shaken off Christianity and joined the multilingual Indian community at Wyoming. When Ohio Delawares slipped through the Alleghenies to raid Pennsylvanians in 1755, Teedyuscung raised warriors to attack British settlements on the upper Delaware River. Rejecting openly the authority of the Covenant Chain, by which the Iroquois had undertaken to maintain control over the Susquehanna Valley, Teedyuscung made it clear that the Susquehanna Delawares, like their Ohio cousins, were fully independent.[58] From Pennsylvania's Susquehanna River to Ohio's Scioto, Delawares, Shawnees, Mingos, and other Indians declared that independence in blood. By the end of 1756, some seven hundred Pennsylvania farming people had been killed or captured, and governance in the province had collapsed.

Effective as the French and Indian alliance around Fort Duquesne was in punishing colonial Pennsylvania, it proved to be but a bubble, expanding beyond its limits before bursting messily. Then it was gone. Disaffection began among the newest of the newcomers, the Susquehanna Valley Delawares themselves, only tenuously connected to the alliance in any case, having had few contacts with the French. These contacts, moreover, had been disheartening. Teedyuscung visited a tattered French garrison at Niagara in 1756 and learned that the French could not supply his men with arms. Trying again the next year, he had no better luck. The French failure to arm his forces was decisive; in conference with Pennsylvanians, New Yorkers, and Six Nations Iroquois at Easton, Pennsylvania, he agreed to a truce, which was followed by a peace in October 1758.

If Niagara was poorly supplied, so was Fort Duquesne, its dependent. Louis-Antoine de Bougainville, aide-de-camp to the commander of France's American forces, first heard reports of Duquesne's lack of munitions in July 1757; by winter he insisted that a real danger of Delaware defection existed and that "there should be a great amount of trade goods at Fort Duquesne to guard against this threat." There should have been— but there was not. Bougainville blamed corruption. Without the matériel to outfit warriors, without the gifts with which to host assemblies and conferences, French officers lost stature on the upper Ohio River. As early as 1757, peace factions among Ohio Delawares sent feelers to colonial Pennsylvania. Even Ottawas would only support the alliance as long as France played its part. Once it became clear that the French could no longer supply the material leadership, the Ottawas refused to do French bidding. In one dramatic episode, the French at Duquesne demanded that the Ottawas attack Delawares who were entertaining messengers from the British. The Ottawas, who just six years before had completed a similar assignment against Miamis at Pickawillany, this time declined. It was a sign that the Great Lakes alliance with France was in jeopardy. It was also a sign that Ottawas had come to identify with Delawares.[59]

In September 1758 a third British army, some five thousand troops under General John Forbes and Colonel Henry Bouquet, was advancing on Fort Duquesne. Camped at Loyalhanna, Forbes's army had already accomplished a feat of meticulous planning and execution. This time the British had with them about sixty Indians, mostly Catawbas from South Carolina, along with a few Tuscaroras. Bouquet hated Indians enough to order that none among the enemy be taken alive, but even he admitted that Indians gave the French certain advantages. Noting that France's Native American allies routinely captured British messengers, he concluded, "Therefore the French may pretty well be informed of our Preceedings [sic]. I am ashamed that they Succeed in all their Scouting Partys and that we never have any Success in ours."[60] Nonetheless, the British did surprise Fort Duquesne and its Indians when, on September 14, eight hundred redcoats and provincials burst upon them at the Forks. The troops were a detachment of Forbes's army, led by Major James Grant, and they had pushed over Chestnut Ridge to approach Fort Duquesne under cover of darkness. They formed, after a fashion, a multicultural force. Scouting parties included fourteen Catawbas, Tuscaroras, and Nottoways. Regulars and provincials passed along orders in Scottish, German, and Chesapeake accents. Grant had planned no assault on the fort. His main task, as Bouquet wrote in French to Forbes, was to "check the boldness of this Indian rabble." Bouquet and his officers, sanctioning Grant's audacious raid, understood that Fort Duquesne was all about Indians. A British victory would, Bouquet believed, "be the means of curing [his troops] of the panic terror they had of them."[61]

On September 14, Grant, at two in the morning, ordered half of his command to surprise Indians camping about the fort. Exhaustion and darkness soon befuddled the soldiers, who stumbled back to Grant's main position without accomplishing anything except to alert the enemy of their arrival. Desperate to boost morale and emboldened to act decisively, Grant threw a detachment of one hundred Highlanders into the open ground, directly toward the gates. In the disaster that followed, practically eight hundred breech-clouted Indians along with some Canadian militia and regulars scattered the Scots, killing their captain and panicking the rest of the British forces, only 525 of whom safely recovered the forty miles to the main camp. Luckless Grant, taken prisoner, was not one of them.[62] His defeat ended the last of the assaults that had approached but never reached the walls of Fort Duquesne. Fort Duquesne's defensive actions had all taken place either on the open ground before it or in the woods well beyond its walls. In every case, Indian warriors had taken action, and in the last two battles they had dominated.

The defeats of Washington, Braddock, and Grant reveal that Fort Duquesne served more to symbolize a French commitment to the region and its people than it did to project French imperium. Instead of a besieged frontier garrison or a provocative Gallic insult to Virginia, Fort Duquesne functioned as a rendezvous, a place of rough fisticuffs and handshakes, shouting and speechifying, scorning and smoking, drinking and regaling, fighting and reconciliation, prayer and despair. Within and outside the walls, Indians of a variety of tribes had come to know one another even as they had come to know the French. The fort was also a supply depot, from which Indians were fed and outfitted and near which they and members of their families worked, slept, and buried their dead as their men prepared for and returned from the dangerous and grim business of raiding and murdering on the British frontier. Among the peoples who met here regularly were the Delawares and the Ottawas, the people of Neolin and Pontiac. It is likely that both men spent some time about its defenses.

Indians did not come to Fort Duquesne simply to be mobilized; their own goals often caused French officers great difficulty. Even after great victories in the early years of the war, when one might expect the flush of success to promote fraternal unity among the various Indian allies, fights over the spoils had erupted. Ottawa warriors, feeling deprived of their share of the plunder from Braddock's defeat in 1755, threatened to abandon their French father and fight for the English, making their point all the more clear by killing and scalping two Frenchmen. Similarly, in 1757 French soldiers and their supposed Miami allies opened fire on each other, leaving several Miamis bleeding to death while their kinsmen contemplated retaliation.[63] French mediation, gifts, and demonstrations of commitment had resolved these dangerous disputes; by 1758, amid dire shortages, this was no longer possible.

The Indians and the French had been victorious over Grant, but the subsequent actions of the Ottawas and their Indian allies quickly turned

WAR UNDER HEAVEN

victory to defeat, at least for the French. In the battle's wake the Great Lakes Indians took what plunder they could and headed homeward toward the Great Lakes, leaving Fort Duquesne itself naked and without its real defenses. Meanwhile, Forbes' army, some forty direct miles away, learned of the defenseless state of Fort Duquesne. The man who revealed this spoke English without a traceable French accent and looked, apart from his outfit, like a European. Virginia provincials had discovered him among the Indian prisoners taken in a blundering clash near Loyalhanna. Despite their outrage, the Virginians kept him alive. British officers determined that he was a British subject who had gone over to the enemy. Death, in an "extraordinary Manner," was promised him, unless he gave accurate information as to the condition of Fort Duquesne. The captive, "Johnson," spoke plainly. By this November day in 1758, the Indians had abandoned the French at the Forks; not five hundred Frenchmen formed the ill-supplied garrison.[64] Forbes' forces plunged forward. The French, well aware that without Indians they were lost, packed their artillery into bateaux, gave away to the Indians what they could not carry, carefully arranged damaged gunpowder about Fort Duquesne's walls, and blew the works to rubble, charred oak, and ash. The troops divided into two parties; one carried its flags downriver to Illinois, and the other went upriver to tiny posts along the Allegheny and the portage to Lake Erie.

Not long afterward, twenty-five hundred British soldiers, an assortment of English, Scottish, Irish, German, Swiss, and colonial soldiers, African pioneers, Catawba scouts, colonial packhorsemen, wives, washerwomen, and lovers stood curiously beside the smoking remnants of what had once symbolized a French-Indian alliance on the Ohio. Forbes, so ill that he had to be carried about on a litter, did not long remain. He dispatched a message to the Delawares, saying that "there should be an everlasting peace with all the Indians, established as sure as the Mountains, between the English Nation and the Indians." After he named the place Fort Pitt, his disciplined men hauled his sick body back over the Alleghenies to Philadelphia, where he would die within earshot of the hubbub from the busy quays of the Delaware River. Commanding at Fort Pitt in his place was Colonel Henry Bouquet, whose life's achievements would come to focus on this place. Within nine days of first laying eyes on this confluence of rivers, Bouquet found Delaware Indians entering his camp, to talk.[65]

They were led by Tamaqua, known to the English as "the Beaver."

Tamaqua had led a neutral faction throughout the war and represented but a minority opinion among Delawares. He refused to declare against the French, but he acquiesced in Bouquet's request that the British be unmolested as they remained at the Forks with a token force of two hundred men under Colonel Hugh Mercer. These troops, Bouquet reassured the Delawares, meant only to protect the traders who would soon come; they had no designs on the land. Perhaps Tamaqua was willing to see British troops remain until the traders' safety was secured; the various records indicate that the Delawares had little desire to have a British army placed permanently among them.[66] Tamaqua also promised to spread the message of peace, a promise he kept, traveling widely over the Great Lakes and Ohio Country in the next year to bring about an end to the fighting.

It was eight months before Delawares and Britons in the Ohio came to something approaching formal terms. This they accomplished, for the most part, through a series of conferences held at Pittsburgh in August. Not all leading Delawares attended—notably absent were the militant Netawatwees and Custaloga—but Tamaqua came with several war leaders. Having himself been to Detroit, he also brought along Wyandots who claimed to speak for the Detroit Indians. Ottawas, Ojibwas, Miamis, and Potawatomis also joined the proceedings, though Ottawas exhibited their continued hostility by scalping two Highlanders. Tamaqua delivered some English captives back into English hands and advised the westerners as well as his own people, "[T]hink no more of war, but go a hunting ... and visit your Brethren the English, and exchange your skins, and furs, for Goods to cloth your Women and Children." Within a month, however, Delawares had reason to wonder about the peace to which they had agreed. By early September backs were bending and straining at the earth all over the Forks, throwing up works and digging trenches that spoke clearly of British intentions. William Pitt, British secretary of state, had authorized the fort's construction in order to "maintain His Majesty's subjects in undisputed possession of the Ohio." No Delaware read Pitt's words, but the new fort, named for Pitt, spoke them plainly.[67]

Though defensible by December 1760, the fort took more than two years to complete; when finished, it would rank among the most impressive of British works in the interior of North America. The walls rose to 20 feet high and squatted 60 feet thick at the base. They spanned lengths of 188 to 272 feet between each bastion, the tips of which gazed at one another over a distance of between 416 and 476 feet. Within the ramparts were two full acres, room enough for a garrison of a thousand men in two-story, brick and frame barracks, which were neatly arranged to offset and display the commandant's brick house. Anyone entering the fort, or gazing upon it from the slopes of today's Mount Washington across the Monongahela, could see that the British meant to stay. Indeed, George Croghan observed that the Indians were "very Jealous seeing a large Fort building here." The Delawares feared they would be "driven further back, as has been the case ever since the white people came into this country." By 1762, traders, Indian officers, and soldiers were reporting that Indians had taken to stealing horses, killing livestock, and killing settlers.[68]

The Delawares felt familiar fear and distrust in the new context of their trans-Appalachian world. Delawares and Shawnees had established good relations with Ottawas and other Anishinabeg during the Seven Years' War, and those contacts continued. Indeed, while the earliest possible record of Pontiac places him at Fort Duquesne in 1757, one informed report about the Delaware Prophet places his home at Cuyahoga, a Delaware community that until 1764 lay within twenty-five canoe-floating miles of the nearest Ottawa town. Delawares could be found in Anishinabe territory as well; a careful British document noted that a Delaware spoke for Ojibwas in council at Michilimackinac, Michigan, in 1761.[69] It was in the creation of new alliances—alliances that arose out of the dual collapse of the Great Lakes alliance with France and the Covenant Chain alliance with Great Britain—that a new, pan-Indian identity was forged among Indians in the trans-Allegheny west. The British, faced with abundant evidence of intertribal activities in 1761 and 1762, continued to view the matters as mere "conspiracies" to be unhinged rather than as evidence for deep changes in the fabric of Indian identity. This was by no means their most serious underestimation of Native America in the three years that preceded Pontiac's War.

CHAPTER TWO

A Worldly War

On September 8, 1760, the governor of New France signed the "Capitulation of Montreal" and formally surrendered his colony, its inhabitants, and all its territories to Great Britain. Although it would take more than two years for Versailles to confirm the surrender, the capitulation effectively ended all French commitments to the Indians of the Great Lakes. Under the terms of European law, it also yielded the Indians and their lands to the sovereignty of the British Crown. The French agreed to evacuate troops from all Canadian posts, including those at Michilimackinac and Detroit. The British promised the French inhabitants security of property, free practice of religion, and general good treatment. They told the French, too, that they would not molest the Indians in their lands as long as the natives remained at peace. Still, they did not invite Indians to discuss the terms.

Although Indians had no part in the negotiations, they were a significant factor at the most explosive point in the discussions. That moment revealed both the deep British hostility to France's native allies and the first stirring of the issue of status, an issue around which would swirl the material interests that precipitated Pontiac's War. The British general Jeffery Amherst demanded that the surrendering French officers pledge to refrain from carrying arms for the full duration of the war. According to the conventions of the eighteenth century, such a return to noncombatant status, while expected for the surrendering rank and file, was waived for ranking officers. French brass bristled with indignation; Amherst stood bluff. He meant to discredit the French leaders for "the infamous part the troops of France had acted in exciting the savages to perpetuate the most horrid of barbarities in the whole progress of the war," and he succeeded in driving his terms home, deliberately dishonoring his French peers.[1] Dishonoring Indians came far more easily, and over the next several years, his decisions, and those of his fellow officers, would drive many a warrior to war.

Five days after the tense signing, Major Robert Rogers and two hundred men gathered into boats and pulled away from Montreal, ascending the St. Lawrence toward the Great Lakes, with orders to take possession of French posts at Detroit, Michilimackinac, and "any others in that district." Rogers proclaimed that the British had been made "masters" of a vast land, "a conquest of perhaps the greatest importance to be met with in British annals." This kind of enthusiasm concerned Indian agent George Croghan, then at Fort Pitt: "The Success of his Majesty's Arms this campaign . . . gives rise to an Opinion generally received in the Army, that we have conquered the Continent." Croghan knew better: "We may say we have beat the French; but we have nothing to boast from the War with the Natives." By October, Rogers and a handful of men had pressed ahead of the rest and had sped southward to Fort Pitt, where the ranger delivered dispatches to the commander, who detached a company of Royal Americans to join the mission. These regulars, commanded by Captain Donald Campbell and accompanied by Croghan, united with Rogers' rangers at Presque Isle. Together they hauled, lugged, and rowed their varied craft—including sleek canoes, sturdy bateaux, and fifteen bulbous whaleboats—as far as the Ashtabula Creek, on the south shore of white-capped Lake Erie, where, weather-beaten, they put in to rest.[2]

Peace, 1760

Rogers still had one hundred linear miles to cover, and not until the end of the next month would he reach Detroit. At Ashtabula Creek, as his forces recovered their strength, an Ottawa party boldly confronted them in the first week of November. The meeting proved to be peaceful. The thirty Ottawas saluted the English, waving the red Cross of St. George and firing an honorary volley. Each party smoothed over the other's rough, suspicious edges with gifts. For five days Indians and rangers transformed the camp into a "plentiful market," and together they smoked, drank, and feasted. Rogers even distributed ammunition to these erstwhile enemies. He later embellished the encounter in his *Concise Account of North America*, placing Pontiac at the center of the meeting; but this is unreliable.[3]

Whoever these Ottawas actually were, they already knew of the Montreal capitulation; Croghan now explained to them its terms. He told them that the French had become British subjects and that they would retain their property on "taking the Oath" to King George. He ceremoniously gave the Ottawas a belt of wampum, promising them a "free Trade" and the "peaceable possession of their hunting Country." "The principal Man of the Ottawas," holding a large belt of wampum, asked the British to take notice of his two principal companions, who were to "transact the Business of [his] Tribe." He formally begged the English to supply the needs of Ottawa women and children, as they were "poor and naked." "[You] are able to do it," he concluded, "and by pitying their Necessities you will win their Hearts." This was the crux of the Ottawa acceptance of peace. Britons were welcome in Ottawa country, as long as they "took notice of" Ottawa leaders and won the Ottawas' loyalty with gifts. When the old man finished, one of the two others, whom Croghan called "the speaker," gave the British officers a pipe of peace, "known to all the Nations" living in his country. It is possible that this was Pontiac.[4]

Rogers' Yankee whaleboats, French bateaux, and Indian canoes plied the Detroit River by the end of November, having lost but one man, drowned. In the flotilla were the leading men of the Ottawa party. Rogers had already sent a messenger ahead of him to bring the waiting French garrison news of the decisions at Montreal. Reaching the Detroit settlements, which stretched out along the shore of the river, Rogers and his men began to set up camp on the present Ontario side in a clearing half a mile away from Fort Pontchartrain. Captain Campbell, meanwhile, ceremoniously approached the immense stockade with an official copy of the Montreal capitulation. The commanding French officer, Captain François-Marie Picoté de Belestre, immediately understood the articles, treated Campbell with "good grace," and agreed to withdraw from the garrison.[5] But on the day before his official surrender, he did something that has been little noted. On November 28, Belestre held a council with the neighboring Hurons, Ottawas, Potawatomis, and Ojibwas. The following June, in Paris, he reported the meeting to his superiors in Paris.

WAR UNDER HEAVEN

Sir Jeffery Amherst, ca. 1765. Engraving based on portrait by Joshua Reynolds. Courtesy Clements Library, University of Michigan. Amherst and several of his subordinates thought so well of their noble, armored domination of the North American interior that they neglected its cultural and human realities.

The Indians opened the council with expressions of grief at his impending departure. They reminded Belestre that they had fought well as his allies and that they had recently, at his request, been "tranquil" around Detroit. They claimed that they had adhered to a promise made to the British at Niagara in 1759 that they would stop raiding the frontier, a promise attached, they said, to a British promise never to invade their country. In fact, Detroit's Indians had not been entirely tranquil: as recently as July, in the company of twenty Frenchmen, they had struck at an invasive British detachment near Presque Isle, killing two men and taking two others prisoner. Now, seeing British soldiers at Detroit, they were "now resolved to send to all the Nations" to gather in the spring to drive the English from their land.[6]

British offenses were already piling up. Fort Presque Isle had been built without permission; the British intention to occupy other French posts in the west was all too clear. That summer, Ottawas and Ojibwas visiting Niagara had discovered that a set of sacred council wampum and calumets, which they had presented the year before in a spirit of peace to Niagara's British commander, had been sent to Amherst as war trophies and curiosities for his cabinet. Detroit's Ottawas wondered if this would happen, too, to the pipe of peace that their speaker had presented to Rogers and Croghan at Ashtabula Creek. Now, as Belestre prepared to yield his stockade to Rogers, Detroit's Indians implored him to deliver to the French king, their "true Father," a sacred calumet "to ask him not to abandon his children." Although they promised to save themselves from "the treachery of the English," they also said they would wait for someone to come to deliver them from their "captivity." They referred to the English as those who had stolen their lands, and they claimed that they would live in sadness as long as they saw the red flag over their land. Belestre promised to deliver to the king their calumet along with their request, and he assured them that the king would not reject their word: "He will have pity on you if you remain always attached to him." Recalling the event five years later, a Miami Indian said that when Belestre left Detroit, "he went away ashamed" but said that the Indians would see him again. In 1763, Ottawas would recall that Belestre had promised them that the British occupation would not last.[7]

This leaves us with an Indian acceptance of the British garrison at Detroit that, at very best, was highly conditional. Detroit's Indians already saw in the coming of British troops a broken promise; already they had begun mooting the possibilities of armed, pan-Indian insurrection under the *drapeau blanc*. Abroad, the Seven Years' War still had years to rage; that Detroit's Indians and its French commander should discuss future collaboration was to be expected. But by 1760 Belestre cut a sad figure. For years he had been promising the Indians a victory, promising them more aid, more men, more matériel, and he had failed to deliver. Indians still hoped the French would assist them against Great Britain, but they also spoke in decidedly autonomous tones of sending "to all the nations" and of freeing themselves from bondage.[8]

Meanwhile, they spoke to the British. The unnamed Ottawas who had met Croghan and Rogers in early November again met the two and Campbell at Detroit in a three-day council held in early December. They were joined by Potawatomis and Wyandots, including the Wyandot speaker, Archonnere. These Indians asked for a flourishing trade and, emphatically, inexpensive goods at fixed prices. The Britons gave them gifts, asked them to look upon Detroit's *habitants* as British subjects, called upon them to return any British prisoners, and promised them His Majesty's protection and "a free open Trade." Ceremoniously, an "Ancient Chain of Friendship" between British subjects, the Six Nations, and these "several Western Nations to the Sun setting" was renewed, brightened, and pledged to continue "as long as the Sun and Moon give light." Detroit's Indians went away with flourishes of gratitude and satisfaction, but not before openly insisting "strongly," and on a full belt of wampum, "that the six Nation Deputys should press their Chiefs to attend the general meeting to be held here in the spring." The British were to be given a chance to prove themselves in Detroit, but if they failed to win local approval, Detroit's Indians were already preparing for a future without them. Captain Campbell, who would command the post with only brief breaks until August 1762, worried, "I shall have a good deal of Difficulty to manage them. . . . They are so much accustomed to come to the French Commandant for every thing they want."[9]

Detroit, 1760–1763

When Belestre formally surrendered Detroit to Rogers on November 29, 1760, ragged, blue-coated French troops lined up in the fort's central parade opposite the ragged, green-coated rangers and red-coated Royal Americans. With rolling drums, the red flag of Britain rose, until it floated above the wooden stockade of the fort to be viewed with resignation. Like most French posts in the *pays d'en haut*, Fort Pontchartrain, which the British would simply call Fort Detroit, had been built to dominate a river, not a people. In 1760, the fort had little artillery, perhaps only four to eight pieces, mostly swivel guns and two-pounders. It stood on a high bank, on the north (Michigan) shore of the Detroit River, commanding "a very pleasant prospect for nine miles above, and nine miles below." From an engineer's perspective, the post was not much, certainly not by the standards of the strongholds at Pitt or Niagara. It was more of an ad hoc affair but well designed for the community it had served at the vital center of the upper Great Lakes alliance. The floor plan presents an odd figure, shaped more like a squatting frog viewed from above than like the conventional star. Three small bastions faced the half-mile-long waterfront; only one faced landward, indicating that the French expected more trouble by water than by land. The British, knowing that Indians resented their presence, saw things differently and built exterior blockhouses to guard the landward gates. From the ground, the oaken palisades, at twelve to fifteen feet in height, evoked a kind of rustic yet imposing grandeur—"one of the best stockades I have seen," said Captain Donald Campbell—while the fort's broad dimensions meant hard work for anything but a full regiment of defenders, which it would never have.[10]

Though it could not rival Fort Pitt in design, though it lacked the stone facing, the dangerous glacis, the moat, and the projecting ravelins, Fort Detroit had more to protect it than its gunnery and pickets. Much as Indians had proven to be Fort Duquesne's best defense, so Detroit would depend in the coming war on forces deployed outside its oaken walls. For one thing, French and Indian supporters, spies, and informers constituted an important shield from danger. Never, even during the coming siege, would the garrison be cut off entirely from the people beyond its walls. Over the course of the nearly three years of occupation preceding the siege, the British would win many allies among the thousands of French and Indian individuals in the neighborhood, and these would serve the garrison well.[11]

Since its founding in 1701, Detroit had been the center of the French-Anishinabe alliance. Some eighty to one hundred houses lay along neat streets within its palisades. Dispersed for more than five miles along each bank of the Detroit River were more white-washed homes. "The country," wrote Croghan in 1765, "is thick settled with the French." There were several hundred families who raised crops and provided dairy products to the garrison and its frequent Indian visitors. Others traded with the Indians, soldiered in the garrison, or labored as voyageurs in the extensive French transportation system, so recently destroyed by the Seven Years' War. Among Wyandots, Ottawas, Potawatomis, and Ojibwas, there were at least 550 local men of fighting age, suggesting a total Indian population of well over 2000.[12] The last several years of the Seven Years' War had put immense strains on this polyglot community.

During the Seven Years' War, the British had elsewhere dispossessed French farmers of their homes and fields, most famously but not exclusively at Acadia in 1755. At Crown Point, in 1759, a small French community had been dislodged, and its petition to reoccupy the lands in 1760 had been summarily rejected. So it is understandable that *habitants* at Detroit entertained skepticism about the British promise to guarantee their lands upon their oaths to the British king. Throughout 1760, disbelieving farmers worried that working their crops would mean leaving them "for the English to reap." Despite these fears they planted anyway, pinning their hopes on the words of the capitulation. French traders and voyageurs had even more to fear, for their livelihoods were not protected by any guarantee. Several fled, some to Illinois, others to Michilimackinac, and still others to the smaller outposts.[13]

Captain Campbell had neither the orders nor the desire to thrust out the French. He found the people in "great want of Every Thing." Meat was a rarity, and flour would begin to run low by February 1761. And this was but a repeat of the previous year's hunger, when the *habitants*, Croghan learned, had been "much Distrest with the want of Provisions." Against the dizziness of famine and the disappointment of British victory, most French *habitants* and merchants had little solace, save that, as long as they adhered to the terms of surrender and assuming the British kept their promises, they would be able to continue to live and work, molested only by this small tribute: they were to provide the garrison with an average of three or four cords of wood per farm each year.[14]

Spared that tax, but otherwise suffering the same shortages as the French in 1760, were the thousands of Ottawas, Potawatomis, and Wyandots whose homes clustered together in several villages up and down each bank of the Detroit River. The previous year, seven Detroit Ottawas had traveled to Fort Pitt, where they told Croghan that the French refused "to Supply them with Powder and Lead, telling them to go to the

English" for what they needed. Now Campbell found them "in great distress for want of Ammunition." On December 3, Indians requested that the English follow the French practice of having a smith mend their guns and a doctor attend to their people when sick. They also wanted to know how soon a trade might be opened. Campbell granted the requests, until "the General's pleasure was known." The doctor was soon overwhelmed.[15]

Though distinct, the French, Ottawa, Potawatomi, and Wyandot communities still saw a cultural cross-fertilization far more pronounced than that in the St. Lawrence Valley or the British colonies. A Wyandot village stood behind the French houses that lined the southern side of the river, almost opposite the fort. Potawatomis occupied a town downstream from Detroit on the Michigan bank, while the Ottawas had at least one town close to Lake St. Clair on the present Ontario side and another on the present Michigan bank near both Lake St. Clair and the River Rouge. Other Potawatomis lived in a village on the Ecorse River. The villagers intermarried frequently across boundaries that were too often and too casually described as tribal. Algonquian-speaking Ottawas, Miamis, Potawatomis, and Ojibwas thought little of intermarrying with one another or even with Iroquoian-speaking Wyandots. Pontiac himself likely sprang from an Ottawa-Ojibwa union. Wyandots told Croghan in 1760, "All the Indians in this Country are Allies to each other and as one people."[16]

As British, Irish, German, and colonial soldiers now occupied Detroit, some readily found comfort and pleasure in French and Indian company. By the time Pontiac's War broke out, a few of the heterogeneous regulars and traders had learned to coexist with their equally heterogeneous Detroit neighbors. Campbell, for example, quickly developed an appreciation for the townswomen, who, in his words, "surpasses our expectations like the rest of America." In the same breath he slighted Detroit's men, but over the next two years he developed an impressive sensitivity. Cut off as they were from their Atlantic British world, soldiers such as Campbell made the best of things. They took up card playing, in in pairs, with the French inhabitants.[17] The ease and familiarity that occasionally ensued won the British factional support from many *habitants* and a few Indians. It was the kind of support that eventually preserved most of these soldiers and traders from destruction—though it could not, as it would later turn out, save Campbell himself.

Never, however, did it appear to Indians that those who were playing cards were genuinely mingling. Before 1760, the Anishinabeg had little known British officers, save as enemies. Over the next few years, they would gain strong impressions about the nature of British military rule in an imperial and aristocratic age. For advice about the British, Pontiac and Detroit's Indians readily turned to those French and Indian peoples with more experience. But the Anishinabeg also listened as certain British officers delivered lessons more directly.

On Bad Terms

Meeting George Croghan when he arrived with Rogers' boats in the fall of 1760, the leading Ottawa had asked British officers to "look upon" two of his headmen. During the first month of Pontiac's War, "an Indian King," Nobaumigate, probably the Mississauga leader Wabbicommicot, visited Fort Niagara. In a phrase that resounded up and down the continent, he complained of being "very indifferently looked upon, whenever he [came] among the English." Later, St. Regis Indians of the St. Lawrence, who allied with the British during Pontiac's War, nonetheless complained that although the British had promised better treatment than that given by the French, they had not seen "the Proofs of it"; indeed, the local commander "had treated the Indians like Slaves." Ohio Indians, enemies of Britain during Pontiac's War, protested, "As soon as you conquered the French, you did not care how you treated us, as you did not think us worth your notice. We request that you may not treat us again in the same manner." Again and again in these Indian charges, blatant British disregard convinced Indians of a British intention to master them. When Pontiac sent for assistance to the French in Illinois, he complained that Detroit's new occupiers both mocked the Indians for their total dependency on British supplies and claimed that such dependency proved British domination: "The English [ask] us constantly, 'From whom will ye get what ye stand in need of?'" The anonymous author of the so-called Pontiac Journal says in his first sentence that the Ottawa planned his attack on Detroit "under pretext of some insult that he believed he had received from Mr. Gladwin, commandant of the fort." And Major Robert Rogers, who arrived at Detroit in July to help defend the post, went so far as to write a play, *Ponteach: or the Savages of America*, in which a fictional commandant of Detroit wildly insults the great Ottawa leader, damning him repeatedly to his face.[18] The play, the commercial failure it deserved to be, nonetheless is important as a thinly veiled attack on Gladwin, a fellow officer under whom Rogers had served in 1763.

The ranger, placing curses and blasphemies in the dramatized mouth of his commander, had a point, for language was critical to the failure of the British and Indians to establish a working relationship. Hugh Mercer, commander at Fort Pitt as the French finally withdrew from the upper Ohio in 1759, put language front and center: "We can now talk to our new Allies in a proper Stile, as their services are not Necessary." When Shawnees complained to a French officer of the "evil speech" or "bad discourse" of the British—"[they] tell us that they regard us as dogs, that they are masters of all the Land, that they have overthrown our French father and they regard him as a dog"—they simultaneously reminded France of their fidelity and accused Great Britain not only of arrogance but also of sedition. *Le mauvais discours*, spoken by *mauvais disants*—speakers of evil—was how speech against the king was characterized in eighteenth-century France.[19] Pontiac's War was as much about speech as it was about such issues as land, trade goods, prisoners, and forts, for speech was a material issue, charging Indian and British struggles over very real power relationships.

Immediate causes of the war varied from place to place, but at the two critical points of Detroit and Pittsburgh, Indians confronted commanders who, like the overall commander, Jeffery Amherst, embodied the drive for an empire of domination. Amherst, as historians have long recognized, radiated contempt for Indians. He thought it foolish to employ Indian interpreters, not putting "the least Trust" in what an Indian might say: "We have too many proofs of their Insincerity." Not all British commanders saw things his way. When Donald Campbell had commanded Detroit, he had been circumspect, often giving Indians proper regard. Other Britons had divided opinions—trader John Porteous expressed well the contradictory sense he had of Detroit's Indians when he wrote to his brother that there was no civil society among Indians and that they concerned themselves chiefly with revenge and theft, while at the same time he praised their hospitality and said that they never stole from their own people, only from outsiders.[20] But Amherst's more thoroughly negative views were shared by Henry Gladwin, the senior officer who arrived at Detroit and took command from Campbell in 1762, and by Simeon Ecuyer, commanding at Fort Pitt. Viewed by imperial historians as rock-solid heroes, these two undeniably brave, even impervious, men helped mightily to bring on the war that gave them fame.[21]

So at least said Detroit's people of Gladwin. An *habitant* named "Pero Barth" in the record called Gladwin "the occasion of this war." Whereas Campbell had been receptive to Indians, Barth said that Gladwin not only refused to give them customary presents but would not even have the fort's smith repair their guns. When the British trader Chapman Abraham had defended Gladwin, saying that the major was only obeying Amherst's commands, Barth shot back: "The General did not order the Major to call them Dogs, Hogs," and then to drive them from his house. Manning Fisher (probably a British trader), after escaping from captivity early in Pontiac's War, told British authorities at Detroit that Gladwin had infuriated Indians by calling them "Hogs and other names, telling them to get along," for he "would not hear them." These charges are only hearsay, but Gladwin did, in fact, terminate gunsmith Abraham Jones' work for the Indians just two weeks before the fighting began, and he did, in fact, later congratulate Bouquet for his successful relief of Fort Pitt and for "the drubbing [he] gave the dogs." During the war Gladwin demonstrated disdain for Indians. When Amherst once prodded him to attack the Ojibwas, Gladwin, undoubtedly correctly, replied that such an attack would be fruitless. But his explanation was ludicrous: Ojibwas had no settlements to burn, they lived off the land, and when food failed, "they frequently [ate] one another." Gladwin was, to be sure, the iron defender of the British fort at Detroit, but he hated the place as a "scoundrel Country, among savages."[22]

Gladwin demonstrated most vividly the severity of British authority in the weeks immediately preceding the war by trying and executing a "Panis" Indian slave woman ("Panis," or Panise, Indians were those whose origins were probably across the Mississippi and who were enslaved to the French) for being an accomplice in the murder of an English trader, her new master. In accordance with orders from Amherst, the execution was carried out in "the most Exemplary and publick manner, that thereby Others [might] be Deterred from Committing such Cruelties for the Future." Only after she had dangled, dead, from Gladwin's scaffold did he worry that the execution had affected "the Temper of the Indians." Back east, Amherst was not worried. It was not in the Indians' power, he wrote, "to Effect any thing of Consequence" against the British. He only wished that the man who had actually wielded the knife had met the same punishment, "for then the Example would have been Compleat."[23] But the example must have been complete enough for Anishinabeg to fear a future of summary and severe justice. During the Seven Years' War, Delawares, while rubbing shoulders with Anishinabeg, were known to have spoken "at length of the chiefs of their nation formerly hanged by the English." According to the French colonel Louis-Antoine de Bougainville, "This is and always will be their excuse for making war."[24]

Indians quickly figured out just where they would fit into the order that the British imperialists were struggling to impose. The garrisons themselves set the example. Nowhere in the British Empire, arguably, were hierarchy and coercion more severe than in the army. Indians accompanying General Amherst in his campaign of 1760 saw him hang a notorious deserter and pardon nine others. In the fall of 1761 Ottawas at Detroit witnessed the one hundred lashes given under Sir William Johnson's orders to Private David Lutts, who had killed one of their horses. In February 1763, at Fort Pitt, Captain Simeon Ecuyer had five hundred lashes laid upon the back of someone who had stolen flour, and an unspecified crime led him to, with one thousand lashes, tear the back off one Childers. In November 1761 Shawnees watched three hundred lashes fall upon Abraham McCoy, who had spread a rumor among them that the colonies were planning to take Indian lands.[25]

Discipline in the army had to be fierce; nothing else could induce men to perform in so dangerous and so badly paid a service. Common British soldiers were poor men, ill clothed, even ragged on the frontier. Bouquet thought his men looked like clowns in 1761; and an officer at Venango thought they "cut a very od[d] figure on Sentry." Indians saw the odd figure, and they received the odd deserter. They knew morale was low. Such conditions and punishments raised questions among Indians as to what British rule portended. Senecas in 1761 stated quite plainly that Amherst intended to "Attempt inslaving them."[26] And it was only two weeks after Gladwin publically hanged the Panis slave woman that Pontiac's warriors stormed his garrison.

British breaches of Indian protocol illuminated such bad discourse and such brutal displays of mastery. Ottawas expected the commander at Detroit to retain the ceremonial pipes they had sent him as reminders of their relationship, but when, shortly before the war, they asked Gladwin if they might see their pipes, the major claimed to know nothing about

Henry Gladwin, eighteenth century. By John Hall. Gift of Dexter M. Ferry Jr., photograph © 1991 Detroit Institute of Arts. Gladwin, portrayed here as the sturdy, clear-eyed defender of Detroit, helped to incite the war through his disrespectful treatment of Indians and his execution of an Indian woman.

them. This was the second time since 1760 that British officers had mis-placed important Detroit Ottawa calumets. During the war, Colonel John Bradstreet would do worse, publicly cutting Pontiac's war belt to pieces, an act Sir William Johnson thought prolonged the war by at least a year. Allied Mohawk diplomats traveling to England found themselves humiliatingly put on open display; their objections eventually reached the House of Lords, which prohibited the "unbecoming and Inhuman" practice of "making a public shew of Indians"—without approval from the Board of Trade.[27]

Insults came easily to Ecuyer, Gladwin's counterpart at Fort Pitt. The letters of this Swiss-born mercenary in the British service reveal other prejudices common to the times. Dealing with a British commissary whom he deeply distrusted, he wrote, "When one is a Jew, one is a Jew, and thus one remains." His discussions with White Eyes, Wingenun, and Yellow Hawk—two Delawares and a Shawnee who represented peace-seeking factions in the early weeks of war—were filled with speeches meant to put Indians in their subordinate place, and William Trent (colonial trader, speculator, and militia officer) noted approvingly in his journal that the discussions left these peace-seeking Indians so "much enraged" and "irritated" that they "would not shake hands with [the British] at Parting."[28]

During the war, British and colonial garrison humor, arrogant and giddy, played upon the Indians' refusal to take a lowly place in the empire. Soldiers and scornful traders mocked the Indians as "gentry," comparing them unfavorably with the landed, rural bedrock of the British ruling class. Indian claims to respect, land, and independence were all swallowed up in the term. "These gentry," "these Red Heads," "those Copper headed Gentry," and these "copperheads" are the terms that pepper the officers' letters and the colonial newspaper accounts of the events of Pontiac's War. Pontiac could be wryly called "General Pontiac," "Marshal Pontiac," "Mr. Pontiac," or even "Monsieur Pontiac," the titles again implying that his and his people's claims to status, dignity, and land were but pompous absurdities. A British veteran of the war later called a Potawatomi chief whom he despised "Mr. Nineway." These were clearly takeoffs on the then common derogatory use of the term *Monsieur* to play upon perceived French pretensions. Even allies came in for such scorn. Michael Byrne, employed by the Indian department to supply Oneidas who were mustering to join a British expedition, said he had to deal with "the most Mutinous Irregular Regulars in America," and he joked that he would "rather be a Tea waterman's Horse, than Commissary for them." Henry Bouquet, considering the use of Indians as allies against Pontiac, hated the idea: "I would rather chuse the Liberty to kill any Savage that may come in our way." Unlike Mr. Byrne, Mr. Bouquet wrote without jest.[29]

Thomas Gage, Amherst's replacement as commander in chief of British forces, also dreamed of such simple and total solutions, at least in his weaker moments. He once instructed Colonel John Bradstreet to sweep Detroit and its outposts of "the [French] Inhabitants," whom he called "trash" and "a vile set." This was exactly what the *habitants* had long feared, and some of them even began building large dugout canoes in preparation for escape to Illinois. Bradstreet, when he arrived at Detroit in 1764, had no power to force out the French; indeed, he saw that he needed their assistance. But the constant uneasiness of these new British subjects sent a powerful message to the far more ambiguously placed Indians. The message of French dispossession vividly reached the militant Shawnee Charlot Kaské in 1765. He was visiting the French governor of Louisiana in New Orleans, petitioning for help in the war, when two hundred Acadian refugees, driven from their homes ten years earlier, arrived, destitute, in the city.[30]

Yet for all the obvious hostility and contempt, British soldiers, traders, and Indian department administrators had wide experience with many Indian peoples by the 1760s, and in many cases their capacities for careful observation and even clear understanding of the Indians of the trans-Appalachian west have to be credited. These were often bright and energetic men, which made them all the more dangerous and challenging for the Indians. The problem was not fundamentally one of cultural misunderstanding; these officers well understood that Indians resented their domineering behavior, but they meant to dominate nonetheless; to do less would have meant shedding their identity as officers of the empire. This is why they commonly characterized Indian postures as "haughty." "No people on the face of the earth," wrote Thomas Mante, a veteran of both the Seven Years' War and Pontiac's War, "are fuller of the idea of liberty, than the North-American Indians." His fellow officers knew this, too, and they saw the Indian idea of liberty as something to be crushed.[31]

Potawatomis allied with Pontiac explained to a French commander in Illinois in 1764 that the British had not afforded the same "advantages" to Indians as had the French. Miamis allied with Pontiac ridiculed Indians allied with Britain for having the "vanity" to think that the English were their brothers: "They are not to be depended upon, as what they deliver to you, comes not from their hearts." Tying bad sentiments to domination, the Miamis added, "You are not your own Masters." When the British spoke with the "tone of the master," there was little choice but war.[32]

A Monster of Ingratitude

The issue of gifts illustrates best the capacity of British officials to understand the Indians' position even as they sought to overrule it. Pontiac's War did not result from a British failure to understand the "old Indian custom" of gift giving; Britons knew well by 1760 that securing the military cooperation of Indian peoples meant regular outlays of gifts by the colonial power at the center of the alliance. The practices of the French in alliance with the Great Lakes and lower Mississippi peoples were widely known and pretty well understood. Nor were the British ignorant of the symbolic dimension of gift giving, for Indians themselves made it plain that a lack of presents for those visiting the posts meant a lack of respect. Historians once saw the war in material terms as a rebellion against British economy, but gifts never were numerous enough or inherently valuable enough to warrant a war. Indians did not go to war to preserve an old custom or to protest an economic policy: they strove to prevent their social and political degradation. When British officials consciously decided to stop dispensing gifts in 1761–62 and to usher in a new regime—a regime in which Indian submission replaced Indian alliance and in which access to the British market replaced customary exchange—the absence of gifts became as dangerous to Indian social and political standing as the cannon sprouting from the walls of Forts Pitt and Detroit.[33]

No one in Europe or America who seriously considered the importance of "presents" saw them as simple, generous offerings unencumbered by social obligation. Such a view would have appalled any respectable early modern European as much as it would a Native American. A young Thomas Hobbes had written in 1620 that gifts and favors were only pleasing if they were "requitable," otherwise they imposed an "intolerable burden" upon the recipient. Throughout the British Atlantic world, the giver of gifts was often expressing a sense of gratitude, which implied a continued obligation. James Sterling, a leading trader and a captain of the British militia at Detroit, exchanged gifts with his business partners back east. He also provided Joshua Loring—a British officer who had helped him to smuggle liquor for the Indian trade—with a gift of expensive furs and finely worked exotic Indian crafts: a shot pouch, knife, and a pair of moccasins. He called these an "acknowledgement of the many Obligations Our Company lys under to you." British officers lived in a world of patronage, in which favors and gifts helped to staff bureaucracies. Sir William Johnson exerted his influence on behalf of many position seekers, receiving in exchange deferential thanks and sometimes gifts. George Croghan, expressing "Greatfull acknoledgmts fer the Honour you have Don Me," sent him gifts of Indian war regalia and specimens of the mandrake plant.[34] Offerings of thanks in British military and administrative culture generally went up the social scale: they were marks of regard. When Indian leaders received gifts from British officers, the nature of the hierarchical relationship was far more at play, but it was clear to all that Indians accepted the presents as tokens of British respect. The British easily understood the meanings Indians attached to gifts; that was the irritation.

By 1760, then, the British understood that gifts played a critical role in Indian relations. In a 1756 proposal for reform of Indian-British affairs, Edmund Atkin had written, "The Exchange of Presents is expected to be made, at all Meetings or interviews upon Publick Business, even among themselves." William Johnson informed his superiors that gifts were the "surest method of proving the reality of words to Indians." George Croghan once reminded Colonel Henry Bouquet that Indian leaders maintained their authority through their ability to give gifts, not commands. Long experience had taught British colonists and officers that gifts were essential and that giving was a complicated business, laden with meaning. Johnson put it best when he wrote to Amherst early in 1763 that the Indians would interpret the sudden withdrawal of presents not as a matter of "good Oeconomy" but as a clear sign of "contempt, dislike, and an Inclination to reduce them so low as to facilitate [the empire's] Designs of extirpating them."[35] He urged that the British continue to dispense gifts to important Indians in the west.

During the Seven Years' War, British and colonial officers had regularly confronted the issue of gift giving. In the slow but powerful campaign against French Fort Duquesne, officers from George Washington to James Forbes had dispensed gifts to warriors from the Savannah River to the Mohawk Valley. Having taken the ruins of Duquesne and built Fort Pitt in their place, the British promised regular presents to the local Indians, so at least Pontiac is said to have recalled. He reportedly visited Fort Pitt in 1759 or 1760 and there learned that "presents from this great King were to be unlimited, that all sorts of goods were to be in the utmost plenty and so cheap." But nowhere had Indians and Britons established anything like a smooth, working relationship. It had infuriated Indian warriors that their alliance with Great Britain was not punctuated with more frequent marks of British "love" and that their services were not met with greater honor. Officers who wrote painful apologies to their superiors for having to give presents to keep Indians in "good humor" could, at the same time, express discomfort that Indians accepted their gifts not with marks of scraping gratitude but with demands for more. Equating Indians with poverty-stricken mercenaries who owed gratitude to the officers for the goods given them, men of rank equated Indian demands for honor and respect with the pretensions of social inferiors.[36]

Far from conceding the Indian understandings of their status as honored allies, Amherst and others determined to invest gifts, key symbols of the empire's Indian relations, with new meanings. Gifts might still occasionally be given to Indians, but they were not to be the gifts of the grateful to the benefactor or of the Indian leader to his honorable followers; rather, they were to be the charity of the gentry to the beggar. British officers, Amherst only one among them, determined to reverse the flow of gratitude. The Indian failure to display gratitude, indeed the Indian demand for it, was intolerable. In 1763, an officer who owed his place in the army to Johnson tried to return him "sutable thenks" but found words "insuficient" to express what his heart meant. Yet he vowed, "When I forget the Obligation may I be Detested for a Monster of ingratitude."[37] Monsters of ingratitude, in the view of Amherst and others, are what Pontiac and his allies became when they started fighting in 1763.

It was not that Indians did not return "thanks" for gifts, for they often did, and sometimes "in a Formal manner." But it bothered Amherst, as it had bothered British and colonial officers throughout the Seven Years' War, that Indians, who theoretically lived under a powerful king's protection, insubordinately demanded gifts as their due, as tribute paid for the maintenance of good relations, as marks of British appreciation and regard. When the fighting began, Amherst first saw in it an opportunity to teach the Indians the folly, madness, and "Ingratitude" of opposing "a

WAR UNDER HEAVEN

People from whom they [had] received so many Benefits." He pledged to wreak "ample vengeance" upon the "Treacherous and Bloody Villains, who [had] so Perfidiously attacked their Benefactors." One "Mohawk Peter" delivered a peace feeler from Johnson to the Ottawas declaring, "Notwithstanding your Ingratitude to him he has still Pity on you." Since Amherst had ordered gifts to Indians stopped well before the outbreak of the war, the occupiers' worthiness of gratitude is a question. For Amherst, the question's answer was clear: Indians were to be grateful because Britons had conquered them, spared them, and given them the opportunity to trade with his dynamic people—"the only People that can be of Use to them, & without Our Assistance they must all Starve."[38] They were to be grateful to the British for their very lives.

When they had acquiesced to the British occupation of French posts between 1758 and 1763, Indians did not have in mind grateful subordination to an empire of trade and troops. They had reason to hope that the British would simply replace the French in the posts, dispensing gifts and accepting the services of warriors going out against mutual enemies. And mutual enemies did exist. Beginning in 1759, Cherokees, enemies of Indians in both the Ohio and Detroit regions, provided a numerous and convenient mutual enemy against whom Lakes and Ohio Indians could fight, aided by the new British garrisons. At Detroit in 1760, George Croghan harangued: "There is your natural Enemies the Cherokees with whom you have been long at War." Throughout 1760 and 1761, as British armies marched from Charleston against the Cherokees' Smoky Mountain homelands, northern Indian warriors, on their way to or from the beleaguered Cherokee Nation, stopped by Forts Detroit and Pitt seeking provisions, arms, and gifts.[39]

Before the conquest of Canada, Amherst had supported the giving of presents to Indians as the only practical way to secure Indian allies and draw Indians away from the French. He had even dined with allied Stockbridge Mahicans in 1759; in 1760 he ordered a ship on Lake Ontario christened in honor of the Onondagas at a ceremony in which he dispensed punch amid good cheer. But these events were exceptional; the very day following the christening of the *Onondaga*, he was already considering how best to stanch the flow of presents to Indians, fearing that if every British post supplied them, there would be "no end to it." Presents, far from regular demonstrations of British affection, were to be targeted to specific tasks. During the Cherokee War, Amherst opined that by bribing Cherokee women with ribbons and paint, he could feed the isolated British garrison of Fort Loudoun. He wished "for a soldiers' feeding for a month on a yard of ribbon." Instead, the garrison was starved into submission—the first of many British posts to fall to Indian assaults during Amherst's disastrous tenure as commander in chief. In April 1760, he wrote a long "talk" to be sent to Fort Pitt, promising the region's Indians "presents in consideration for the lands" upon which posts in the west would be built. The talk also implied, however, that the presents would be payments—given once—and not annual outlays. Undiplomatically, he tied threats to his proposals: he would retaliate "tenfold for every breach of treaty or outrage [the Indians] could be guilty of." Christian Frederick Post, a knowledgeable mediator between the British colonies and the Ohio Indians, knew better than to deliver the message, which he feared might be "misunderstood."[40]

After the capitulation at Montreal, Amherst decided to reduce British gift giving to Indians. If the presents were cut off, he reasoned, Indians would be more industrious; deprived of regular outlays of ammunition, they would be weaker, more submissive, and "More regular." He did not intend "ever . . . to gain the Friendship of Indians by Presents." He had decided, but he could not so act, for the Cherokee War gave officers in the west too good a reason to continue gift giving, which they were learning was essential to good relations with Indian allies. By the late spring of 1762, with that war ended, Amherst issued his order. Northern Indians, particularly Mingos in the Ohio and a greater number of Great Lakes and Illinois Indians, were perplexed. They and the Cherokees were still at war. They still needed arms and ammunition to ensure their success. Again and again, their demands for arms were tied to their expeditions against the Cherokees.[41]

Mingo and Seneca Indians, almost starved as they were returning to their homes in the summer of 1762, found garrisons reluctant even to feed them. The commander of Fort Venango, Francis Gordon, discovered his eight capable men surrounded by thirty-six armed warriors, who requested provisions, according to established custom. They said that they had not eaten for three days, and they presented Gordon with a certificate from George Croghan. Under Amherst's orders, Gordon at first refused to help, but the starving Iroquoian gunmen plundered sheep and forced him to yield. They had hoped to be polite, but they would have the food one way or the other. Gordon soothed them with "all the Reterick [he] was Master of," but the damage was already done. "They told the Dela-wars that I shude Not Stay longe here that they would Come Soon and burn the Fort." Ten months later, Venango was in ashes, its soldiers killed to a man.[42]

Amherst ended the practice of dispensing presents to the Indians in the face of warnings of trouble from men such as Donald Campbell, George Croghan, and Sir William Johnson. Johnson, calling the Indians "a mercenary people," later intimated that Indians saw the new regime in light of its material "disadvantage" to them. Historians have often fol-lowed suit. But the Indians' response was not simply a reaction to a diminishing financial prospectus. They repeatedly said that they were "greatly surprised," "disappointed," and "much Displast" with the meager British outlays because they made it clear that the British, quite literally, "sett so little store by thire frendshipe." Indians saw in the ending of British gifts an assumption of British conquest. The British, complained Ohio Mingos at Fort Pitt, were now a "Welthey pople," who could well afford to give the Indians "butt Litle" of the booty they had taken from the French. The British had promised to supply the Indians, but their failure to do so now made the area's Indians jealous and suspicious of British intentions. Simeon Ecuyer, commanding Fort Pitt, may have despised Indians, but he nonetheless saw the delicacy of his position, caught be-tween, on the one hand, the demands of his superiors for economy and authority and, on the other, the power of Indians who continued to de-mand customary respect: "That causes me embarrassment; I refuse, at other times I give them a little, and sometimes I don't know on which foot to dance."[43] The steel-tipped arrow that pierced his leg later in the year settled the dancing question, but the primary issue—the social and politi-cal status of Indians in the new British empire—could not be so crudely resolved. "Bad discourse" and the struggle over gifts had revealed the stakes clearly to Indians and Britons.

Bad Markets

Back in early November 1760, after Robert Rogers had beached his whaleboats and rested with his rangers on the north shore of Lake Erie, he and Indian agent Croghan assured Ottawas on a belt of wampum that "all Nations of Indians shou'd enjoy a Free Trade . . . and be protected in Peaceable Possession of their Hunting Country." The assurance that, compared with the French, the English "were better able to supply them with all manner of necessaries" pleased the Indians. When Rogers' party reached Sandusky, Croghan repeated the performance, and Wyandots as well as Indians from the Detroit region agreed to be peaceful, expecting that the British would establish a "free and oppen trade . . . for the Support of [their] Women and Children." Later still, at Detroit, some of the same Indians told Croghan that they meant to hold him to his promises. Things would be well, they said, if the prices of goods were settled so that they would have them cheaper from the British than they had from the French, which was what the British had often told them.[44] Both Indians and British colonists expected trade to be central to their relations.

Amherst assumed that a flourishing trade would reduce the Indians' demands for presents. He believed that his restrictions on gifts would foster industry and peace: "As their minds are on business they will not have leisure to hatch mischief." Like many others in British North America, he held that trade was the key to the peaceful regulation of Indian affairs. Once Indians understood their dependence on Britons for goods, once errant, abusive traders had been brought under good order, relations with neighboring tribes could be well managed. Authorities could answer Indian outrages with trade embargoes, reminding Indians of their utter dependence on their British neighbors. As long as the French or Spanish had presented Indians with rival outlets for Indian hunters' furs and skins, British colonists recognized that the ideal could be realized only imperfectly, but the late victories of the Seven Years' War, by promising Great Britain control of the continent east of the Mississippi (save New Orleans and its environs), raised new possibilities in the early 1760s. When Bouquet in 1762 imposed an embargo on Shawnees who had stolen horses and who had not yet delivered prisoners taken during the Seven Years' War, Amherst enthusiastically supported him. Such an embargo, he said, had recently forced the Cherokees to return their prisoners.[45]

Amherst determined to make the most of British advantages. Attempting to control traders, he urged, with others, that all trade be limited to the posts, and he considered limiting it to Detroit, Niagara, and Pitt. In this specific and ill-conceived policy, he had William Johnson's support. Attempting to limit Indian power and increase Indian dependence, he further restricted the sale of ammunition to Indians, and he outlawed the trade in rum. Yet rum and powder, both quickly consumed, were constantly in demand. And while rum might be seen as a luxury, ammunition was essential both to hunting and to the northern Indians' defense against such enemies as the Cherokees, whom the British had encouraged them to fight. At Detroit, Indians had been shrewd consumers of ammunition, insisting on the best, "hardest Corn'd" gunpowder. Amherst's orders hit them hard. "I am certain," wrote Detroit's Captain Campbell, "if the Indians knew General Amherst's sentiments about keeping them short of Powder it would be impossible to keep them in temper." As ammunition remained scarce in the Lakes region, alienated Indians found it "strange" that "the traders [were] not allowed even to take so much Ammunition with them as to enable those Indians to kill sufficient game for the Support of their families." Wabbicommicot, a Mississauga visiting William Johnson at Niagara in 1761, said his people had been impoverished by being "debarred the liberty of purchasing ammunition to kill game." Meanwhile, Indian complaints about high British prices for goods rang in from both Forts Detroit and Pitt. Campbell hoped that the general would "change his present way of thinking. . . . If they were supplyed with ammunition it would prevent them from doing mischief." Amherst did not change, however. After repeated warnings from knowledgeable authorities, Amherst dismissed the possibility of war. "Our Suspicions of their Plots," he wrote a month before the outbreak, "are Meer *Bugbears*." Indians were so dependent on the trade that if the British withheld "Friendship from them," it would be the "Greatest Misfortune" that could befall them.[46]

The misfortune fell instead on Amherst's scattered and undermanned garrisons, most of which Indians took in rapid succession between May and June 1763. It also fell on at least seven traders in the upper Ohio, sixteen at Fort Sandusky, and many more in a convoy en route to Detroit. Hundreds of British subjects were killed, and their ammunition stolen, at the outbreak of the war in May and June. Even as warriors stormed outposts and killed captive soldiers, some found it necessary to explain to the British "the Reasons which induced them." At Venango, it was later reported, they forced the officer to write on paper those reasons, among which was this: whenever they had complained about the price of powder, "they were Ill Treated, and never Redressed." When the officer put the pen down, they killed him.[47]

Johnson and Croghan consistently complained about several of Amherst's retrenchments. Croghan voiced his opposition to restrictions on presents as early as 1760 in letters not only to his immediate superior,

Johnson, but also to Henry Bouquet, hoping the latter might shield Croghan's continued gifts from the knowledge of the commander in chief. Johnson wrote to Amherst, to the general's subordinates, and over Amherst's head to the earl of Egremont. He and other members of the Indian department had, of course, their own reasons for wanting Amherst to provide them with greater resources, and their complaints were dismissed, as were those of military subordinates. James Gorell, isolated at Fort Edward Augustus in Wisconsin, could not find words to describe his "trouble" at being unable to give presents to Indians. Once the war did erupt and post after post fell into Indian hands, an entire corps joined Croghan and Johnson as they beat the drums against Amherst, until he was finally recalled in the fall of 1763. The most effective criticism was that he had placed handfuls of soldiers in weak outposts with neither the strength to dominate Indians nor the means to curry Indian favor. Learning of Amherst's recall, Ecuyer observed, "He is greatly regretted by the entire army. . . . Bumpers of Madeira are drunk to his prompt departure."[48] Incapable of managing Indian affairs as he was, Amherst was also hamstrung by the imperial demand for greater economy. Nor did he alone give Indians reason for war. Gladwin and Ecuyer, as we have seen, were equally contemptuous of Indians, as were many other officers in the field. Johnson sought to maximize his authority through that of the Six Nations. And even he and Croghan expected eventual Indian subordination. Both, along with Amherst, had their eyes on Indian land.

Possessions

The "bad talk" of the British, the misplaced calumets, and the hostile restrictions on presents and trade reinforced Indian fears that the ultimate British aims were to possess Indian land and enslave Indian people. Historians have often pointed to the obvious expansionism of the British colonies as the most important cause for the war. As early as 1766 General Thomas Gage considered that it was "the chief occasion of the defection of the Indians," pointing out, as have many since, that this was particularly true in the Ohio region. The threat to the land was real; the fear of dispossession was widespread. During Pontiac's War, even Great Lakes and Illinois Indians who had yet to face landed British colonial expansion sometimes declared that it was a cause of their war.[49] But since actual loss of land west of the Appalachians, before or in the immediate wake of the war, was limited to a very small proportion of lands held by Pontiac's allies, the manner in which Indians came to be convinced of the bad intentions of the British toward their lands needs examination.

Indians in the 1760s had some reason to hope that the British would hold back the settlements. In December 1761 the British Privy Council issued special instructions to New York, New Hampshire, Nova Scotia, North Carolina, South Carolina, and Georgia that forbade further land purchases by those colonies. As a war measure (the Seven Years' War had yet to conclude in Europe), the king signed those instructions on December 9, prohibiting new settlements in the west without the approval of the Board of Trade. Around Fort Pitt, the army backed these fair words with scattered deeds, standing against British "Outlaws," "Idle People," and "country people"—"the scum of the Neighbouring Provinces"—who were moving into the region to settle, hunt, or traffic in liquor. In the spring of 1762, Bouquet, who understood that mastery of the Indians implied mastery of the settlers as well, was burning British colonial huts.[50] Officers in the early 1760s adopted the authoritarian pose of those who would protect Indians from scoundrels, and they would do so again after Pontiac's War, but the pose should not mislead us. The army itself was the problem.

The army presented the most immediate threat to trans-Allegheny land. By 1763 it had taken over and garrisoned the former French posts at Niagara, Detroit, Miami, St. Joseph, Ouiatenon, La Baye, and Michilimackinac. It had rebuilt recently abandoned French posts at Pitt, Venango, Le Boeuf, and Presque Isle and constructed a new post near the long-abandoned French one at Sandusky. It also built new posts on the Niagara River. Sandusky stood out sorely. The French had not had any post in the region since 1753, so it was difficult for Indians to see the English rationale in planting one there. Amherst ordered the construction of the post in 1761. In early 1762, the headman of the nearby town of Coonudute told Sandusky's commander, Ensign Pauli, that the fort would be burned in the spring (he was off by one year). Not only did the army establish these posts throughout the Ohio and Lakes regions, but it also invited farmers to settle nearby and along some of the communications connecting these imperial outposts to the Atlantic World. In addition to provisioning the garrisons, farmers would supply the horses, oxen, forage, and even wagons necessary for land carriage. Bouquet wanted taverns established on the road from Pennsylvania to Fort Pitt. At Fort Pitt, when Bouquet found that the army's and the settlers' hogs were rooting in the fort's earthworks, he had them run free beyond the King's Gardens, where they threatened instead nearby Indian fields. The garrison also raised its own wheat in fields that lay well beyond its walls.[51]

In the winter and spring of 1761, Mingos, Shawnees, and Delawares, sensing betrayal in the rise of Fort Pitt, took steps to slow down its construction, stealing horses on which the British relied for much heavy work, such as hauling the heavy molds and the firewood needed to form and bake bricks. They stole from the army as well as from the settlers. At Forts Pitt and Le Boeuf, shots were exchanged as soldiers gave chase to Mingo horse thieves. Bouquet imposed an embargo on the Shawnees for horse theft. He forbade settlers from buying stolen horse bridles, saddles, hobbles, and bells from Indian thieves. Faced with illicit trade, he had to pull down the houses of two settlers, whom he banished from the region. For posts dependent on the carriage of supplies over the mountains, horse theft was a grave concern, and Bouquet repeatedly addressed it in his talks with Indians at Fort Pitt. There were "thieves" among the soldiers, too, at least as the Indians saw it. British soldiers occasionally hunted on Indian lands. Three Indians arrested a soldier from the outpost of Le Boeuf in 1761, fining him by taking his powder horn and bullets and ordering him "not to come out there any more."[52]

Shortly before the outbreak of war, Fort Pitt threatened further military expansion as the Monongahela Valley rang with the sounds of carpenters building thirty large bateaux meant to carry four hundred men downstream to secure the Illinois Country. Taking Illinois, the British would cut off the Upper Ohio Country from its last links with New Orleans. Jeffery Amherst intended settlements to follow, for it would not do to have the British Illinois garrisons too dependent on either the local *habitants* or the Indians. Croghan worried that the Indians would not "relish such Settlements," and he speculated that Amherst would never even acquaint them "with his Designs." Elsewhere, Amherst infuriated Johnson by condoning the plan of several merchants and retired officers to take control of the Niagara carrying place: a critical portage in the trade with the upper Great Lakes, one then held largely by the Senecas. Johnson was certain that the plan, which was already under way, would convince Indians that the British meant to root "them out of their Country."[53]

Ultimately, that is exactly what the empire and its colonists, including Croghan and Johnson, meant to do. Croghan kept journals as he conducted his Indian diplomacy, and when in new places he looked upon them more as a developer than a trader, noting the "Good Soil," "fine Bottom," and "Pleasant Barrens of good Food," all "Clover and wild Timothy." Johnson, too, was an active speculator. He would receive gifts of acreage from Indians (even gifts contrary to the king's Royal Proclamation of 1763, discussed in Chapter 6), and he would participate, as would Croghan, in speculative real estate ventures.[54] Ohio Indians placed little trust in any of the men with whom they had to deal, and they conveyed those sentiments westward.

East of the mountains, settlers and colonists, poised to mop up what remained of Indian holdings, posed the most serious threat to Indians. In the Susquehanna Valley, from which many of the Ohioans had migrated, Delawares, Nanticokes, Conoys, and others suffered an organized invasion, sponsored by the Susquehanna Company. By the early 1760s, few outside the company itself recognized the validity of the shady deal through which its shareholders claimed title, yet the company sent settlers anyway. In the fall of 1760, Pennsylvania Indian agent Richard Peters feared that the company would "kindle an Indian War in the Bowels of this poor province."[55] The Treaty of Easton in 1757 had granted the Wyoming section of the valley to the important Susquehanna Delaware leader Teedyuscung, and the province of Pennsylvania had built cabins for him and for some of his followers there; now all this was in jeopardy.[56]

In August 1762 these Connecticut settlers' activities loomed over the treaty proceedings at Lancaster, attended by Six Nations Indians, Susquehanna Indians, Ohio Delawares, Shawnees, Mingos, and Wabash-area Kickapoos, Weas, and Miamis. The negotiations were supposed to be about trade and the return of captives still living among the Indians. Trade was discussed, and some prisoners were returned, but there was poison in the air. At one point, an Oneida negotiator and leader, Thomas King, threatened to undo decades of diplomacy by insisting that the Delaware Valley lands now being settled by New Englanders did not belong to his own Six Nations but to the Munsee Delawares themselves. If that had been acknowledged, many earlier British purchases from the Six Nations would have been invalidated. Croghan managed to contain that outburst, but British colonists failed to achieve one of their major objectives. Pennsylvania's Governor James Hamilton had requested free-trade rights for his colony in the entire Susquehanna Valley; the Six Nations flatly refused. When King journeyed homeward through the

Susquehanna Valley, moreover, he ordered settlers around Wyoming "to go away, and quit the land." Tamaqua, the Ohio Delaware leader who had done so much to secure the peace in 1758, also openly objected to the Susquehanna Company's settlements and spurned a present offered him by Governor Hamilton, who sought concessions in the valley. Not long after, as Tamaqua returned homeward, colonial bandits stole his horses. Once in the Ohio Valley, he found that his willingness to negotiate with colonists was costing him authority, and he lost influence to the rising leader Netawatwees, who would be influenced by militants with a millennial message.[57]

William Johnson and Governor Hamilton worried that the Connecticut settlements at Wyoming would mean war. But Johnson had no army, and Hamilton, who considered forcibly removing the Yankee settlers, decided instead to wait on General Amherst. In April 1763 Teedyuscung died in the flames of his burning cabin, likely a victim of colonial assassination. A month later, his son, Captain Bull, was in Philadelphia angrily protesting the settlement. By then, Pontiac's War had already erupted in the west. There is an oddity here: at the very moment that Pontiac, who had little to fear from British colonial farmers, was besieging Detroit, Captain Bull, whose dispossession was actually taking place and who believed that colonists had just burned to death his own father, was not fighting but was appealing for justice. Land was at stake in Pontiac's War, but no pattern establishes it as the overriding issue. The first Indians to rise, those under Pontiac at Detroit, saw only theoretical threats to their land. Some of the last to rise, the Susquehanna Valley peoples, were actually under landed invasion. Thomas King, who repeatedly challenged the Susquehanna Company, would never turn against the British; he would even take up arms for them, eventually capturing Captain Bull. To be sure, Indians of the upper Ohio, many of them of eastern origin and in that sense already among the dispossessed, felt threatened by the squatter camps mushrooming in the shadow of the forts and along the roads to the forts from the east. The Ohioans' villages, though, were under no immediate threat of dispossession.[58] Pontiac's War was not an inevitable conflict pitting expansionist Anglo-American farmers against Native American defenders of the soil. The first issue was not land but authority and submission. The Indians' determination to resist slavery, voiced as frequently as their determination to defend their lands, has been largely overlooked, probably because history did not so thoroughly bear out predictions of enslavement as it did those of dispossession. At Detroit and in many parts of the Great Lakes region, however, Indian slavery had been both practiced by the French and supported by Indians. When Henry Gladwin had given new meaning to that form of slavery by publically hanging a Panis woman in 1763, he created a palpable image of what might lie in store for the region's Indians under British subjection. Should Indians lose the struggle against domination, they knew that the loss of their land would follow.

Men, Women, Children, and Love

Personal matters of individual identity aggravated relations as British authorities and Indian headmen found it difficult to come to agreeable terms. British policies appeared to threaten the identity and roles of whites living among Indians, of Indian hunters, and of Indian women. Love, and its failure, figured in the origins of the war.

The most vexing of issues complicating relations between the British and the upper Ohio Wyandots, Shawnees, Delawares, and Mingos was an intractable matter of the heart—the return of captive family members, especially children, to the British. Even as Indians considered peace with King George in 1758, they rumored that the British would demand the return of all persons whom they had torn from the colonies during the war. Counterrumors also had it that any captive who wished to remain among the Indians would be permitted to do so. By mid-August 1758, months before the fall of Fort Duquesne, the British position was clear: Indians must deliver every captive among them. George Croghan made the same point at Detroit in 1760.[59]

The issue was less troubling at Detroit than in the Ohio Country. Seventeen captives were returned to the British within the first month of the British occupation. The Anishinabeg and Wyandots of Detroit had probably taken fewer English prisoners than had the Shawnees and Delawares, who lived so close to the colonies. Given their longer history of relations with France, when the first two peoples did capture colonists, they were more likely to seek ransom than adoption. But even at Detroit, Britons could find it difficult to have particular prisoners returned. Sir William Johnson had to pay a very high price for an English woman whom, he wrote without explanation, the Indians had used "barbarously." The family to which she now belonged was reluctant to part with her, for she had taken the "place" of two young men "killed by the English."[60]

Powerful emotions ran behind the British demand as family members in the colonies worried in the night about their lost children, their wives, and their mothers. Some wrote directly to British officers, begging that their children be located and returned. James McColloch, a poor Pennsylvanian from the neighborhood of Fort Loudon, sent a close description of the various moles and "mousemarks" on the bodies of his two stolen boys. He had gathered information as to their possible whereabouts, and he pleaded for their return. Since their capture, McColloch and his wife had been "truly wretched," and they now presented "their distressed case to all Charitable and well disposed Christians." Though he possessed very little, McColloch also promised "any reward in his power."[61]

Delawares, Wyandots, and Shawnees knew these sentiments, found them affecting, and did return some prisoners. But it was a terrible thing to return children who had, over perhaps half a dozen years, become their own. Wyandots told Croghan they would return only those who did not "have a mind" to live with them. Delawares returned three children who went unwillingly, crying "as if they would die when they were presented" to the British, something the officials understood well. These were the most delicate of all negotiations, and in the end there was no good deal. A crowd of Indians came with a small girl to Fort Pitt in February 1759. A man stepped forward to demand whiskey for himself and a present for the woman who headed the child's Indian household. Captain Hugh Mercer initially declared in high tones that he would not purchase his own people, that the Indians would have peace only if they returned every prisoner. But he soon found himself looking upon the woman with charity, and he gave her a coat.[62]

Years passed, British subjects and their children remained among Indian people, and the issue still hampered diplomacy. Shawnees still held scores of captives in 1762. British officers threatened, cajoled, and placed embargoes on the trade for the release of all captives, but with little result. Shawnees remained deeply suspicious of British intentions. Rumors circulated that the army meant to attack the Shawnees and was seeking first to weaken the tribe by both reducing its numbers and dividing its distressed families into camps for and against headmen compliant with the British. George Croghan heard that the Shawnees thought the reason the British spoke so much of the captives was that they intended to "fall upon them" once the captives were returned.[63]

In the early 1760s, Indian men in the region of Fort Pitt were more worried by colonial hunters than they were by colonial settlers, and with good reason. Hunting, central to the identity of most Indian men and central to the Indian exchange economy, was failing, as it was harder to find game in the Upper Ohio Country. Even worse, prices for European manufactured goods proved to be higher after the Seven Years' War than they had been before. The general economy of the Ohio Indians had been severely disrupted in the late 1750s. When Forbes' army advanced in 1758, Indians neglected their fields, and the harvest was a disaster. At the year's end, Fort Pitt's Captain Mercer reported that the Indians had stripped the cornfields at abandoned Logstown and that the Indians were "in a likely way of eating [the British] up too, especially in the Article of Flower." The following summer, Ohio Indians were starving. Bouquet complained that the British continually had "4, or 500 Indians to feed at Pittsburgh." The famine forced Indians to seek food in the woods, leading to overhunting as Indians devastated already depleted deer herds in order to get meat as well as skins to trade for food, clothing, ammunition, metal goods, and rum. As the regular trade became reestablished in 1761, the deerskin harvest was unexpectedly small. James Kenny, in his first year as the official Pennsylvania Indian factor, shipped off only "19 Load of Skins." Trade, he observed, seemed dull-"Many people has left it."[64]

In the fall, a different complaint about the game shortage was heard in the Ohio Country. In October 1761 Sergeant Angus McDonald of Fort Burd, on the Monongahela, sent word to Bouquet that the "Crowds of Hunters" coming from the colonies were so large as to fill the woods. This disturbed the Indians "very much," for they believed that the white people killed "all there [sic] deer." After 1761 the key reason they opposed the colonial invasion of the Monongahela was that it threatened their hunting. Mingos told Croghan that they were moving downriver in search of better game. Shawnees and others complained "bitterly" to Henry Bouquet that white men had "Distroyed a Great quantity of game." As a Mingo put it to George Croghan, "You settling here in the Heart of our Country has made our Game Scarce," and it convinced Indians that the British had "some bad designs against them."[65] Conflict over hunting south of the Ohio had long been a source of warfare with the Cherokees; now it threatened to involve Indian men with colonists.

In early 1762, Shawnees brought three scalps from backcountry Virginia to Sandusky, causing alarm at Fort Detroit. Traders at the Shawnee towns on the Scioto River calmed official fears, persuading Henry Bouquet at Fort Pitt that this was only the rash act of one small band and that the rest of the nation was "very peaceable." Two more settlers, hunting along the Monongahela, were soon killed, and again Shawnees were implicated, but this time the killers' identity was uncertain. What was certain was that the killers had stolen two fine rifles from the victims. Bouquet noted that the victims had been out "contrary to orders."[66]

Colonial hunters, armed and proficient, were seen by Indians as dangerous men. But men alone did not threaten the deer herds. So did cattle and, even more, hogs. Many of these were owned by Indians, but more were owned by the migrating colonists and the British garrisons, who let them run wild. The first colonial settlers of the Ohio and Appalachian regions depended heavily on their semiferal livestock. The hogs of these hog drovers, like the deer, sought woods forage and mast, particularly acorns and chestnuts. Regions that had once been noted for an abundance of deer, such as southern Ohio, Indiana, and Kentucky, would be transformed by the early nineteenth century from thick deer country into outstanding hog country.[67]

One old Delaware faced the matter in a dream. Carried upward to a heavenly mansion, he spoke to the Great Spirit, who explained that the Indians were failing to summon the animals with the correct ritual language. They had used the wrong words; they had misnamed all the animals. The Creator then taught the man the proper names, calling the animals "One after Another with a mighty Sound." This was how to get the animals to appear, for they "take notice of their name when called." Far to the west, Pontiac, raising warriors for the war, relied on another Delaware holy man's encounter with the Great Spirit. The Prophet had reported that the Master of Life was punishing the Indians: "I led the wild animals into the depths of the forests. . . . Ye have only to become good again, . . . and I will send back the animals for your food."[68]

The British sense of hierarchy, the poor conditions of trade, the demand for the return of captives, and the destruction of the hunting economy all involved relations between men and women in ways that signaled impending Indian degradation. When British officers demanded the return of captives, they spoke to Indian men, yet women determined a captive's fate in most of these societies. Stress within families and town councils was inevitable. British officers were demanding, in effect, that Indian women relinquish both family members and a key social power. Adopted captives had also played crucial mediating roles in Indian societies, serving as interpreters between their original and adoptive people. Captives, in many cases, were the very people who could provide crucial services and knowledge to Indian peoples dealing with the empire.

A British decision in 1761 to restrict trade to the posts also aggravated concerns about the nature of the developing relations with the British, not only because of the inconvenience of having to travel to British posts but also because the regulation spoke of the British fear of intermingling with Indians. Bouquet wrote from Fort Pitt that the Indians did not "complain of anything, except that the Traders [were] not permitted to go to their towns." French traders, and British traders in the southeast and in Hudson's Bay, frequently lived among the Indians, often enough intermarrying with them according to the "custom of the country" and sometimes even with the blessing of the church. Short of intermarriage, godparenting provided an important and meaningful form of kinship linking French people and what Indian Catholics remained in the Great Lakes region. To block such relations by forbidding traders to dwell in Indian towns was to send the powerful message that the British were unwilling to see their people join in common humanity with Indians. Ohio Shawnees complained that the British, while willing to trade with the French in such French towns as Quebec and Detroit, did not "look upon" Shawnees "as brothers and freinds [sic]."[69]

For women to travel to the posts was more than an inconvenience, though that it was. Women had heavy responsibilities in and near the village as the primary cultivators and gatherers and as the heads of matrilineal households in many of the societies. But inconvenience became peril at the posts as women confronted the largely male garrisons, accustomed to prostitution. Bouquet denounced one brothel at Fort Pitt as a "Colony sprung from Hell." But his fellow Swiss countryman and subordinate, Captain Simeon Ecuyer, could wax bawdy of his Saturday night parties, attended by the "prettiest ladies" of the garrison: "We regale them with punch, and if it is not strong enough, the whiskey is at their disposal. You may be sure that we shall not be completely cheated." Ecuyer wrote with evident satisfaction that a prostitute had given "the itch" to a man Ecuyer disliked. The next year, William Grant wrote from the same fort that he had to send eastward an ensign's mistress who had become "a most infamous Harlot." Grant observed that "all the ladies of her profession" were "very troublesome at an outpost"; still, one lieutenant insisted on keeping his mistress at Fort Pitt.[70]

Some of these women may have been Indians. In the letters just quoted, Grant and Ecuyer joked about soldiers keeping "Dulcineas," perhaps pointing to the dark hair and dark eyes, to say nothing of the low status, of the women. In neither case were these Dulcineas sent back to the settlements, which suggests that they had not arrived at their employment from that direction. Be that as it may, sexuality emerged as a definite issue between Britons and Indians. When Miamis took Fort Miami in 1763, they deployed a ruse involving the Indian lover of the garrison commander. And in the first violence of the war, on the St. Clair River far north of Detroit, Ojibwa women would use seductive gestures very effectively to entice willing British boatmen into the gun sights of hidden Ojibwa warriors. In these instances there are hints that Indians resented a British assumption of sexual access to Indian women.[71]

With forts replacing Indian villages as the only venues for interaction between Indians and Britons, Indian women were losing influence over public affairs, and Indian societies were losing authority over intercultural sexual relations. In addition, Indian women rarely met with British colonial women in any setting outside the Moravian missions (where the colonists spoke German). Perhaps that is why, when a group of Delaware women met a group of English Quaker women in 1761, all embraced and openly wept.[72]

British policies also troubled Indian manhood. With the Seven Years' War over and the Cherokee War fizzling to a close, there was no place for the warrior. This itself need not have been a problem. Indians celebrated peace and had a variety of ways, ceremonial and practical, of turning warriors into hunters, family men, and neighbors. The end of the wars would have been a relief, had hunting been possible. But with the gross restrictions on ammunition everywhere, the poor hunting conditions around Fort Pitt, and the high prices of goods, this was increasingly a doubtful option. Husbands had little access to the goods that might please their wives, and wives themselves had little access to the traders. Leading Indian men felt dishonored and their leadership threatened as they were not given the kind of presents that signaled British respect and that they needed to redistribute as marks of their respect for their followers.

During a meeting with leaders of the Iroquois League in July 1763, Sir

William Johnson learned that the Senecas had sent to the rest of the Six Nations asking them to attack the English. The Senecas, Johnson learned, had "given a lease to their Warriors, and desired they would do the same." He also learned that "the Women of the Senecas, spoke with a Belt to the Women of the other Nations desiring they would persuade their Men to do the Same."[73] At Forts Detroit, Miami, and Michilimackinac, women played key roles in the opening events of the war.

Though wars have reasons and though rational people fight wars, war is never reducible to reason alone; powerful sentiments—senses of loyalty, honor, hatred, jealousy, vengeance, and fear—must be invoked to bring men and women to kill and to risk death. Summoning strength, warriors and soldiers summon concepts that complicate reason: honor, the sacred, the country, the cause. Some analysts insist that reason must be worldly and material; Pontiac's War had, to be sure, a worldly, material, reasonable dimension. Indians reasonably feared British landed expansion; they reasonably found the trade inadequate to their needs. But these were the kinds of measurable and quantifiable issues that might have been negotiated had it not become so clear that other issues, pressing matters of the heart, were beyond discussion. British officials clearly conveyed their intention to dominate and to master a conquered continent; to intend less would have been to shed their identities as British imperial leaders. Indians demanded recognition, honor, and respect. Conflicts over foul language, insults, Indian captives, women, patterns of authority, trade, and, perhaps above all, presents revealed clearly that an unbridgeable distance lay between each party's dimming hopes for peace. When Pontiac began his war at Detroit, his example was followed rapidly and with great violence. In the course of the war that then began, Indians looked to another world.

CHAPTER THREE

An Otherworldly War

Listening to Pontiac's invocation of the Delaware Prophet as he appealed for a war against the British in the spring of 1763, the Anishinabeg already knew much of the story. But they were quiet that late April evening as Pontiac described the Prophet's journey to the Sky World and his encounter with the Master of Life, who showed the Prophet the Indians' way to salvation in heaven and on earth. Over the next year, Pontiac preached the message to Anishinabeg, to Wyandots, and to French soldiers and Indians in the Illinois Country. The anonymous "Journal of a Conspiracy" calls the message "the reason of the attack upon the English."[1]

Delawares had more reason than most Native Americans to doubt the possibilities of peaceful coexistence with British North America. Their long peace with Pennsylvania had come at high costs in land and autonomy. They had felt directly the expansiveness of the colonial population, the intricacies of the British-Iroquois Covenant Chain, the mobilizing capabilities of the British and colonial military. Having moved to the Ohio not only for better hunting but also to escape the tightening grip of the colonial-Iroquois "chain of friendship" and having taken up arms in 1755 to defend, in alliance with France, their recently restored autonomy, Delawares in 1763 felt powerless, by themselves, to resist the imposing British presence at Fort Pitt. As familiar disruptions threatened again, Delawares turned to their western allies of the late war, and they turned, too, to sacred power.

The Anishinabeg by 1763 appreciated the Delawares' vast experience with the British. Commonly traveled trade routes had long linked Detroit to the upper Ohio, and Delawares and Shawnees had maintained diplomatic contact along those paths with the Great Lakes Indians. One report places Pontiac himself in the upper Ohio in 1757, another in 1759 or 1760, and although neither is very trustworthy, we know that many Anishinabeg had operated out of Fort Pitt during the Seven Years' War. On the eve of Pontiac's War, Delawares and Shawnees were similarly active near the Great Lakes. In late March 1763, for example, Fort Miami's Ensign Robert Holmes sent word to his commander at Detroit that a "Bloody Belt" calling for war had been delivered to the Miamis by the Shawnees, Delawares, and Senecas. Holmes managed to secure the belt, perhaps with the help of his Miami lover, and forward it to his superiors.[2] When, far to the east, George Croghan first learned of the outbreak of the war, he suspected Delaware provocateurs. The next winter, Detroit Indians themselves sent word to the French in Illinois that they had listened to arguments from the upper Ohio: "All that the Delawares and Shawannays told us is now come to pass. . . . The Delawares told us this Spring, that the English sought to become Masters of all, & would put us to death. They told us also, Our Brethren, let us die together. Seeing the Design of the English is to cutt us off, we are Dead one way or another."[3]

The Delawares had for at least a decade sought safety in Indian numbers. As early as 1754, some had invited Shawnees to join them in a polyglot settlement, and the Shawnees passed the invitation down the Ohio River to the Indians of Illinois and up the Scioto River to the Miamis near the Great Lakes: "Come to see us all, my brothers, and . . . be united as one people." The message of unity surfaced again in 1758, when the Delaware Indians Shingas and "Delaware George" protested to a British emissary that they alone could not make peace with the British: "[Since] all the Indians, from sunrise to the sunset, are united in a body, it is necessary that the whole should join in the peace." The "whole" included "all the Indians, a great way from this, even beyond the lakes." After Pontiac's War had ended, Sir William Johnson recognized that Delawares and Shawnees had become "much more respected by the rest than formerly." He attributed their rising prestige to their having fought well in the Seven Years' War; but there was a deeper foundation.[4]

The Anishinabeg placed their own origins far to the east, along the Atlantic, and they conceived of coastal Algonquians as both relatives and ancestral peoples. The east, Waban, was the most sacred of Ottawa directions, and the Delawares, whose home was in the east, possessed the honorific Wapanachki (easterners). Shawnee myths report that the Creator had made the Delawares before making the Shawnees, an acknowledgment of the special Delaware place. Other central Algonquians commonly called the Delawares their "grandfathers." Between the late 1730s and the 1760s, Delawares and their neighbors were busily reinventing and renewing their religious traditions, adding to their already established reputation.[5] History and sacred tradition lent authority to Delaware voices, especially when they spoke of the British.

The Anishinabeg of the Great Lakes remained open to sacred appeals throughout the period of great violence that began in the 1750s. French colonel Louis-Antoine de Bougainville, an astute observer of his Indian allies during the Seven Years' War, reported much native religiosity among the Anishinabeg. It should not be surprising that, during Pontiac's first open assault on Detroit in May 1763, Britons observed the Ottawas performing "incantations" to see how they might advance without suffering great casualties. Ojibwas who captured John Rutherford that month shaved most of his head and "carefully put by" his hair. They also ritually sacrificed a dog. The next year, Captain Thomas Morris, attempting negotiations with Pontiac on the Maumee River, heard that one of the Ottawas was able to speak directly with the Great Spirit. Morris passed Ottawa sites where he "saw their offerings of tobacco, made by every individual each morning, ranged in the nicest order." He also saw their sacred bundles: "[They] carry their God in a bag, which is hung in the front of their encampment, and is visited by none but [their religious specialists.]" Archaeology, too, suggests persistent native spirituality: native burial practices, not Christian practices, dominated in the region until about 1800. Alexander Henry, among Ottawas during the first year of the war, witnessed one such Ojibwa burial in Michigan in 1764.[6]

The Delaware Prophet's message tapped a vibrant Anishinabe spirituality, something the Indians' British opponents could recognize almost despite themselves. John Porteous, a British trader stationed at Detroit, had little good to say about Indian culture, which he abhorred above "all other ways of life." He once wrote to his brother in England that Ottawas and Ojibwas in the area had no religious festivities and no priesthood, and then, in the next stroke, he described both. The Indians, he wrote, held "solemn sacrifices," which could last a whole night. The ceremonies were led by "one, two, three, or any number of rever'd conjurers." Shaking tent rituals—key features of Anishinabe and central Algonquian worship—accompanied these ceremonies. Gathered around a tent or cabin in which a shaman awaited the visit of spiritual messengers, onlookers heard winds that they could not feel rise and shake the structure. As the shaman called out questions, the witnesses heard sacred voices provide answers, before the mysterious turbulence passed and the shaman emerged. Porteous had heard that one of the so-called conjurers could shake a cabin that "four men could not budge." He had seen the specialists bind men, bury them under blankets, and then order them to rise again. He had seen holy men touch worshipers with their sacred otter skins (variations of Nanabush's earth divers), causing the individuals to fall "as if dead for at least half an hour" before being reborn. In short, Porteous had seen Detroit's Indians involved in the Midewiwin rites, in which "individuals were initiated . . . by being symbolically killed. Revived from this ritual death, the initiate became a newly born member of the society," a *mide*.[7]

The master of stratagem, Nanabush, was a key figure in Midewiwin ceremonies, and Great Lakes warriors took vital cues from him in 1763. Ruses worthy of the Great Hare brought down several of the British posts in the region, most notably Michilimackinac, taken by surprise as the British watched Ojibwas and Sauks play lacrosse, a game favored by Nanabush. On May 8, the night before the first assault on Detroit, Ottawas, Ojibwas, Potawatomis, and Wyandots gathered at Pontiac's village also to play "a great Match at Cross [lacrosse]," part sport, part ritual of regeneration, part ritual of war. Such a stratagem was even a ritualized way of dealing with powerful, potentially dangerous sacred beings. During the hard winter of 1763–64, Alexander Henry and his band of famished Ottawa protectors sought ritually to deceive a threatening spirit world: "We were often twenty-four hours without eating. . . . The custom was to black our faces with grease and charcoal, and exhibit . . . a temper as cheerful as if in the midst of plenty." Pontiac's allies among the Sandusky Wyandots made it clear to the British that trickery could be divine when turned against British soldiers: "Their God tells them that they must make War . . . for seven Years, at the end of which by force of treachery . . . the English would be drove away." Of "sagacity and stratagem" Sir William Johnson warned his superiors: the Indians were "no wise inferior."[8]

Delawares did not practice Midewiwin ceremonies, but they shared much faith with the Ottawas. A Munsee Delaware word for shaman was *medea*—a cognate of the Anishinabe word *mide*. Both peoples referred to a sacred power as a *manitou*. Ottawas and Delawares together respected such manitous as thunderers and great horned serpents. They saw something sacred in some varieties of sea shells and sought to obtain blessings from certain animals through elaborate ceremonies after the hunt. Religiously wary of snakes and admiring of rabbits, they related the adventures of the Great Hare and honored the more distant Great Spirit. In the 1760s, Ottawas and Delawares alike told stories of how the world had been rescued from watery chaos: some Delawares in the late 1760s told missionaries that the task had been accomplished by the Great Hare and an earth diver, exactly as the Anishinabeg had it. They believed, too, in death, rebirth, and transformation. Both peoples had traditionally believed in a kind of heaven, but decades of colonization and encounters with Christians convinced many among them that hell might also await one in the afterlife.[9]

Death was a major concern in the Indian villages around Detroit in the winter of 1762–63. Diseases claimed an unusually high number of Indian lives, which the Ottawas began to "ascribe to the Conjurations of the English," who were "a sett of Barbarians, Wizzards, [and] Conjurers," who could trouble "the Air" and send illnesses "to kill all the Indians." The same idea had circulated in 1757, when smallpox broke out among Great Lakes Indians who returned from their victory at Fort William Henry. That outbreak, they believed, was caused by the English poisoning them, for which the Indians owed them "an everlasting ill will." Like Ottawas and other Anishinabeg, Delawares often attributed disease to witchery, and in the early 1760s they saw much such abomination among the British.[10] When the Delaware prophecies reached Detroit, they found a receptive audience.

The Delaware Prophet

On October 15, 1761, the Pennsylvania Quaker and fur trader James Kenny first recorded the teachings of the Delaware Prophet, whom he called the "Imposter." They amounted to a total rejection of white people and their culture; even heaven was empty of whites. Kenny noted that the Prophet drew on skin or paper a chart that placed this world at the bottom and heaven at the top, with a road leading from one place to the

"Indians giving a Talk to Colonel Bouquet." Engraving based on a Benjamin West painting. From William Smith, *An Historical Account of the Expedition against the Ohio Indians, in the year MDCCLXIV, under the command of Henry Bouquet, Esq.* . . . (Philadelphia, 1765; London, 1766). Courtesy Burton Historical Collection, Detroit Public Library. An Indian orator points to the heavens as he speaks to a confident Colonel Henry Bouquet against a backdrop of uncertain warriors, neat British tents, and the American forest.

other, which the Indians' ancestors "used to ascend to Happiness" before an assortment of obstacles—white people and the sins they had taught Indians—had blocked the way, forcing Indians to hell. The Delawares had to "learn to live without any trade or connections with the white people, clothing and supporting themselves as their forefathers did." For a time, good relations with whites, "good talks," would continue. But war would eventually come. By March 1763, shortly before the war, the Prophet had elaborated what Kenny called the "new Plan of Religion," and a rigorous plan it was. Boys were to be taught the use of the bow and arrow and raised on a special diet: for seven years they would drink a bitter emetic. Old men and women would eat only corn. But for all the plan's rigor, it is noteworthy that trade with whites would continue until the period of sustained ritual fasting and purging had come to an end; then, and only then, would commerce be cut off.[11] These were difficult articles of faith, but they would have allowed Indians to hunt, use firearms, and trade for a while.

Of all the relatively direct renderings of the Prophet's teachings, Kenny's most implies a categorical rejection of all things European; he records no special exception for the French. Historians have similarly registered antiwhite sentiment as an aspect of Pontiac's War. Yet even Kenny's rendition permits temporary trade with whites, and other reports of the Prophet's teachings, those taken from regions with a deeper French influence, do not lump all white people together. Pontiac's own version of the message, spoken in a Detroit that still supported a significant and influential French-speaking community, clearly distinguished between the *habitants* and the English. The discrepancy between Kenny's record and the Detroit record has led most historians to accuse Pontiac of manipulating "the Prophet's message" to exempt the French from spiritual condemnation or, in a more cynical spirit, employing the message to "rationalize his assault on Detroit." The implication is that Pontiac stood outside and above the religious movement yet harnessed it to achieve his practical objectives.[12]

There is reason, however, to think that even the Delaware Prophet himself was more favorable to the French than Kenny suggests. Eighteenth-century Delawares had a word for Europeans in general (*Schwonack*), for Anglo-American settlers (*Choanshikan*), and for the French (*Pelaciman*, derived from the English word *Frenchman*). Even if we assume that the Prophet employed the term *Schwonack* when he taught his followers, he still may have been understood to mean British subjects, by far the most common Europeans in the Delaware experience.[13] The fullest source for the Prophet's influence on Pontiac is that anonymous "journal" attributed to Robert Navarre. Throughout at least July 1763, Navarre lived among the *habitants* and Indians near, but not within, the fort. He was in direct contact with Pontiac and tried to serve as a mediator for peace, even writing down a few of the messages that the unlettered Ottawa wanted sent to the fort's commander.[14] The journal describes Pontiac as "craftily" using the Prophet's religion to inspire warriors, but it also states that Pontiac believed the Delaware's vision "as an article of faith." According to the journal, the Master of Life chided the Indians for relying on the French but permitted the French to live among Indians, declaring of them, "I love them." The Master professed, however, not to love the English at all: "They are my enemies, and the enemies of your brothers [the French]."[15] The absence of similar defenses of the French from most other records of the Prophet's teachings lends support to the conventional wisdom that Pontiac manipulated the Prophet's teachings, but a different section of Navarre's journal suggests that the Delaware Prophet had more to say about the French.

Six weeks into the siege of Detroit, Ojibwas from the north and Delawares and Shawnees from the Upper Ohio Country arrived to coordinate their efforts with Pontiac's warriors. All three visiting groups denounced Pontiac for attempting to force Detroit's *habitants* to support him. According to the journal—the very source that scholars employ to demonstrate Pontiac's twisting of the Prophet's vision—the visiting Delawares revealed to the Ottawas that they, like Pontiac, easily distinguished the French from the British. They claimed, "The Master of Life by one of our brother Delawares . . . forbade us to attack our brothers the French." Not only that, but they identified themselves as French: "Thou art French as well as we." The Delawares did not want to put themselves "in a bad light with [their] Great Father," the king of France, by violating his sensibilities. The Delawares, when in the neighborhood of *habitants*, separated the French speakers from the British, and, like Pontiac, they did so at the behest of the Master of Life.[16]

The first French officer to mention the Delaware Prophet was the commander of Fort de Chartres, Illinois, Chevalier Pierre Joseph Neyon de Villiers (de Neyon). By December 1763 de Neyon had been trying for several months to persuade the Indians that the French were, in fact, at peace with the British, so the warriors should lay down their arms. One "Sieur de Beaujeu" reported to de Neyon that his efforts were not appreciated by Potawatomis on the upper Illinois River. De Beaujeu maintained that a prophetic spirit had been "introduced among the Abnaki" (meaning the easterners, in this case, the Delawares) and that the Prophet had had "no difficulty convincing all his own people, and in turn all red men, that God appeared to him." The Master of Life told the Prophet that Indians should no longer "suffer the English" to live among them, for the English only meant "sickness, smallpox, . . . poison," and death.[17] By the spring, Pontiac himself was in Illinois, pleading with de Neyon not to abandon the region but to resume the war: "My Father thou goest against the Master of Life. . . . I pray thee to talk no more of a Peace with the English, because I hate them." It was the Master of Life who had ordered the Indians to fight against "this bad meat that would come to infest" their lands. Pontiac pointed out that this was not his belief alone but that of "the Abenakis [Delawares] the Iroquois and the Sawanoes [Shawnees] the Saulteurs [Ojibwas] in short all the nations of the Continent."[18] The French-language records, whether recorded in the Great Lakes region or the Illinois Country, show not only that Pontiac adhered to the Prophet's teachings but also that those teachings distinguished the British from the French.

In one other way, too, they differ from the English-language records taken or recalled from the Ohio Country. They do less to suggest a longing to resurrect the precolonial past. James Kenny and John M'Cullough, a captive among the Delawares in this period, both wrote about the Prophet's insistence that Indians abandon white manners, but French documents show the Prophet attacking certain Indian traditions as well. Both the Detroit journal attributed to Navarre and de Beaujeu's message relayed by de Neyon agree that the Prophet ordered an end to polygamy. More provocative, he challenged certain indigenous rituals. In de Neyon's report, the Prophet ordered Indians to abandon their "altermats and your manitoes," while in the Detroit piece he tells his followers not to make medicine. There is evidence that Pontiac's followers continued to employ traditional medicine bundles in their forms of worship, though it appears that these bundles belonged more to groups than to individuals. There is not much evidence to suggest that the Prophet or Pontiac intended an assault on communal forms of worship. Rather, Pontiac and the

Prophet appear to have exalted collective worship and to have subordinated individual access to sacred power.[19]

A more decisive innovation was the incorporation of Christian cosmology. Pontiac's rendition of the Prophet's vision takes up what may be the Christian imagery of the spiritual journey as a kind of pilgrimage, a long walk down a road, yet there is something almost universal in that image, and Native American mythology contains many heroic journeys to the Sky World. Kenny's description of the Prophet's spiritual chart has been taken by some to mean that the Prophet was imitating the Bible, which is doubtful, since this was not a book at all but a single, large image on a deerskin. Native Americans are well known to have drawn maps, charts, and other graphic representations, so one may dismiss the claim that this was an imitation of Christian Scripture. Still, Christian missionaries also deployed graphic representations of the roads to heaven and hell; it is these, not the Bible, that may have provided the model for the Indian prophets. The Delaware Prophet's representation of an easier road to hell than to heaven bears a strong resemblance to John Bunyan's famous Pilgrim and to the favorite missionary text of the Presbyterians, whose influence among the New Jersey Delawares was already historic: "Enter ye at the strait gate: for wide is the gate, and broad the way, that leadeth to destruction, and many there be which go in thereat: Because strait is the gate, and narrow is the way, which leadeth unto life, and few there be that find it" (Matt. 7:13–14).[20] This text was more popular among Calvinists than Catholics, though missionaries of both Christian denominations could cite it.

The Prophet likely had some experience with Awakened Calvinism: there were Mahican refugees from the New England border among his people, and a number of Delawares themselves had been converted by David and John Brainerd in New Jersey before being scattered. The Presbyterian Charles Beatty encountered some of these former Christians when he visited the Prophet's own village in 1766. As for other Protestants, the Prophet almost certainly had met Moravian Indians and missionaries. The Prophet definitely thought well of Quakers, for he sought them out in 1765. There is also a chance that he had encountered or heard about two German-speaking hermits and pacifists, Gabriel and Israel Eckerlin, who had, with Indian permission, lived in the upper Monongahela Valley for twenty years, until they were taken into custody in 1757 by Ottawas near Fort Duquesne and brought to Niagara. These men were "genuine and truthful and were venerated by the Indians of those regions." It is possible that the Prophet knew of the Jesuit who traveled to Fort Duquesne in 1757, the same year for which we have some evidence that Pontiac was at the post, or he may have heard from Delawares who met with a Jesuit at Fort Niagara in New York, also that year. The Prophet's life, in short, had provided abundant opportunities to hear, reform, and incorporate Christian doctrine of the Catholic, Calvinistic, pietistic, and mystical varieties into his teachings.[21]

British army and Indian department officers noticed Indian religion as the war approached and during its course, but unlike James Kenny or Robert Navarre, they could not take it very seriously. Eight months before the first shots, a Six Nations Indian warned British Indian superintendent William Johnson that a local visionary prophesied sacred retribution against the British for their theft of Indian lands. Johnson dismissed the speech with the kind of "bad language" that had so angered Indians in the west: "Your romantic Notions, Custom of Dreaming, and Seeing visions, . . . cannot but appear in a very ridiculous Light to White People, who will Consider it, only a Scheme set on foot by some designing Persons to answer their Purposes." Jeffery Amherst simultaneously ridiculed women and native religiosity: "The dream of a squaw was sufficient to determine them to any belief"; and he had heard that "the Indians above Detroit had butchered ten prisoners from a squaw having dreamt ten men must be killed." The first imperial official to note the Delaware Prophet may have been Captain Jehu Hay, in his Detroit diary entry for July 18, 1763. His garbled report on the existence of a prophet includes the grisly and false detail that the Delawares had killed all their English prisoners. Hay also heard from his source, a Wyandot named Andre, that the Prophet opposed the torturing of prisoners to death, which is possible, given the dearth of reports of such torture during Pontiac's War, and which concurs with evidence in the so-called Pontiac Journal from about the same time. Major Robert Rogers, at Detroit during the latter part of the siege, would write that religious imposters were "not less frequent among the Indians of America, than among the Christians of Europe," and he spent scores of words describing them, but in such vague and general terms that he cannot have paid them much mind. French officers, French traders, British traders, and colonial missionaries took the most notice of the prophetic movement. British officers did not write much of, probably did not know much about, and certainly did not care much for the Delaware Prophet.[22]

The Prophet's name does not surface in the British imperial record until the early fall of 1764, but when it does, it emerges evocatively. His name was "Neolin," which meant, says the document flatly, "four." This, a sacred number, identifies the Prophet with the spirits of the four cardinal directions and also with the winds, sacred to Delawares as well as to Ottawas. The winds were particularly influential among the Anishinabeg and central Algonquians, who practiced shaking tent rituals in which spiritual winds buffeted the shaman's hut while he or she sought the winds' advice, knowledge, and power. "Neolin" suggests a powerful intermediary with benevolent spirits. The name may also have emphasized that the Master of Life wanted unity among Indian peoples from all directions of this world.[23]

Neolin was a young man when he had his first visions in 1760–61. The visions resembled others that had already come to other Native Americans from the Susquehanna Valley to the Great Lakes over the past several decades and would again come over the next half century. During Neolin's religious ascendency, too, there were other minor prophets whose visions resonated with his. James Kenny recorded the prophecies of an old Delaware in 1762, who, like Neolin, was led to a building in the heavens where he met the "Great Creator . . . sitting an [sic] a Glorious Seat . . . like the King of the White People."[24] The visions came to Neolin while he sat alone one night by a fire, greatly concerned about his people's evil ways. Exactly where he was at the time is uncertain. Moravian missionary John Heckewelder recalled much later that Neolin was living at the town of Cuyahoga, near Lake Erie. This would make sense in the light of his obvious Ottawa connections, but Heckewelder also notes that the prophet traveled a great deal.[25] Most reports put him at the village of Tuscarawas. By the spring of 1763 Neolin had achieved intertribal influence, even among the Six Nations. Genesee Senecas attended to his message, only to be chided by league authorities for admiring "Wizards." Neolin's influence "spread from village to village, and finally reached Pontiac," who, one writer records, "believed all this."[26]

Pontiac recited Neolin's vision and message as he laid out for Ottawas, Hurons, and Potawatomis his plans for an assault on Detroit. His listeners were ready for what he had to say, and as he said it, "they listened to him as an oracle."[27] He described how Neolin, through incantations, had fallen into a dream. In that state, the Prophet journeyed to "Paradise," equipped as a contemporary hunter, complete with firearm, trade kettle, and ammunition. For eight days he walked, camping at night. On the eighth evening, as he set up his camp, he saw three wide roads open before him, so he boldly set out along the "widest," which he found led to nothing but fire. Taking a narrower road, he again found fire. So he took the third, which led him uneventfully for a full day as far as a "mountain of marvellous whiteness," at which the road disappeared. He had no idea how next to proceed, until a seated woman, clothed in radiant garments, appeared and spoke to him in Lenape.

She told him to leave everything behind, right down to his clothes, which presumably were also trade items. Before continuing up the mountain, he had to bathe. Then, naked, he began his climb, permitted to use only his "hand and his left foot." At the top, he at first saw nothing of interest, until he discerned three villages at a distance toward his right, so he set out toward the most attractive of the three. When he paused, fearing to enter a village while stark naked, "a voice" encouraged him onward. The village was barred by a "gate," which opened, and "a handsome man, clothed all in white," led him to the Master of Life.

The Creator grasped his hand and then "gave him a hat all bordered with gold" and asked him to sit on it. The hat, with its gold lace, pointed directly to the colonies and to their worst flaw, greed. Hats represented the British colonies clearly enough; during Pontiac's War, Timothy Horsefield, a Pennsylvania justice of the peace, would insist that Moravian Christian Indian men in the Lehigh River region wear hats to distinguish them from enemy Indians. But a more pointed meaning also suggests itself. At the end of the Lancaster treaty council held in Pennsylvania in 1744, between the Six Nations and Pennsylvania, Maryland, and Virginia, the colonies gave the Six Nations councillor Canasatego a scarlet coat, and they gave his countryman Gachradodow a gold-laced hat. Since by that treaty Virginia gained what it saw as an Iroquois quitclaim to the very Ohio Country that Neolin called home, Gachradodow's gold-laced hat would be a fitting symbol both of the Anglo-American peril facing all Indians and of the particular dangers that the British-Iroquois Covenant Chain presented to the Delawares.[28] Neolin at first hesitated to spoil a thing of such value, but the Creator insisted, and the Prophet did as he was told. Then the Master of Life spoke.

He was the Creator, and he loved the people. He forbade adultery, polygamy, and fighting among Indians. He opposed the medicine dance performed before war, for this dance honored the evil manitou. He opposed the occupation of the land by "whites." He admonished the Indians for relying even on the French for goods, though he professed his love for the French. He reminded Neolin that Indians had once lived without any Europeans, but now they were "given up to evil." As punishment, the Master of Life had withdrawn the game.

The Creator forbade drinking to drunkenness, but not drinking outright. By Neolin's time, alcohol was abundant in Indian country. Brandy and, later, rum had befogged minds and fed bad tempers since the arrival of traders. It had spread poverty, as hunters traded for liquor instead of for essential materials, such as clothing. It had also led to violence. After an Indian near Fort Pitt, who had been "abused here in his Liquor by the soldiers," retaliated by killing a Virginia provincial in the spring of 1760, George Croghan urged that the trade be curtailed. The trade was soon forbidden, but traders, inhabitants of a colonial culture that had a high tolerance for smuggling, found the means to avoid the ban in the very soldiers whom it was meant to protect. Rum, as a standard part of the soldiers' allowance, could be brought to the western posts under official cover. At Detroit, trader James Sterling bribed the commander of the sloop *The Michigan*, who brought up rum under the pretense that it was for "his and his sailors' use." In but one example, Sterling imported upwards of thirty gallons of rum and brandy for one lieutenant's personal use. In another, he sought to bring in nine hundred gallons "for the use of the French Inhabitants," whom he said numbered three hundred families, when in fact there were no more than two hundred families at Detroit (and they may well have made their own brandy). Donald Campbell, who had earlier asked that the liquor trade be closed down, gradually relaxed, and he petitioned Amherst to allow Sterling to pursue it. Legally or illegally, the trade continued, catching some Indians in a web of dependency and poverty that did nothing to improve relations with the British and led to the Delaware Prophet's condemnation of overdrinking.[29]

In the anonymous journal, the Creator denounces the English for "rum and their poison." Was this redundant? Was rum itself the poison? The journal does not comment, but it is doubtful that Neolin's followers entirely rejected the use of alcohol. It is true that British officers, whose pen portraits of Indians already represented them as self-destructive drunkards, tended to see rum as a potential Indian killer. During the war they would playfully dream of using rum as a weapon of mass destruction. Henry Gladwin saw "the free sale of rum" as the best and cheapest way to rid the world of Indians, for it would "destroy them more effectually than fire and sword." Sir William Johnson agreed that liquor, the "greatest gratification to all Indians," should be sold in plenty, "to let them shorten their Days . . . by the immoderate use of it." Johnson's aim, in fairness, was less widespread death than it was trade, for he knew that rum attracted hunters to trading posts and increased the Indians' dependence on the British: "Without it, the Indians can purchase their clothing with half the quantity of Skins, which will make them Indolent, and lessen the fur Trade." The use of alcohol as an Indian killer, then, was perhaps more a matter of racist joking than of British policy. It is hard to think that rum smuggler James Sterling was serious when he proposed in 1765 that if soldiers wanted to sleep in security they might place rum barrels all around the fort about a hundred yards away from the stockades: "For I'll be hang'd if even one [Indian] offers to come past them till the last Drop is expended."[30]

There was no such bigoted humor in Indian complaints about alcohol, but neither were Indians calling for total abstinence. In 1765 Pontiac would tell Croghan that his people had left Detroit in 1763 for the Miami River in order to escape the plague of alcohol issuing from the post, but he would also insist at the conclusion of their meeting that Croghan unstop the rum barrel, so that the Indians might "drink and be merry."[31] The Master of Life, according to both Pontiac and Neolin, promoted reform, not rejection.

Finessing the French and moderate on alcohol, Pontiac's version of Neolin's Creator was unequivocal on the British: "As to those who come to trouble your lands,—drive them out, make war upon them. I do not love them at all." To throw out the British was not to throw out all things European. Indeed, the Creator had decided that it was time for Indians to become literate. He gave Neolin a written prayer, causing the embarrassed Prophet to protest that he could not read, to which the Creator replied that Neolin's village chief would be able to read the prayer. The Indians were to memorize it and repeat it morning and night. As a final touch, he told the Prophet that Indians should shake hands when greeting one another, but using the left hand, "which is nearest the heart."

Neolin returned to this world following the same route by which he left it, picking up his clothes and equipment at the bottom of the mountain along the way. Enjoined not to speak with anyone until he delivered the prayer to the village chief, he sought out the man, probably Netawatwees, right away. Delawares then began to pray. Within three years, they and factions of Indians—from the Susquehanna River in Pennsylvania and the Genesee River in New York to the Ohio, to all the Great Lakes, even to the countries of Illinois and Arkansas—would be at war with British North America.

Conspiracy Theories

Pontiac's War first claimed lives at Detroit on May 9, 1763, and it spread so rapidly that it seemed to many at the time (and still seems to some historians) that there must have been a plan, conceived and laid by Indians or Frenchmen. The search for a single origin to the war is useless. For years there had been steady intertribal talk about dangers and insults that came from the British. There had been plots against the garrisons, as well as talk of an armed French return to the Great Lakes. When British policies and arrogant commanders convinced Pontiac that no accommodation could be reached, he attacked Detroit, and he sent to others to do likewise in their localities. What ensued was a struggle for the loyalties of Indians and *habitants*. In the end, this was clearly an Indian, not a French, fight. Despite the direct and expanding rhetoric about the French king's imminent return, Pontiac and his allies won far more extensive help from Indians than from the ethnic French in the American interior or from the remaining French officers in the Illinois Country. Most striking was that Catholic Indians, who could be viewed as those most connected with the French, gave Pontiac little assistance. Whether in mission villages on the St. Lawrence, in remote stations near Lake Michigan, or in Pontiac's own immediate neighborhood, Indian Catholics offered Pontiac the least support—indeed, they threatened to become his enemy.

One theory credits the Senecas, and the leadership of the Six Nations, with coming up with a plan for a concerted uprising in 1761. On June 16, 1761, a Wyandot informed Detroit commander Donald Campbell that Seneca emissaries were in the vicinity. Two of them, the Seneca-Mingos Kiashuta and Tahaiadoris, were at the west end of Lake Erie, delivering war belts and speeches in the hope of promoting an intertribal war against Britain. Campbell took quick action, dispatching a detachment to rescue threatened traders at Sandusky. As it happened, the Detroit-area Indians were then unenthusiastic about the Seneca proposal, partly because they mistrusted the Six Nations, partly because they still had a potentially lucrative war against the Cherokees to pursue. So the plot failed. On the basis of this Seneca-Mingo plot, it has been suggested not only that Senecas originated the idea of a united attack on the British but also that they did so with the knowledge of the central Onondaga council of the Six Nations Iroquois League.[32]

There are fatal problems with the argument. First of all, when Pontiac's War did break out in 1763, it did so in Anishinabe, not Seneca, country. Second, the Detroit-area Indians have an equally good claim to having initiated the early intertribal discussions that led to the rebellion. As early as November 28, 1760, Detroit's last full day under the *drapeau blanc*, Ottawas, Potawatomis, Hurons, and Ojibwas laid plans to throw out the British when they promised the departing French garrison that they would gather an intertribal coalition in the spring of 1761 to force the British out. The peoples pleaded with the French commander (not vice versa) to join them. Less than a week later, as the British occupied the fort, George Croghan learned that Detroit Indians were inviting the Iroquois to come west in the spring. Late in the appointed spring, Seneca-Mingo militants, with Shawnee and Delaware support, carried to Detroit both the anti-British plan and apologies for the killing at Niagara of several Anishinabeg by Six Nations warriors in 1759. On this Seneca mission rests the claim for an Iroquois origin for the uprising, but these Senecas may have only been responding to the Detroit Indians' call. And if this not enough to establish a plausible Detroit Indian origin for the "conspiracy," there is the fact that the two Seneca-Mingo militants apologized to the Detroit Indians in 1761 for not having responded sooner to the westerners' invitation. The evidence for the "Seneca plot," in short, points as convincingly to the Anishinabeg as to the Iroquois.[33]

If a single Seneca, or Seneca-Mingo, origin is doubtful, even less likely is active involvement by the central Onondaga council. The two most prominent of the Senecas who carried the war belt to Detroit, Kiashuta and Tahaiadoris, were heartily disliked at the league's central council fire at Onondaga; they had long been too hostile to Britain, growing close during the Seven Years' War to their Mingo kinsmen, to Shawnees, and to Delawares, most of whom had defied the Six Nations and had turned against Britain by 1755. Tahaiadoris identified strongly with a group of

Senecas that had leaned toward the French since the 1720s. His father, in fact, had been French and a very influential negotiator. Finally, the Seneca "deputies'" claim to speak for the league was contradicted by vigorous Six Nations' denials.[34]

Militant Indians from among many peoples and militant *habitants* throughout the region talked with one another during these years, as they had before, of uniting against the redcoats who threatened their lands, but whether the talk amounted to a web of concerted intrigue remains a matter of speculation. If the Indians did intertribally conspire to throw out the British, if Indians from the Alleghenies to Lake Superior did stealthily lay plans to rise up together in the late spring of 1763, they kept their secrets well and conspired effectively, for we do not have a clear record of them.

An older but still vibrant tradition has French inhabitants and French officers still in Indian country stirring up the troubles. Francis Parkman and Howard Peckham both share this view.[35] Like the British officers and traders from whom they draw most of their evidence, they see French intrigue behind Indian action. Although neither ignores other factors, they nonetheless both place French influence in the foreground, leaving Indian objectives in the shadow of the imperial struggles. Parkman implicates the French *habitants* of the Great Lakes region and Ohio Country as well as (though less directly) the French military establishment in Illinois. "The French declared," he writes, "that the King of France had of late years fallen asleep; that during his slumbers, the English had seized upon Canada; but that he was now awake again, and that his armies were now advancing up the St. Lawrence and the Mississippi." Parkman's credulous Indians were further provoked by the "arms, ammunition, clothing, and provisions, which the French trading companies, if not the officers of the Crown, distributed with a liberal hand." Parkman does not tell us where the strapped French traders obtained their goods; nor does he explain what advantage the French trading companies would gain from "liberal" handouts. He assumes without analysis that the desire for vengeance as well as some calculation of their interest in the French empire lay behind the "trading companies'" action. To support his accusation, Parkman relies on "many passages from contemporary letters and documents" written by Britons. As "a good example," he quotes a letter written some six weeks before the outbreak of Pontiac's War by Lieutenant Edward Jenkins, at Fort Ouiatenon on the Wabash, to Major

Gladwin, commander of Fort Detroit. Jenkins wrote that the Canadians that were there were "eternally telling lies to the Indians" and that "in a short time (showing them when the corn was about a foot high) . . . there was a great Army to come from the Mississippi." The strength of Parkman's conspiracy thesis rests on the letter's timing, shortly before the conflict. But Jenkins continues: "This I am informed they tell from one end of the year to the other," a point that considerably reduces the importance of the document's date. We can, moreover, distrust Jenkins' own source. As Parkman neglects to tell us, although the full letter reveals the fact, Jenkins received his information from an English peltry trader anxious to muscle in on the trading networks still controlled by merchants operating out of French-occupied Illinois and Louisiana.[36]

Such self-interested British traders formed a rich source of information for the British Indian department, which left Parkman most of his evidence. Sir William Johnson concluded from traders' letters that their French counterparts, in addition to acting as "faithful and even useful agents" for France, had assured the Indians that the French would come "with a great Fleet and army and retake the country." Relying on such reports, Johnson was ready to believe, as early as July 1763, "however extraordinary" it may have appeared, that the French had been "principally instrumental in creating these present disturbances." By 1764, again on the basis of these reports, Colonel Henry Bouquet joined Johnson in the conclusion that the French were behind the uprising. Bouquet admitted, however, that, where French officials were concerned, it was not "easy to prove this."[37] It is no easier today.

Howard Peckham, in the only major twentieth-century scholarly monograph devoted to Pontiac's War, reasons that "the evidence of French instigation is indirect, yet fairly conclusive. We do not know it from French sources, but both the British and Indians blamed the French, and their accusations cannot be laid entirely to prejudice in the one case or the desire to exculpate themselves in the other." Peckham, like Parkman, leans on evidence provided ultimately by an English trader, in this case George Croghan. Peckham also points to the Indian claim that symbolic "war belts," circulating among the tribes immediately before the outbreak of war, originated with the French in Illinois. But as with Parkman's reliance on Jenkins, there is the problem here of timing. If the belts had been issued during the American combat phase of the Seven Years'

War, that is, before the close of 1760, their French origin is dubious evidence that the Illinois garrisons provoked Pontiac's War in 1763.[38]

If the motives of the British traders compromise their claims that France was behind Pontiac's War, so does the context of Anglo-American hostility to Roman Catholicism, far more violent in Pontiac's day than even in Parkman's, a hostility reinforced by persistent historic animosities within the British Isles, the frequent wars with France and Spain, and the immigration to British North America of severely persecuted Continental Protestants. Indeed, in the colonies, the Seven Years' War had been, on one emotional level, a war against Rome. So the Reverend Thomas Barnard thought in 1763, as he recounted for his congregation the history of obstacles that his Protestant nation had just surmounted. Great Britain was once "at the Brink of being swallowed up by an invincible *Armada* of *Spain;* once nigh remediless Confusion, thro' the infernal Arts of *Rome,* in the infamous Powder-Plot; and for a Century past, [it has been] constantly endangered by the insidious Arts of *France,* the unceasing Enemy of her Tranquility." Nonetheless, it had triumphed, through the grace of God.[39] Such anti-Catholic attitudes promoted the charge that France was somehow behind Pontiac; at the same time, those attitudes blinded the British to a striking reality.

Pontiac and his allies got little but trouble from Roman Catholic Indians. The vast majority of the Native Americans living in missions from the St. Lawrence River's reserves westward to the shores of Lake Michigan either remained neutral or supported Great Britain. At best, only two groups of Indian Catholics gave, or may have given, Pontiac some support, and even among these it is impossible to measure the level of support or to find evidence that religious animosities compelled them. First were the Wyandots in his immediate neighborhood. Their village, according to John Porteous, was "pretty large with good square logg houses regularly built," and they had a priest and "a good Church." They were the last of Detroit's Indians to join Pontiac; they were also the first to leave him, making peace with Gladwin after less than two weeks of fighting, claiming "they had been forced into the war by the Ottawas." Their pastor, Father Pierre Potier, clearly opposed the war from its beginning, with considerable support from the local French speakers. These Wyandots kept to the peace thereafter. One of their leaders, Odinghquanooron, or Baby, confirmed the peace twice again, with both Gladwin at Detroit in May 1764 and Sir William Johnson at Fort Niagara in July 1764. Another leader, Teata, faced the scorn of the non-Christian Wyandots from Sandusky, who declared that their "Gods" had ordered them to fight the English. In 1765, Irish-born George Croghan, who had no taste for Catholicism, noted the Detroit Wyandots' "particular attachment" to the Catholic Church, and he also noted that they were "remarkable for their good sense and hospitality." Nothing motivated Catholic Wyandots to oppose Britains, not Rome, not French priests, not anti-Protestant sentiment.[40]

The most likely exception to this pattern were the so-called Catholic Potawatomis of the St. Joseph Valley (in what is now southwestern Michigan and north-central Indiana), for the Potawatomis of that valley were among the most ardent supporters of Pontiac's cause, and they continued to wage war even after Pontiac had made peace. Baptismal records from the intermittently maintained St. Joseph mission, however, indicate that only a handful of Potawatomis, mostly women, received and survived baptism in the years from the establishment of the mission in 1720 to the end of Pontiac's War. An uncertain but probably larger number received deathbed baptisms. Since missionaries maintained high standards for the baptism of healthy Indians, it is possible that more Potawatomis thought of themselves as Catholic than the baptismal records reveal. Still, nothing in those records suggest that Potawatomis were Catholic to any significant degree before the American Revolutionary era. There were indeed "Catholic Potawatomis" in the St. Joseph Valley, but they lived in a later era.[41]

Catholic Indians, then, stood consistently apart from Pontiac. He did not win over his fellow Ottawas at L'Arbre Croche, some of whom were Catholics. They had a long Catholic experience, and not only did they withhold their support from Pontiac, but they rescued captive British troops and traders from Ojibwas and Sauks who took Fort Michilimackinac on June 4, 1763. They brought Captain George Etherington to L'Arbre Croche until they could deliver him safely to the English at Montreal in August. While at L'Arbre Croche, Etherington corresponded with the famous Métis leader and Catholic Charles Langlade, who had campaigned brilliantly against the British in the 1750s. Langlade was also the maternal nephew of the important northern Ottawa leader La Fourche. Etherington deputized Langlade as symbolic commander of Michilimackinac in his absence, and Thomas Gage later praised Langlade and his Jesuit priest, Father Pierre du Jaunay, for saving so many English lives. While Etherington remained at L'Arbre Croche, awaiting the formation of the Ottawa convoy that would bring him to Montreal, he spent pleasant days, as he described them, with Langlade's Ottawa uncle. When Daniel Claus, Indian agent at Montreal, welcomed Etherington and his men a month later, he wrote that the officers and traders could "not say enough of the good Behaviour of these Ottawas." They had not only ransomed the troops at considerable expense but had also escorted them safely to Montreal. Again, these Ottawas were hardly uniformly Catholic; Alexander Henry, captured and taken under the protective wing of Ottawas at the same time, recorded little evidence among his rescuers of Catholicism and much of traditional spirituality. But as there was more Catholicism among the Ottawas of L'Arbre Croche than among most other Great Lakes Indians, so too was there less sympathy for the prophetic, anti-British cause.[42]

General Thomas Gage, then with Claus at Montreal, agreed that a reward was in order, and they distributed some gifts to the Ottawas, for which Amherst rebuked them: "Justice they shall have; but no more, for they can never be Considered by Us, as a People to whome We Owe Rewards." Worse for the L'Arbre Croche Indians, British officials shut down all legal trade between their colonies, including Canada, and the Great Lakes. The neutral Indians protested this; some even offered to become allies. After a year, the British lifted the embargo on everything except arms and ammunition, but these two items were essential to hunters. Alexander Henry, who returned to the colonies after his months among the neutral Ottawas, attempted without success to raise an Anishinabe army against Pontiac. He later wrote that the neutral Ottawas "never overcame their disgust, at the neglect with which they had been treated, in the beginning of the war."[43]

From mission or reserve Indians on the St. Lawrence River, France's best allies among Indians until 1760, no known warriors joined Pontiac. However much Britons such as Henry Gladwin at Detroit may have charged that the Indians of the reserves "certainly knew of what was going on" and that they intended to join the "insurrection" at "the least shadow of help" from France, the fact is the reserve Indians not only kept the peace but also enlisted in the British war effort. In August 1763 colonial Britons could read with relief that the Indians of the St. Lawrence showed "not the least Disturbance" and continued to trade "in the most amicable Manner." The following spring, Indian agent Claus and Canada's governor, General Ralph Burton, began raising Kahnawakes for Bradstreet's expedition. Welcoming Burton to their village on May 5, 1764, the Kahnawakes "hoisted up . . . union flags, and red flags, and saluted him with a discharge of pateraroes," lightweight cannon mounted on swivels.[44]

If ever there was a body of Indians under a kind of persistent "French influence," it was that in the "mystical body" of the Catholic Church. Yet that body opposed Pontiac, Neolin, and the millennial movement to drive Britain from the trans-Appalachian west. Pontiac, to be sure, went to an occasional Mass, and he seriously hoped for assistance from Catholic France, but from the church he got nothing, and from those few communities of Catholic Great Lakes and Canadian Indians he got, variously, brief support, neutral opposition, and armed confrontation.

The interpretation that French encouragement led to the sieges of the British posts is further compromised by evidence that a French betrayal triggered the war. Indians in the Great Lakes region and the Ohio Country had received news of the preliminaries of the Peace of Paris, in which France ceded the region to the British, in the months preceding their assaults. On April 24, two weeks before the outbreak, George Croghan wrote from Fort Pitt that both Ohioans and Great Lakes Indians were "uneasy" and said "the French had no right to give up their Country to the English."[45] Because the Indians knew of the treaty's preliminaries, they must have suspected that France had forsaken them; because the Indians knew that France had given their lands to Britain, they must have had strong reason to resent the French and little reason to follow French direction. It is difficult to understand how Indians entertaining such suspicions could have believed uncritically in the French promises that Parkman, Peckham, and others have considered the primary cause of the war. Jeffery Amherst's response to news that Indians were upset about the Peace of 1763 was characteristic: "Whatever Idle notions they may Entertain in regard to the Cessions . . . it is in their Interest to Behave [sociably] and while they continue to do so, they may be assured of His Majesty's Protection."[46]

If the French cannot be credited with conspiring to organize the Indian war, if Indian defensive motives, sacred beliefs, desires for autonomy, and awareness of hostile British sentiments must be fully grasped and appreciated, we are nonetheless left with that disturbing, repetitive skip in the record. We are left with all that talk of the French, much of it from the lips of Indian speakers. We are still left with those rumors that the French king had awakened and was sending his troops to rescue New France. We are still left with Native American claims that a French revival of power was in the making.

The idea has been widely noted, but it had little to do with French manipulation of Indians; the idea's exponents even condemned Frenchmen. Miamis, for example, proved in 1765 that they could believe in the return of French power and yet not believe the word of particular French commanders. While circulating rumors that all Europe was leaguing against the English and that the British had already lost battles on the lower Mississippi and in the neighborhood of Quebec, they also claimed that de Neyon, who had attempted to convince the Indians to make peace in the fall of 1763, "loved the English," and for that, he had been ordered out of Illinois, had "had his Cross of St. Lewis [sic] taken from him," and had been taken to France to be hanged. The powerful idea of the French return reflected less an example of artful French puppetry than it did an Indian attempt to manipulate France. Indians and *habitants* did declare during Pontiac's War that France would return to the Great Lakes. The Indian combatants did so because they could, as easily as the French, imagine the second French coming. However much they had once resented French pretensions to the ownership of the Ohio and Great Lakes regions—pretensions newly manifested in the French cession to the British[47]—Pontiac and his Indian allies nonetheless desired to restore the French king as a counterweight to Anglo-American expansion. To meet that end, Indians adopted a strategy at once military and ceremonial.

Deeply held religious traditions inspired in Pontiac and his followers the conviction that they could defeat the British by stratagem, manipulate France (as they had in the past), and transform their world through sacred and profane means, perhaps in the manner of their great cultural hero. Recent experience with the honored Delawares and the rise of prophets among that people gave additional hope to the Great Lakes' Indians that sacred forces would deliver them from British mastery. Delawares, experienced with the British, underscored the urgency of such deliverance, and the British sent their own highly material and highly emotional lessons. The result was a worldly and an otherworldly war.

CHAPTER FOUR

Besieging Britons, 1763

Without a mastermind or master plan, Pontiac's War unfolded with cruel logic and clear purpose. Unsupported by European powers, Native American forces, often intertribal in composition, attacked imperial armies and colonial settlers from Ontario and New York to Arkansas, from Wisconsin to South Carolina. Though there was no single Indian "side," and though the more massively organized Britons were riven by provincial and imperial jealousies, it is possible without denying the divisions to gain a sense of deliberation in the chaotic events of 1763. Pontiac and his allies left no written record of their strategy, but with flintlocks they inscribed their intentions both into the British fortifications studding their homelands and into the social landscape of the middle-Atlantic backcountry. Viewed analytically from the distance that time provides, their deadly assaults coalesce into a clear picture.

Great Lakes and Ohio Valley Indians sought, above all, to drive British troops back across the Alleghenies. Their strategy, as it rapidly evolved, was to take what trans-Appalachian forts they could; to cut the communications to the forts they could not take; to denude the countryside surrounding the communications they could not cut; and to intimidate those settlers they could not kill or capture into leaving and avoiding the trans-Appalachian west. They sought, too, to impress their prowess and fidelity upon the French garrisons remaining in the Illinois Country in an effort to draw them as allies into the war. These large aims Pontiac and his allies pursued with great violence, but both the aims and the violence had limits. They killed many of their prisoners—but their record on this score may well be better than that of their adversaries. They made no effort to kill or drive away all "whites." They did not attack the region's established French inhabitants, unless to press them for goods or to punish them for aiding the British. There was no uniform assault on the British colonies; but neither were the assaults random or simply opportunistic. Forts, communications and supply lines to the forts, regional granaries providing the provisions, livestock that might be driven westward as soldiers' food on the hoof, draft animals that might haul military supplies, stored forage for feeding these animals: all were caught in the Indians' sights. Although Great Lakes and Ohio-area Indians called upon and summoned the assistance of sacred powers, although vengeance, too, doubtless inspired some warriors to mount isolated attacks, such appeals and motives concurred with an overall strategy. It was an aggressive defense, meant to drive out British armies and colonists.

Unlike the Indian plans, the evolving British strategy is stated in thick volumes. In 1763 the ultimate objective was harsh, intimidating punishment, which ran like a theme through British correspondence. It could be summarized in the following phrasing, a composite of letters of four British and colonial officials: "I wish we could once flog those Devils heartily" for their "temerity," "perfidy," "rage," "insolence and pride" and "rascally" "Insurrection."[1] Achieving that end proved difficult, and British strategy developed in ways that are better read in action than in writings. To protect the colonial backcountry and to project imperial authority, British officers meant to maintain and to reinforce the forts at Detroit, Pitt, and Niagara. Three vulnerable lifelines tied these posts to the British Atlantic world: Braddock's Road, from Fort Pitt to Virginia; Forbes' Road, from Pitt to eastern Pennsylvania; and the water passage from Detroit to the Niagara portage to Lake Ontario, from which other, safer communications led to Montreal or Albany. Willing to tolerate high losses and under orders to take no prisoners, the British concentrated their military efforts along these three exposed routes. Once Detroit, Pitt, and Niagara were secured, massed armies were to punish Indians so severely as to prevent such an outbreak in the future. Settlers, encouraged by hefty bounties on Indian scalps, might raise militia bands to pursue and punish marauders; officers might dream up and deploy unconven-

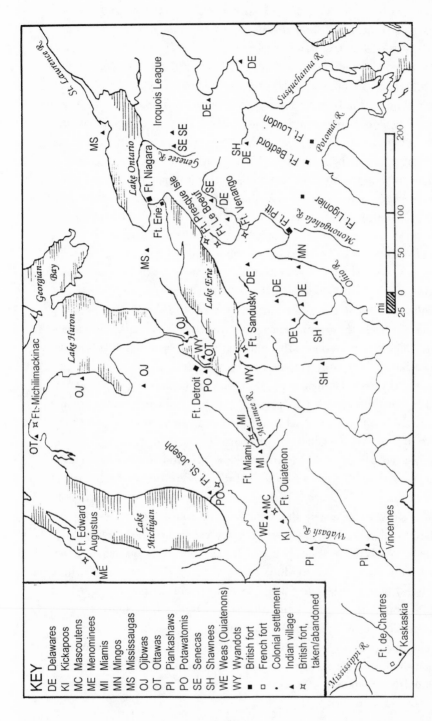

KEY
DE Delawares
KI Kickapoos
MC Mascoutens
ME Menominees
MI Miamis
MN Mingos
MS Mississaugas
OJ Ojibwas
OT Ottawas
PI Piankashaws
PO Potawatomis
SE Senecas
SH Shawnees
WE Weas (Ouiatenons)
WY Wyandots
■   British fort
□   French fort
•   Colonial settlement
▲   Indian village
⚔   British fort, taken/abandoned

Map 2. Pontiac's War, summer 1760 through late summer 1763. Approximate locations of sieges, Indian villages, imperial forts, and colonial towns in chapters 3 and 4.

tional weapons of mass destruction, but British troops would ensure the safety of their communications before mounting any punishing invasions of enemy villages.

The war assumed two overlapping phases in 1763: first, the assault on the western posts (May to August 1763); second, the harassment of the British along the routes to the interior (from May onward). Warriors understood that the British advantage lay less in absolute numbers than in the capacity to supply and reinforce troops. The numbers were, on one level, overwhelming. Not counting the millions of British subjects in Europe, there were probably a million and a half such subjects in the colonies by the war's end. Among all the Indians between the Great Lakes, the Mississippi River, the Ohio River, and the Appalachian mountain range, numbers may not have reached—at Sir William Johnson's estimate, which was probably low—10,000 warriors or, say, 50,000 people. Even if Johnson was off by as much as a factor of four, the Indians were greatly outnumbered. In terms of men whom the British and the Indians could deploy, however, the match was more even. At the opening of the war, General Amherst's forces in the west did not number 2,000 men, and many of these were killed in the early assaults. In North America as a whole he commanded some 8,000 men, but 3,650 of these were tied down in the St. Lawrence and another 1,700 in Nova Scotia and Cape Breton, places from which the British were loath to move them, given their uncertainties about the local French and Indians. Of the rest, 450 were in South Carolina and Georgia, having just concluded the Cherokee War, and several hundred awaited orders in the vicinity of New York City. These could more easily be moved to join the 1,250 Britons stationed in upper New York from Niagara to Lake Champlain, the 400 in western Pennsylvania, and the 350 in Michigan. They would oppose the probably no more than 3,500 men capable of bearing arms among the peoples allied with Pontiac—never that many at any one time. In short, at the outset of the war, the numbers of men ready to engage on either side were fairly close.[2]

If Pontiac and his allies had reason to doubt the immediate numerical advantage of the British soldiers, they knew from personal experience that the British army had vast supplies and a steely technological edge, particularly in defensive fortifications, gunnery, and sailing craft. They probably understood that provincials and militias, though slow to mobilize, would eventually enter the fray. They knew, too, that the British army was now well skilled in forest warfare, after deep experience with such fighting in the Seven Years' War. But Indians had also learned much in that war: lessons of laying siege, challenging gunboats, cooperating across cultures on the battlefield, mobilizing and maneuvering on a regimental scale. Having fought beside Montcalm and Lévis, many of them knew what it took to move a large army; they knew how regiments might be worn down. Still the best light infantry their European counterparts had ever seen, the warriors could well hope to overcome their disadvantages not only through surprise and stealth but also through targeted destruction.

Tricksters at the Gates

On April 27 and again on May 5, 1763, Pontiac presided over councils: the first, at his own village some ten miles southwest of Detroit, called Indians to war; the second, at a Potawatomi village but three miles from the English garrison, arranged a definite plan of action. In both meetings, he laid out before the attending Ottawas, Ojibwas, Potawatomis, and Hurons all the "insults which he and his nation had received from the Commandant [Henry Gladwin] and the English officers." He preached on the Master of Life's commands to the Delaware Prophet. He spoke of France, both claiming that his "Great Father" had sent him war belts and comparing the current British economic regime unfavorably with that of the French in the recent past. He demanded the secrecy needed for surprise. The first meeting established that ten men under Pontiac would reconnoiter Fort Detroit on May 1. The second meeting designed the plan to take the fort by stealth on May 7 and to send messages northward and eastward to raise Ottawas, Ojibwas, and the related Mississaugas. Since Miamis, Piankashaws, Delawares, Shawnees, and Mingos were also talking of war, Pontiac had little need to summon them. Besides Pontiac, leaders at the meetings included the Potawatomi Ninivois, the Wyandot Takay, and the Ottawa Mackatepelecite. Teata, a headman of Detroit's Catholic Wyandots, attended but gave little support to the project.[3]

According to plan, on May 1, Pontiac and thirty to fifty others appeared at the gates and persuaded Major Henry Gladwin that they wished to perform a ceremonial dance for the garrison's entertainment. Within the walls, while the dancers and singers distracted the garrison, ten individuals stood apart to study the locations of the powder magazines, commissaries, and barracks. When the drums stopped, Pontiac arranged with Gladwin for a general council to be held on Saturday, May 7. Early on that Saturday morning an eager party of fifteen warriors arrived at the gates, gained easy entry, and casually asked the whereabouts of English trading houses. As the time for the meeting approached, "a great many Indians" paddled across the Detroit River to join them. Some three hundred Anishinabeg and Wyandots, hiding beneath their robes guns that had been sawed "into Pistols," entered the fort and dispersed to street corners adjacent to the English stores, waiting for Pontiac to hold up a particular wampum belt and then turn it from its white to its green side, the signal to attack the British garrison of 120 men. But if the king's men were outnumbered that day, they were not outfoxed. Posted advantageously on the ramparts and in full battle array with weapons charged and ready, they prepared to turn the parade, now filled with milling warriors, into a slaughter pen. Pontiac and fifty other leading men, outmaneuvered and probably outgunned, had little choice but to hold awkward council with Gladwin, pledge their friendship, and deny any hostility. Pontiac, saying that he was "greatly surprised" at seeing so many guns pointing at his men, imagined "some bad Bird" had spread a malicious rumor about his intentions. He never turned the belt over, and he and the warriors left Detroit "Discontented."[4]

Various local legends concern the identity of Gladwin's informer or informers. The stories pointing to a militia officer's Indian lover fit a pattern with a long history, for such informers exist in legends surrounding the English in Jamestown, in Dublin—and even in stories of the French earlier in Detroit. The documents closest to the events reveal much concern about Gladwin's sources, though he never revealed their identities. Yet if he had indeed been informed, Gladwin put those informers at risk. In the tense council of May 7, boldly challenging Pontiac's claim to innocent intentions, he told the warriors "that he had certain Intelligence that some Indians were Projecting Mischief." When the Indians returned to their villages, a search for the traitors ensued. That evening six warriors dragged an old woman to the gates and charged her before the garrison with having fabricated dangerous lies about an Indian plot. Trader John Porteous identifies her as "Catherine an old Popish Squaw of the Poutewatamy Nation" (another example of Catholic Indian opposition to Pontiac). Gladwin called down that she was no informer. To be sure, he said, the informer was an Indian, but they had fingered the wrong one. His concern registered negatively. The woman was beaten with a lacrosse stick to within an inch of her life; it was later said that Pontiac himself administered the blows.[5]

Pontiac knew how serious was his failure to surprise Detroit. Not only had he lost the chance to eliminate the post, but he had not gained the arms and munitions that filled its magazines and shops. At this point, poorly armed, he could only hope to take Detroit by storm or starve it into submission; it was better, perhaps, to await another time. The next day, he went to the post and offered to restore good relations. Gladwin, who hated this remote British outpost, refused to have anything to do with him. Captain Donald Campbell, who had a greater attachment to Detroit and its peoples, gained permission to talk over a pipe with the Ottawa leader, and the two agreed that "all the Nations would come to Council" the next morning. Campbell thought he had secured a promise that only the chiefs would come; instead, the next morning some four hundred people glided across the Detroit River in canoes. The gates remained shut. Gladwin, through interpreters, insisted that everyone save fifty or sixty leading men return to their villages. Pontiac demanded that all the people be allowed in, adding that he would destroy the fort's cattle if refused entrance.[6]

If we credit Gladwin with seeing the folly of admitting the hundreds, we may also credit Pontiac with knowing that admittance was out of the question; that opportunity had passed. But by bringing four hundred warriors to witness Gladwin's refusal, Pontiac dramatized the *causus belli*: the imperial forces despised them and would, if allowed, enslave them. The Indian-hating commandant had spurned Indians on the preceding day, he had spurned Indians repeatedly before, and he was spurning them now. Pontiac wrote the script, Gladwin played as scripted, and the disgusted warriors took note. So did "All the French Women and Children with many of the Men" who "left the Fort [that] forenoon." These "white" people felt safer outside the walls than within them. In his diary, a British officer noted that "everything put on a hostile appearance."[7]

Later that day, painted men opened fire on the fort and on the two vessels that were moored at each end of the fort's palisades. The fighting lasted through the night. British energies were severely taxed as the soldiers and traders worked the lengthy walls and "lay on their arms at night." Pontiac did his best to "cut off the Communication from the Fort to the [French] Inhabitants" on each side of the river. Anishinabe parties paddled off to nearby Hog Island, where the British army kept twenty-four bullocks under a guard of three. The Fisher household, consisting of a servant woman, a mother, her husband (a retired sergeant), and their four children, was also there when the warriors arrived. Only two or three children survived the attack—as captives. One of these, a girl, would later be murdered. Pontiac himself would be listed among those accused of her death. French suffering also began when the warriors killed a French builder whom they had mistaken for an Englishman.[8]

After several hours of gunfire on the morning of May 10, a party of Wyandots appeared before the walls and offered to mediate between the hostile Anishinabeg and the British. Later in the day, this group returned to the fort in the company of Ottawa, Ojibwa, and Potawatomi chiefs, together with three prominent Detroit *habitants*, who suggested that the more affable Colonel Campbell come out with another officer to negotiate. Gladwin, short of pork and flour and seeing in the proposed truce an opportunity to replenish his mess, agreed. Campbell, game for the undertaking, was joined by Lieutenant John McDougall, and as they emerged from the fort, two Potawatomi hostages were taken into it.

When the two officers arrived that day at the house of Antoine Cuillerier, where they understood negotiations would be held, they found that there was little to discuss. Some of Detroit's citizens seemed to be leagued with the Indians, recommending that the British immediately withdraw to Niagara. The Wyandots, instead of mediating, sang "the War Song" as they allied with Pontiac. A party of Indian and French men agreed to go to the Illinois Country to summon help from its French commander, de Neyon. A messenger was dispatched to Gladwin to demand that he surrender his fort, its munitions, and the two vessels. Campbell and McDougall were declared prisoners. Campbell, as portly and nearsighted as he was genial, never attempted to flee. Agile and fit, McDougall managed to escape after almost two months. McDougall's reports to his superiors in Detroit reveal that Pontiac believed that he could encourage France to return in force to North America. Historians have long interpreted these texts as demonstrating French instigation of Pontiac's War, but if examined under different assumptions, the reports can lead us to quite different conclusions. If read with an eye toward ritual action, they suggest that Indians sought French intervention and not the other way around

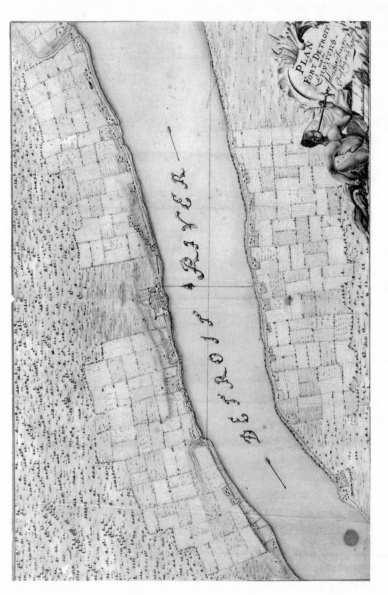

Fort Detroit and Its Environs, 1763/1764, by John Montressor. Founders Society Purchase, Gibbs–Williams Fund, photograph © 1991 Detroit Institute of Arts. Its image of a relaxed Indian a stark contrast to the war still raging, this map of the Detroit region places the fort—with its more elaborate riverside defenses—at the center; the *habitants*' homes and fields along both shores, and the Wyandot village on the southern (Canadian) bank at the lower left. Indian arrows direct the river's flow. A white fleur-de-lis points northward.

(an analysis that even a more traditional approach supports).[9] They also suggest that Indians and the few ethnic French most alienated by the British sought together to bring about the return of French power.

One report was taken in August 1763 at a court of inquiry held within the walls of Fort Detroit, where McDougall described his meeting, chez Cuillerier, with Pontiac. The lieutenant vividly recalled Cuillerier's insubordinate deportment. The prosperous but common trader, a half brother of the former French commander of Detroit, kept his seat at the entrance of the British officers, wore a laced coat, and denied the officers the customary honor of removing his laced hat, keeping "covered during the Congress." The full significance of Cuillerier's utter lack of deference became manifest in the midst of the meeting, when Pontiac invested the trader with the command of Detroit. Together, Pontiac and the *habitant* symbolically restored French power in Detroit, and they wanted the British to know it. Pontiac declared that he now recognized Cuillerier "as his Father come to life and as the commandant of Detroit until the arrival of his Brother," Captain François de Belestre, the former commandant.[10] What's more, Pontiac invested Cuillerier with the office, a sign of the Ottawa's authority and initiative. The performance suggests that he sought to bring about the return of the French through acts of ritual invocation, as well as through military victories that might encourage France to abandon the peace.

Antoine Cuillerier, a visible member of Detroit's French-speaking community, was a likely vessel in which to cast anew the departed French father. Pontiac's very phrasing ("Father come to life") resembles adoption speeches recorded by the missionaries, officers, and travelers which stress the ceremonial resurrection of the dead. Invoking transformative powers, like those of Nanabush, Pontiac and his allies sought to bring about a new world—or rather, a restored world—in which Ottawas prospered in alliance with France.[11]

These utopian dreams came during the war, and the war drowned them in violence. Two days after McDougall's escape, in retaliation for the battle death of the son of a Saginaw Ojibwa headman, a party of Indians under the Ojibwa chief Wasson seized Campbell, stripped him, marched him to their village, and killed him. Wasson, from Saginaw, did not well know the affable and accommodating Campbell, whose murder reportedly infuriated Pontiac.[12] The fate of Fort Detroit's Indian prisoners is generally a mystery. In mid-June, well before Campbell's death, four Potawatomis attempted to negotiate with Gladwin for their two hostage kinsmen, still in his hands. Potawatomis held, by that point, fourteen British prisoners. But instead of gaining the release of their two tribesmen, the two emissaries found themselves captured and imprisoned. Detroit's scribes, according to standard practice, did not record their fate, and in the face of such notarial silence we can only guess. By June 22, in any case, Amherst had directed Gladwin to put "Every Indian in your power, to *Death*" (emphasis his).[13]

Pontiac's forces expanded throughout June. Potawatomis and Ottawas arrived from the St. Joseph River, Ottawas and Ojibwas from Saginaw Bay, Hurons from Sandusky, Ojibwas (including Mississaugas) from the Grand and Thames Rivers of Ontario—even an Abenaki from Montreal visited the Ottawa leader, as did Shawnees and Delawares from the upper Ohio. The besiegers possessed all the ground beyond rifle range of the fort, they raided the communications between the fort and the east, and they regularly harassed the garrison itself. Although they did little damage to those within the walls, the fear grew with the summer that "this affair [would] be general ere long."[14]

By the time Gladwin had written those words on June 26, thirteen other British garrisons had either evacuated in the face of an Indian threat or come under direct assault. Fort Niagara and its dependent posts on the way to Lake Erie, Forts Schlosser and Erie, were never besieged, but they faced much fighting in their environs. The British evacuated two forts, Burd and Edward Augustus. Three withstood direct attacks (Pitt, Ligonier, and Bedford). Eight fell to the Indians (Sandusky, Miami, St. Joseph, Ouiatenon, Michilimackinac, Venango, Le Boeuf, and Presque Isle). Apart from Michilimackinac, these last were small posts, and it has to be wondered why they existed at all. Each post had its mission. Fort Edward Augustus was meant to maintain relations with the far western Indians; Forts Miami, St. Joseph, and Ouiatenon were outposts on the way to the Illinois Country, which the British had yet to occupy. Forts Venango, Le Boeuf, Presque Isle, and Sandusky had been garrisoned in order to secure the communication between the large Forts Pitt, Niagara, Detroit, and Michilimackinac, the great symbols of British domination. Taken together, the mission of the posts was clear enough: to establish and embed in Indian minds the British claim to authority.

They could do nothing of the sort. The smaller posts were too ill supplied with presents to win the Indians over with generosity and too understaffed to dominate the local warriors with force. Amherst expected his officers to punish local Indians for crimes against the British: "By such treatment only, will it be possible to deter them from evil and keep them within due bounds." He had such contempt for Indians that he could not imagine them capable of taking a garrison of any kind. When presented in 1760 with the fact that Cherokees had forced the capitulation of the starving British garrison at Fort Loudoun in what is now Tennessee, Amherst dismissed the evidence before him and instead blamed the commander for capitulating to inferiors. He simply refused to believe that "one of the King's Forts could yield to a parcel of miscreants, without artillery or apparatus capable to reduce it, if properly defended." Since then, the British general had placed a good many more of his men in perilous places and had assigned them impossible tasks.[15] Indians had come to see the outposts not only as insults but also as easy targets, and in the spring of 1763 they trained guns on them.

The assault on the outposts came in two quick waves. In the first, between May 16 and June 2, Ottawa, Wyandot, Ojibwa, Potawatomi, and Miami Indians captured five posts by stratagem before the garrisons even knew that Pontiac had besieged Detroit. They took Forts Sandusky (May 16) and St. Joseph (May 25) by the very technique that had failed at Detroit: after gaining entry to the forts under the pretense of holding a council, they killed or captured most of the soldiers (at Sandusky, they slaughtered a great many English traders as well, gaining an immense booty: one hundred horseloads of trade goods, including arms and ammunition). Indians killed roughly one hundred British traders and their workers in these early days of the war. Warriors employed a variation on the theme at Ouiatenon (June 1), luring a good part of the garrison out for a council and then taking it captive in the open air.[16]

At Fort Miami, the ruse was more elaborate. Lieutenant Robert Holmes, commander of the garrison, had formed a sexual relationship with a Miami woman; the record says that he "lived with" her, or "kept" her. On May 27 she entered the fort and implored Holmes to come to her village to bleed her ailing sister. Although he already suspected trouble, he agreed, only to be shot dead as he approached the village. A bold but incautious sergeant pursued the sound of gunfire, only to be captured. The nine remaining soldiers closed the gates and huddled hopelessly within the small palisaded structure, while a large crowd of Indians gathered outside and demanded that they surrender. They could do little else.

Following the surrender a white French flag was seen floating above the garrison.[17]

As at Fort Miami, women played a key role in the taking of the largest garrison to be surprised by an Indian force at the outbreak of Pontiac's War: Fort Michilimackinac, located on a sandy stretch of land on the south side of the Straits of Mackinac between Lakes Huron and Michigan. Built and rebuilt by the French of cedar pickets and enclosing two acres, the post contained thirty small, neat houses and a church. The British had been in it only since late 1761, and if they meant to dominate the region, their garrison—with fewer than forty soldiers—was far too small.[18] So common were rumors of Indian conspiracies against the garrison that Captain George Etherington had come to ignore them. Ojibwas frequently met outside one of the gates to play the high-stakes sport of *bag'-gat'iway*, a kind of lacrosse.[19]

On the cool morning of June 2, 1763, Ojibwas and visiting Sauks assembled in large numbers near the fort. Blanketed women, weapons concealed, gathered to watch the game; men disrobed and prepared for the rough sport. For several hours they played with spirit. At close to noon, a player threw the ball toward the open gate, where Lieutenant William Leslie and Captain Etherington casually admired the onrushing players—then saw with a start that the women were passing out tomahawks and short spears. These meager weapons, wielded with surprise, skill, and overwhelming numbers, captured the strategic post, killing some sixteen British subjects, all but one a soldier. The warriors made captives of all the British traders and all the remaining soldiers, five of whom they later executed. When, some days afterward, an English trading canoe landed at the fort, the Indians seized it and "beat, reviled [and] marched" the stripped civilians to captivity. Although one English trader had been killed in the initial onslaught on the post, it is worth noting that none were killed thereafter. The Indians who had taken this post without firearms now had considerable weaponry, including fifty barrels of gunpowder.[20] At Sandusky, a major trading center, Wyandots and Anishinabeg had also taken many stores.

Michilimackinac was the greatest, and last, prize gained by surprise. By mid-June, during the second wave of assaults, Senecas, Ottawas, and Wyandots confronted an alarmed British military, yet they would still overpower every post on the line between Fort Pitt and Lake Erie, effectively isolating Fort Detroit from the British presence in the Upper Ohio

Country. This string of posts, and the road it defended, had long been a source of grievance to the Senecas, Mingos, Shawnees, Delawares, and Wyandots, having been established by the British without any serious Indian consultation. Indians had upbraided George Croghan in 1760, as he noted to William Johnson: "[They said] I tuck a very good Method to first Make a Road Throw thire Cuntry and then Aquaint them I was going to Do itt." A colonial official had dismissed such complaints. However the Indians might fret about the posts, he wrote, the "murmur" would "grow fainter and gentler every day."[21]

Thirty Senecas proved him wrong on June 18, 1763. Lodging themselves in an outbuilding near the British post of Fort Le Boeuf, they blasted away at the garrison of twelve. Shooting fire arrows at the blockhouse roof, they set the post alight. Commander Ensign Price and five troops escaped through a window, evading the Indian force, and reached the safety of Fort Pitt on June 26. The next day, a woman and four more men also made it to Pitt. Two went missing. In their flight, Price and his men had passed the charred ruins of the blockhouse at Venango. Unlike the survivors of Le Boeuf, not one of Venango's defenders, who numbered about twelve, returned to British lines to tell the story of its fiery end.[22]

Once the extent of the war became apparent, few officers were surprised by the Indians' successful elimination of such tiny posts such as St. Joseph, Miami, Sandusky, Ouiatenon, Le Boeuf, or Venango. More formidable was Fort Presque Isle, a powerful blockhouse attached to a palisaded fort sheltering perhaps sixty men. Two hundred fifty Indians carefully surrounded the timberwork on the night of June 19. They represented an intertribal coalition of peoples spanning Lake Erie: Ottawas, Ojibwas, Wyandots, and Senecas. Many, veterans of the Seven Years' War, showed their experience. Occupying small hills to the east and north of the post, they dug trenches and leveled their weapons. Shortly after daybreak, well-placed parties opened a "pretty smart" barrage and sustained it into the next day, covering others who dug approaches not only toward the palisades but even beneath the walls and into the parade. From the trenches warriors shot glowing lead from "fuzees," and they let fly fire arrows, igniting all the structures except the corner blockhouse, where the terrified defenders were now confined. The soldiers returned fire and managed to kill several attackers; but they had little chance. For a time they could hope for relief from the British schooner *Huron*, which they could see hovering two miles offshore, but the vessel, unable to find a suitable mooring, could neither bombard the Indians nor cover a landing party. The choking garrison, "fatigued to the greatest extremity," soon recognized that the Indians could ignite the blockhouse at will. A former English colonist, long ago adopted by and fighting beside the Wyandots, helped to negotiate a surrender. British commander Ensign John Christie and his men were to be permitted "to go to Fort Pitt, or where they pleased." Most went to their graves, attacked and murdered soon after they emerged from their forlorn post. Wyandots took Christie, four of his men, and one woman captive. These they carried to the Detroit region, where Christie, the woman, and one soldier were delivered to Gladwin. Presque Isle was the last British post to fall to the warriors. The news left Colonel Henry Bouquet, who had built the place, in "unspeakable astonishment."[23]

The rapidity and success of these assaults should not obscure the fact that they divided Indians; that Gladwin had received warning of the plan against Detroit is but one piece of evidence. At Michilimackinac, Ottawas from L'Arbre Croche on Lake Michigan arrived to condemn the Ojibwa action. They redeemed most of the English captives and eventually escorted them to Montreal. Charles Langlade, perhaps the most prominent Métis in the region, cooperated in their rescue. At Presque Isle, Wyandots pleaded with the very troops they were successfully attacking that they had been forced into action by the Detroit Ottawas; they, too, managed to deliver some English soldiers to safety. At Sandusky, St. Joseph, and Ouiatenon, Indians worked to spare the lives of captured men. The easternmost Mississauga villages refused to strike the British; as early as June, Pontiac was reported to have been alarmed by their insistence that they would remain neutral, as would the Six Nations. Far to the west, soldiers at Fort Edward Augustus, or La Baye (Green Bay, Wisconsin), secured the protection and escort of Menominees and Ottawas at odds with Pontiac and made their way to Montreal with the Michilimackinac captives during the months of June and July.[24]

Among the Delawares, these divisions and doubts gave Fort Pitt weeks to prepare for the first assaults on its stone-faced walls. Premonitions of trouble came on May 27. A patrol discovered that a Munsee Indian town, seven miles up the Allegheny River, had been precipitously abandoned, its flourishing cornfields lying open. Delaware Indians that day also came to Fort Pitt, trading with "uncommon dispatch and indifference of what they took" for the skins. Two days later, Delawares killed

WAR UNDER HEAVEN

two soldiers at the fort's sawmill, and the garrison learned that Delawares under one "Wolfe" had killed five colonists, including two women and a child, on the nearby Youghiogheny River. Soldiers found at the site a "war club [Cassé Tête] or Tomahawk," which the commander of Fort Pitt, Simeon Ecuyer, took to be "a declaration of war."[25]

Late in the afternoon of May 30, a British packhorseman brought to Fort Pitt rumors from Shawnee country that "Detroit was taken, the post at Sandusky burnt, and all the garrison put to death, except the officer whom they made prisoner." The exhausted and panicked reporter was an employee of Thomas Calhoun, an Indian trader who had led a packhorse train to the town of Muskingum (sometimes called Tuscarawas town). The survivor thought Calhoun and his men had been killed. Over the next twenty-four hours, more men from Calhoun's party arrived at Pitt. Calhoun, whom the packhorseman had thought to be dead, himself arrived at about six o'clock the evening of May 31, but he confirmed most of the rest of the story.[26]

The Delaware leaders Tamaqua, Shingas, Weindohela, and Daniel had met with Calhoun at Tuscarawas town on May 27. They misinformed him that Detroit had been taken, told him of other attacks on Britons, and urged him to flee. They provided but three men as an escort for his fourteen disarmed men, and those three vanished as the party came under fire at Beaver Creek. Only four colonists, including Calhoun, escaped. Calhoun believed that he and his men had been set up for an ambush. Yet before he had left Tuscarawas, one elder, Daniel, had pulled him aside and given him a remarkably accurate account of the siege of Detroit, telling him that the fort had been attacked but not taken, that the Indians were unsuccessful but "strongly persisted" in their efforts.[27] If this was betraying the lies of some fellow chiefs, it was but one indication that Delawares were divided. Alexander McKee provides another. This trader and agent with strong Shawnee connections reported to William Trent what Shawnees had reported to him: "The Capts and warriors of the Delaware pay no regard to their Chiefs," who were cautioning against the war now begun at Detroit.[28]

Delawares Shingas, Tamaqua, and others, hoping to encourage the British to withdraw from Fort Pitt without much bloodshed, harassed the British with words. They told stories of the fall of Detroit. Delaware war parties hid themselves near the fort, awaited the sentinel's "all's well" cry, and then called out their mocking echo: "All's well." In the meantime, the garrison at Pitt prepared for an attack, burning outbuildings that might offer assailants shelter, piling packs of deerskins for extra cover on the bastions, and in general "repairing and strengthening the fort." On June 10, Indians sniped at a platoon that had been dispatched to build a fence at a rifle shot from the fort's walls. They did not attack the post itself until June 22; even this attack seemed halfhearted, as if the Delawares knew it would fail.[29]

On June 24 and 26, Delaware leaders Turtle's Heart, Mamaltee, Shingas, Wingenun, and Grey Eyes tried words again. They claimed that all the posts as far east as Fort Ligonier had been "destroyed, that great numbers of Indians," including Six Nations warriors, were coming to attack Fort Pitt, but that the Delawares would permit the garrison to evacuate safely if it did so quickly.[30] In the meantime their gunfire occasionally peppered the fort. Another serious assault did not come until July 28, and it was belated and brief. That day warriors carefully surrounded the fort, dug trenches in the banks of the rivers that flanked the post, and opened a "very smart fire." Their marksmen aimed at any exposed man, and they managed to kill one and wound seven. Captain Ecuyer took a steel-tipped arrow in the left leg. The barracks and the commander's roof were set alight by fire arrows. But most of the 330 men, 104 women, and 106 children within the walls went unscathed. Firing stopped on the first day of August. Conditions in the fort were poor—fuel for cooking was short, parsnips were rationed, dogs that were a nuisance were killed—but not desperate. Total casualties sustained by soldiers into August were low: twelve killed, thirteen wounded, two missing. Ecuyer believed that his men had killed and wounded at least twenty Indians.[31]

By late June and early July, Delaware Indians were also launching unsuccessful assaults on Fort Ligonier, deep in the Alleghenies, and Fort Bedford, east of the mountains. Attacking warriors sent word to the defenders that they thought that "all the Country was theirs," that "they had been Cheated out of it, and that they would Carry on the War 'till they had burnt Philadelphia." Ligonier and Bedford, critical to any resupply of Fort Pitt from Pennsylvania, held out, but other posts were evacuated. The garrison at Fort Burd, at the mouth of the Redstone Creek on the lifeline between Fort Cumberland, Maryland, and Fort Pitt, withdrew to Fort Cumberland in mid-June. Outposts at Bushy Run and Red Stone Creek "were abandon'd for want of men."[32]

Pontiac had no direct role in these attacks. If his example stimulated

them, he did not coordinate them. Still, Pontiac's influence reached beyond Detroit. He had sent word northward of his plans to attack Detroit,
which spurred the Ojibwas of Michilimackinac. His emissaries were present at the capitulation of Fort Miami. Detroit and Maumee Valley Ottawas were present at the attacks on Forts Sandusky, Miami, St. Joseph,
and Presque Isle, and from these posts the Indians carried a good many
captives to the Detroit-area Indian villages. The use of deception and the
type of deception used suggest further connections among the assaults
west of Sandusky.[33] In less than two months Great Lakes and Ohio Indians had reduced the British presence west of the Niagara region to
Forts Pitt and Detroit. These posts were too strong to be taken by storm;
their garrisons would have to be starved out. That fact altered the nature
of the war.

Cutting Communications

It is easy to forget that colonial Detroit was, in a very real sense, a
maritime community. Its very name (from the French word *étroit*, meaning "strait") says as much: it existed to dominate a narrows. French
settlers along the shore, their farms laid in strips behind them, were
known as people "of the coasts." Colonial lieutenant Jehu Hay opened
many of his journal entries with notes about the wind, just one indication
that Detroit and its fort depended on waterborne supplies and reinforcements. At the beginning of the British occupation, Lake Erie and the
Detroit River were regularly cruised by hundreds of bateaux and large
canoes, mostly under the muscle power and control of Indians or former
subjects of the French king. Because of their solid plank construction,
bateaux were difficult to portage. But they worked well both in shallows
and, when the weather was good, in deep water, and they could carry up
to twelve tons of lading. Big oar craft, with flat bottoms, they looked
much the same from bow or stern and could move as easily forward as
backward. Canoes were less commodious but lighter and ideal for portage. The biggest of them could carry five well-placed tons, including
men. Alexander Henry described a four-tonner he saw in 1761 as "32 feet
in length and 4½ feet in greatest width, made of birch bark a quarter of
an inch thick, lined with small splints [probably cedar], and further
strengthened by ribs of cedar wood." Sewn together with a spruce fiber
called *wattap* and calked with pine gum, a large trading canoe could be

carried by but four strong men. For deepwater travel, French and Indian travelers had rigged such canoes with sails during the Seven Years' War, and Captain Campbell had successfully rigged out bateaux. But neither canoes nor bateaux had the draft or stability to make them very reliable sailing vessels, especially in bad weather, which the Great Lakes have in abundance. Their crews, moreover, had to come ashore to cook and to sleep, a serious disadvantage in wartime.[34]

Aware of this, British officers advocated the construction of larger, sailing gunboats. British traders mistrusted the French voyageurs, resented having to pay them for their labors, and sought an independent carriage as a way of cutting both costs and labor trouble. They knew that the French had sailed such ships on Lake Erie as recently as 1760, when the last French vessel was wrecked on the north shore. Lieutenant Robertson supervised the construction of two such vessels in the summer of 1761. One, the sloop *Michigan*, carried six four-pounders and eight swivels; the other, the schooner *Huron*, carried four four-pounders and six swivels.[35] Sailors aboard either vessel, protected by the thick timbers from the Indians' small arms, could load their larger weapons with grapeshot—devastating against bark canoes at close range.

From the very start of the war, Pontiac sought to cut Detroit off from reinforcements and supplies. Efforts against British communications, far more than siege, had been the specialty of Ottawas, Potawatomis, and Ojibwas assisting the French during the Seven Years' War, and the Anishinabeg again did well against convoys in 1763. On May 13, Wyandots lured ashore and entirely captured an unsuspecting trading party of five bateaux and canoes under one Rackman and Chapman Abraham. These traders had been smuggling liquor, which several warriors drank until women, perhaps influenced by the religious movement sweeping the region, convinced the leading men to stave in the barrels. No one objected to the appropriation of the seventeen barrels of gunpowder.[36]

In late May, when scouts reported the approach of a British military convoy of one hundred rangers in ten fully laden bateaux carrying "one hundred thirty nine barrels of provisions," Anishinabe warriors hurried eastward to take it. Late in the evening on May 27, they concealed themselves as the convoy made camp. They first killed a man and a boy who had strayed from the camp about one hundred yards to gather firewood. The exhausted rangers, alarmed by the shooting, formed for defense, but the unseen warriors—protected by a hill—outflanked them and emerged to deliver a crippling fire. The surviving rangers fled to five of the boats, which they boarded chaotically, losing oars, floating helplessly, while Indians pounded them from both the shore and the remaining bateaux. The Anishinabeg forced the surrender of all but two boats, which pulled away across the lake with thirty or forty men. On board one of these was the expedition's commander, Lieutenant Cornelius Cuyler. Cuyler and his men made for Sandusky, which they found destroyed, then for Presque Isle, where six were left to strengthen the garrison, only to perish in the later assault. Cuyler himself reported the disaster to his superiors at Niagara and soon sailed back for Detroit. The Anishinabeg, meanwhile, took their prize of eight bateaux and forced the captured rangers to row them to Detroit.

It was a dreadful display the Anishinabeg had planned for Gladwin and his garrison: the bateaux were to ascend the Detroit River and pass before the walls of the fort under the power of miserable captives—rangers, the cream of British counterinsurgency. But the four soldiers pulling the first bateau upriver refused to cooperate. As they came opposite the fort, they rose up, threw overboard their guards, and made for the moored *Michigan*, which assisted them with a covering barrage. One of the four took a fatal bullet, but the others gained the sloop, saving not only themselves but also a bateau loaded with pork and flour. Anishinabeg could console themselves that they retained rich supplies and a good many prisoners. But the three rangers' escape significantly diminished the terror they had hoped to inspire in the garrison.[37]

If deception, assault, and terror had failed to bring down Detroit, then it had to be strangled. In council at Pontiac's village on June 1, Ojibwas, Potawatomis, Wyandots, and Ottawas determined that "no more assistance could reach the English." They sent their warriors to "prowl around the lake" and capture any British subjects they might find there. The next day, far to the east, Ojibwas, quite independently, did just that. Near the mouth of Ontario's Grand River, only forty miles from the Niagara River, a small party of under twenty men, painted black and red, opened fire on an English trade convoy headed by John Wendell and "one Van Veghten," which had come ashore for the night. The onslaught killed several traders. A few managed to flee in boats; pulling furiously away from shore, they could see eleven to fourteen of their companions submitting to Indians. The Ojibwas gained at least four bateaux loaded with gunpowder and wine. The day after that, Indians attacked another trading party only ten miles from the Niagara River.[38] They did not capture it, but they did turn it back.

These small victories might have promised to blockade Detroit, but they could not blind the Indians to the sight of the two sailing craft that aggressively cruised Lake Erie and the Detroit River. On June 30, as the schooner *Huron* sailed past a Wyandot village, it sprayed grapeshot at people "standing with folded arms, wrapped in their blankets, at the doors of their cabins," wounding several. A week later, the sloop *Michigan* bombarded Pontiac's village itself. This time no one was hurt.[39] Since Indians could easily move out of range, the vessels had limited offensive value. But for resupply and communications, keys to Detroit's survival, they meant everything.

The *Huron* set sail in late May for the Niagara region in order to secure reinforcements, arriving on June 15 and returning on June 30. After fighting its way past entrenched Indians on Turkey Island, sustaining about five wounded, it delivered to Detroit fifty men, all Queen's Rangers under Lieutenant Cornelius Cuyler and Captain Joseph Hopkins, who would be Detroit's most successful commander of small operations beyond the walls. Just as critically, it delivered one hundred barrels of provision and thirty barrels of ammunition, which put the garrison "in good Spirits." Twelve days later it was off again, but it was never far from the minds of the defenders of Detroit. Lieutenant Jehu Hay, recognizing how he depended on the craft, spent several days describing the winds: "fresh at N.W," "westerly," blowing "fresh all the next day." Thus he "imagined the Schooner must have been at the Niagara River" sometime during the night of July 15 or, at the latest, on July 16. The craft was back at Detroit on August 5, delivering twenty-five more troops, along with supplies. By October 3 it had made voyages worth almost four hundred barrels of flour and pork. Amherst counted it "very lucky" that the British had these vessels; otherwise there would have been no possibility of reinforcing Detroit or sending provisions until he could collect such a force "as would be able to attack all the Indians in their passage." A soldier at Detroit noted that the monthly flow of supplies to Detroit caused the Indians to see that their attempts would prove "Abortive."[40]

The Indians knew that the vessels were Detroit's best defense. On May 14 and again on May 21, Jehu Hay recorded that Pontiac's followers concentrated as much or more firepower on the vessels as on the fort. Whenever the *Huron* cruised the lower Detroit River, Indians fired on it from entrenchments. On May 23, when it ran briefly aground on a sand-bar while descending the Detroit River, Pontiac, backed by Potawatomi and Ottawa warriors, offered from the shore to exchange the captive Captain Campbell for the vessel. The offer was spurned, and the crew freed the boat. Indians held a council on June 8 solely to discuss ways to capture the two craft.[41] In July they sent fire rafts drifting downriver toward the *Michigan,* but the men aboard managed to deflect these. The use of such rafts raised British speculation that French *habitants* were behind the scheme, but Indians could easily have come across the technique during the siege of Quebec in 1759.[42]

Gladwin recognized that the ships also had a defensive function. They gave him control of the stretch of the Detroit River fronting the fort. So he kept one vessel, the *Michigan,* near the fort until July, when the arrival of another type of gunboat freed him to send the *Michigan* to the Niagara portage for supplies. The new gunboats were four "row galleys," mounted with swivels or six-pound mortars. Captain James Dalyell had led them across the length of Lake Erie in a convoy of twenty rowing craft, mostly bateaux. His 260 men had stopped to burn Indian villages near Sandusky before proceeding to Detroit. They had sustained fourteen casualties, wounded while fighting their way up the Detroit River, but the spray of grapeshot from their swivels ensured their arrival at Detroit with fresh troops and supplies.[43]

Pontiac was having little success in forcing the surrender of Detroit. At the end of July, he intimated to the garrison that he would consider negotiating a peace to put an end to what was becoming a pointless war. Dalyell, very much an Amherst protégé, argued urgently that punishment, not peace, was what Pontiac deserved. He easily persuaded a like-minded Gladwin to allow him to lead a surprise attack on Pontiac's sleeping men, camped some two miles from the fort, "that they might be . . . totally Routed, and drove out of the Settlement." He would strike well before sunrise on the morning of the last day of July.[44]

Pontiac was ready for this, having good intelligence concerning English intentions. He placed watchmen along the route from the fort to his camp and set up breastworks and entrenchments in advantageous places where French houses did not provide cover. Crouched, prone, silent, the warriors were ready for the 247 soldiers who sallied from the garrison at a quick march, two abreast, in the dark of the night. As the soldiers hit a bridge where the road crossed a brook, concealed warriors delivered such galling fire that the stream has since been called Bloody Run. The crack regulars maintained order and counterattacked, but determined Anishinabeg refused to yield their ground. The fighting attracted warriors from other camps, who crossed the river to swell Pontiac's forces. Dalyell's men suffered terribly, and Dalyell himself took three bullets—the third a fatal one—while organizing a retreat, which survivors effected under the covering fire of two row galleys. At eight o'clock in the morning, the battered survivors of the expedition returned to the post, leaving behind some twenty dead, sustaining some forty wounded; almost a fourth of the force had been rendered incapable of combat. The Indian casualties are unknown.[45]

News of the Indian victory raced through Indian country. Pontiac was reinforced by one hundred Indians in early August, and the British reported that more were on their way. Gladwin fully expected to be "invested by upwards of a thousand." By December, he had only 212 active men. Bloody Run erased British plans for offensive operations around Detroit in 1763. Detroit's defenders worried that the war was "not likely to end in haste," and they grew furious with the local French population, widely suspected of fomenting the war and particularly implicated in informing Pontiac of Dalyell's march. Of the "rascally French Settlement" trader James Sterling claimed to "know enough to hang a dozen of them," and he was sure that "all the rest (except three or four) merit[ed] at least transportation." Gladwin, contemplating his chances against the Indians, thought he would need close to fifteen hundred men to punish them, and even that might not be enough: "Things are expected of me that cant [*sic*] be performed; I wish I had quitted the service seven years ago, and that somebody else commanded here."[46]

Pontiac was equally stalled. The red flag still waved over Detroit while four gunboats and the *Huron* threatened from the Detroit River. British naval efforts were not all successful. The *Michigan* broke apart with eighty barrels of provisions amid high winds and whitecaps on August 28 at the eastern end of Lake Erie. News of the wreck disquieted the embattled garrison at Detroit and confirmed the impossibility of large-scale offensive operations. In fact, given his limited stores, Gladwin had to reduce the size of his garrison and send men east.[47]

The *Huron* was almost also lost. On September 4, facing unfavorable winds, the schooner moored in the river and was attacked by 350 warriors, who strove to board the vessel from canoes under cover of darkness.

Several managed to clamber up the bow and the stern, only to be speared and shot by sailors and soldiers. The attackers killed the ship's master and one seaman, and they might well have taken the vessel had not a warrior cut one of the two moorings, causing the vessel to rotate unexpectedly into the current, away from his fellows and in such a manner that the crew could unexpectedly fire broadsides of grapeshot at the canoes. Favorable winds later rose to propel the *Huron* upriver with its cargo of provisions, to the Detroit garrison's "Great Joy." Gladwin made the crew a present of one hundred dollars, and he renamed the ship the *Victory*. Never did the Indians capture it.[48]

Genesee Senecas identified the Niagara portage as a potentially weaker link in the British chain of communication from Fort Niagara to Fort Detroit. The British knew it as the "Carrying Place"; Senecas who labored there as burdeners called it, with harsh workers' poetry, "Di-jih-heh-ah,"—"walking on all fours." Since the Niagara River was not navigable, the road formed a critical landed connection between Detroit and the Atlantic world. It stretched along the churning Niagara River from Fort Niagara on Lake Ontario to Fort "Little Niagara" (or Schlosser) near the falls. Pro-French factions had long existed among the Senecas of the region, but Pontiac's War found most Senecas neutral, including those who lived along the portage. These had suffered the king's loaded ox wagons to pass. The Senecas of Genesee and several other villages, commonly lumped together as the "Genesees," remained strongly anti-British.[49]

On September 14, as twenty-five to thirty soldiers struggled with oxen along the edge of a deep gorge, several hundred Genesee Senecas fell upon them. The gunfire, resounding in the rugged terrain, attracted two companies of reinforcements; Senecas cut them down, killing more than seventy, in one of the worst defeats the British suffered at Indian hands in America. Genesees stripped the dead, threw corpses down among the rocks, and carried off horses, arms, and ammunition. More to the point of the attack, they destroyed a good many horses, oxen, and wagons, making the further delivery of "supplies to Detroit very difficult." British troops around Niagara found their workloads vastly increased as they had to carry supplies on their own shoulders and under heavy guard. News of the Seneca victory spread widely and amplified with the distance. When the French and Indians heard about it in the Illinois Country, they thought Senecas had killed fifteen hundred troops.[50]

British officers thought the "Slap" they had gotten at Niagara "a Severe one," and they struggled to resupply Niagara with oxen and wagons from Oswego. Indians, meanwhile, continued to hit parties along the portage. In mid-October they silently killed or captured four men. Shortly after that, they killed another nine, beheading one and leaving his head "within sight of" the small post at the landing. They stole oxen and harassed the region well into the next year. Such tactics so hindered British efforts that not until late October 1763 could redcoats mount a major relief expedition for Detroit. By then it was dangerously late in the season.[51]

Six hundred troops under Major John Wilkins left the Niagara portage area on October 20, 1763, with twenty-two bateaux and some fifty barrels of provisions. As the two rear vessels cast off into Lake Erie, a party of Indians brought them under a smart fire from ashore, killing or wounding all aboard. The convoy proceeded, but in a matter of days winter fell upon it in a violent storm that engulfed the lives of two officers and seventy men, forcing the battered survivors to turn back. For the British, the dark storm clouds had this silver lining: they had spared them likely defeat by Pontiac, who had organized seven hundred warriors to intercept the flotilla. Robert Rogers and Joshua Loring, familiar with the fighting skills of the Anishinabeg, had been uneasy about the expedition all along. Its failure forced Gladwin to ship still more troops eastward. To the east, Mississauga factions showed increasing hostility to the British, who feared they might raid the St. Lawrence River, interrupting supplies to Niagara.[52]

Potential Mississauga assistance from the far country north of Lake Ontario could not compensate for the absence of France. The definitive Peace of Paris had been signed in February; the official news reached New York on May 4 and Detroit in early July. Since the news lacked official French confirmation, the Indians could doubt it, just as they might doubt what had been said of the preliminaries. On May 16 Pontiac had sent messengers, accompanied by two *habitants*, to Illinois to seek French assistance and to verify the rumored results of Anglo-French negotiations. What his messengers learned was discouraging. The French commander of Fort de Chartres announced in September that a definitive peace had been made, and he urged them to "leave off . . . the spilling of the Blood of . . . the English." He addressed letters and belts to Detroit's Indians, confirming the Anglo-French peace.[53]

WAR UNDER HEAVEN

Without French help, Pontiac could not maintain the siege. The Indians lacked "every necessary, particularly Ammunition." Between October 12 and November 1, the Ottawas and Gladwin negotiated what was essentially a truce. Gladwin "made them no promises," and, under orders from Amherst to kill Pontiac if he could lay his hands on him, Gladwin "judiciously refused" to allow the Ottawa to enter the fort. But he did tell his enemies that once Amherst was convinced of their sincerity "all would be well again." In the meantime, he purchased food. Pontiac promised to ask "all the nations concerned in the war to bury the hatchet." For several months, there was occasional cattle killing, some firing on the schooner, and the odd attack on bateaux, but most of the fighting at Detroit had stopped. The British estimated that Pontiac had lost ninety men around Detroit, but that was only a guess.[54]

After the harvest, Pontiac and something like 150 of his Ottawa and Ojibwa followers left Detroit to resettle a village some ninety miles to the southwest, a dozen miles above the rapids of the Maumee River. Thirty miles farther up the river, something like 40 Ottawa warriors and their families established a second town. One can estimate that the total population of both villages would have been 800 to 1,000. Pontiac's Wyandot allies also settled in the region. At one level, the resettlement reflected a typical seasonal dispersal; winter was the hunting season. But these were large villages, not hunting camps, and Pontiac had not yet given up on the French: his new village lay along the main route from Detroit to Illinois. Far from ready for peace, as he had appeared to be in the fall of 1763, Pontiac by the spring of 1764 exhibited renewed confidence. Since he could expect the British to reinforce Detroit and to attempt further retaliations in the spring, his new location would force them to fight him on his terms: without waterborne guns. Although he was surrendering Detroit to the British, at least until he could persuade the French to reengage, without Indians Detroit was but a remote French hamlet. The British could dominate the straits, but they could not dominate the warriors, who simply withdrew from reach.[55]

The year 1763 ended in a stalemate along the Detroit-Niagara line. Indians had prevented the British from mounting the kind of punishing offensives that Amherst desired, but they had failed to take Detroit. British naval strength on Lake Erie was the deciding factor in the post's survival, a fact the British recognized as they built still more vessels. By the summer of 1764 they had launched three. Two of these, it was found, could pass into Lake Huron and sail to Michilimackinac.⁵⁶ With the *Huron*, these vessels presented Pontiac with a cruel fact that Indians had faced since beginning of colonization: Europe had the capacity to resupply its desperate outposts with arms, provisions, and people. Like many of the struggling colonial beachheads that had preceded it, Detroit had a lifeline to the east that stretched across waterways, adding a maritime dimension to Pontiac's War, a dimension that gave the British a critical edge.

Fort Pitt's lifeline was very different. It stretched across mountains and through thickening colonial settlements. The Indians' struggle against it meant trips through high country and attacks on farmsteads, navigating old memories and new hatreds. Shamokin Daniel, a Delaware war captain, was no stranger to the mountains and valleys east of the upper Ohio River. In 1758, Daniel had escorted Pennsylvania's peace seeker, Christian Frederick Post, westward to the Ohio. His people crossed the Alleghenies after they abandoned their Susquehanna Valley town, Shamokin, in 1756. Neither was he a stranger to the British, whom he repeatedly charged with land grabbing. In 1758 he had berated Post and the British: "Damned you, why do not you and the French fight on the sea? You come here only to cheat the poor Indians, and to take land from them." An ineffective double agent during the Seven Years' War, Daniel had tried to sell Post to the French at Duquesne, only to be stopped by other Delawares, who valued him more highly as a warrior than as anything else. Because he was well known to many Britons, we can follow him and his raiders east into Pennsylvania in 1763.⁵⁷

Pontiac's War had been raging for about six weeks when Daniel and eighteen Delawares left their Ohio Country homes to kill settlers in the Susquehanna Valley. Traveling by horse during the day, they slept without benefit of fire by night, vulnerable to insects, mice, and chills. They ate little, occasionally taking an uncooked concoction colonists called green powder, a mixture of parched cornmeal, herbs, and salt. Counting on stealth and surprise, they moved toward the isolated but armed and wary settlements. On July 10 Daniel's band approached the Juniata River, a tributary of his beloved Susquehanna. Ten years earlier, this had been Delaware country; now it was freckled with Yankee, German, and Scots-Irish families—or to put it better, with the men of those families, as the women and children had already, for the most part, gone downstream and out of range of the anticipated violence.⁵⁸ It was early morning when

Daniel and his men trained their guns on the home of William White, whom they drew to the door with a soft sound. In a moment White lay dead on the front step. Delawares immediately fired the house and slew two men who appeared armed at the doorway. They shot dead a fourth man as he climbed out of a loft window. Their last victim, a wounded boy, they took alive. His father, William Riddle, broke through the roof and slipped away amid the smoke, the gunfire, and the groans of the dying. White's neighbor, one McMachen, rode to the scene, only to take a bullet in the arm as he turned his horse to flee the clear disaster.

Quickly destroying the livestock, burning the outbuildings, and plundering what they could safely carry, Daniel's men were on the move again by midday. A mile and a half away, having crossed the Juniata, they burst into the home of Robert Campbell, surprising six men at their midday meal. Daniel lost a man to the swift counterfire of the one settler who escaped. The Delawares slaughtered the rest. By evening they were five miles farther up the river, attacking and killing William Anderson and two children.

Early the next day Daniel's men united with another party of at least eight raiders, and they moved to a pass in the Tuscarora Mountain between the Juniata and Sherman Valleys, where they sent out scouts and waited for the anticipated retaliation. Twelve colonial men, mostly Juniata settlers, obliged, five of them fatally. The net result was this: a mere twenty-six Delawares in two parties had penetrated the Pennsylvania countryside and killed at least eighteen colonists, three of them children. They wounded an additional two men and carried off one captive. They suffered one fatality. Only twenty miles from Carlisle, well to the east of several Pennsylvania forts, colonial families mourned lost children and men. Animals that might feed troops or carry supplies lay dead. Vast fields lay untended as panic cleared out the countryside.

In small parties, almost always under fifty men, often as small as seven or eight, Delaware and Shawnee Indian raiders left the colonial backcountry in a state of terror even though they were vastly outnumbered and outgunned. Carrying but few supplies—with a few horses, perhaps, but for the most part on foot for the sake of silence—they had to live off their enemy. They could strike only a few targets, and these had to be hit rapidly because word would quickly spread and a retaliatory force would soon gather. In thirty days they might cover three hundred miles and raid a farmstead or two, but a small party can take only so much plunder and so many prisoners across the mountains, and it would have to return home quickly.

George Croghan's oft-cited claim that Indians had, in "the space of four Months" in 1763, "killed and captivated" at least "two thousand of his Majesty's subjects" was only an uneducated, wild guess, and it cannot be taken seriously. Croghan was in London when he offered it. The public and personal papers that he would have had at his disposal do not bring the number anywhere near that high. But numbers killed cannot be the sole measure of the Indians' effectiveness. What parties such as Daniel's had accomplished by August was to crowd the larger backcountry villages with grieving, fearful, and often furious refugees; Shippensburg alone had almost fourteen hundred, "obliged to lie in Barns, Stables, Cellars, and under old Leaky Sheds." The chill of terror went beyond the backcountry as urbane Philadelphians read that "Above a thousand Families [were] driven from their Houses and Habitations" and that the Indians were traveling "from one Place to anther, along the Valley, burning the Farms, and destroying all the People" they met. Panic erupted as far east as Orange County, New York. There the sounds of gunfire—from colonial hunters shooting wild fowl—triggered the flight of "near 500 Families" from the Wallkill Valley near Goshen.[59] Even inadvertently, the Delawares were emptying their old valleys of settlers, disrupting the British war effort, and sending the message that Delaware power was not to be treated with contempt.

"Never," wrote the *Pennsylvania Gazette* in August, "was Panic more general . . . than that of the Back Inhabitants, whose Terrors, at this Time, exceed what followed on the Defeat of General Braddock." By the end of the month, even South Carolinians "Crowded into Houses . . . building Forts." A minister said that the "enemy" had even killed the Catawba "King Hagler," a close ally of the British, causing "such Terror, that there was nothing but running and flying, wherever safety could be had." The panic clearly spread widely, even creating imaginary theaters of war. Doing so, it pinned down colonial militias and Indian allies who might have been deployed to counter Indians in the war's real theater. New York was so rife with rumors of an entire Six Nations' uprising that the assembly became convinced. Sir William Johnson found it difficult to counter "one of the late New York Papers," which had implicated his loyal Mohawks in an attack on the "Borders of Pennsylvania." The writer of that story claimed to know Mohawks by "their Caps and manner of cutting their Hair," to which Johnson retorted, "The Mohawks do not wear caps." Into the next spring, Oneidas were accused of hostilities against the English, and false rumors circulated that Joseph Brant, the rising Mohawk leader, had "gone over to the Enemy." In the face of such uncertainty, New York could offer little help elsewhere. The same was true in New England, were Massachusetts governor Francis Bernard had to consider sending two hundred men to Maine to overawe its Indians, in case they listened to appeals from "the Western Indians."[60]

Daniel's raid, and the many more that took place even closer to the heavily defended Forbes' Road, had other purposes than inspiring such terror, useful as it might be. Plunder attracted some Delawares, who had for several years been very poor. The raiders prized firearms above all else, but other hardware could also be loaded onto stolen horses, which constituted another prime objective. Oxen, cattle, and hogs, more cumbersome, were for the most part killed.[61]

Seeking to gain plunder and spread terror, the assailants had deeper purposes, evident in the locations they chose to strike. The raiding was not random but concentrated in revealing ways. Fully two-thirds of the raids on the settlements fell on an area defined by three roads. Braddock's Road ran from Fort Pitt southeastward to Fort Cumberland, Maryland, where good roads carried on to the Shenandoah Valley of Virginia. Forbes' Road ran from Fort Pitt eastward through the fortified depots of Forts Ligonier, Bedford, and Loudon before reaching the towns of Shippensburg and Carlisle. The third road, the "Virginia Road," intersected with the first two, running along the eastern edge of the Appalachians from Winchester, Virginia, northward across the Potomac through the Conococheague River settlements of Maryland and Pennsylvania and then toward Shippensburg, Pennsylvania. The three formed an acute triangle whose sharpest point pierced the Indian country at Fort Pitt.[62] Critical routes of correspondence, resupply, provision, and carriage for the British, the roads and the farms around them became targets for warriors.[63]

Beyond the triangle, two patterns emerged. Early in the war, Shawnees devastated the Greenbriar River valley settlements (now in West Virginia), which marked a dangerous westward thrust of British settlement. By the end of the war, Shawnees held more Greenbriar captives than those from any other place; only the nearby Jackson's River settlements saw as much devastation, and for the same reason. Land was certainly an issue in these areas, where settlers had crossed the Appalachians. Shawnees sent a clear message that they would brook no British farmers west of the mountains. The second pattern belongs to the Susquehanna Delawares. Only in the Delaware villages along the Susquehanna River did Indian raiders conform in any manner to the Parkmanesque stereotype of revenge. Far more than the Shawnees and Ohio Delawares with their calculated raids, the Susquehanna Delawares appear to have reacted to the spilling of the war over the Appalachians and to the opportunity to strike at the settlers that had taken their lands. These Delawares came late to the war. Ottawas, Ohio Delawares, Genesee Senecas, and others had taken to arms within the space of a month in the spring of 1763; Susquehanna Delawares did not strike until the end of the summer, when they attacked New Englanders at Wyoming, that lovely stretch of valley so recently and fraudulently taken from them by the Susquehanna Company of Connecticut. The foul wind of their retaliatory war blew even to the neighborhoods of Fort Allen and Fort Henry, with the easternmost strikes of the war on the Delaware River itself and its small tributary, the Lackawaxen.[64]

Fear of the Susquehanna Delawares spread into New Jersey, and in New York it raised the specter of an Indian-slave conspiracy. The British rarely discussed the capture of any Indians, but when runaway slave Sam Tony fell into their hands, his name appeared in the writings of William Johnson, General Gage, New York governor Cadwallader Colden, and the *Pennsylvania Gazette*. Johnson thought the Delawares had "many Rifles" and "some Negro's [*sic*]." Rumors reached Albany that some sixty families had been destroyed in the Delaware Valley, and Albany citizen David Van der Heyden rumored that his own slaves had told him that the Indians were corresponding with slaves, reassuring them that they "would be in no Danger" when Indians attacked.[65]

Ohio Delawares and Mingos did not consider striking so far to the north or east; they had enough work along the triangular arteries that sustained Fort Pitt. Sometimes they hit heavily armed convoys, but since their parties were small, they generally attacked expresses, wood-cutting parties, harvesters, and families, in a calculated effort to keep British troops pinned down: ill supplied, without carriage, preoccupied with defense, and ignorant of Indian movements. Such raids had increased after it had become clear, probably as early as July 1763, that neither storm nor stratagem would win Forts Detroit or Pitt for the Indians. The only hope was to cut the posts off. British contemporaries understood the Indians' strategy. William Eyre noted that though Indians could not take the larger forts by storm, they could "more or less ... cut off the Communication to them," which was "taking them in Fact, or rendering them useless." For a year after Daniel's raid, Indians targeted both supply lines to Forts Pitt and Detroit, and they struck hard at the western Pennsylvania, Maryland, and Virginia granaries. As far east as Fort Bedford, Pennsylvania, the Indians in the summer of 1763 were so well deployed "that neither messengers nor any thing else could escape them." They had killed or captured eighteen members of the garrison and kept the British in "total want of intelligence."[66]

The intelligence was theirs. Delawares, Shawnees, and Mingos carefully observed the mounting of the first British effort to invade their country. Colonel Henry Bouquet had gathered a force of close to five hundred Royal Americans at Carlisle. Determined to stop him, Indians struck hard at the countryside "through which the army was to pass," emptying it of people, save for wretched families fleeing eastward along the roads. "By this confusion," a British officer later wrote, "the supplies for the expedition became more and more precarious." The troops reached Fort Bedford, completely deprived of "intelligence of the enemy," in midsummer. Bouquet there stored his wagons and a good many supplies and strengthened the garrison with thirty of his weakest men. At the next post, Fort Ligonier, he again reduced his force and his supplies. Leaving Ligonier, he had 460 soldiers, "many of them convalescents," and 340 packhorses "loaded with flour."[67]

Delawares, Shawnees, Wyandots, and Mingos, who had harassed Fort Pitt for most of the summer, began to besiege it on July 27, but without success. They broke off after several days to converge, as a "considerable body," on Bouquet's expedition. The advanced British guard collided with them at Edge Hill on August 5. The Indians, fighting with "uncommon bravery" but handicapped by a lack of ammunition, concentrated their energies on the packhorse train but were unable to take it from the British. From early afternoon until nightfall they unleashed several coordinated attacks, surrounding the British and keeping them on the defensive. The next morning they resumed the attack but were deftly outflanked by a company of light infantry. Their powder running low, the warriors withdrew, having killed fifty and wounded sixty of Bouquet's troops, including many officers. Kikiuskung, one of the Delaware leaders, was among the Indian dead, whose numbers will never be known. His son, Wolf, was also killed.[68]

The battle has come to be called Bushy Run, because it took place a mile from that stream. It has generally been treated as a heroic British victory, often as the decisive battle of the war; but its results were mixed. If the Indians meant to keep Pitt from being reinforced, they failed. If they meant to prevent it from being resupplied, they had considerable success. Bouquet's 390 survivors, many of them sick and wounded, made it to the fort, but they did so without most of the flour, which had to be abandoned if the wounded were to be carried to the fort. The Indians exacted so high a price that Bouquet discovered, to his "great mortification," that he was unable to assist either forces from Niagara in an effort to reestablish Fort Presque Isle or Gladwin at Detroit in any material way. Amherst pressed Bouquet to go on the offensive, suggesting that he link up with Virginia volunteers to do so. This was out of the question. Bouquet could not feed any additional mouths; he instead sent eastward all noncombatants and even some soldiers to ease the demands on his commissary. He dedicated troops to the task of escorting all traffic on the communications. As the officers and troops awakened from the proud dream of setting Indian villages afire to the harsh reality of another winter penned up in a garrison, Bouquet had to combat a "spirit of discontent and desertion."[69] Discouraged, too, however, were his enemies, who by the end of August had surrendered their own proud dream of eliminating Fort Pitt.

Although the defenses of Pitt and Detroit and the British efforts to reinforce those posts received most attention from the British officers who kept the diaries and who made the official reports of the war, the Indians' war was more typically one of small but violent raids, and these continued, particularly in Virginia. Pennsylvania seems to have been safer after August 1763, at least in the sense that there were fewer casualties; on the other hand, with the countryside largely abandoned, there were fewer people to kill. Pennsylvanians and Virginians were all too familiar with this kind of warfare. They knew to "fort up," to harvest under arms and in teams, but they could do little themselves to seal off their long roads and dispersed settlements from isolated attacks. They called upon their governments to bring the war to the enemy: even such a moderate Philadelphia paper as the *Pennsylvania Gazette* concluded its report on Shamokin Daniel's raid with: "Today a British vengeance begins to rise in the Breasts of our Men."[70]

For the British, the year 1763 had been one of reaction as they struggled to defend, reinforce, and resupply their posts and as they launched only minor counterstrokes, some in the form of raids by regular detachments from Detroit, others in the form of the blasting of ships' cannon along the Detroit River, the most common in the form of militia mobilizations and provincial attacks on Indian villages in the Susquehanna Valley. For the Indians, 1763 had been a year of initiative, initial success, and disquieting stalemate. Although they had eliminated a good many posts and had put a full stop to colonial expansion, they had failed to dislodge the major posts and were short of ammunition. Most disturbing was the human dimension: they had failed to win the support of France or of the French *habitants* generally. They had also never succeeded in securing the aid of the Catholic Indians domiciled near Montreal and Quebec or the Catholic-influenced Ottawas of L'Arbre Croche, and they had lost the support of the Catholic Wyandots of Detroit. Strong factions of Senecas had joined them and scored victories, but the Iroquois League as a whole was drifting against them.

CHAPTER FIVE

Defending the Villages, 1764

Pontiac and his allies appeared to be losing the struggle for potential loyalties during the first winter of the war. They faced the weapons not only of British soldiers and colonists but also of Canadian militia and Indian scouts from the St. Lawrence Valley. The Six Nations, apart from the Genesee Senecas, were pondering their Covenant Chain. Individual Indians already worked as British agents. Andrew, a Huron, regularly took messages between Fort Pitt and Detroit. He sometimes lost them, and he sometimes bragged among Detroit Indians of his having been among the attackers at Venango, so many distrusted him. But his employers remained confident of his allegiance. Two Mohawk "captains," Daniel and Aaron, also accompanied the British; the first was singled out for praise in a brief firefight that followed the wreck of the *Michigan*, when the survivors had entrenched on the shore and then had repulsed attackers. Over the course of 1764, four Mohawks—Peter, his two sons, and Jacob—also carried letters for the British, in this case between Detroit and Sir William Johnson's elegant, fortified home in the Mohawk Valley. All these Indians ran high risks. Duplicity was part of their job, and they were the objects of suspicion on all sides.[1]

As for raising Indian warriors in the British alliance, Lord Jeffery Amherst scorned the idea. It was not that he was unfamiliar with warriors; he had tolerated them, even deigning to dine with them in his 1759 campaigns, but by 1760 he had had quite enough. When Stockbridge Indians—who had in the late war performed as great a service to the

British, man for man, as any group on the continent—offered on July 23, 1763, to campaign against Pontiac, Amherst "would on no Account whatever think of Engaging" that "Worthless Tribe." When Six Nations warriors and Kahnawakes of the St. Lawrence appeared ready to assist Crown soldiers, Amherst would "not employ them," for he would never put "the least trust in any of the Indian Race." Sir William Johnson, who envisioned a broad North American force of "Brisk Canadians," colonials, and Indians, could not change the general's mind. Johnson sought the fabled Indian skill at guerrilla warfare less than he sought to "intimidate the Enemy" and "animate the Troops." He greatly feared that if Amherst obstinately refused to employ Indian auxiliaries, the potential Indian allies would become enemies. Fortunately for Johnson's efforts, Amherst did not remain in office but was recalled to England toward the end of 1763.[2]

His replacement, Major General Thomas Gage, shared Amherst's broad contempt for Indians, but he was more willing to cooperate with other officials, particularly Johnson, whose advice he took seriously. When Johnson gingerly felt out Gage's views on the securing of Indian allies, Gage readily concurred: "They know the woods, Dwellings Grounds of every Nation; They can lead us to Them, & Secure us from Surprise which the Troops know, & will give them a Confidence." With that, Johnson moved swiftly to form his force.[3]

Johnson had great sway among the Mohawks, who formed the eastern "door" of the Six Nations Iroquois League. This gave him influence with the league as a whole. A wealthy planter, Indian trader, baronet, and land baron, Johnson was also the veteran of the Seven Years' War who had—with a thousand Indians at his side—led the successful British siege of Niagara in 1759. He had been superintendent of Indian affairs in the northern department since 1756, and, critically, he was the husband by Iroquois reckoning of the influential Mohawk Mary Brant. One British official exaggerated when in 1758 he called Johnson the "stateholder" of the Iroquois, but Sir William could expect a good hearing from the Six Nations as he made Great Britain's case. His main difficulty was, as always, the western "door" of the league, the divided Seneca Nation, several villages of which had allied with Pontiac. But he hoped initially to persuade the others to send men against the Delawares and the Shawnees, whom he represented as insurgents against the Anglo-Iroquois Covenant Chain.[4]

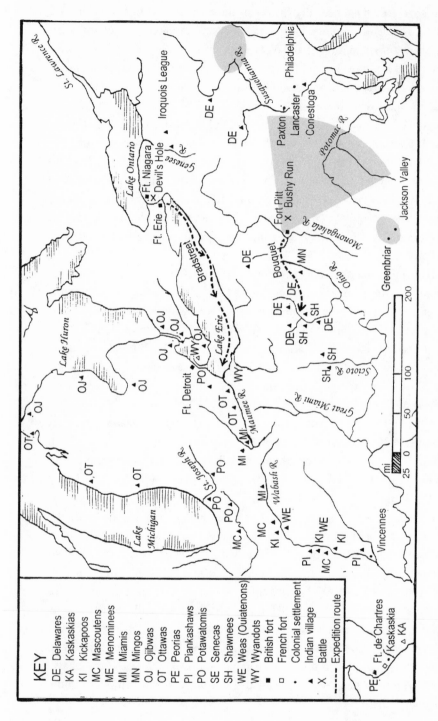

Map 3. Pontiac's War, late summer 1763 through 1764. Approximate sites of battles, Indian villages, imperial forts and expeditions, and colonial towns in chapters 4 through 6. Shaded zones were targeted by trans-Appalachian Indians.

The stakes were high. If the Susquehanna and Ohio Delawares and Shawnees were to gain legitimacy in the eyes of the Six Nations as the rightful, independent holders of the upper Ohio or Susquehanna lands on which they lived, British claims to western lands would be enormously complicated. The Six Nations, too, would lose the influence in British councils on which rested both their own independence and Sir William's authority. Johnson readily argued that the Delawares and Shawnees "were certainly the first authors of the present disturbances" and "greatly" deserved British resentment. He acknowledged that the Genesee Senecas were equally culpable, but punishing them was impractical, since they were members of the Six Nations. Early in 1764, he extended generous peace offers to the Genesees. At the same time, he gained Gage's support for retribution against the Delawares and Shawnees. The singling out of the Shawnees and Delawares requires some explanation. At some level, Johnson believed that the Delawares and Shawnees were at the "bottom" of the trouble, but he was never clear on this; he just as often pointed fingers at Ottawas, French traders, or (without the least shred of evidence and against hard facts) Jesuits. At another level, he knew that these two peoples had brought the greatest misery to British settlers. But Johnson's push to punish Delawares and Shawnees was actually less a matter of justice or revenge than of policy: to end the war, he would reunite the Six Nations, come down cruelly on the neighboring enemy nations, extend olive branches to more distant enemies, and in the process both divide Pontiac from the Ohioans and shore up the Six Nations' Covenant Chain, which gave him such power. In this manner he could establish British authority in the west and, not incidentally, vastly increase his own command.[5]

Oneidas and Tuscaroras, members of the league, visited Johnson in January and February 1764, gaining arms, paint, and ammunition. Johnson posted bounties for the heads of various Delawares, particularly the Squash Cutter and the Long Coat. A party of only ten, under the Oneida Thomas King, shed the "first blood"; surprising nine Delawares on March 9, they killed one and took three prisoners. This kind of action, wrote Johnson, would "greatly distress" the Britons' enemies, "as well as . . . disunite them."[6]

So much for blood. A much larger party of more than 140 Indians and some colonial rangers, headed by Henry Montour, had already taken a different tack against the Delawares, one that reveals the limits and the extent of Johnson's authority. Montour, accompanied by William Hare and John Johnson (son of Sir William and his former housekeeper, Catherine Weisenberg), had left Johnson Hall armed and ready for action against the Delawares of the Susquehanna. On their way southward, they paused for several days at Montour's own settlement, Auqvauge. There they learned that a large party of Delawares was approaching the village in peace. Seven of the Delaware chiefs, including "the famous Captain Bull," visited Auqvauge on February 27, where Montour's men seized them that evening and "bound them hand and feet." The next day, Montour's party surrounded and surprised the unsuspecting Delawares camped nearby, taking captive eleven men, eight women, and three children. Johnson received the news quickly, and as he relayed it to other officials, he omitted the fact that Bull and his men had been seized while guests in Montour's own village. Further misrepresentations of the event had Montour surprising a single Delaware village at daybreak, a more honorable Indian way of war. The twenty-nine captives somehow soared in the record to forty-one. Fourteen of the captives, all men, Johnson gained and sent eastward as prisoners; the rest, mostly women and children, were distributed among the Six Nations, save a woman whom the Six Nations warriors "gave Sir William . . . with a belt of Wampum to replace his father lately deceased." These and the other captives taken by the Six Nations, notably, are the only known war prisoners—apart from hostages who surrendered themselves to guarantee their people's fulfillment of treaty obligations—the British made any effort to keep alive.[7]

The fourteen captives sent eastward and eventually to New York included Captain Bull, whom Johnson described as a "Villain of the first rank," rumored to have "with his own hands killed 26 English since the Spring." The allegations were in part political, for Bull and his late father, Teedyuscung, had in recent times worked with the Pennsylvania Quaker party both to embarrass that colony's proprietary government and to gain recognition for Delaware independence of the Six Nations. Johnson's political allies, Thomas Gage, Witham Marsh, and New York governor Cadwallader Colden, were all delighted to see Captain Bull behind bars, and they hoped to milk his association with Quakers for everything it was worth. Marsh went so far as to visit the Delaware in the prison in New York City in early April, and he pressed him and his countryman, Joe Nutimus, to admit that "some *quaking Devils*" were the originators of the "Delaware Scheme." Colden, writing to the earl of Halifax, noted that Bull had been "much caressed" in Philadelphia, and he believed that the Six Nations had taken Bull's party in order to chastise it as a band of rebels.[8]

After they had first captured Bull and the Delawares, Montour's men descended the Susquehanna Valley, destroying abandoned enemy towns along the way. A special target was Kanestio town, a "Nest of Villains composed chiefly of Senecas, Shawaneses & a few Delawares." Johnson suggested to Gage (his report made it into the *Pennsylvania Gazette*) that the escaping Delawares would take shelter with Indians to the south or west. This was deception; the refugees fled in neither direction but instead to the north, to dwell in sympathetic villages among the Cayugas, a Six Nations people. Had this been widely known, it would have reflected badly on Johnson's ability to manage the Six Nations. By the end of July the British learned that these refugees, living on wild roots, were still strongly "for War."[9]

Facing Bradstreet's Expedition

The Iroquois refused to march in lockstep behind Johnson. Not only did Genesee Senecas continue to show signs of hostility, but Cayugas gave shelter to enemy Delawares, expressly against Johnson's wishes. Johnson's Indian warriors, in spite of his generous outlays of gifts, killed very few of his enemies. In talks with the Six Nations, Johnson himself expressed surprise at the "Backwardness" shown by some of the league's people. Throughout the spring and into the summer, he steadily beat the war drum, so that by the end of June he was able to marshal an impressive force at Niagara of 650 Indians who would accompany almost 1,200 British troops, most of them provincials from New York, Connecticut, and New Jersey, in an expedition west under Colonel John Bradstreet.[10] Johnson hoped the expedition would demonstrate his influence over the Iroquois and, by projecting Iroquois power westward, demonstrate the importance of the Six Nations. Six Nations warriors, pursuing their own agendas, would disappoint him.

Niagara lay in the territory of the divided Seneca Nation. The sight of the impressive British colonial army and its growing Indian auxiliary force, composed largely of their Six Nations countrymen, inspired many Genesee Senecas to change their ways, or so William Johnson came to believe by early August. Genesees delivered ten British captives to the baronet; what is more, twenty-three Genesees agreed to join Bradstreet's expedition. Johnson made formal peace with village leaders and exacted from them both a promise to deliver any Delawares harbored among them and the cession of the Niagara carrying place to the king. The cession was a serious matter, and it would in the end be one of the most important land cessions actually obtained by the British in the course of the war. Johnson readily acknowledged to Gage that, beyond this cession, his peace with the Genesees had punished no one, not even recent killers of Englishmen. But he argued that isolating the Genesees and mobilizing the Six Nations would render "Pontiac with his Adherents . . . verry Submissive. . . . The Shawnese and Delawares [would] also be Staggered at the Indians Joining [British] Troops, and probably make all necessary Submission."[11]

Other Indians also converged on the gathering expedition: Ottawas from L'Arbre Croche, Mississaugas from north of Lake Ontario, Nipissings from north Ontario, and Ojibwas from Sault Ste. Marie. Some pledged to support Bradstreet. On July 14, eighteen of the Ojibwas agreed to accompany the troops. In Johnson's inflated rhetoric, they had become part of the Covenant Chain. Soon Johnson was able to report to Gage that forty-two Ottawas and Ojibwas from L'Arbre Croche and Sault Ste. Marie had expressed a particular readiness to attack the Shawnees and Delawares. He would later recall that they sang "their War Song against" the Ohioans and "expected nothing else than proceeding by the way of Sandusky and attacking them."[12]

Yet doubts about Indian loyalties clouded the expedition before it got under way. When a British soldier, isolated on the Niagara portage, was found killed, provincials wondered how his killers had managed to escape detection by the hundreds of vigilant, supposedly British-allied Indians in the region. Indians had troubling questions of their own; when one of their parties, marching and singing past the outpost of Fort Schlosser, saluted the garrison with a harmless volley, panicky soldiers opened fire—severely wounding three. More routinely, allied Indians faced "the Soldiery bestowing Curses &ca. verry liberally upon them at the Posts, and often giving them much worse treatment." What were they to make of "those indiscreet Expressions concerning Indians so customary amongst the Soldiery"? What were they to make of the British officers' reluctance to "admit them into their Rooms" and hear what they had to say, "the Indians being used to much freedom with the French Generals and Officers"? The "bad discourse" of the new regime became further evident to those Anishinabeg considering the British alliance in mid-July, when Bradstreet judged "it proper to assume a high tone," chastised his allies for their lack of discipline, and drew this Ojibwa rejoinder: "It is not good for a great Warrior to be cross to his Warriors, it discourages them." Ottawas and Sault Ste. Marie Ojibwas soon deserted en masse.[13]

Losing his Anishinabe allies, Bradstreet still had with him Mahicans, Kahnawakes, and Six Nations warriors when he launched his expedition on August 6. His first objective was Detroit, where he was to reinforce Gladwin and bring Pontiac and the Indians to terms. Gladwin suggested that Bradstreet should strike the Maumee River villages before the harvest and "cut up the Outawas['] Corn, which [would] distress them more than fire and sword." Bradstreet liked the idea, noting that he intended to fall "upon Mr. Pondiac's Friends and . . . march for that first." By the time he got under way, his mission included a host of objectives that he chose to construe as options. Johnson and Gage wanted him to descend from Sandusky to the Scioto River, advancing on Shawnees and Delawares from the northwest, trapping them in a pincer movement as Colonel Henry Bouquet marched from the east. To Gage's later disappointment and anger, Bradstreet abandoned that idea even before he left Niagara, reasoning that a march to the Scioto would overextend his force. With the Wilkins disaster in mind, he left the Niagara region in large, newly designed, seaworthy keel boats, each forty-six feet long, carrying twenty-seven men and three weeks of provisions. Pontiac, meanwhile, remained in his village above the rapids of the Maumee River. He hinted that he wanted peace, but he did not come to talk peace himself. At the same time, he sent "belts and messages everywhere." He had at least three hundred men in arms around him as Bradstreet's force of twelve hundred troops and some six hundred Indians headed his way.[14]

Six days later, strong, contrary winds forced the expedition to camp at L'Anse aux Feuilles on the south shore of Lake Erie. There a delegation of Shawnees, Delawares, Sandusky Wyandots, and Mingos approached peacefully, and they agreed with Bradstreet to a tentative, conditional peace—a peace, it should be understood, that was to be voided in twenty-five days if the Indians did not fulfill its terms. The Indian delegates granted the British *possession* of claims not only to all existing forts but also to any unspecified future forts and to all lands within a cannon shot around these. They left six principal people as hostages. They promised to surrender to the British any person who thenceforth committed hos-

"Indians delivering up the English Captives to Colonel Bouquet." Engraving based on a Benjamin West painting. From William Smith, *An Historical Account of the Expedition against the Ohio Indians, in the year MDCCLXIV, under the command of Henry Bouquet, Esq.* . . . (Philadelphia, 1765; London, 1766). Courtesy Burton Historical Collection, Detroit Public Library. Engaging our sentiments, the artist and engraver have the children leave Native American embraces for the colonel's open arms, backed by a row of bayonets.

tilities. In an idea that harkened back to William Penn, that person would be tried by a jury, half "of the same [Indian] nation with the Offender," half British. In mid-September Bradstreet and these Ohioans pledged to meet again at Sandusky, where Indians were to deliver all prisoners. A commission composed of six Britons, six Canadian new subjects, and six Indians would then investigate all the towns to make sure all prisoners had been released. Bradstreet promised to send immediately to Fort Pitt to have Bouquet suspend his imminent attack on the Delawares and Shawnees. He concluded the treaty by claiming authority from General Gage, saying: "I Grant Peace."[15]

The last few points—the jury, the commission, the suspension of Bouquet's expedition—raised a chorus of official indignation. Bouquet registered "astonishment" that Bradstreet had not sent the delegates to beg for Bouquet's mercy; the younger officer had instead unilaterally promised to stop a senior officer's expedition, already in motion, working its way toward Fort Pitt from Pennsylvania. Gage and Johnson joined Bouquet in denouncing a peace that contained "not the least satisfaction" and that would halt two armies now poised to "penetrate into the heart of the Enemy's country." Delawares and Shawnees deserved punishment, a punishment Bradstreet threatened to abort. Bradstreet, stung by the harsh criticism, wondered why Johnson's peace at Niagara with the Genesee Senecas, "Masters of Treachery and Butchery," was more fitting than his at L'Anse aux Feuilles.[16] It was a good question.

Johnson had long been at odds with Bradstreet, and he may have felt slighted, too, when the officer granted peace without proper consultation. Gage accused Bradstreet of usurping the authority "to conclude any Peace, and [to] dictate the Articles thereof, Agreeable to his own Judgment." Yet Gage himself had empowered Bradstreet "to bring those tribes to conclude a formal peace," one that would be "sincere and lasting."[17] The fury inspired by Bradstreet's peace had two deeper sources. First, there was a great suspicion that Indian treachery was at work. Johnson convinced a more ambivalent Gage that the Shawnees and Delawares would not live up to their engagements. These Indians were still enemies and should be treated as such. The Indians who made the "peace" with Bradstreet, were not, except for the Seneca-Mingo Kiashuta, prominent figures, a fact that further convinced Gage that the peace had merely been another Indian ruse to fend off an attack and to watch the motions of the army.

Second, and far more important, Shawnees and Delawares, unlike the others, were illegitimate peoples in Sir William's view. Their proper place was in subjection to the Six Nations, who were themselves bound to the British by the Covenant Chain. Bradstreet's peace said nothing of the Covenant Chain. In its discussion of lands, it stunned Johnson and Gage, who believed that "as for their Lands," the Shawnees and Delawares had none to give the British. Johnson and the Indian department he headed conveniently viewed the upper Ohio as part of an Iroquois empire. That very summer, Johnson's deputy, George Croghan, was in London seeking support for a British boundary with the Indians, one that would recognize Iroquois lordship over lands and "dependant" tribes northwest of the Ohio River. Making peace with Shawnees and Delawares, Bradstreet had tangled himself in a complicated imperial web. The Shawnees and Delawares, Gage declared, were "the last" with whom he would have "any Transactions." He voided Bradstreet's peace and ordered Bouquet to attack the Ohio peoples and "to extirpate them, unless they both deliver[ed] up the Promoters of the war" and sent deputies to make peace with William Johnson. The Delawares' and Shawnees' failure to appear at Sandusky at the end of September in conformity with Bradstreet's peace seemed to confirm Gage's estimation, though Bradstreet's defenders pointed out that Bouquet's continued preparations for an Ohio campaign kept the Indians in the Ohio Country and prevented them from traveling to Sandusky.[18]

Bradstreet's maligned peace angered Johnson for another reason. The Indians the superintendent had so strenuously raised, and on whose success his reputation rested, claimed that Bradstreet's treaty made it impossible for them to engage in any kind of offensive. Six Nations leaders, in fact, questioned the propriety of Bouquet's continuing advance. Johnson took pains to explain that since Shawnees and Delawares had defrauded Bradstreet, there had been no peace. But he was not certain that he had been convincing: the leaders only "Seemed" to acquiesce. They had their own worries. As eager as Johnson to see the Six Nations' authority projected westward, they were not eager for extensive war against Shawnees and Delawares, whom they had long viewed as props of their league. Ideally, the Six Nations sought to lead through mediation, through the making of peace. Senecas had for months been pleading with Johnson to forgive the Delawares, advising him not to let the army, with its "large foot, . . . tread upon [their] Nephews, the Delawares." Those Iroquois who accompanied Bradstreet, though clothed in the raiment of war, hoped to bind the western Indians to the Covenant Chain through negotiation.[19] Even Johnson was never able to control his allies.

Ignorant of all criticism and still en route to Detroit, Bradstreet and his troops put in at the mouth of the Maumee River. There he dispatched Lieutenant Thomas Morris, accompanied by a small party under the Oneida Thomas King, to carry news of the L'Anse aux Feuilles peace to Pontiac. Morris and King hoped that news of the defection of his Ohio allies would persuade Ottawas to give up the war. The two would then proceed to the French posts still in the Illinois Country, where Morris would formally relieve the remaining French officers of command. Morris, King, and several Oneidas ascended the Maumee on August 26 and reached the first village, above the rapids, the next day. Five or six hundred of Pontiac's followers seized them, separated them, and carried them through nearby villages. They treated Morris roughly but did him no serious harm. Other Indians worked on King and his followers, calling these Indians servants of the English and taunting them with English misdeeds. They attempted to disengage the Six Nations from the British, and with this group they claimed some success. The French, in Illinois, heard rumors that King's party pledged "to betray" the English "when the time should come."[20]

At Pontiac's village the Anishinabeg reunited Morris and King. There they met a "native of old France," one St. Vincent, who, by his bearing and uniform, "appeared to be a French officer." Morris later learned that the man had never been more than a drummer in the French army. Another source pegs St. Vincent as "a Canadian Indian." Stepping in for French brass, St. Vincent led Morris to a meeting ground to await Pontiac, repeating the story that the French army would return to free the Great Lakes region from the British yoke. What Pontiac said was equally alarming. Scoffing at Bradstreet's peace, which purported to disarm the Ohio Indians, Pontiac declared that he had received fresh war belts from the Senecas, Shawnees, and Delawares. Against Bradstreet's 1,200 troops and 650 Indians, Pontiac claimed that he expected assistance from France. Far from proclaiming peace, the Ottawa proclaimed the French king's revival: the English had lied in claiming that the French king had been "crushed." Pontiac showed Morris a letter regarding the French; it was full, says Morris, "of the most improbable falsehoods." Morris's account of the letter is corroborated by King's report from the same year that

Pontiac "had received a Letter from the King of France with Account that he had been dead and risen again and that he should send directly 60 Sail of Vessels up the River Mississippi with every Necessary to supply them for carrying on the War."[21]

A later version of Morris's journal adds to this account a more detailed picture of the appearance of Pontiac's village, a picture that suggests elaborate attempts on the part of both the Indians and the local French to reconstitute New France. Morris claims that as he approached the village he was "astonished to see a great number of white flags flying." Nothing in either version of Morris's journal suggests that he saw flags as indications either of peace, often represented by things white among the woodland Indians, or of surrender, as a European might have it. Neither peace nor surrender would have "astonished" Morris, for he still believed, on this second day of his journey, that peace was in the offing. Morris saw in each flag the *drapeau blanc*. Raising the flag, Ottawas may have recalled their declaration to the French at Detroit in 1760: "Our hearts will be sore so long as we see the Red Flag over our land—we who have always loved the White."[22]

Pontiac, in the presence of British officers, had announced the return of the French king while accompanied by an unofficial French "officer." He displayed forged French letters and even copied French flags. These facts, once interpreted as revealing that Pontiac's allies had been manipulated by the French, indicate almost the reverse: far from being under French control, Pontiac's allies sought together to influence France. A group of French and Indian people stood near the Maumee River, performed ceremonies, displayed things French, and carefully considered their military options as they attempted to summon the French king to come with his troops and his goods to America. Through the notion that French power could be appropriated spiritually, Great Lakes and Illinois Country Indians of the 1760s came to imagine a world free of English domination, a world with plenty of room for a French counterweight to the British, a counterweight provided, in large measure, by French goods but also by less material forms of French power.[23] In such a world, Indians, not Europeans, would control Indian destinies.

Morris and King had learned in the summer of 1764 that Pontiac saw no reason to submit to Britain. But Pontiac did promise to consider peace, and he gave permission to Morris and King to advance to Illinois. Morris thought Pontiac a "sensible Savage," with "absolute" command, who "might be made a faithful subject of the King of England and become of Infinite Service." Morris and King proceeded as far as the captured Fort Miami, where French *habitants* were installed. There, on September 9, Miamis refused to permit them to pass to Illinois, sending them instead to the army at Detroit.[24]

After Bradstreet had sent Morris up the Maumee River, he had made for Detroit. Several Ottawa and Ojibwa leaders, including Wasson—the Saginaw Ojibwa who had executed Donald Campbell—met him there and petitioned for peace. "Last year," they claimed, "God forsook us, God has now opened our Eyes. . . . It is God's will also there shall be Peace." They argued that the war stemmed from bad decisions made by the "old Chiefs." They, the "Young Chiefs," now would "break all their old Chiefs," who would "never be allowed to act." Bradstreet, in a departure from protocol, got these Indians to acknowledge themselves to be subjects of the British king, and according to some reports, he demonstrated Pontiac's weakness by destroying a belt that the Ottawa had sent. These Anishinabeg claimed that Pontiac was "heartily ashamed of what had happened, and if he could be forgiven he would be very thankful." In a measure that would further infuriate Johnson and Croghan, who wanted to shut the ethnic French out of the trade, Bradstreet opened that trade, which the Indians desperately needed. Bradstreet granted the Indians peace on their good behavior, and he said that he looked forward to meeting Pontiac, whom he promised to pardon, at Sandusky.[25]

When Bradstreet returned to Sandusky on September 18, 1764, hoping to meet the Ohio delegates and Pontiac, he received Gage's icy letters condemning the peace he had made with the Delawares and Shawnees. Settling matters with Pontiac surely would end the war and restore his reputation, but neither Pontiac nor the Ohioans appeared. Hoping to make things up with his commander in chief, Bradstreet sent what Indians he could to attack the Shawnees and Delawares. A party of Ojibwas went out, but they struck no one. Oneidas under Thomas King refused to go out at all. King and Wadori (or Tannawhonega) would later tell Johnson that the treaty with the Shawnees and Delawares at L'Anse aux Feuilles had prevented further hostilities. King and others also reported to Johnson that Bradstreet had treated them poorly, had "ruled . . . in a more absolute manner" than they had ever experienced before. Still others, including Henry Montour, averred that peace with the Shawnees and Delawares had been their primary objective from the start.[26]

At Sandusky, Bradstreet negotiated another peace, this one with the region's Wyandots. It conformed in most particulars to the agreements he had already made at Detroit. It differed mainly in calling for the Wyandots' removal the following spring from Sandusky to Detroit, farther away from the influence of the French in Illinois and away from the council fires of Pontiac on the Maumee River. Bradstreet believed that while most Indians genuinely wanted peace, the French in Illinois were still telling "such Tales as turn[ed] them most to their Advantage." On October 18, 1764, Bradstreet steered again for Detroit. There his most important acts were to relieve Gladwin, get a sailing vessel into Lake Huron, and send a force that successfully and peacefully reestablished British control over Fort Michilimackinac.[27] These were real achievements, but he received very little official credit for them, in part because he was reviled by his superiors, in part because he left the region in only dubious peace, but mostly because he attacked no one.

His twelve hundred troops had destroyed no Indian villages and had spread no terror. Low on ammunition, Great Lakes Indians had instead used words, for the most part effectively, to defend their villages. Throughout the winter and into the spring of 1765, they continued to use words to keep the British off balance. At Michilimackinac, commanding officer Captain William Howard heard regularly of renewed French-Indian conspiracy, of armies converging on the Great Lakes from Quebec, Crown Point, and the Mississippi, of Indian deception in feigning peace with the English. Great Lakes Indians were still able to negotiate from strength.[28]

Bouquet's Ohio Expedition

The Delawares and Shawnees in the upper Ohio region were in a weaker bargaining position, but they too would rely on words as other powers failed them. In the fall of 1764, amid disease and shortages of ammunition, they faced the approach of a large, well-equipped force under Colonel Henry Bouquet. The plan, as Bouquet, Gage, and Johnson had drawn it, was to bring the war to Delaware and Shawnee towns, to offer a harsh peace, and to attack if they rejected these terms: deliver up for British punishment all men guilty of killing settlers and traders in 1763; compensate surviving traders for their material losses; surrender all colonists still held captive, even those individuals with no wish to repatriate; submit to the authority of the Six Nations; and renounce all claims to lands east of the Ohio. The last condition, Bouquet understood, "would facilitate the Purchase," by the proper authorities, of more lands. Gage, who agreed in every particular, ordered him to "extirpate the Shawnese and Delawares" if the Indians did not come to terms. He could trust Bouquet to follow these orders.[29]

Ohio's Indians carefully monitored Bouquet's movements westward through Pennsylvania. In mid-August, while he was still well to the east of the Allegheny ridge, his men spotted small scouting parties watching his army. Not until mid-September did Bouquet's Royal Highlanders, Royal Americans, and Pennsylvania and Virginia provincials reach the neighborhood of Bushy Run, site of an abandoned outpost and close to the scene of Bouquet's costly "victory" of the previous year. There he received the ghoulish news that a British messenger's head had been discovered, impaled on a stake along the path from Fort Pitt to Detroit. As Bouquet reached Fort Pitt and readied his men for the campaign against the Ohio peoples, he wrote to Gage, "If the Delawares and Shawanese refuse to deliver the Promoters of the War, I shall attack them." To attack meant a one week's march to the principal Delaware and minor Shawnee towns on the Muskingum River, then a longer march to the principal Shawnee towns on the Scioto, before returning to Fort Pitt, hopefully by December.[30] Bouquet was dreaming, and he was too careful a general not to know it. Such objectives were far beyond his force's capacity. As he undertook the actual campaign, which was hardly the unqualified conquest it has too often been deemed, he prudently and quietly revised both the plan of march and the terms of peace, implicitly recognizing that the Ohio Mingos, Shawnees, and Delawares retained considerable power and independence.

Bouquet hated working with Indians; he had far fewer Indian auxiliaries than accompanied Bradstreet, and he failed to recruit adequate interpreters. Mohawk and Tuscarora commandoes raised by Johnson never reached him; news of Bradstreet's abortive peace at L'Anse aux Feuilles had arrested their progress. That peace also confused those few Indians who were with Bouquet; they had, after all, intended more to mediate between the Ohioans and the British than to make war. They attempted to persuade Bouquet that the Delawares and Shawnees genuinely desired peace. When he refused to believe it, they turned the tables on British prejudices and wondered openly if it was vengeance that inspired the colonial campaign. A chastened Bouquet dispatched two expresses, accompanied by only two Indians, to carry messages to Bradstreet at Detroit. Delawares welcomed these messengers into their towns, and, permitting the British-allied Indians to carry the letters forward to Detroit, they asked the two soldiers in the party to carry back to Bouquet the Delawares' own offers to meet with him in peace.[31]

The British force, 1,150 men strong, floated across the Ohio River and clambered up the northwest shore on October 3, to begin the march to the Muskingum Valley. Over the next ten days, Indian scouts closely followed the army but offered it no resistance. On October 15, at the Delaware town of Tuscarawas, Bouquet met the Seneca-Mingo Kiashuta and his delegation; the next day they delivered eighteen captive British subjects. Following suit, the Delaware Custaloga delivered forty-two sticks, which he said represented the prisoners among his people, and the Delaware Tamaqua delivered forty-one sticks. It is noteworthy that the prophet Neolin is listed among the names of the prominent Delawares who promised to "think nothing but good." Somehow, the failure to take Fort Pitt and the penetration of Bouquet's army had not marginalized him. The Delaware leaders asked Bouquet to delay any negotiations until the Shawnee leaders arrived, but Bouquet insisted on treating with each people separately. Over five mid-October days, Delawares and Mingos held a series of meetings with Bouquet. Shawnees arrived on October 20. All left him with hostages to their good behavior until they could all gather for full negotiations in two weeks' time down at the forks of the Muskingum near the Shawnee town of Wakatomika. There the Indians were to surrender all people they had ever taken captive, whether white, black, English, French, man, woman, or child. Additionally, they were to surrender all children born to any woman who had been taken captive.[32]

The troops reached the forks of the Muskingum and made camp on October 25. Cold nights warned of winter as Bouquet revised his objectives. He still might inflict heavy damage on Delawares and Shawnees in the Muskingum region, but a march to the lower Shawnee towns, some eighty-five linear miles away, and a return through hostile country was unthinkable with winter setting in. Food for his troops would soon be a problem; as for forage for his animals, he would have none. He gave up the idea of insisting on the surrender of the "Authors of the War, to be put to death," previously a key ingredient in the recipe for Indian submission. To seize these men, he saw, would engulf him in great "Violence," putting it out of his "Power to bring afterwards the Savages to submit to any terms." To destroy their towns and fields would drive them, by necessity, "to fall upon [British colonial] Frontiers." He had recently learned, moreover, of a trade in "Ammunition" between the lower Shawnees and the French in Illinois. He admitted, in short, that the Indians could not yet be conquered. The point was violently driven home on November 7, when one of his soldiers was found killed in the woods; Bouquet promised revenge on the Delawares if they did not deliver the murderer, but they deftly deflected the blame to a marauding and absent Wyandot, and negotiations continued.[33]

If Bouquet did not conquer the Ohioans, neither did they dictate the terms. With troops already in their villages, Delawares and Mingos were ready to negotiate, and the negotiations did not come cheaply. The Delaware sachem, Tamaqua, sought an immediate opening of the deerskin trade, but Bouquet declared that any trade would have to await a more formal peace with Sir William Johnson. Bouquet insisted that they and the Shawnees give fourteen hostages, to be held until they returned all the captives taken since the opening of the Seven Years' War. The Indians were also to appoint deputies to treat with William Johnson for a formal end to the war in the spring. Delawares and Mingos complied with the demands, naming hostages among their prominent men and delivering almost two hundred captives, most of whom were now full members of their nations. Several were fully orphaned children born of captive women, children with little claim to a place in colonial society. Shawnees bristled at the demands, and they had to be persuaded by the others to comply, which they eventually did on November 13, but only enough to be rid of Bouquet. They delivered forty persons and promised to deliver almost ninety more—even allowing parties of Virginians to accompany them to their towns to collect them. They also sent along six principal men as hostages and negotiators.[34]

Bouquet's collection of "upwards of 200 Captives," who marched with the British army to Fort Pitt in mid-November, was a signal achievement. It demonstrated a degree of British power over Delawares, Mingos, and even Shawnees. Gage was pleased, believing the Shawnees and Delawares, now "reduced and humbled," ready for "proper Management." But "management" was out of the question. Mingos continued to steal horses. Even the redeemed captives presented difficulties. "Many of them part from them with the greatest reluctance," wrote Bouquet, who had to post guards to prevent their escape "to their Savage Masters." For those among the redeemed whose bonds to colonial society were most severely shattered, for children with no remaining ties, there was a grim future ahead. Once back in the east, under the care of the Pennsylvania government, those who were not reunited with families within a mere six weeks of February 21, 1765, were, if boys, to "be bound out to Trades" and, if girls, to be "so disposed of, that they [might] be no further Expense to the Public." One can only speculate about the fate of the children so alienated from their colonial identities that they knew nothing of their family names: Cawachawache, Conongoniony, Joseph (Red Jacket), Simon, Peter, Jemmy, Pompadour, Tawanima, Crooked Legs, Sour Mouth, Kitty, Peggy, Christina, Irena, Phebe, Flat Nose, Betty, Polly, Dorothy's Son, and Dorothy's Daughter. Perhaps some of these children found their suffering families; perhaps others left Indian freedom for colonial servitude. Bouquet was particularly insistent on obtaining the children of women captives, and Johnson concurred: "That mixed Race[,] forgetting their Ancestry on one side[,] are found to be the most Inveterate of any." In a phrase suggesting that Indian depopulation was an intentional benefit for the British, Johnson added that these children would "greatly Augment their numbers."[35]

An advertisement in the *Pennsylvania Gazette* underscored the difficulty some colonial families had in gaining access to these captives. One Ulrick Conrad, settled on the South Branch in Augusta County, Virginia, had lost his wife and five children in 1760 to Indian raiders. He was eventually reunited with his wife and one son, and he knew of the deaths of two of his other children. He also knew that his sixteen-year-old daughter, Barbara, had been delivered to the English, yet he could not locate her as late as September 1765. He offered three pounds and any reasonable charges to the person who delivered her to him.[36]

If some of the captives were double victims, by virtue of their initial captivity and their highly uncertain reentry into colonial society, there were fewer of these among the Shawnees than among the Delawares and Mingos. Two of the forty people whom the Shawnees had delivered as captives to the British quickly escaped. What's more, almost ninety still remained in the Ohio region. Bouquet's firm position that Shawnees return all prisoners as a precondition for peace dissolved as he lost strength at Fort Pitt. Without adequate provisions for the oncoming winter, he had to send much of his force to the provinces. At the same time, the

Mingo hostages stole eight British guns, and all escaped. Bouquet sent the Shawnee, Delaware, and Ohio Caughnawaga hostages off as delegates to treat with Johnson, but once outside the gates of Fort Pitt in the first days of December, these Shawnees, save one, fled westward. The colonel quickly dispatched some Canadian Indians, in the company of David Owens, to demand their return.[37]

Owens, one of Bouquet's interpreters, was a poor choice; trusted by few, he was indeed untrustworthy. A deserter from the colonial service, he had been captured by Indians in 1759. By the spring of 1764, he was among Shawnees, traveling with a party of three men, two women, two Indian children, and one recently captured white child. He later claimed that this was a raiding party—though its composition suggests otherwise. One night, as the party lay sleeping, he killed all the Indians, including the children and his Shawnee wife, and escaped with the white boy to the settlements, spreading the false rumor that nine hundred Indians were mobilizing to descend on the province. Not surprisingly, Owens was not welcome among the Shawnees. When he and his party caught up with the fleeing hostages, a gunfight ensued; a Shawnee fell dead, but Owens and his warriors returned to Fort Pitt empty-handed.[38]

Bouquet's foray into the Ohio Country, which most historians have portrayed as a victory bringing the war to a virtual close, had instead convinced the British that only further negotiation, not force, would restore order. Although Bouquet did gain well over two hundred captives from the Indians, his negotiations with the Ohioans, particularly the Shawnees, had come to little more of a conclusion than had Bradstreet's dealings at L'Anse aux Feuilles. Mingos and Shawnees remained un-cooperative. William Johnson feared that the Delawares were also backing off from peace; he reported that they viewed the agreements with Bouquet and Bradstreet "in so trifling a light" that they would be "easily induced to prosecute the War with Vigour." Johnson heard from Colonel John Campbell at Detroit that supplies of ammunition and arms were coming up the Mississippi and finding their way throughout the Ohio and Great Lakes regions; as a consequence, he believed that the Shawnees and Delawares were still enemies of the British. In fact the Ohioans were neither simple enemies nor friends but were bargaining for their advantage. When a party of Virginia volunteers visited the Shawnee towns seeking the return of the ninety-odd captives still among them, only to become snowbound and bewildered on their return, Shawnees rescued them and brought them safely to Fort Pitt, with but nine of the promised ninety captives. Led by Benevissica, the Shawnees explained to the commander at Fort Pitt that the remaining eighty-odd prisoners would stay in the Shawnee villages, because of, he said, the severity of the winter. He said the Shawnees might return half the remainder in the spring, but the indications are that the Shawnees returned to the British few of the captives who were unwilling to leave them. Shawnees remained beyond British rule; this was even truer of peoples to their west.[39]

The Struggle for Illinois

Pontiac and his allies understood by the end of 1763 that they would not dislodge the British from Forts Detroit and Pitt; keeping the British out of the Illinois Country, bounded by the Mississippi, Ohio, and Wabash Valleys, was another matter. By the Treaty of Paris (1763) Britain had gained France's paper claims to Illinois. Three summers would pass before British efforts to garrison Illinois would stake those claims to the ground, and even then the troops would bring little in the way of British rule. In the meantime, Pontiac and his allies impeded British efforts with rumor and intimidation more than with force; lives, to be sure, were lost in fighting, but battle deaths did less damage to the British struggle for Illinois than did bad talk.

The Indians of the greater Illinois Country went by many names: Illinois, Kaskaskias, Cahokias, Peorias, Metchis, and Tamoranas along the Mississippi and Kaskaskia Rivers south of the Illinois River: also Kickapoos, Mascoutens, Piankashaws, Weas, and Miamis of the Wabash drainage. Some Shawnees were also settled in the region. Perhaps three thousand people inhabited the French villages, a staggering one-third of whom were Panis Indian or African American slaves, a ratio of slave to free then comparable to Virginia's. Among French adults, men predominated by a margin of almost two to one, which contributed to a relatively relaxed attitude toward marriage or cohabitation with Indians, especially among traders and voyageurs. The region stretched from Cahokia (now East St. Louis, Illinois), where the French had built a fort in 1720, to Vincennes (Indiana), where the French had operated a post since 1731. Dominating Illinois militarily was Fort de Chartres, a large stone structure that bristled with twenty cannon, capable of holding three hundred men. The land was fertile, fruitful, and healthful; its French habitants made "passable Wine" and "very good" beer. Despite the presence of French commandants and troops, they retained a high degree of independence from official French control. After 1763, in any case, that control had slipped considerably; the commandant, having exhausted his supply of Indian gifts, wrote in 1765: "I am destitute."[40]

Dominating the Illinois Country economically was remote New Orleans, or, more accurate, the long Mississippi that lay between it and New Orleans. Twice a year, huge convoys—armed to the teeth against, and laden with presents for, Indians along the way—plied the great waters in between. These convoys continued during Pontiac's War. The eight bateaux and one pirogue that departed New Orleans in August 1764 carried 132 people, 19 of them slaves. A convoy of five vessels had preceded it in April, and another "very large Convoy of Goods" followed it in February. Through such means, Illinois's *habitants* imported goods that gave them a high colonial standard of living and presents that maintained their alliance with neighboring Indian peoples. In return, they exported grain, grown prodigiously on long lots stretching out from the rivers. Through such trade, worried the British southern Indian superintendent, John Stuart, the tribes at war with the British were supplied: "This is the Channel, by which Pondiac and his Party have been Enabled to Carry on the War."[41]

Hoping to cut that channel, Major Arthur Loftus arrived in New Orleans on January 23, 1764, and dined with Governor Jean-Jacques-Blaise D'Abbadie the next evening. D'Abbadie shared with Loftus and the other British officers all the letters sent to him from the Illinois Country, whose garrisons he hoped soon to evacuate. It took but one month for Loftus to form a convoy of ten bateaux and two pirogues, carrying as many as 381 people, including 30 women and 17 children. Three hundred and twenty men of the British Twenty-second Regiment were commanded by Loftus; French pilots, interpreters, and guides accompanied them as far north as Pointe Coupée.[42]

By then, Loftus had so cruelly treated his men that thirty to fifty had deserted and seven had died—one man's head had been crushed by a comrade. Four or five days later, at Roche à Davion (modern Fort Adams Landing, Mississippi), the river narrowed, Loftus later recalled; thus a boat was never more than twelve yards from the wooded, flooded shores that spread along both banks, commanded on the east by the great rock after which the place was named. There, early one morning, two advanced pirogues came under heavy fire from Ofogoula, Choctaw, Avoyelle, and Tunica Indians stationed on each bank. Six men died immediately, and seven more were wounded. When the devastated party descended the river to rejoin the convoy, Loftus reversed course and gave up the expedition. D'Abbadie, who became extremely critical of Loftus for his despotic and rigid character, later claimed that the attackers had consisted of only thirty men who could have been dispersed with a few rounds, but Loftus had decided the river was not wide enough for a successful ascent. As he descended the river, Loftus further enraged the Tunicas by firing on one of their villages; and he had to bear the indignity of remaining camped before New Orleans while the governor treated in the capital with the very Indians who had fired upon him. Rumor had it that at least one of the expedition's many deserters had been killed by Quapaws.[43]

Indians had stopped the British occupation of Illinois; European diplomacy made matters even more ticklish. While everyone involved knew of the Treaty of Paris, with its cessions to Britain of both French claims east of the Louisiana Territory and Spanish claims to Florida, rumors were circulating that another vast cession had been made overseas. In November 1762, by a secret provision in the Treaty of Fontainebleau between France and Spain, Spain gained claim to the vast Louisiana Territory. Although it took almost two years, until September 1764, for French authorities in New Orleans to receive official word of Spanish rule, rumor had moved faster, and the governor thought the cession probable as early as April.[44]

Thomas Gage in New York first learned of the rumored cession, "a very extraordinary Piece of good News," in January 1764, but he was still uncertain of it in July. In the meantime, he worried that he did not have the resources to take the Illinois colony by force. The colonial governments were doing little, in his view, to support the mustering of Bradstreet's and Bouquet's forces, despite the task of these two armies to drive "the enemy from their doors." The assemblies, therefore, could not be expected to support an army "at such a distance" as Illinois. Yet the Illinois region is where Pontiac was active in 1764, raising Indians and providing a refuge for those already hostile to Great Britain. Gage credited the Indians with understanding "their political interest extreamly well, ... to have a door open to treat with and trade with another power." "I need not explain the Consequence it will be of to us the Possessing of the Ilinios," Gage wrote Bouquet. "If we get a quiet Possession, and reconcile the Indians of the Ilinois to us, everything below will by their means soon be quieted." Archibald Robertson had been more direct earlier in the year: "The possession of these posts in a great measure cuts off all communication between the french [in New Orleans] and the Indian Nations living in the vast Countrys water'd by the [Wabash, Ohio, and Illinois Rivers]. The Indians finding themselves inclosed, will be more intimidated . . . and sooner reduced to reason."[45]

The Indians understood all this. Wea and Piankashaw diplomats hurried to seek French assistance in March, paving the way for a delegation led by Pontiac. They attempted to deliver war belts and two English scalps, but when these were spurned by the embarrassed Commandant de Neyon, the warriors simply left them in the officer's hall. News of the repulse of Loftus's large army reached Illinois with the arrival of Pontiac in mid-April 1764 and threw de Neyon's Indian diplomacy into further confusion: "[Pontiac] has succeeded in an hour in destroying in the hearts of our domestic Indians what I believed I had inculcated in eight months." Pontiac denounced all efforts at peace with the British, a peace that meant slavery. The French, he said, might stay at peace, but the Indians would continue to organize against the British and would brook no French meddling. Pontiac repeated that he had heard the British insult the French, just as they insulted Ottawas, calling them "hogs." Pontiac even attempted to play on religious differences between Catholics and Protestants. De Neyon was impressed, but he could do nothing but confirm the word that he had sent Pontiac in the fall. The French were indeed at peace with the English; the French and the English in Illinois were now as one people. Pontiac and his allies thought they could prevent the British from gaining ground in the interior.[46]

Indian diplomats were busy in Illinois that spring. Headmen from the Miamis, Kickapoos, Mascoutens, Weas, Piankashaws, Shawnees, Potawatomis, Ottawas, and others visited the French posts, demanding gifts and assistance; they sent war belts southward along the Mississippi, where they succeeded in influencing the Quapaws of Arkansas. When de Neyon happily retired from the Illinois region on June 15, he was succeeded as commandant by Louis St. Ange de Bellerive (St. Ange), previously commander of Vincennes. St. Ange obliged visiting Indians from north-central Illinois and Indiana with "a little powder" because of their "sad condition." But whenever he spoke of peace with the British, "they replied that they preferred dying." Pontiac did not move the French commanders, but he had succeeded in bringing over to his cause "all the Illinois nation." Even after he left the region on July 1, Pontiac kept his gaze fixed on it, sending a huge, six-foot-long war belt that displayed all the Indian nations that were "in his interest." He and the other "movers of the conspiracy," St. Ange wrote in November, were expanding their alliances, "working continually to interest all the most distant nations." St. Ange felt that they would "succeed very perfectly." In New Orleans, the governor became convinced that Pontiac was "the firebrand of all the nations" and it was he who excited them against the British.[47] Illinois, even more than Detroit, made Pontiac's reputation with the Europeans.

Indian parties and French officials kept the British abreast of events in Illinois over the spring and summer of 1764. In early June, "a small Party of Potawatomies" gave Gladwin at Detroit a generally accurate report of Pontiac's meeting with de Neyon, though it differed from French accounts in rendering de Neyon as more hostile to Pontiac and the Illinois Indians as less enthusiastic in their support for him. Throughout July, as Bradstreet's and Bouquet's armies made their preparations in the northeast, Gage hoped these forces might even take Illinois, but his confidence was shaken by rumors that the French were arming the Indians, and the general grew increasingly concerned about the "despotick" character and influence of the "Rascal" Pontiac, the conspirator "at the Bottom of the whole." Pontiac, wrote Gage, "should be gained to our Interest, or knocked in the head, He has great Abilities, but his Savage Cruelty destroys the regard we Should otherwise have for him."[48]

Rumors and misinformation drifted down the Mississippi to New Orleans, where British officers continued to visit the French in the hope of mounting another expedition northward. In New Orleans, rumors greatly exaggerated the British losses of 1763: fifteen hundred British troops had been defeated at Niagara; the Wilkins expedition, defeated in fact by storm on Lake Erie, had lost twenty-two bateaux and all hands had been massacred on shore. Combined with accurate word of the hostility of the Illinois Indians and the real experience of the defeat of Loftus, the rumors inhibited British negotiations with the Mississippi Valley's Indians. Loftus tried to organize a second ascent but never effected it. Lieutenant Philip Pittman sought in June and again in August to ascend the river with a French convoy, but he, too, never made the trip. He did, however, meet with a delegation of Tunica Indians, the same peoples who had attacked Loftus and who had been bombarded on Loftus's return. Pittman persuaded them to agree to a peace, on the condition that the English "not be ingrates" and give them "something." Deploying rumors of his own, Pittman alienated the French governor. In August, the lieutenant assembled voyageurs in New Orleans and told them of the cession of Louisiana to Spain, giving "out as a fact . . . a popular rumor. . . which was foreign to his purpose." D'Abbadie protested Pittman's actions to Gage, but Gage approved of them as "very necessary" for the interests of the British. As Gage understood it, the French would lose influence with the Indians who came to believe in the intended cession.[49]

Words and gifts moved peoples as much as did ships and guns, and by the end of 1764 the British had yet to deploy any of these forces successfully in the Illinois Country, where Pontiac retained the advantage. The Quapaws of Arkansas still blocked the British ascent of the Mississippi. Great Britain's Major Robert Farmar, looking forward to an expedition to Illinois the following year, decided he would have to do far more to prepare the ground with "soothing and cajoling methods occasionally intermixed with threats, and softened by presents, than with any force of Arms." He understood that his enemy lay in the sentiments and "prejudices" of those along the river. What he failed to see was that those prejudices lay partly in an accurate Indian reading of British expectations. Even as Farmar hoped to please his "Master," independence of British mastery lay at the heart of the Indians' cause.[50]

The British had opened the campaign of 1764 intending to punish Ottawas, Ojibwas, Shawnees, Mingos, and Delawares. White flags would be lowered and red flags raised in Illinois. Pontiac and other leaders would be captured and punished, towns burned, warriors brought to their knees, and captives all redeemed. The British achieved only the last point, and that in limited measure, with intentions as punitive as they were humanitarian. The rest of the goals disappeared in the face of the reality that Great Britain was not yet strong enough to dominate the Indians of the interior. As the mastery of Indians eluded the empire, Pontiac's War confronted it with the fundamental question of the Native Americans' status.

CHAPTER SIX

Mobs, Germs, and the
Status of American Indians

Waging Pontiac's War, Indians directly challenged the presence in their homelands of a new imperial administration that had proven, through repeated insults, that it sought nothing less than lordship. That much is both obvious and well established in the literature. What is less obvious, and less studied, is that the war confronted colonials and their imperial officials with the issue of the status of Indians in the emerging British Empire. To the degree that the issue has been examined, backcountry settlers wishing only to drive Indians out appear to have squared off against imperial administrators willing to incorporate them (in relationships of power that would be reciprocal, if asymmetrical) into the empire; such distinctions between farmers and officials grow largely out of the administrative record, which masks both a vast imperial failure of imagination and a much darker reality. Though there were debates and even violent confrontations over Indian policy, settlers and authorities shared in the conviction of British superiority and in the expectation that Indians would, before long, surrender their homelands to British subjects who were racially white.

A powerful recent interpretation has argued, as one of its many subordinate themes, that as the British occupied the western garrisons in 1760, they sought to make British "subjects" of the Indians, and indeed some officers and agents unsystematically applied the word to the western Indians.[1] But they did not do so often, and in their more careful writings and official pronouncements they recoiled from the usage, and for good reason, by their lights. The word *subject*, by 1760, presented Britons with a dilemma. To be a British subject was, even then, to have a claim to a lofty status. After two seventeenth-century English revolutions and after the securing of the Protestant succession in the early eighteenth century, the word *subject* had become invested with new meanings, having less to do with "subjection" to a monarch than with the Protestant monarch's responsibilities to subjects whom history had invested with liberties. A highly charged word it was, and very few officers, administrators, or agents applied it after midcentury to Native Americans, whom Britons, including British colonists, deemed to lack whiteness, Protestantism, and the capacities for constitutional liberty. Those who did call Indians subjects spoke a dead language.[2]

The Indians' uncertain status emerged, especially in Pennsylvania but also in the officer corps, as a divisive issue among those who would and could call themselves British subjects. The issue was not, as it is too often portrayed, a matter of contention between officers supporting a benevolent rule of law that might protect Indians and unruly backcountry Indian killers bent on doing what killers do best. Official policy, highly confused though it was, tended to place Indians far beyond the rule of law, and it intended, even in the long run, to keep them there by pushing them away from any civil jurisdiction in the colonies.

There is a sense in much of the literature, even in recent material, that the period saw an increasingly accommodating, though unsuccessful, attempt by the imperial administration to restrain the land-hungry settlers. Yet Pontiac's War first broke out in regions where land was not an immediate issue and where British and colonial officials, far more than frontier folk, brought it on. During the war, moreover, these officers urged, ordered, and approved the indiscriminate slaughter of Indians. As they tried to imagine a world without Indian warfare, fixed boundaries separating colonists from Indians became their dream. Backcountry settlers, for their part, were increasingly hostile to Indians, but their hostility—indeed, the racism they shared with their imperial governors—was not simply "riot and murder." Although hundreds were cruel and cowardly, striking at unarmed Indian innocents, others showed remarkable

Sir William Johnson (1715–74), by John Wollaston (working 1736–67), oil on canvas, ca. 1751. Albany Institute of History and Art, Gift of Laura Munsell Tremaine. Johnson would gain his title only several years after this painting was done, yet even here he is the colonial gentleman on the move.

courage and organization as they deployed controlled, even legalistic, violence not against Indians but against the imperial army itself. The issue was Indian policy.[3]

Subjects, Sovereigns, and Tribes

The British colonial administration seated in offices along a London street named Whitehall was not known for frequent and close consideration of American Indian affairs. Since midcentury the metropolitan government had been reviewing, if only in a desultory manner, proposals for organizing the empire, and many of those proposals discussed Indians. For years dust had gathered on plans to draw a boundary between aggressive colonial settlers, viewed by the Board of Trade as disturbers of the peace, and those Indian peoples who still exercised considerable independence. The capitulation of Montreal in 1760, to be sure, had guaranteed the formerly French-allied Indians the possession of their lands against encroachment, as had, many thought, the Delawares' Treaty of Easton of 1758. But the final peace with France and the outbreak of Pontiac's War in 1763 had made it clear that more regulation was needed, and both events encouraged the British Board of Trade to shift from casual review to fast action. The chief result was the Royal Proclamation of 1763, which, although best known for drawing a line down the crest of the Appalachians in order to hem in colonial settlement, also placed Indians outside the status of "subject" yet under the king's "protection." For Native Americans, the protection confirmed no fundamental, or even British, rights or liberties; and it effectively denied native sovereignty. King George III made his proclamation on October 7, 1763; three days later, printed copies were sent to America.[4]

The proclamation promised to regulate trade with Indians, ban settlement west of a boundary line, and forbid the purchase of any Indian land without Crown approval through its Indian superintendents. The boundary, which had to be redrawn several times in the next several years, lay at the headwaters of the rivers flowing into the Atlantic, save in the few areas beyond that watershed where the Crown already recognized colonial settlements. All persons already settled on the vast lands the Crown now reserved for the Indians were ordered "forthwith to remove themselves." General Thomas Gage, assuming the post of commander in chief in North America, thought it "a salutary measure and if fallen upon some years ago would have prevented the Grievances" that brought on the war. But others were not so sanguine. Land speculators were horrified at the effects the proclamation would have on their claims to the west. Squatters may have worried about the legal security of their stakes, but since they had been violating official wishes in any case, they would go right on squatting once peace was restored. Enemy Indians, who had heard such promises before, were unimpressed, and the proclamation certainly did not acknowledge the justice of their war. Most notable is that even the king diminished the importance of the document, conceding that it was a temporary measure.[5]

The Royal Proclamation of 1763, though temporary and ineffective, is a landmark in North American history. Scholars will continue to debate its role in fostering a rebellious spirit in the colonies, but whatever its importance for the American Revolution, it is of high importance for American Indian history and law. John Marshall, the great jurist who would render several of the most important legal decisions in American Indian history, pointed directly to the proclamation as he defined the peculiar status of Indian peoples within the United States. Similarly, though generally with opposite results (until quite recently), Canadian authorities would look to the proclamation when attempting to define the status of Canada's First Nations.[6]

The proclamation also remains a testament to the emerging imperial understanding of the Indians' constitutional status. Unlike the former French subjects in the newly conquered regions, Indians would be treated as separate peoples, not as newly minted subjects of the king. The famous borderline protecting Indians from expansion unsanctioned by the Crown also sets them apart from His Majesty's people. At least twice the proclamation distinguishes clearly between the king's "loving subjects" and Indians who live in "such Parts of Our Dominions and Territories as, not having been ceded to, or purchased by Us, are reserved to them." In drawing up the proclamation, the Board of Trade sought to regulate relations between the British and the Indian "Tribes and Nations" that were now "under His Majesty's immediate protection." The proclamation itself expressly concerned "the several Nations or Tribes with whom [the British were] connected, and who live[d] under [British] Protection." It reserved all Indian lands west of the line for "the use of the said Indians," under the Crown's "Sovereignty, Protection, and Dominion." It promoted the idea, which remains a key feature of American Indian law, that Indian nations and tribes existed as separate entities within the British dominion. Though distinct nations, the tribes were under the king's protection; he was sovereign.[7]

The proclamation had reached America by December, and in the winter months that followed, as the army and the Indian department prepared for a summer campaign, Sir William Johnson stressed the importance of treating Indian nations as entities unto themselves, distinct both from British subjects and from one another. "Whenever it may happen that peace is agreed upon," he wrote, "it will be Expedient to treat with each Nation separately . . . for could they arrive at a perfect union, they must prove very dangerous Neighbours." Gage was in complete agreement, as was Colonel Henry Bouquet. When Bouquet marched into the middle of Delaware country in 1764 to pacify the Delawares, Shawnees, and Mingos, he insisted that each of the "Tribes" send "Deputies" to Johnson. The empire was groping toward the position that Indian nations and tribes, though under the sovereignty of the Crown, had a status apart. Their relations with British subjects, as well as with one another, were ideally to be managed by Crown officials. Pontiac's War was proving the dangers of a "perfect union" among them. As Johnson put it a little too simply: "As long as they Quarrell with one another, we shall be well with them all. And when they are all at Peace, It's the Signal for us to have a good Look out."[8]

In 1764, Whitehall sought further to bring order to the "present vague and uncertain administration" of Indian affairs by drafting a governing plan. Most of the "Plan for the Future Management of Indian Affairs" considers the regulation of trade, but it also struggles to fix Indians clearly within the empire. Curiously, nowhere in the draft are Indian groups referred to as "nations," as they had been in the proclamation and as was one common usage. Instead, the draft prefers the less civil term *tribe*. The draft, like the proclamation, does not call Indians "subjects." Instead, it plainly distinguishes the tribes from British subjects, while placing them plainly "under the Protection of His Majesty" and within "the British Dominions in North America."[9]

Bringing Indians within the realm, some went further and called the Indians subjects outright, a term that had earlier, in the seventeenth century and early eighteenth, been frequently applied to Indians in the king's claimed realm. As late as 1760, Indian agent George Croghan had told Detroit's Indians that they should attack only one Indian people, the

Cherokees, as all other Indian nations had become "the subjects of Great Britain." But elsewhere in the same meetings, Croghan isolated His Majesty's subjects from Indians, whom he called upon to be "faithful allies." John Bradstreet, in the treaties he made with the Detroit-area Indians in September 1764, demanded that the Indians acknowledge themselves as "Subjects and Children" of the king. When Indians hesitated and referred to the English as "brothers," Bradstreet insisted on his usage, and Wabbicommicot of the Mississaugas acknowledged that his people were "Subjects and Children of the King of England, which they should always in the future call themselves." Lieutenant Thomas Morris, returning from his difficult meetings with Pontiac on the Maumee River at the same time, thought that Pontiac could become "a faithful subject of the King of England." The next year, Lieutenant Colonel John Campbell, also treating at Detroit, promised the St. Joseph River Potawatomis, "As soon as you become true, and faithful Subjects to his Britannic Majesty, your Father here will always be ready to hear your complaints, and redress your grievances."[10] The word *subject*, a once popular song sung out of tune with the times, could still be found on British lips.

Exactly how these officers and the Indians with whom they treated understood the term *subject* is difficult to know; only Croghan made a career out of Indian diplomacy, and in his extensive dealings with Indians he did not again call them "subjects." By the 1760s, British political thought and constitutional practice had removed much of the British subject's subjection—so much so that Britons found the term *subject* to have outgrown its fit with Indians. They had less problem clothing conquered Europeans, even North American Catholics, with the status. In the conquest of Canada and in the efforts to take over the Illinois territory, the British administrators made it clear that the French inhabitants would "become subjects of His Majesty" and would "enjoy the same rights and privileges, the same security for their persons and effects, and the liberty of trade, as the old subjects of their King." By 1766, French Catholics were admitted to jury service and to the bar, liberties their Catholic counterparts in Britain and Ireland did not enjoy. No Briton on either side of the Atlantic contemplated such rapid arrangements for Indians. They were to be allies under the king's protection and within the king's dominion, or they would be enemies. Beyond that, their status was shaky.[11]

At the other extreme from those few who would anachronistically call

Indians "British subjects" were those who would impose a more drastic kind of subjection, obliterating the Indians as peoples and reducing those few who remained alive to the marginal status of alien vagabonds without social or civil legitimacy, individuals fit for slavery. General Amherst, although powerless to realize the kind of complete domination over scattered individuals he envisioned, fruitlessly advanced that position as he grew infuriated by the war.[12]

Sir William Johnson, superintendent of the northern Indian department, was never happy with Amherst's policies, but he had to be careful about what he said to and about the general before Amherst's departure in December 1763. About Bradstreet's insistence in 1764 that Indians adopt the term *subject* Sir William was free to wax apoplectic. He denounced the usage in several letters to Thomas Gage and to the Board of Trade. "The very word would have startled them," he explained. The "very Idea of Subjection" would have filled them "with horror." Its meaning was "repugnant to their Principles": "No Nation of Indians have any word which can express, or convey, the Idea of Subjection." He implied that Bradstreet had inserted the word into the treaty without adequately conveying its meaning to the Indians and that, as Indians grew aware of this, they became "alarmed at the specious Words of Subjection and Dominion."[13] Sir William perhaps accurately captured the Indians' refusal to concede British rule, but he had other concerns, too. If Indians were subjects, would they suffer trials? Were they to be "governed by the laws liable to the punishments for high Treason, Murder, Robbery and the pains and penaltys on actions for property on Debt"? These suggestions were simply "impossible" for Indians, who, a disingenuous Johnson added, had "no ties amongst themselves but inclination." And then, too, were they to have access to courts? The Catholic inhabitants of Sir William's native Ireland, being British subjects, had limited legal access, which could occasionally trouble authorities. And in America, Sir William read—but did not support—petitions from Long Island Indians willing to "do the Duty bear the Burthen and be entitled to the Privileges and Rights of faithful Subjects," precisely because they hoped to secure their lands by a "Title as [might] be maintained in the King's Courts of Law."[14]

Bradstreet's loose use of the term *subject* hit Sir William in a sore spot, because the Board of Trade was just then in the process of attempting to establish legal procedures for certain cases involving Indians. Earlier in the year, Johnson's southern counterpart, John Stuart, had suggested to the board that Indians gain a limited access to colonial courts, access of the sort, perhaps, enjoyed by British women and Catholics: their testimony should be admitted. The Board of Trade listened to Stuart and incorporated his suggestion into its "Plan for the Future Management of Indian Affairs, 1764." Article 16 of that draft would have ordered that "the evidence of Indians . . . be admitted" in criminal cases both in colonial courts and in special courts that the plan would have established. These new courts would also hear civil cases. Again, the article is consistent with the rest of the plan in that it distinguishes Indians from subjects: if the testimony was proved false, Indians would suffer the "same Pains and Penalties . . . as his Majesty's Subjects." The board did not in Article 16 explicitly propose making "subjects" of Indians, and it was far from extending English law over the tribes, but some feared it might be heading in that direction.[15]

After the board sent that plan to the colonies for comment, Georgia's Royal governor and later loyalist James Wright jumped on the proposal to admit Indian testimony in colonial courts, saying it would lead to the "very worst Consequences": "Surely no man who knows what Indians are, would ever think of admitting their Evidence as Legal, in Courts of Justice, in any Case either Civil or Criminal." Johnson, more circumspect, concurred in part; he suggested that the proposed article be whittled to a very narrow reed: only the testimony of Indian Christians, whose faith and church attendance had been certified by a missionary, "might be taken," and then only in the special courts. Indians capable of understanding the nature of the oath or the penalties for perjury, he observed, were so "few in number, . . . [that] this Article should not extend to capital offences or [Colonial] Courts of Justice, unless . . . under great restrictions."[16]

The Board of Trade's draft would have empowered superintendents and their commissaries to act as justices of the peace in the special courts. In their respective districts the superintendents would have the authority summarily to adjudicate civil cases disputing less than ten pounds in cases involving traders, even when Indians were also involved. There were no provisions for appeal, effectively depriving colonial courts jurisdiction in such cases. Johnson supported this proposal. Superintendents, he thought, should also have the power to try cases "relative to claims or titles" to land. He felt that perhaps they should do so in collaboration with "the Governor or some other person of the Province concerned" but that they should have the power to settle such matters "in a summary way," as

WAR UNDER HEAVEN

these cases could not "speedily or satisfactorily be determined at Common Law, . . . frequently turning in favour of the White people." Any appeal should bypass the common-law courts and go to the "King in Council, or otherwise." In the event, the Plan of 1764 never became law, and it never extended its limited legal access to Indians.

If British officials had seen Indians as legal subjects in the 1760s, then the captured allies of Pontiac might have been legally tried for treason. This was considered, in fact, for Euro-American men who were alleged to have supported Indian militants. In 1764, Bouquet's expedition separately seized the brothers Gershom and Levy Hicks "on the Strongest suspicion that they came with Evil Intentions." Gershom had appeared at the gates of Fort Pitt on April 14, 1764, claiming to have escaped from Indians. The garrison believed—on weak evidence—that he had a "known Attachment to Indian life," that he was a spy whose mission was to gather information about the fort. Captain William Grant, then commanding at Fort Pitt, ordered Gershom interrogated, a confession was "extorted from him by threats of Death," and he was even marched under arms to the place of his hanging. Gage, fully aware of the mode of interrogation, which was dutifully recorded, at first suggested that he be tried by a general "Court Martial for a Spy." And if he did turn out to be a spy, he was to be hanged. But months later, after Gershom's brother, Levy, had also been taken and the two had languished together in irons at Fort Pitt, Gage reversed his decision. For one thing, he felt the evidence of their being spies was too slim, and the testimony under threats of death too tainted, for the army to render a judgment. More important, the military could hang a spy in time of war, but "Rebels in Arms" were tried by the civil courts. As rebels, then, the brothers Hicks were sent to Pennsylvania's Cumberland County jail to await trial. The hearty correspondence discussing these "white" men has no counterpart for captured western Indians, for the brothers Hicks were taken to be British subjects, while captive Indians were not subjects, not rebels, and not white. Britons might in the 1760s bring a "domestic" Indian to trial for an isolated crime against British settlers; but to bring a Muskingum Valley Delaware or a Maumee Valley Ottawa to trial for fighting a war was unthinkable.[17]

Another case starkly displays the assumption that to be a British subject was, in the 1760s, to be "white." Shortly after William Johnson had sent fourteen Delawares, captured not by the British but by Oneidas, to jail in New York in 1764, he sent to Albany three more prisoners, recently surrendered to him by the Genesee Senecas. One, "Roger," was a Delaware. A second, known variously as the "Negro," the "Indian Negro," "Tony," or "Sam Tony," had "fled many years ago" from a southern colony and then lived in a polyglot town on the Susquehanna River, where he spread "dangerous, and Treasonable" rumors that alienated Indian "Affections from the English." The third, John Eice (or Eyce), was a "German captured in Virginia years ago"; he likewise was reported to have done the British "much harm." The three were in the Albany jail in May 1764, but Johnson feared that they might be released "for want of white Evidences" against them. Gage agreed that the colonial courts would not proceed adequately against the men, and he reminded Johnson that the "Negro and the Indian" might "easily be disposed of"—easily and profitably, for they could go to the West Indies as slaves. Eice was another matter. Gage could not summarily dispose of the German. Had Eice been either a deserter from colonial forces or the spy of a European power, he might have been tried by "a General Court Martial": "I think he would sooner meet with the Punishment which Such a Traitor Deserves, from a Military than a Civil Court." Instead, he was a white captive of Indians, taken as a "Young Lad," so a military court was out of the question.[18] "Roger" simply disappears from Johnson's and Gage's papers. Eice and Tony languished in the Albany jail throughout the next year—Johnson's worries about the lack of "white Evidences" notwithstanding. In July 1765, the two were sent from Albany to New York. Noting their arrival in the city, Gage planned to send the "Negro" to the West Indies. He wished that fate for Eice as well, but in this German's case he decided to seek the concurrence of the civil authority, so he asked New York's lieutenant governor, Cadwallader Colden, to settle the matter. Colden applauded Gage's decision to sell off Tony, and he gave Gage permission summarily to dispense with Eice by sending him in servitude to British Pensacola or to the Caribbean.[19] From Eice's point of view, this was a grim outcome. Eice, not only a renegade but a "German" to boot, did not get the trial by jury that he should have been able expect as a British subject. Yet even this judicial miscarriage, by the racist standards of the day, demonstrates that Eice, as a white Indian, stood apart from his two fellow Indians, Roger and Tony. More thought and direct civil intervention went into his disposal. Had there been "white Evidences" against him, Eice would have stood trial; without that evidence, the authorities considered the law, bent it to their satisfaction, and shipped him off to misery. Gage, Johnson, and

Colden needed no such creativity in the horror they devised for Tony. And the unanswered question remains: What did they devise for Roger?

Imperial authorities came to a rough conclusion regarding the status of most of the Indian nations now at war with Great Britain. When at peace, they were separate peoples inhabiting tracts of lands "secured to them under the Sovereignty Protection and Dominion of His Majesty, . . . living in Friendship with his Majesty's Subjects in America" but not subjects themselves. They possessed "the highest notions of Liberty of any people on Earth," and they retained a violable independence over their internal affairs. Sir William expressed the hope that the proclamation, once understood by the Indians, would "induce them" to a conviction that His Majesty was "well disposed to favor and protect them." "Allies and Friends," outside the status of subject yet tied to Great Britain by "Interest," Indians stood within the king's realm as protected, semi-autonomous peoples, at least for the present.[20]

The imperial authorities never expected their arrangements with Indians to last: eventually a fuller domination would follow. Sir William understood that the arrangements would end when the empire became "formidable throughout the country." The officials did not bestow the idea of full sovereignty upon Indian nations—they certainly did not treat them as they would European nation-states; the general disregard of Indian peoples at formal treaties in Europe underscores the point, and Indian treaties themselves never held much status in London, its suburbs, or its European counterparts. Nations these may have been, but they were, to use a phrase that would not have startled a man like Sir William, dependent nations. After 1763, Indians east of the Mississippi were seen as dependent on Great Britain for protection and trade. Indians regularly appeared in the record as "depending on" a colony, the Crown, or a European enemy. Britain already claimed full sovereignty; dependence was the claim's road to fulfillment.[21]

Domestic Nations, Dependent Nations

Those Britons who closely considered Indian matters in the American northeast gave particular attention to the Six Nations League of Iroquois, with whom the colonies were connected by the Covenant Chain. Johnson, Colden, and others put literal stake in the notion that the Iroquois, through their legendary conquests of lands and peoples to the West, held legitimate title as far as Kentucky and Illinois. The notion that western Indians such as the Potawatomis, Ottawas, Miamis, Wyandots, or Illinois had accepted the domination of the Six Nations and had become bound by the Covenant Chain did not meet with wide acceptance, though it was popular in New York (where it was the basis for the colony's western territorial claims). The western Indians themselves would have found it preposterous, and other colonies gave it little credence. But most colonial officials accepted the notion of Iroquois dominion when it came to the Delawares and Shawnees. These nations no longer, according to the standard argument, stood on a par with other Indian nations. The Shawnees and Delawares—according to a legal fiction accepted by the British Indian department, the British army, and the colonial governors—were indeed subjects, but not British ones. Rather, they had subjected themselves to the Six Nations at an undetermined time in the past.[22]

Delawares had come under heavy Iroquois League influence in the early eighteenth century, and they gained the status of fictive "women," a term that did less to explain their place in the so-called Covenant Chain than to provide a point of debate. The Delawares-as-women held an uneasy position, because the status became a feature of their relations with the British, who had vastly different concepts of womanhood. Women, it is certain, could exercise considerable political influence among both Algonquian and Iroquoian peoples in the mid-eighteenth century, yet European notions of a more dependent womanhood were coming into diplomatic play. In April 1757 in Montreal, the French governor had met with Iroquois Indians from the reserve mission town of La Presentation in a council that "ended with the presentation of wampum belts to the council women," whose "gravity . . . deserves to be noted." The French colonel Louis-Antoine de Bougainville decided that council women "had the same standing among the Indians that matrons formerly had among the Gauls and Germans." On the basis of such evidence, some have suggested that, as designated women, Delawares were to have a special role in the Susquehanna Valley. Much as women might decide the fate of strangers entering a village, the Delawares could claim that the status entitled them to mediate relations between the Iroquoian Six Nations League and other migrants to the valley, especially other Algonquian speakers. The designation "women," in short, did not clearly mean subjection. Yet in council deliberations before Europeans, both Delawares and members of the Iroquois League understood European notions of

WAR UNDER HEAVEN

womanhood, and in those settings the Iroquois creatively deployed degrading notions of their own. Bougainville had news from Niagara in 1757 that French-allied Delawares openly objected to figuratively dressing at council in the *machicoté*, the "piece of cloth" that women wore. Bougainville saw the *machicoté* as "degrading them from their status as men." And in that council, the Delawares declared they would no longer wear it, suggesting that the Six Nations, still at peace, should wear it instead. The Six Nations rejected it as too "filthy." If there is ambiguity in the Indian understandings of Delaware womanhood, European understandings of it are clear: it was a mark of their status as dependent subjects under Iroquois League dominion.[23] As women, Delawares held what was for the British the perfect designation of dependency: here, if ever there was one, was a *domestic*, dependent nation in the offing.

As the English idea of womanhood infected the Delawares' body politic, that idea met with uneven, convulsive, and, eventually, feverish rejection. Ohio Delawares had begun to fight in 1755; Susquehanna Valley Delawares joined them the next year, and Pennsylvania's lieutenant governor declared them to be "Enemies, Rebels, and Traitors" for having broken the commands not of the British but of "the Six Nations," to whom they owed "Obedience and Subjection." The same logic allowed Governor John Penn to declare the Shawnees and Delawares "Enemies, Rebels and Traitors" in 1764. Sir William Johnson thought the Delawares and Shawnees should be harshly punished. Their attempt to throw off the Six Nations was rebellion and, simultaneously, an attempt to throw off Britain. Genesee Senecas had committed the same treason against the Six Nations, which permitted Sir William to include them once in his suggestion that they, along with Delawares and Shawnees, should be tortured when captured. But he would later see advantages in offering mercies to Genesees—who were, after all, members of the Six Nations—that he would not extend to the others. When he met in 1765 with Delawares from the Ohio as well as the Susquehanna to confirm the peace made by Bouquet the previous fall, he included in the resulting treaty an acknowledgment of their part in the Covenant Chain, which gave the Six Nations explicit authority over their lands. Sir William, representing Great Britain, thought Delawares and Shawnees were properly subject to the Six Nations. Gage, considering Sir William's intelligence, ordered his subordinates to treat with Delawares and Shawnees, and to gain "satisfaction" from them, but not to treat for lands.[24]

Far more common than fictive womanhood was fictive childhood, and here the tradition in North America reached far back, having special power and meaning among the seventeenth- and early-eighteenth-century Indian allies of France. Throughout most of the colonial history of the Northeast, British officers had been generally unable to gain the title of "father" and had instead been called "brother." At several of the treaties made during and at the close of Pontiac's War, the British managed to gain the title "father," but as they did so, the Indians made it clear that certain obligations were fixed to the role. The father had to "take Care of them," "be tender to" them, and, most important, "make up the differences subsisting between them" and other Indian allies of Britain—or as another put it, to "restore tranquility among all Nations, that your Children unborn may enjoy the blessings of a lasting Peace." This role of the mediating father is one the British would agree to adopt, even as they would push forward a policy of divide and rule.[25]

The household metaphors would have a long future. Though no one speaks seriously today of the federal government as the Great Father to his Indian children, the domestic metaphor is embedded in law. In 1831 and 1832, when the U.S. Supreme Court would, in the Cherokee cases (*Cherokee Nation v. State of Georgia* and *Worcester v. Georgia*), attempt to define the legal standing of Indian nations in the United States, Chief Justice John Marshall called Indian tribes within the territory of the United States "domestic, dependent nations." He found it necessary to modify *dependent nations* with the word *domestic*—a curious usage that still puzzles jurists—because in his day, as in the mid-eighteenth century, "dependent nations" did not necessarily mean "domestic nations." In 1763, not all dependent nations were "domestic," "domesticated," or "domiciled," though all might be within the king's dominion. British officials could distinguish between, on the one hand, Indians who—while under British sovereignty and dependent on trade—were still, somehow, to be treated as allies and, on the other hand, those who were under and "reconciled to" colonial authority, regardless of whatever autonomy they might have had within the surrounded borders of their confined hamlets. Among the former were the Six Nations, who had their own dependents, the Delawares and the Shawnees. Most of those Anishinabeg and others attacking the British garrisons in 1763 were also such dependent nations, however illogical that may seem. Among the "domestic," "domiciled," or "settlement" Indians were much smaller groups scattered from the suburbs of Savannah, Georgia, to those of Montreal and Quebec, Canada. Those groups who lived "near the Sea" in the colonies from the Chesapeake through New England no longer had, as far as Sir William Johnson was concerned, any "importance to his Majesty's interest." They were generally too weak to be taken seriously by colonial authorities, as Sir William made clear when he said he would not concern himself in land disputes on behalf of any such domestic tribes that were not "either by themselves [or through their] connections capable of resenting" mistreatment. In other words, the Crown's Indian department would secure justice only for the strong.[26]

Most "domestic" Indians' efforts against land fraud would meet with little assistance from the Indian department, and their status declined for many years. Johnson and Gage both decided that the Kahnawakes, Lorette Wendots, and other Indians settled near French towns on the St. Lawrence had no claims to the land that the British were required to respect, since they had only been "invited to *Canada*" and had not been the "original" proprietors. The extreme poverty of settlement Indians in the colonies from New England to the southern regions alarmed the still "free Indians" who saw themselves approaching the edge of such degradation. Mohawk women, opposing in council a vast land swindle in the spring of 1763, declared to the British that "they would keep their Land, and did not chuse to part with the same to be reduced to make Brooms." They knew where such impoverishment could lead; for one Albany Indian, "Margrett Van Cealen," it had led to slavery. In 1763, she legally signed away her own person and all her posterity to cover her debts. If it was true, as Thomas Augustine Arne had taught Britons to sing it in 1740, that "Britons never never shall be slaves," then these domestic Indians, though under the protection of the colonies, were no more British subjects than were the more distant "dependent" nations.[27]

British officers saw Indians as standing beyond other forms of the pale as well; their correspondence is littered with imaginative methods for killing enemy Indians. Colonel Henry Bouquet sought to use bloodhounds; Captain Simeon Ecuyer, beaver traps and "crow-foot traps . . . pointed enough for their moccasins." The commander in chief ordered several times that there be *"No Prisoners"* (emphasis his) among *any* Indians, an order later repeated by Sir William as he sent his Iroquois allies out against Delawares. The warriors of the Six Nations ignored the order. Soldiers had to obey. Records of Indian warriors captured in action by British troops have yet to come to light—save for one, reported in the *Pennsylvania Gazette.* On August 6, while Bouquet's army succeeded in repelling the two-day assault on his troops at the Battle of Bushy Run, it captured "only one Prisoner, and after a little Examination he received his Quietus."[28]

At Fort Pitt during the first summer of fighting, Captain Ecuyer thought the Delawares should be "exterminated," and he wished he could devise a way to do it at "one single stroke." The story has often been told. Smallpox had broken out in his garrison, and he knew enough about the disease to set up a quarantined hospital "to prevent the spreading of that Distemper." Only the "doctor and the people attending" the sick could go near them, and those were to "be very careful" not to go near any person who had not had the disease. On June 24, 1763, when two Delaware leaders visited him for talks, he gave them as a present two blankets and two handkerchiefs from the hospital. A receipt, initialed by top British brass, notes that the purpose was "to Convey the Smallpox to the Indians." William Trent noted in his journal that the gift was a genuine sign of his and Ecuyer's "regard," and he hoped it would have the "desired effect." Smallpox did break out among the Indians, and though the disease may easily have come to the Delawares and Shawnees through other vectors, it is plain that Indians were well beyond European laws of war, which held, "from old times," that it was "not permissible to kill an enemy by poison."[29]

Given the blunt hostility and loathing for Delawares and other enemy Indians which governors, Indian superintendents, and British officers expressed, it is hardly surprising that the Royal Proclamation's insistence on the protection of Indians, even as a matter of contingency, fell upon deaf ears among the colonials when it was announced in December 1763, particularly in areas that faced the smoking barns and maimed survivors of war. A great many colonists saw little good coming to them in the imperial vision for an orderly westward procession of the frontier, with eastern land barons organizing and profiting from expansion while frontier folk paid stiff rents and suffered heavy blows. They saw hypocrisy and greed in the Indian department's and colonial government's mismanagement of Indian affairs. They knew that imperial officials were no more ready than were they themselves to see the western lands remain in Indian hands forever, and some determined to take vicious local action against Indians in their midst.

Murder, Removal, and Status

One form the action would take was predictable, for it had taken shape before. The *Pennsylvania Gazette* reported in 1756 on the colony of New York's effort to protect its "settlement Indians" from Ulster County and Orange County men enraged by a series of Indian attacks. The settlement Indians were ordered to New York City, where they were offered protection. In early March, however, Samuel Slaughter, a colonist at the head of "a Party of armed Men," murdered four men, three women, and two children among the protected Indians. Fearing that such murders would alienate New York's Indian allies, the government issued a proclamation calling for Slaughter's arrest and ordering colonial officials to give assistance to settlement Indians seeking protection from His Majesty's subjects. In the neighboring colony of Pennsylvania the next month, Edward Shippen wrote to the governor that Indians allied to the British, including the steadfast mediator John Shickellamy, had huddled for safety in McKee's Fort for fear of being murdered by settlers.[30] Throughout the Seven Years' War, hundreds of domestic Indians had lived uneasily within the bounds of the growing colony. Some of these lived as Moravian Christians in communities served by Moravian missionaries, others as ethnic enclaves amid German- or English-speaking neighbors. As Pontiac's War erupted, these all became targets.

On September 15, 1763, missionary John Brainerd placed an advertisement in the *Pennsylvania Gazette* denouncing rumors that members of his New Jersey Delaware congregation had joined the enemy. Rumors continued to spread, however, and Christian Indians grew everywhere fearful. John Heckewelder, a Moravian missionary to the small Indian communities at Nain and Wequatank in the forks of the Lehigh and Delaware Rivers, later recalled that many settlers were embracing the doctrine "that the Indians were the Canaanites, who by God's commandment were to be destroyed." Even the *Pennsylvania Gazette*, which was something of an organ for the Quaker Party–dominated assembly, contributed to the atmosphere as it resounded in 1763 with calls for "Revenge for the Butcheries committed by the Barbarians."[31]

The smiting began on August 20, 1763, when militiamen killed four Moravian Indians—"Zachary," his wife, their child, and another woman—who had come to trade pelts at Fort Allen on the Lehigh River. The aggressors broadcast their intention to kill any other Indian who crossed their path. Soon thereafter, two Conoys and one Nanticoke were found murdered near Fort Augusta on the Susquehanna River. Then came the news that a party of British-allied Cayugas had been attacked in Virginia, with five fatalities. Though this was more a case of mistaken identity than of willful murder, Sir William worried about the effects the killings would have on the fidelity of the Six Nations, who claimed all these dead as their dependents. His worries soon intensified.[32]

One group of so-called domestic Indians, the Indians of Conestoga Manor, lived on the proprietors' own lands southeast of Lancaster. This community of twenty-two "Conestogas," composed of intermarried Susquehannocks, Senecas, Delawares, and others, had occupied their four-hundred-odd-acre parcel with the governor's blessing since 1717. Long since, the rest of the manor had been sold to German and English settlers, most of whom adhered to religious principles of nonbelligerence. The Conestogas' immediate neighbors neither feared Conestogas nor gave Conestogas cause for fear. As Thomas McKee soon wrote from Lancaster, just eight miles away, "These Indians have lived all their Lives . . . in Peace and Quietness with their Neighbours, and I do not believe were ever concerned against us."[33]

But not far to the northwest, the colonial inhabitants of the towns of Paxtang (commonly called Paxton), Donegal, and Hempfied threatened the Conestogas and other Indians who lived within the blanket of British settlements. The region's spiritual and martial leader, at least in the eyes of its authorities, was the Presbyterian minister Reverend Colonel John Elder, commissioned to raise companies for Pennsylvania in July. In September 1763, Elder, who easily referred to Africans as "the Progeny of Ham," recommended the "immediate removal" of the Conestogas. John Penn, the newly arrived governor and a proprietor of the colony, saw these Indians as his dependents and himself as their guardian, and he refused the recommendation on the grounds that the "faith of this Government" was "pledged for their protection."[34] Penn would soon reverse this position.

In October, Elder got word that a "murdering party" of enemy Indians was roving higher up the Susquehanna Valley, and he dispatched two companies of men northward. They came upon the mutilated corpses of New Englanders who had settled in the dangerous valley under dubious grants from the Susquehanna Company. Although Elder's militia failed in its mission "to intercept" the killers, it returned to Paxton with gruesome news of families massacred. Elder charged bitterly that Moravian Indians of Wyalusing had sheltered, supplied, and warned the Indian raiding parties. He again urged that the Pennsylvania reaches of the Susquehanna River be cleared of Indians. His charges and demands sounded through-out the counties suffering Indian attacks. The government concluded that since there might be truth to the charge against the Moravian Indians, they should all be confined in Philadelphia for their protection. As Penn put it to his brother, "We have been oblig'd to order the Moravian Indians down to Philadelphia to quiet the minds of the Inhabitants of North-ampton County who were determined either to quit their settlements or take an opportunity of murdering them all." As one band made its way in November to the city, a mob put its village to the torch. On December 8, when Penn received and published the Royal Proclamation, all its high tones about Indians under the king's protection made little sound in the chaotic theater of war.[35]

Rumors circulated in the town of Paxton that the Conestogas had harbored enemy spies; still the Conestoga Indians, inhabiting their little plot amid their peaceful immediate neighbors, remained unmoved. On December 14, more than fifty mounted Paxtonians burst upon their "town," killing the six people they could find there. Most of the rest of the Conestogas, as they returned from their chores and gathered what had happened, fled to the protection of the Lancaster workhouse. By Decem-ber 21, the governor's council concluded that Conestogas, Wyalusings, and Moravian Indians should be concentrated in Philadelphia "for their better Security." Before that order was carried out, all the Conestogas in the Lancaster refuge were dead.[36] On December 27, in little more than ten minutes, Paxtonians took the workhouse by force, killed the fourteen Indians, and left the mangled bodies helter-skelter about the yard. A company of Royal Highlanders, then at Lancaster, did not intervene: they had no orders to suppress civilians, and they may well have been unfit for duty, but their inaction cast doubt on the willingness of the king's troops to protect Indians from British subjects. It is often asserted that the dead represented the last of the Conestogas, but, as is usual with such "Last of the Mohican" stories, there were survivors. "Michael" and "Mary" had previously left Conestoga Manor to work for "Christian Hershey at his plantation in Warwick Township." Hershey, a Mennonite, "hid them in his cellar, where they had to stay all winter until the excitement had somewhat abated." They never returned to the manor.[37]

The murderers, ever since known as the Paxton Boys, accomplished the task of "removing" Indians in the cruellest sense of the word, but what alarmed British officials is that they also threatened to disrupt the alliance with the Six Nations, already angry at the accidental killings of several Cayugas in Virginia. When one Cayuga "struck some English" in retaliation for those killings, Sir William was obliged by the Paxton enormities to "bury"—that is, to pledge to forget—the Cayuga's deeds in formal council. John Penn issued proclamations calling for both the seizure of the killers and the protection of the Indians who remained at peace in the colony. He offered two hundred pounds for the arrest of the ringleaders and pardon to any follower who would turn them over to authorities. He had no takers. When Elder protested that he had both tried to stop the party and did not know "one person of judgement" who had joined it, Penn, wondering why he would not name those who lacked judgment, discharged him from active service. Meanwhile, Penn acted to protect the 140 settlement Indians who had already come to Philadelphia.[38]

John Papunhank—a Mahican by birth but recently an inhabitant of the Delaware, Munsee, Nanticoke, and Conoy town of Wyalusing on the Susquehanna—was among those Indians who received such protection, who had removed themselves from their homes to become virtual prisoners in Philadelphia's smallpox quarantine, which lay on Province Island in the broad Delaware River. Papunhank, swept up in the waves of visionary spirituality that had washed down the Susquehanna Valley since the 1740s, had become a prophet of peace; he had involved himself with the Moravians, and he had enjoyed long conversations with the celebrated Irish Quaker Susanna Lightfoot. By 1760 he had emerged as the leading Indian advocate of nonbelligerence, even sustaining wounds in his efforts to stop feuding among Indians along the Susquehanna. As Pontiac's War broke out, he and his people took up no arms—but they did inform Colonel James Burd of Fort Augusta, near Shamokin on the Susquehanna, of the movements of enemy warriors. It was Papunhank, in company with Job Chilaway, who identified Shamokin Daniel as the leader of the band that was out raiding in July 1763. In November, Chilaway had further warned the soldiers and colonists in the neighborhood of Bethlehem of the movements of a party of Munsee warriors. Governor

Penn called Chilaway and his fellows from the Susquehanna River town of Wyalusing "really our sincere Friends." Papunhank did not want this confinement, but it was the only protection Penn could offer.[39]

The Paxtonians responded to Penn's first proclamation with threats to kill the Indians harbored by the government. Knowing that he could not trust the refugees' defense to his provincials (they had already refused to allow the Indians to be stationed in their barracks), Penn sent to Thomas Gage at New York for imperial help. He even suggested that the three Royal companies stationed at Carlisle for frontier defense might be ordered to Philadelphia to protect Indians. But before Gage could respond, Penn decided on a more drastic course of action. To protect the Indians, he would remove them from the colony. Lewis Weiss, a strong advocate for the Moravian Indians, had already proposed that the colony fund a temporary sojourn for the refugees in England. Penn chose another direction, and he became an early advocate of a policy adopted by the United States in the nineteenth century: permanent removal deeper into Indian country to preserve peace.[40] Like the Paxtonians, Penn and many other imperial officials were moving toward the position that Indians and British subjects were best kept apart.

On the night of January 4, 1764, the 140 Indians on windswept Province Island were awakened, guided into boats, and taken back to Philadelphia, where they were met by their escort, seventy British Highlanders from a regiment that had seen fierce action against the Cherokees just four years before. They safely crossed into and through New Jersey as far as Perth Amboy, despite taunts and threats from mobs along the way. Penn hoped that from that port they could sail or otherwise travel to Albany and continue unmolested to some haven among the Six Nations Iroquois. Yet Penn had sent them on their way without first consulting New York's officials, the Indian department, or the Iroquois.[41]

Colden, his council, and Johnson "unanimously" stood in the path. They feared the consequences of releasing Indians "full of Resentment" among the Iroquois. Better to keep them under guard as "a Sort of Hostages" than to let them spread their anger. The evacuees, Colden wrote without explanation, were "the most obnoxious to the People of this Province of any," and there was no guarantee that they could "safely pass" through it. When Gage learned of New York's decision, he dispatched three companies of Royal Americans under Captain J. Schlosser from Albany to Perth Amboy with orders to escort the refugees overland back to Philadelphia. There was economy in the measure; the troops were preparing to join Colonel Henry Bouquet's western expedition in any case. Schlosser accomplished the task and placed the Indians under guard in the city barracks. But before he had done so, he observed that many in New Jersey and Pennsylvania were "very much incensed against" the dispossessed Indians; he even asked his commander he might fire "at those who would fall upon them."[42]

It was a good question, for, as he wrote, three hundred settlers were mobilizing to kill the refugees, demand greater representation for newly settled regions in the legislature, and gain greater protection for the frontier. Led by Matthew Smith and James Gibson, they got as far as Germantown, where they learned that they would confront a mobilized urban populace and the king's troops. The assembly passed a riot act, and the governor ordered Schlosser to use force if necessary. Benjamin Franklin had raised some five hundred citizens to act against the Paxtonians, but before any fighting could occur, he and other prominent men negotiated with the leaders of the outnumbered and outgunned insurgents. The Paxtonians agreed to submit a petition to the governor and the assembly; officials agreed to allow a Paxtonian to visit the barracks and to name any known murderer among the refugees. He named none. The vigilantes, facing not only the armed Philadelphians but British Highlanders and Royal Americans, realized that they had not a chance of achieving their objective at a reasonable cost with force. Gage took credit for the marchers' dispersal, claiming that although they would have challenged any militia or provincial units that might have tried to stop them, they could not bring themselves to cross the king's own troops. Since the Indians were under His Majesty's protection, and not merely that of Pennsylvania's government, Gage confidently informed his superiors that the rioters would leave them alone.[43]

The Paxtonians' murders and armed march to Philadelphia precipitated a furious pamphlet war in which writers fought over the virtues and deficiencies of taxes, Quakers, Presbyterians, proprietors, Royal governments, the representative system, the history of the defense of the province, and a host of issues that had little to do directly with the shooting and tomahawking of unarmed innocents. But when the pamphleteers did broach the murders themselves, they confronted the vexing issue of the Conestoga and Moravian Indians' place in Pennsylvania society. How were Pennsylvanians to view these people? Paxtonians clearly saw all

WAR UNDER HEAVEN

Indians as enemies. Opponents of the Paxtonians called the Indians in their midst, variously, fellow subjects of the king, friends, allies, neighbors, sojourners, and strangers—a range of terms encompassing a range of relationships to the colony and the empire.[44]

Charles Read, chief justice of the New Jersey Supreme Court, took the position that the Conestogas, despite their "yellow" skin, had become "subjects" and therefore deserved the same treatment "as other subjects in like Circumstances." Another, anonymous pamphleteer was less systematic and almost casually called the Conestogas subjects, neighbors, and Christians deserving of protection. Thomas McKee, an Indian agent who knew them well, argued that the Conestogas had assimilated enough, "had in Manner . . . become white People, and expected the same Protection" from the British. The murders personally affronted John Penn, for the Conestogas had been living under the protection of his government, "on Lands assigned to them for their Habitation," that is, on his land. Although he never called them subjects, he did say they "were as much under the Protection of the Government, and its Laws, as any others" among the colonists. Only for Read did the assertion of the Indians' access to the "same" protection of the law rest on a consistent claim that the Indians were "subjects," a word others avoided. The anonymous author of "A Serious Address" at times seemed to imply that the Conestogas had the status of a separate, friendly, nation, and at other times he suggested that they had agreed by treaty in 1701 to live with the colonists "as one People." Benjamin Franklin and another writer took a more narrow tack and called them "strangers" or "sojourners," who, without any explicit liberties, deserved what Franklin called the "Sacred Rites of Hospitality," including at least protection. Franklin was closest to the developing imperial line, which in Gage's words treated the "domestick" Indians as a separate people "under His Majesty's protection."[45] Together, the anti-Paxtonians failed to fix the "domestic Indians'" place clearly. They argued for the Crown's duty to protect Indians, but that was as far as they could agree, and they did not directly note their disagreements. The status of Indians remained wobbly; the writers did not consider it deeply.

In consistency, if not in humanity, they were outclassed by the defenders of the Paxtonians. These writers claimed variously but unanimously that the domestic Indians had become enemies—by virtue, as some writers alleged, of individual misdeeds and bad character or, as others alleged, of race. One went so far as to advocate the killing of Indian women and children, anticipating nineteenth-century advocates of genocide on the High Plains when he pointed out that "out of a SERPENT'S EGG, there should come . . . a fiery flying SERPENT." But the pro-Paxtonians all agreed that Indians had no place in the British nation and were undeserving of the government's protection. They said it was not in the proper power of government to give shelter to its own enemies and that it was an indignity for "Free-Men and English Subjects" to become tributary to such Indians as were then being supported by the government in Philadelphia. One seized directly on the autonomous character of Indian communities as a reason for their elimination: to permit these "independent Commonwealths," who "never came under [British] laws nor acknowledged Subjection to [the British] King and Government" and who still corresponded with the enemy, to "live in a Time of War" within the colonies was "contrary to the Maxims of good Policy"; states within a state were dangerous. Andrew Jackson, the not-yet-born future president of the United States, would never put it better during his administration. By 1764, imperial and colonial officials were coming to agree that the best policy was the expulsion of all Indian communities to the west of a hardening (but westward-shifting) frontier line.[46]

On almost every count, the Paxtonians won the contest over the status of Indians. Nobody faced charges for the Conestoga murders. Before those killings, the government had been reluctant to reimburse locally organized bands that went out to patrol the frontiers; in the same month as the Paxtonians' march, the assembly agreed to reimburse two such bands. By the end of the winter, the government had embraced the policy of Indian removal and was struggling to carry it out. The Paxtonian desire to kill the confined Indians in Philadelphia was also partly met, for smallpox broke out in the barracks, and 56 of the 140 died by September. Six Nations spokesmen claimed the Conestogas' widowed lands as their own and hoped now to profit from their sale. John Penn acceded to the Paxtonians' demands that a scalp bounty be placed on enemy Indians, and Penn's bounty included premiums for the scalps of women and children above ten years of age. The bounty made certain that Pennsylvania would remain a dangerous place for any Indian, friend or enemy, for the duration of the war, and it advanced the cause of removal.[47]

"Immediate removal" had been the Paxtonians' aim since before the Conestoga killings, and it was a keystone of the "Declaration and Remonstrance" that they submitted to the government at Germantown. As a pamphleteer put it, "It would be well[,] ... as the White People most in General hates any Thing that Savours of the Name of Indian, that they were remov'd to their own Country." In March, more than twelve hundred inhabitants of Cumberland County, well to the west of Paxton and a place where Shamokin Daniel had raided in 1763 and where more raids would come in 1764, signed a petition. It urged that the refugee Indians in Philadelphia, who were but "Pretended Friends," be "immediately sent away." Penn soon agreed. As Pennsylvanians debated the Paxton affair, Penn saw it as "more than ever necessary, that all the Indians should be removed out of the Province, in order to put a Stop to the present Disturbances and Murmurs of the people, and lest their rage may not be restrained ... from venting itself still, in the destruction of these Indians." He appealed to Sir William to convince New York to give the refugees safe passage to "their own Country," which he still deemed to be among the Six Nations, where they had never lived. Papunhank supported the idea, but in March New York again refused to comply. Penn also considered sending the refugees under an armed guard up the Susquehanna to Six Nations territory, but that could well have meant civil conflict with Paxtonians, and he gave up the idea. The refugees continued to be "detained" in the city throughout most of 1764.[48]

Anti-Paxtonian pamphleteers strangely avoided the topic of removal; the voice in the wilderness again belonged to New Jersey's Charles Read, who believed, uncommonly, that the Indians were Crown subjects with "the same Right of Living on Lands of their own, or of other People's, by the Owner's permission," as other subjects; therefore he knew of "no Law to oblige them to remove." Most others, however, including Penn, Johnson, and Gage, hoped to sweep the Pennsylvania segments of the upper Susquehanna Valley of Indians. Already the war was emptying it of peoples. Delawares had driven off the New England settlers, and Sir William's allies had in early 1764 driven out many Delawares, for which Gage commended the superintendent, adding, "I hope no more Tribes will be suffered to make their Nests either on the Susquehanna or Delaware, or any Branches of those Rivers." Sir William, who noted that the Indians were "all very fond of that Country," promised to take up the matter with the Six Nations: "[The Indians'] Claims to Lands are at present only under the Six Nations who sell them at pleasure, but the removing them from being such near Neighbours is a matter worthy of consideration, and I shall endeavour to effect it."[49]

To effect removal would, as it turned out, take another decade and another war—the American Revolution—a fact attributable far more to Indian perseverance and Moravian religious witness than to imperial protection. As Pontiac's War wound down in 1765, Delawares, Nanticokes, Conoys, and others repopulated portions of Susquehanna. Among them were the Moravian survivors from Philadelphia, some of whom gathered a mile below Wyalusing Creek in a new town called Friedenshütten. A delegate from the Six Nations invited them to move to the head of Cayuga Lake, but these Moravian Christians, like many of their non-Christian Delaware counterparts, refused, and removal stalled.⁵⁰

Murder, meanwhile, proceeded apace. In Staunton, Virginia, a place that had suffered direct attacks by Shawnees, twenty to thirty "Augusta Boys" mounted a dawn assault on ten Cherokees, who, at peace with the British, were surprised while sleeping in a barn. Unlike the Conestogas, these Cherokees were warriors. Now allied with the British, they were on their way to raid Delawares and Shawnees on the Ohio. The Virginians killed five, including Nockonowa, the party's leader, and another who was the son of the important headman Standing Turkey. The rest escaped homeward; along the way, two killed a colonial woman and her blind husband and wounded another man, whose horse they stole. Six years earlier such incidents had helped to spark the Great Cherokee War (1759–62), a fact that gravely concerned leading Cherokees and Virginians as the news spread. Southern superintendent John Stuart had to work very hard to keep the Cherokees at peace. Virginia authorities arrested two Augusta Boys, James Clendening and Patrick Duffy, but could not hold them. A crowd freed Clendening before he ever reached jail; another broke Duffy free. Virginia's lieutenant governor, Francis Fauquier, issued proclamations calling for the arrest of the killers, and he even identified them with the Paxton Boys, reporting that those Pennsylvanians had offered to assist the Augusta Boys in resisting arrest. But the Augusta Boys were not Paxton Boys; they never professed the righteousness of Indian killing. Instead, they stubbornly insisted, against all good evidence, that they had killed enemy Shawnees and Delawares, not Cherokees, whom they acknowledged as "Friends."⁵¹

The murders of three Anishinabeg at Detroit in 1765 and 1766, a Seneca near Fort Pitt in 1765, a Delaware boy on the Pennsylvania frontier that year, a Six Nations warrior near Fort Cumberland in 1766, an Indian "vagrant" in Ulster County, New York, in 1766, and "Seneca

George" on the Susquehanna River in 1769 do not complete the dreary list of high crimes against Indians that went unpunished by British authorities in the closing years and immediate aftermath of Pontiac's War. William Johnson, shocked and worried at the turn of events, grimly calculated in June 1766 that British subjects had murdered "no less than 15 Indians" within the past few months, several of whom had "always been faithful and well disposed." When Frederick Stump and John Ironcutter—consistently and pointedly referred to in the record as "Germans"—killed ten Indians on a tributary of the Susquehanna on January 10 and 11, 1768, their act repulsed some frontier folk: their victims were mostly women and children. Stump's neighbor, William Blyth, testified against him, and frontiersman William Patterson gathered nineteen men from Juniata Valley to arrest the two killers. Patterson, Blyth, and the nineteen others, backcountry folk all, helped to commit Stump and Ironcutter to the Carlisle jail. A week later, a large crowd of seventy to eighty men armed with guns and tomahawks set them free. Stump was said first to have fled west, then east to his father's home in Tulpehoken. The usual proclamations, warrants, and lamentations were issued, but he was never arrested. Indeed, when John Penn wrote to Sir William of the murders, he appended not only the names of the Indians killed—they were related to the Genesee Senecas—but also the murders that had been committed on Pennsylvanians since the end of Pontiac's War, every one of which had taken place west of the Alleghenies and could have had little to do with these Susquehanna Valley Indians.[52]

Fear of renewed Indian war, along with a stern insistence on the government's duty to uphold the law and a personal desire to placate the Six Nations, led New Jersey governor William Franklin to take truly extraordinary measures when he faced several murders of Indians in his own colony. In the spring of 1766, an Oneida man came down the Delaware River from New York to trade at Minisink, New Jersey. The Oneidas, many of whom were Congregationalists, had long been in good standing with the British. This victim, who is not named in the record, was apparently well known to people at Minisink. He had even fought beside the British in the Seven Years' War. Nonetheless, two colonists murdered him and made off with his gun and goods. One of the murderers, Robert Seamor, boasted of the deed, saying that "he would destroy any Indian that came his Way." Seamor was arrested on April 2, but twenty-five armed men broke open the Sussex County jail and set him free.

Late in June the same year, two local Delaware women, one of whom was pregnant and close to term, went to Moorestown, New Jersey, to purchase some cloth. They encountered James Anin and James McKinzey, two travelers en route from the western frontiers to New York. McKinzey had been the servant of a Scottish officer recently killed in Pontiac's War. The men were poor, begging for meals while on the road. Both were eating breakfast outside a Moorestown home when they noticed the two Delaware women in the village, and they harassed the women with foul language. The women made their purchases, left the town, and rested in a nearby wood, where McKinzey and Anin surprised them. That afternoon, two miles from the town, McKinzey sold a blanket and a piece of new linen, and Anin sold a woman's shift. For three days the women's bodies lay near the road, but travelers who saw them claimed they thought the women to be sleeping. When death's stench finally, inescapably, drew the attention of more intrepid passers-by, they discovered that both had been bludgeoned, and the younger woman's body "had marks of shocking treatment." Anin was quickly arrested and placed in the Burlington County jail. It took a week to find McKinzey, who had fled to Philadelphia.[53]

The killings did not surprise anyone familiar with the recent rash of murders committed against allied Indians throughout the thirteen colonies. In no colony had an arrest yet led to a conviction. The Minisink mob that freed Seamor from the Sussex County jail demonstrated that New Jersey might be no different. Governor Franklin was determined to break the mold. He offered one hundred dollars for the rearrest of Seamor and appointed special courts of oyer and terminer to convene grand juries in Burlington County to bring the murderers to justice. Franklin has been rightly praised for his energetic prosecution of the murderers, but he had personal interests at stake; he needed Iroquois support for his speculative ventures and could not tolerate the murder of an Oneida in his colony. Delawares, too, had relations with the Iroquois League that the governor had to keep in mind. Franklin would in 1768 receive the title "Dispenser of Justice" from the Iroquois, even as he received Iroquois title to land.[54]

The Moorestown case of the two murdered women was settled first. Anin and McKinzey, rapists, vagabonds, strangers to New Jersey without local connections, were found guilty, sentenced, and hanged within six weeks. Just before the floor dropped from below him, Anin, fifty-four years old, declared it a "Duty to extirpate the Heathen." For him, clearly, the fact that these women were Christian made no difference. William Johnson exaggerated when he called this "the opinion of all the common people," but Anin's words did reflect a vein of colonial sentiment. Seamor and David (or Robert) Ray, the two killers of the Oneida in Sussex County, proved more difficult to bring to justice. Ray counted on clemency, which he sought and received. He escaped the gallows by confessing and gained a painful brand on the hand. Seamor counted on the protection of his Sussex County neighbors, and indeed it took a sheriff from a neighboring county to arrest him and a trial in distant Burlington County to convict him. He was hanged in December. Presiding over his trial was Charles Read, the clearest advocate during the Paxton crisis of the idea that the Conestoga Indians were British subjects.[55]

Nowhere else in the 1760s from the middle colonies to the Florida border did a colonial governor so force the issue. Here, killing white Indian killers, William Franklin was *sui generis*. But even he determined to prevent the like from happening again by keeping Indians out of his province. Franklin opined, "Some of the worst People in every Colony reside on the Frontiers, and it were to be wish'd that the Indians could be persuaded to avoid coming among them." Franklin joined with the emerging imperial position that a line between settlers and Indians was the answer, and while settlers were to be hemmed in on one side, he would happily invest with Johnson, Croghan, and their assorted partners and competitors in speculative claims to lands on the other. The line, he believed with his father, would be temporary and mobile, and its westward shift would mark the Indians' decline even as it marked the rise in his and his empire's wealth.[56]

Imperial Indian Policy in the Backcountry

If the imperial elite had little claim to genuine disinterestedness when it came to Indian policy during and in the wake of the war, neither were the backcountry colonists all Paxton Boys writ large, driven by Indian hating to murder. To the west of the Susquehanna toward the end of Pontiac's War, the settlers of the western section of expansive Cumberland County formed yet another movement challenging Pennsylvania's and the empire's Indian policy. These Cumberland folk organized themselves into a body, variously called the Brave Fellows, Loyal Volunteers, or the Black Boys, the last because they blackened their faces and dressed in Indian costume during their actions. Like the Paxton Boys, like the governors of Pennsylvania and New Jersey, and like Thomas Gage and Johnson, they advocated Indian removal from the settlements; all accepted rigid divisions between Indian and white, as the terms were then understood and generally used. But this group of Cumberland folk, inhabitants of the Conococheague Valley, can be distinguished from the Paxton Boys. The Brave Fellows did not set out to kill allied or neutral Indians; indeed, their leader, James ("Black Boy Jimmy") Smith, spoke the Mohawk and Ottawa languages, having spent much of the Seven Years' War as a captive among a group of Ohio Kahnawakes. During the Paxton crisis, Smith had been busy working as a scout for Henry Bouquet. Smith would later write a great deal about Indians; his writings would condemn other such wanton killers. After the Revolution, during which American militiamen rounded up and murdered Christian Indians at the town of Gnadenhütten (Ohio), Smith would call the massacre "an act of barbarity" beyond anything he ever knew to be committed "by the savages themselves." In 1790 he would write that, in generosity, Indians shamed those who professed to be Christians. Later still, in 1801, the Presbyterian Smith, smitten during the evangelical frontier revivals that climaxed that year in Kentucky, would spend three months "in the Indian towns as a missionary, conversing freely with them in their own tongue." Notwithstanding his admiration for certain facets of Indian life, Smith shared in the nascent white supremacism of his day. He believed, like the imperial authorities, that Indian lands would eventually be taken by colonists and that the Indians would come under colonial sway. He was determined that settlers, not imperial authorities or speculators, would benefit from the expansion.[57] There is no record that he condemned either the Paxton Boys or the many who took part in their movement; nor is there recorded evidence that he condemned Frederick Stump, John Ironcutter, and the men who rescued them, even though these actions would take place on the eastern fringe of his own county.

Cumberland County, which braced Forbes' Road from eastern Pennsylvania to Fort Pitt, suffered frequent raiding during Pontiac's War; particularly hard hit had been Smith's own Conococheague Valley, which formed the northeastern point in the triangle of concentrated Indian assaults. In the most notorious of these assaults, a war party had descended in the summer of 1764 upon a little schoolhouse, slaughtering master Enoch Brown and ten of his pupils and enraging the weary settlers. Their rage was directed at the government as well as the Indians, for in the summer of 1763 the people of the valley had petitioned the legislature for the support of James Smith's thirty scouts, "a Body of intrepid, resolute Fellows, under the Command of one who was Captive with the *Indians* for several Years." The petitioners thought Smith's men more able than regular or provincial soldiers, who were "not acquainted with the Country, or the *Indian* manner of fighting" (emphases in original). The petition was rejected, but Smith and some of his fellows were able to assist Henry Bouquet's expedition in 1764.[58]

When news spread in February 1765 that the government was sending presents to Fort Pitt in the wake of Bouquet's Ohio negotiations, there was renewed anger in the county. Formal peace had yet to be concluded with the Ohio Delawares and Shawnees; Shawnees had yet to return all their captives; Pennsylvania had yet to formally lift its embargo on the Indian trade. Nonetheless, as the country people rightly understood, trade goods, including weapons, were hidden among the burdens that packhorses were carrying through their county. James Smith believed that well-connected men seeking profits were endangering his neighbors, and he mobilized the Brave Fellows. William Smith, a local justice of the peace and James Smith's brother-in-law, did not join the volunteers, but he supported their actions. On March 6, they three times stopped the long packhorse train as it headed westward. The volunteers repeatedly asked the packhorsemen if they were carrying gunpowder, and they were shown invoices denying it. They ordered the packhorsemen to unload, but the train went on. At the third encounter they issued a warning: proceed and you will be attacked at Sidling Hill, a slow ascent into the mountains, roughly between Forts Loudon and Bedford.[59]

When the train, eighty-one horses long, began to climb Sidling Hill, two hundred men—armed with rifles, faces blackened, in Indian dress— emerged from the brush and shot dead the leading horse. They ordered the drivers and packhorsemen to dismount, and they gave them fifteen minutes to gather their personal belongings, take the horses, and leave. Stealing nothing, they attached themselves to a tradition of British protest that honored property even while destroying it. Yet they also claimed an American nature: dressed as Indians, they ran "about the Hill hollowing and Shooting" as the packs took fire. Signaling their clear contempt for Indians, they neither destroyed, stole, nor drank of the eighteen loads that consisted "chiefly of liquor." The goods they did destroy were of enormous value: sixty-three horseloads went up in smoke; John Penn guessed the cost to be twenty to thirty thousand pounds, a vast sum of money.[60]

Penn could not be more precise because, in a conspiratorial wrinkle, many of the goods had been shipped illegally; indeed, the convoy had taken a circuitous route in order to avoid inspection at Forts Loudon and Lyttelton. A good part of the correspondence surrounding the affair involves the illegal effort of George Croghan, the Wharton, Bayton, and Morgan trading firm, and the mercantile house of Callender and Company to use the king's service as a means of being first on the ground at Fort Pitt and the Illinois Country when trade with the Indians resumed. It appears all were guilty, and even Henry Bouquet was accused of violating the letter of the law in order to uphold the spirit of his November 1764 peace with the Ohio Indians. Croghan's reputation, along with that of the Indian department he served, was badly tarnished by the affair. Croghan complained that the destruction of the trade goods, however illegal those may have been, endangered the peace that was only beginning to settle on the upper Ohio Valley, where Indians needed to gain something other than rum in exchange for their peltry. The Brave Fellows' action also threatened to undermine the efforts the British were making to establish peace with the Indians of Illinois, the destination for most of the king's "presents."[61]

The riflemen's attack at Sidling Hill on March 6 was only the first of a series of local actions that unsettled the British garrisons of Fort Loudon and Fort Bedford well into the next year and beyond. Of the several justices of the peace in the county, most supported the Brave Fellows, which gave them a veneer of legality. That the destroyed packhorse train had been carrying contraband added to their case. One justice of the peace, James Maxwell, did oppose them. On March 9, a crowd suspecting that he was in business with George Croghan paid his home a visit, demanding his powder and lead but insisting that they would do him no harm. They then broke open his storehouse and discovered eight hidden barrels of gunpowder, which they carried away and blasted.[62]

When the army took the part of the injured and corrupt trading company rather than the settlers whom it was meant to protect but who had also just destroyed the king's goods, the incident became an early sign of the imperial crisis about to beset North America. In the immediate aftermath of the assault, twelve soldiers sallied out from Fort Loudon to bring back what they could of the destroyed goods. They managed to confiscate eight rifles and seize two of Smith's Brave Fellows, whom they confined in the fort. The "country men" responded by marching—two-hundred strong, armed and led by James Smith—on the garrison. Fearing "a Civil War," Loudon's commander, Lieutenant George Grant, released his two captives on bail, but he kept the firearms in an effort to establish the owners' identity. In retaliation, other Brave Fellows flogged packhorsemen attempting to supply Fort Loudon and killed five of their horses. This drew another sally from the fort, which met resistance in a short firefight in which one volunteer, James Brown, was wounded. The Brave Fellows then turned to their community, and, with the support of William Smith and two other justices of the peace, they ordered the arrest of Sergeant Leonard McGlashan, who had led the last sally. Grant refused to obey the summons. The volunteers continued to harass the fort's communications with the outside world. They intercepted and treated "cruelly" an express from Carlisle, and they attempted to stop another heading in the other direction. On May 10, they marched again; 150 to 200 Brave Fellows appeared threateningly before the garrison and demanded both the confiscated rifles and permission to inspect the damaged goods that the army had recovered from the wreckage at Sidling Hill. They insisted that Indian agent Croghan and the Philadelphia trading company had acted illegally.

Just how serious they were became evident on May 28, when they waylaid Grant as he was riding alone, "taking the air." James Smith, John Piery, and Sam Owens kept him up all night in the woods, and they forced him to sign a note promising to deliver the arms or face a legal penalty of forty pounds. Smith also handed him a warrant for Sergeant McGlashan's arrest. Rumors of this unprecedented, legalistic colonial assault on a British officer reached Fort Pitt—Grant was said to have been killed—causing a company of forty-five soldiers to race eastward to oppose a feared rebellion. That force turned back on news that Grant was safe, but the trouble around Fort Loudon continued. The two Smiths, William and James, drew up and issued commissions authorizing crowd action to prevent westbound convoys from carrying firearms or other weapons to Indians; they drew up passports to be given only to wagons and convoys that passed the volunteers' inspection. The only Indian trading good to be allowed was alcohol. Pennsylvania authorities, unable to take stronger action, revoked William Smith's commission as justice of the peace and futilely ordered James Smith's arrest; Conococheague folk continued to threaten the trading companies.[63]

To cut the Indians off from arms, the Brave Fellows consciously adopted the Indian method of raiding the communications. Smith recalled that he found two men, former captives like himself, and had them gather and lead the companies: "We dressed them uniformly in the Indian manner, with breech-clouts, leggings, mockesons, and green strouds. . . . In place of hats we wore red handkerchiefs, and painted our faces red and black, like Indian warriors." November 16 witnessed a peculiar Brave Fellow fusing of British and Indian practices. At seven that night, the volunteers for a third time marched on and surrounded the fort, this time with "firing and hooting," in clear imitation of Indians. They did not stop their mock assault until morning, when, reinforced, they made camp around the fort. Grant guessed that they numbered two hundred men. The next night they again peppered the palisades with lead. Their actions were extreme, their demands very modest: deliver up the seized guns in exchange for a written acknowledgment that weapons' owners would not recover them until the governor's pleasure was known. Grant, by now under orders to evacuate Fort Loudon—an order unrelated to the regional turmoil—agreed to give the guns to a local gentleman, William McDowell.[64]

Philadelphia's Wharton, Bayton, and Morgan trading company, whose own illegal actions had in part precipitated the Brave Fellows' protests and whose directors were anxious in March 1766 to win over the trade of the entire Ohio Valley, claimed that it could not ship its goods as long as "lawless Banditti" were able to check its operations and threaten its property "with destruction." By then, the Brave Fellows did little more than circulate rumors and threats, for formal peace with the Ohio Indians had been concluded, the Conococheague Valley was again secure, and the farmers had crops to put in. Still, Gage complained to his superiors, "The Ringleaders as well as the rest are known, but I have not been able to get any Satisfaction."[65]

Nor was he ever satisfied; his dissatisfaction would only increase in August and September 1769 when, amid renewed fears of Indian war, men from the Conococheague Valley waylaid another packhorse train, destroying powder, rifles, and clothing bound for the Indian trade. Fort Bedford's Royal Highlanders responded by arresting several of the rioters, arousing James Smith, or so at least he later recalled, to another unprecedented action in the history of the eighteenth-century British colonies. He gathered his best followers, and with them on September 12, 1769, he surprised the British garrison of Fort Bedford, captured it, harmed no one, freed his arrested neighbors, and withdrew. Years later, lightly gilding the lily, he would point out that this was the first British fort to be taken by colonists in the era of the American Revolution.[66]

The commander did not report the incident, yet there can be no doubt that Smith was near the fort that September or that he had drawn the ire of its garrison. Rumors circulated that month that "the Black Boys intended to attack" the British troops then marching toward Fort Pitt. Small parties of the insurgents were said to be moving about the countryside, among them James Smith and two companions. Four men from Fort Bedford went in pursuit of Smith, found him, and ordered him to surrender, and somehow in the ensuing struggle Smith's friend John Johnson was shot dead. The soldiers seized Smith and accused him of manslaughter. By September 22, Smith was in the Carlisle jail, perhaps in the same cell that had held Frederick Stump twenty months earlier. Over the next two days, crowds of men with blackened faces sped toward Carlisle, putting the authorities "in great Confusion." But Smith was not Stump; he himself calmed matters by insisting, first by letter and then in person, that he would face his trial, at one point extending his hands through the barred windows of the jail and imploring the men to go home. Grumbling, they obeyed, and Smith stood his trial. No doubt to the army's dismay, a special court of oyer and terminer acquitted him after serious doubts were raised that his rifle could have been the weapon that killed Johnson.[67]

Although the events surrounding Smith, the Brave Fellows, and the army were extraordinary, they were extraordinarily forgotten: overshadowed by the Stamp Act Riots in the port cities. Years before Lexington and Concord, these Pennsylvanians organized by the hundreds, fired on regulars, arrested regular officers, and captured a British garrison, and neither the colonial government nor the imperial army could stop them. Because of the romance that could surround a man like Black Boy Jimmy Smith in an age that accepted his frequent hostility toward Indians, writers in the early twentieth century found him interesting. Those in the second half of that century, however, largely abandoned him; his actions have been mostly ignored or, worse, fully identified with those of the Paxtonians. Indeed, historians from Francis Parkman to our own day have equated and confused the two movements, calling the "Black Boys" the "Paxton Boys." This is not only factually wrong but interpretively misleading, not least because the Black Boys took far greater risks and, unlike the Paxtonians, displayed real bravery. Where the Paxtonians had cited Scripture to support the indiscriminate killing of unarmed Indians, the Black Boys circulated legal documents and dressed in Indian garb while threatening—though never killing—British soldiers. Though they operated in Cumberland County, they did so far to the west of Frederick Stump's actions, and nowhere is a James Smith listed among the "daring and riotous persons" who broke Stump and Ironcutter out of the Carlisle jail. Since Smith was by then well known in the county, it seems inescapable that he had no part in the Stump affair. No one at the time identified him with it.[68]

The Black Boys' opponents, capitalizing on the volunteers' own self-fashioning as Indians, portrayed them as drunks and as pagans. It was likely an opponent who posted the following "Advertisement," a broadside that, taken to be authentic, infuriated the Pennsylvania council. It pledged the volunteers' loyalty to men who would, in the words of the broadside, "come to our Tavern and fill your Belly's with Liquor and your Mouth full of Swearing," to men who "have a mind to join us, [with] free toleration for Drinking, swearing, Sabbath breaking, and any outrage we have a mind to do, to let those Strangers [in the British army] know their place." This does not sound like Black Boy Jimmy Smith, who carried with him a "Psalm Book and Watkins upon Prayer" and who, unlike those involved in the Stump affair, admired legal order to the point of securing summonses and refusing to be broken out of jail. He claimed to be an Indian fighter; he could be contemptuous of Indians and racist toward African Americans. But his experiences as a captive among Indians gave him the wherewithal to view his own society critically, and he knew it. He wrote with evident affection of individual Indians whom he had come to know as a captive. The Indians generally, he would come to argue, were not "oppressed or perplexed with expensive litigation." He wrote further: "They are not injured by legal robbery—They have no splendid villains that make themselves grand and great on other people's labor—They have neither church nor state erected as money-making machines." His own society, he argued, had far too many of these. James Smith cautions us that the backcountry was at least as complicated in its variety of attitudes toward Indians as was the Indian department.[69]

But even if we were to allow the equation of James Smith with the Paxton Boys, the dichotomy of a sober imperial and colonial elite willing to protect Indians and a wild colonial frontier ready to kill all—a dichotomy apparent in many works—breaks against hard facts. During Pontiac's War the top echelons of the army, whose own arrogant disregard for Indian honor, custom, and right had brought on the war in the first place, not only contemplated but also committed and sanctioned atrocities of the first order. Officers and superintendents ordered that no quarter be given to captured Indians, and the army obeyed. Fort Pitt deliberately infected negotiators with smallpox in a manner approved by two commanders in chief, Amherst and Gage. The smallpox-infected blankets were handed out by William Trent, himself a gentleman and a member of the very trading house most suspected by the Brave Fellows of putting trade before the interests of the frontier inhabitants.[70] Pennsylvania's governor placed bounties on the heads of enemy women and children, and, joined by New Jersey's governor, he embraced and advanced Indian removal. The frontier folk, the "country people" seen from the east to be Paxtonians writ large, understandably shared a widespread hostility toward the Indians whose lands they were taking and whose raids they were suffering. But hostility is not always hate, and hate is not always murder. Paxtonian murderers killed Indians in the name of God; Black Boy rioters imitated Indians, to the point of besieging British garrisons with bullets and war cries, in the name of the law, with the limited purpose of restoring their families and forcing the army to attend to their interests. As they did so, their leader openly admired certain facets of Indian life. This admiration did not make him a "friend of the Indian," just as the increasing tendency of British Indian department officials to sport moccasins and beadwork did not disguise their efforts to dominate Indians and profit from the hearty speculation in Indian lands.

Of British and colonial atrocities that have made it into the books, two—the deployment of smallpox at Fort Pitt and the massacre of peaceable Indians by the Paxton Boys—occurred in 1763 and within the official bounds of the colony of Pennsylvania, that great offspring of William Penn. The two events, examined together and in a broader context, serve to remind us that as the British and the British colonists contemplated and fought over the status of the Indians within their emerging empire, they came up with nothing satisfactory for the Indians involved. Almost all people, Indian, colonist, or imperial officer, could agree that Indians were not British subjects in the fully charged meaning of the word. Almost all contemplated, with sentiments that ranged from desire to fury, the continued westward expansion of the British Empire, at Indian expense. The idea of the Indians as inhabiting a kind of protectorate within the realm was, even in the minds of its proponents and progenitors, at best a temporary solution implying a current Indian dependence and a foreseeable Indian reduction that no Indian nation could gladly abide. When peace came in 1765 and 1766, it was barely a peace at all. It was, at best, an amorphous armistice that brought little clarity or order to British-Indian relations and which few expected to last.

CHAPTER SEVEN

Uneasy Conclusions

Dating precisely the beginning of a war is often easier than dating its end. Many wars conclude without a decisive battle, definitive treaty, and persuasive peace. Pontiac's War had none of these. Thomas Gage hesitantly declared the war over on December 13, 1764: "A general, and it's to be hoped, lasting Peace is concluded." Yet no agreements had by then been made with the Indians of the rivers Wabash, Maumee, Illinois, and Arkansas or even with Pontiac; Gage was not even sure that the Delawares and the Shawnees would "keep the Peace" they had made. The next six months erased his declaration and confirmed his fears. In June, blaming Bradstreet, not Bouquet, he proclaimed the entire campaign of 1764 a failure: "We neither attacked them, or made Peace with them. Pondiac was thought to have lost His influence, . . . And when it was found that he was still powerful, No means were taken to make Friends with Him."[1]

Eastern Delawares, living now in the Susquehanna and Genesee Valleys, did formally come to terms with Sir William Johnson in May, and there were some Ohio Delawares in attendance. But this was hardly a definitive peace: Johnson knew that these Indians still had captives and deserters among them, so he kept four hostages until the Delawares and Senecas complied with his demands. Especially doubtful were the Ohio Delawares. When Squash Cutter, one of the most prominent of the eastern Delaware hostages, later died of smallpox, Johnson felt compelled to release the others. Rumor warned that an Ohio Delaware war faction had risen to denounce the peace faction and to spirit others against the

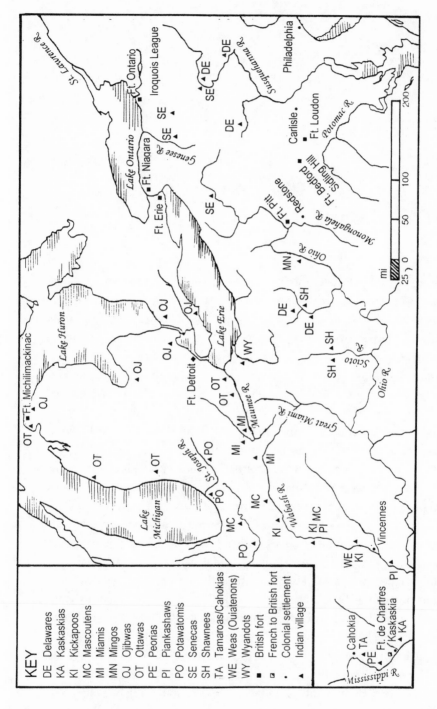

KEY

DE Delawares
KA Kaskaskias
KI Kickapoos
MC Mascoutens
MI Miamis
MN Mingos
OJ Ojibwas
OT Ottawas
PE Peorias
PI Piankashaws
PO Potawatomis
SE Senecas
SH Shawnees
TA Tamaroas/Cahokias
WE Weas (Ouiatenons)
WY Wyandots
■   British fort
◩   French to British fort
•   Colonial settlement
▲   Indian village

Map 4. Pontiac's War, final years. Approximate locations of Indian villages, imperial forts, and colonial towns in chapters 6 through 8.

empire. For several weeks in April, moreover, the peace faction bargained for better terms and sought Quaker mediation. The prophet Neolin, who remained "in good repute among the Delawares," informed the British that "the Great Spirit" had ordered him "to make peace with the Quakers," a proposal the British flatly rejected. Only in May did Ohio Delawares, amid "great Confusion amongst themselves," confirm a peace at Fort Pitt, sending delegates on to treat more formally with William Johnson at his home in the Mohawk Valley.[2]

From the end of Bouquet's expedition through early 1765, the British continued to fear the Shawnees. Sir William had intelligence that the Shawnees "were not hearty" in the peace they had made with Bouquet, "above the half of them being against it." When Maryland volunteer James Bon murdered a Shawnee "hostage" in December, all but one of the remaining Shawnee "hostages" fled from Fort Pitt, taking with them immediate prospects for a formal peace. Bouquet sought to have Bon brought to justice, but the governor of Maryland refused to pursue a crime committed "without the limits of Maryland,"—a strange decision, since Bon was under Maryland's military authority. Well into May 1765, Johnson worried about Shawnees' correspondence with ordinary French inhabitants of Illinois who, it was rumored, took on "the garb" and "Character of Officers" to deceive the Ohio Indians with presents and war belts.[3]

Peace-minded Shawnees also tentatively treated with the British throughout the spring. As Croghan and Major William Murray looked on, Shawnee delegates ceremonially approached Fort Pitt on May 10, "beating a Drum and singing their peace song" and escorting forty-four "English prisoners," about half of those whom the British understood to be still among them. Thirty of these unfortunates had been in Shawnee villages since the Seven Years' War, and of this group, half did not know their European surnames. Several did not even know their given Christian names; these must have been effectively full members of Shawnee families. Fourteen had been taken during Pontiac's War; only two of these were ignorant of their full European names. All of these more recent captives had been quite young—under eight years of age—when first violently seized from their families. As devastating as the return of these children was to the Shawnees, the British triumph in their recovery was incomplete: Shawnees still retained roughly forty captives—about whom the British officers, eager to settle matters and willing to blink at strict details, no longer complained, to the continuing outrage of backcountry colonists. Moreover, whereas Delawares and Mingos were sending impressive delegations to treat with Sir William Johnson that spring, Shawnees sent but one man. When Croghan did assemble a larger group, the individuals were of so little note that the agent could write at length only of sway wielded by the Seneca-Mingo Kiashuta, who, though no Shawnee himself, accompanied the Shawnee party. Kiashuta, it will be recalled, had accompanied the Ohio delegation that, treating with Bradstreet just a year before, had been so widely condemned by the Indian department. Anxious to put some conclusion to the war, that same Indian department would settle for this delegation.[4]

Three years later, the Shawnee diplomat Nimwha would describe the conditional, halting Shawnee decision for peace: "When you talked of peace to us at the times we were struggling in War, we did not hearken to you at first; you mentioned it a second time to us, we still refused to attend to you, but after repeating it to us several Times, we consented to hear You." Referring to Bouquet's expedition, he cast the peace in terms of Shawnee initiative: "We then looked at you and saw you holding Instruments of War in your Hands, which we took from you and cast them into the air out of our Sight." Emphatically denying British lordship, he asserted Shawnee independence and sovereignty: "You think yourselves Masters of this Country, because you have taken it from the French, who, you know, had no Right to it, as it is the Property of us Indians."[5] Nimwha was no militant, but he understood that peace was less a settled condition than a process, one that took negotiation, concession, and marks of mutual respect.

The peace process accelerated in July, as the odd delegation of Shawnees and the respectable delegation of Ohio Delawares, including such leaders as Turtle's Heart, Wingenum, and Tedabaghsika, arrived at Johnson Manor to mark the articles of peace with Sir William. The prominent Delaware "Captain," Killbuck, had already agreed to the terms. Two carefully worded, almost identical passages defined in highly ambiguous language the status of the Delawares and Shawnees: "[They were] Children of the Great King of England, . . . deeming themselves thereby closer linked to the British Crown, to whom they will pay all due submission and subjection so far as the same can be consistent with the Indians['] Native Rights." Subjection they agreed to, but they were "children," not subjects. Native rights they retained, but those rights went unwritten. In Sir William's understanding, the rights were neither those of British subjects nor those of native sovereigns.[6]

Instead, the Delawares acknowledged a subordinate place in the Covenant Chain of friendship with the British. One passage, by granting permission "to all His Majesty's troops or other His Subjects" to pass through their country, clearly distinguished them from Crown subjects. Most critically, they yielded to the Six Nations the right to determine through mediation with the British the boundaries between themselves and "His Majesty's Subjects."[7] The idea of a negotiable boundary, mediated by British authority, dividing lands over which the Crown was sovereign even as it divided Indians from subjects, was fixing itself in Anglo-American conceptions of Indian management. By the time of this signing, the Susquehanna Delawares and the Genesee Senecas had brought in twenty-five captives to Sir William, who called them, wrongly, "the last that remained Prisoners in their Hands."[8] Such details as a few captive settlers no longer worried Sir William, and by the end of July 1765, peace with several leading Delawares and Genesee Senecas had been formalized and established. It had been formalized with the Shawnees, too, but less adequately.

Shawnees were no more a single, unified, political entity than were any of the others; they were, in fact, even less so. Shawnee villages could be found among the Creeks, the Delawares, and, most significant in the spring of 1765, the Illinois. Both Delawares and Senecas had in recent months been relaying rumors to the British at Fort Pitt that the French in Illinois were still "encouraging Shawnee hostilities." Charlot Kaské's name rode on the rumors' wings.[9]

Shawnee Mission to Illinois and New Orleans

Charlot Kaské, a Shawnee "beloved man," civil leader, and close ally of Pontiac's, was known among "all the nations for his Sense." Going beyond Neolin's proscriptions, Kaské never drank alcohol of any sort. According to one report, his father had been a German who had instilled in his son a hatred of the English. However true that may be, Kaské loved the French, or so he repeatedly said.[10] Kaské spent most of Pontiac's War in an energetic but futile effort to arouse France against Great Britain; like Pontiac, he was more successful at rousing the Indians. He first surfaces as Pontiac's messenger to commander de Neyon in Illinois, but he also often spoke for himself. On October 27, 1763, he delivered to de Neyon Pontiac's war belt and message, and then he listened with disappointment as de Neyon, rejecting both, demanded to hear why Shawnees refused to abide by the peace between France and Great Britain. De Neyon knew that the continued French military presence in Illinois gave the Indians continued hope for French assistance. The commander had long advocated the withdrawal of all troops from Illinois; but until he had orders to leave, he could only insist that the Indians stop the war.[11]

In the summer of 1764, Kaské again descended the Ohio River from the Shawnee towns to seek the assistance of the French at Illinois. By early November he had met with the new French commandant, Louis St. Ange de Bellerive (St. Ange), who provided few goods and no promises. Undaunted, Kaské decided to petition a higher authority, and, in the company of his wife, he boarded a convoy for New Orleans on November 9, 1764. Kiashuta, the Seneca-Mingo leader who had come to terms with the English, probably referred indirectly to Kaské when he reported that the Shawnees and Delawares had aroused nine Indian nations in Illinois to agree "to carry on the War." Kiashuta rumored that the local French had supplied the Shawnees with arms and ammunition and that St. Ange had "approved much of their resolution to defend themselves from Slavery, and their Country being settled by the English." Kiashuta said that even after the peace they had made with Bouquet, the Shawnees on the Scioto River harbored three French traders.[12] Never did Kiashuta mention Kaské by name or say that one Shawnee had gone on to New Orleans. Those two details would come later, and in a very unpleasant form, to the British.

Kaské arrived in New Orleans and stood before Governor Jean-Jacques-Blaise D'Abbadie on December 20, 1764. Having already been to the city during the Seven Years' War, he remarked how much had changed. Describing a vast sadness about the place, he noted that many of its important people had departed, and he said he was saddened himself. He claimed to represent forty-seven villages, each of which was marked on the great belt "of five branches" that he offered the governor: "I ask you, my father, to help your children, the Shawnee, who have always held the Frenchman's hand. Our warriors, our old men, our wives, and our children are sad because they see the French no more. . . . The French came to settle there only to protect us and defend us as a good father protects and defends his children. You put the tomahawk in our hands to strike the English, which we did; and we shall preserve it forever." D'Abbadie, who by this time knew well of the cessions of Illinois to Great Britain and of Louisiana to Spain, could only insist on peace.[13]

As Kaské wintered in New Orleans, he must have been further saddened, for D'Abbadie died on February 4, 1765. The succeeding governor, Charles Aubry, agreed to hear the Shawnee, but when Kaské entered the chamber, he was dismayed by the presence of several visiting British officers. Kaské pleaded with the French, in the name of the Master of Life, to protect the Indians against the land-hungry English, who wished only to enslave his people. He was willing to shake the hands of the British officers then in New Orleans, but he did not wish to see them in his own villages on the Scioto. Aubry could only recommend that the Shawnees make peace and engage in a prosperous trade with the British. The Louisiana record, in short, reveals total diplomatic defeat, which Kaské artfully deployed, when back in Illinois, as victory.[14]

He returned to Illinois by convoy in mid-May 1765, carrying a large belt and powerful words, and with those he disrupted British diplomacy. Even while French officials in the Illinois Country made plans to abandon their posts, even while the news circulated that France would officially leave not only Illinois and Canada but also Louisiana, Kaské predicted the revival of the French king and emphasized the coming of a vast French cargo. As *habitants* unloaded supplies from the convoy, and as someone distributed rum to a party of Indians congregating about the beached bateaux, Kaské announced that "the french had made peace with them [the English, but] they were in a few months to begin the war again, but peace or war that they [the Indians] might depend on being well supplyd with arms and ammunition."[15]

British Efforts in the Illinois Country

Kaské had rivals for the attentions and loyalties of the peoples of the Illinois Country. Several representatives of the British had made their way to the troubled region even as Kaské had been in New Orleans. The first envoys, well connected with the Indians of the Great Lakes, were "new subjects" of King George III. Alexander Maisonville had accepted the English occupation of Detroit since 1760, and he would work energetically as both diplomat and interpreter to negotiate a peace. His companion, Jacques Godfroi, accused of aiding the Indians in the capture of Fort

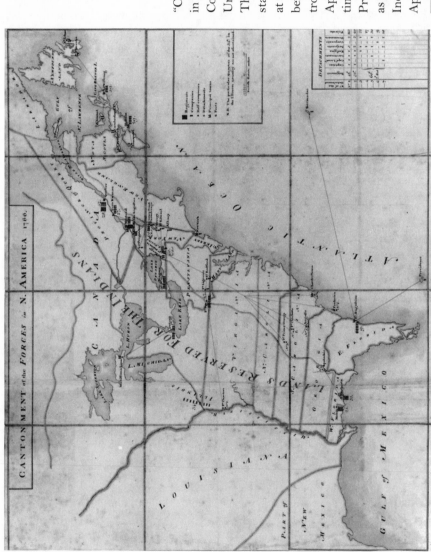

"Cantonment of the Forces in N. America, 1766." Courtesy Clements Library, University of Michigan. This map represents the stationing of British forces at the close of the war, just before drastic reductions in troop strength west of the Appalachians. At the same time, it misrepresents the Proclamation Line of 1763 as fixing a reserve for Indians behind the Appalachians.

Miami in 1763, had been pardoned by Bradstreet. Godfroi was also well connected, and today his surname is common, in a different spelling, among the Miamis of Indiana. Maisonville and Godfroi accomplished little, but they did accurately report on the divided sentiments of the peoples of Illinois. Far from at one with the Indians, French Illinoisans complained of insults at Indian hands, and some hoped for English protection. The Indians, too, far from united in hostility to Britain, were divided over the prospect of peace. Cahokias and Kaskaskias patiently listened to peace proposals but "gave them no positive answer." The peoples of the Wabash Valley seemed more favorably inclined. The Piankashaw leader Black Fly and the Mascouten leader Washion assured the two envoys that their peoples would remain at peace with the British. The Wea Indians of the Ouiatenon neighborhood also seemed favorable. Maisonville and Godfroi were back at Detroit by February 21, knowing that peace in Illinois remained unaccomplished but equally convinced that it was possible.[16]

The first British officer to make the trip to Illinois under orders was Lieutenant John Ross, who traveled overland with trader Hugh Crawford northward from Mobile through Choctaw and Chickasaw country, arriving on February 18, 1765. Ross, less sensitive than Maisonville to local complexity, had even less success. He assumed St. Ange to be culpable in enraging the Indians against Great Britain, and he heard rumors, which he feared were "but too true," that Pontiac was on his way to the Illinois with three thousand armed followers, determined to prevent any British occupation. St. Ange arranged for Ross to meet with Indians, but the meetings went badly. Ojibwas from Michigan presented the Briton a peace calumet but yanked it away in a "contemptuous manner." A Kaskaskia spokesman declared that Indians had "unanimously agreed to continue the war." He said that whenever the Indians weighed the Frenchman against the Englishman, the Englishman weighed more, "because he is filled with wickedness and has not the white heart like our father." He concluded, "We will never receive the English on our lands." St. Ange soon warned Ross that Ojibwas and Potawatomis intended to seize him and Crawford as their prisoners. On this news, the two envoys fled down river to New Orleans. En route, they passed the struggling huge convoy of "between 4 & 500 traders" with many goods and, unknown to them, with Kaské aboard. The day after Ross's departure from Fort de Chartres, Pontiac and another Indian, Minweweh, themselves approached that

French garrison. Kaské, Pontiac, and Minweweh—Shawnee, Ottawa, and Ojibwa—here was an unfortunate convergence for the British.[17]

At winter's end, at the other end of the Ohio River, Lieutenant Robert Fraser and George Croghan waited at Fort Pitt for the arrival of a long pack train, loaded with legal presents and illegal trade goods, some for the Indians of Illinois. Fraser was itching to descend the Ohio to Illinois; Croghan, ignorant that the pack train had surrendered on March 6 to the hoots, hollers, and gunshots of Cumberland County riflemen at Sidling Hill, insisted on waiting. On March 21, 1765, the arrival from Detroit of Maisonville, an experienced multilingual Indian mediator, gave Fraser the chance to shake off Croghan. The very next day, Fraser, Maisonville, Andrew the Huron, and two unnamed Indians formed a party. The five men, in the company of eight boatmen and one "young lad," made their way downstream in a single, large bateau. Fraser's hope was to encourage the *habitants* of Illinois to take oaths of allegiance to King George III.[18]

At abandoned French Fort Massac (opposite what is now Paducah, Kentucky), Fraser divided his command. He sent the bateau on toward Fort de Chartres under the command of a sergeant, while he, Maisonville, Andrew, and a few other men hurried overland to reach the French village of Kaskaskia on April 17. A good road linked Kaskaskia to Chartres. Fraser obtained a horse and buggy, left most of his small party in the village, and drove on to his destination with Andrew. He passed through Indian villages unmolested—but at a good clip. Reaching Chartres, Fraser met with St. Ange and the village priest. He lost no time in warning the French that the British would penalize them for their support for Pontiac and his allies. St. Ange coolly responded that he was powerless to control the Indians, and he politely invited Fraser to supper. The meal was less eventful than its afterglow, during which "Pontiac with eight of his followers rushed into the room" and seized Fraser. St. Ange, an elderly man commanding no more than fifty men, intervened and persuaded Pontiac to release the Briton, at least to allow him to spend the night in the fort. But the next six weeks found Fraser at Pontiac's mercy.

The next day, Fraser and Maisonville met with Pontiac and Illinois leaders. Five hundred Indians attended, charging one another with initiating the war, which led Fraser to hope for peace. Pontiac also softened, or so it appeared. If it was indeed true, as Fraser maintained, that the Shawnees, Delawares, and Mingos had made peace, Pontiac promised that he, too, would make peace. Four "Principal Chiefs" of Illinois and some of their warriors agreed to travel to the Wabash River with Maison-ville to intercept and escort George Croghan, who was then en route, Fraser hoped, to Illinois. They kept their promise and departed a week later. Despite such good appearances, the Indians and the *habitants* never gave Fraser much confidence. Over the next month, he found he had to pay an "Extravagant Price" for any provisions he purchased from the local farmers and merchants. Worse, Pontiac's "ruffians" assaulted him more than once, striking him and threatening at times to "scalp or burn" him. Maisonville, too, felt imperiled, and both he and Fraser were en-gulfed in wild rumors. As the lieutenant put it, "I am every day threatened with some Story or other."[19]

To the east, in the British colonies, Fraser's journey to Illinois began to receive wide attention, as rumor flew through British correspondence and into the public prints that he was burned, boiled, perhaps eaten. As the stories proved to be groundless, British colonists had a ready expla-nation for them: French traders in Illinois sought to corner the market in furs and skins. "These accounts . . . were hatched by Traders to serve their own Purposes."[20]

Just as the New Orleans convoy carrying Charlot Kaské arrived in Illinois, Fraser was again attempting to assemble a peace delegation, which would include Pontiac, to follow the first Illinois delegation and to find Croghan. Kaské got to the new delegates before they departed. He showed them a great belt, which he claimed embodied the call from Governor Aubry at New Orleans to "strike the English," who only "wanted to impose upon them, and enslave them." Kaské promised his listeners loads of presents, and he said that New Orleans would continue to supply them with presents, traders, arms, and ammunition. He opened a large cask of rum. "[The] Story has made a very great Change" wrote Fraser, who charged St. Ange with a reticence to contradict it.[21]

Rumor thrives on ambiguity; ambiguous was the diplomatic climate in the entire Ohio Valley that spring. Pontiac and the Indians of Illinois, amid the haze of groundless reports, had thoroughly undermined Fraser's authority, confidence, and mission. A few days after Kaské deployed his rumors in Illinois, Maisonville returned from the mouth of the Wabash with the disappointed and angry delegation of Illinoisan "Chiefs," who had just wasted twenty-four days hiking long trails and waiting for Croghan's arrival. Local Indians rumored that the British had promised the Illinois Country to the Cherokees and that Fraser was aware of British complicity in Cherokee attacks on them. That the Shawnees and Delawares, far up the Ohio, had not made peace was constantly bandied about. Pontiac at one point stood apart from the others, pledging to Fraser that he would wait ten or twelve days for Croghan's arrival; Fraser, despite himself, began to learn the lessons of his own dependence on Pontiac. Pontiac became for him the "most humane Indian [he] ever saw, . . . careful of [him] and [his] men." In a marvelous role reversal for an officer accustomed to patriarchal hierarchy, Fraser said that Pontiac treated the British in his protection "as if [they] were his own Children."[22] The would-be father had become a child.

Under these circumstances, while in "Pontiac's Mercy" at the village of Kaskaskia, Fraser penned letters that contributed strongly to the myth of Pontiac as the Indian genius at the head of the western tribes. "He is the most sensible man among all the Nations." "He is in a manner ador'd by All the nations hereabouts, and he is more remarkable for his integrity and humanity than either Frenchman or Indian in the Colony." Pontiac made the most of Fraser's growing insecurity and sense of dependence. Fraser, fearing for their safety, sent most of his men away to New Orleans on the night of May 18. The next day, Pontiac and his party further whipsawed the lieutenant's confidence, bursting into his quarters, seizing him and a servant, and fighting among themselves over the pair's fate. "All night they did nothing else but sing the Death Song," and were it not for a single Ottawa "Indian who was sober," Fraser felt he would not have survived. In the morning, the saw again whipped back—"they thought proper to let us escape"—and Pontiac urged Fraser to leave the dangerous Illinois Country, going either northeastward to Pontiac's own village on the Maumee River or southward "by the Sea" (the Mississippi) to New Orleans. The second suggestion Fraser quickly embraced. On May 29, he boarded a "pettiauger," a small canoe, and had a few last words with Pontiac, who stood on the bank. Two weeks later, he was in New Orleans, "yet alive," as he put it, "thank God and Pontiac."[23] Pontiac had given a remarkable performance. He had managed to convince Fraser of his power, humanity, and rationality while keeping the lieutenant off balance and denying to the British the prize of Illinois.

Shortly after Fraser had fled, another pair of envoys in the British service arrived in the Illinois, this time coming from New Orleans. They made little impression. Harpain de la Gauterais, a former French Illinois militia captain, had signed up with the British in 1764. He accompanied deputy southern Indian agent Pierce Acton Sinnott, and they traveled in secret, under cover of being Frenchmen (Sinnott spoke French with a Scottish accent and was passed off as La Gauterais's cousin). Rumors, meanwhile, preceded them. From Vincennes, a French settler wrote that Pontiac was preparing to cook them. Sinnott had recently been described by a countryman as "a stranger to the art of pleasing," and when he got to the Illinois Country, he failed to please the Indians. They plundered him and sent him packing with his comrade.[24]

Illinois eluded British authority throughout the summer of 1765, as Pontiac and his allies, short of ammunition and without the French assistance they so desired, still fought off British conquest with rumor, a weapon of the psyche. Gage knew the danger in Indian talk. Of Fraser he wrote, "Some Idle Reports had like to have cost him his life"; and: "He ran a great Risk, from the different Storys that were propagated." Britons tended to believe that the French had set the stories in motion, but if the origins had not been obscure, then the reports would not have been rumors.[25] Telling tales was waging war; the lesson was not lost on George Croghan.

Croghan, Illinois, and Divide and Rule

Croghan left Fort Pitt for Illinois late in May, and as he descended the Ohio, he described its frontage with the eye of a speculator: "The soil rich, the country level . . . the soil . . . is prodigious rich." Croghan never reached Kaskaskia or Fort de Chartres. On June 8, at dawn, eighty Kickapoo and Mascouten Indians fired on his camp, stealing everything and capturing the survivors. Three of the five dead were Shawnee diplomats. Croghan himself took a glancing hatchet blow but survived: "My scull being pretty thick the hatchett would not enter." The Shawnee speaker Nimwha, his thigh clearly pierced by a bullet, escaped into the woods and watched the scene in throbbing pain until he had discerned the identity of the attackers. He then boldly emerged to accept captivity, and he announced to the startled Kickapoos and Mascoutens that they had just committed an act of war on an important group of Shawnees, for which the upper Ohio Indians would retaliate. Likewise, when the attackers brought their prisoners to Vincennes and then to Ouiatenon, local Piankashaws and Weas criticized the entire action. Kickapoos and Mascoutens, finding themselves isolated, pleaded that they had been spirited against the English by the French, who had warned them that the English were leagued with the Cherokees, bent on enslaving all Illinois peoples and on taking Indian land. They said that they had mistaken Croghan's Shawnee and Delaware escorts for invading Cherokees, and they released all their Indian captives. Still, they kept the British as prisoners. Croghan, who during his captivity continued carefully to observe the productive capacity of the land and the indolence, in his view, of its Indian and French inhabitants, hoped that the incident would lead to a war between the upper Ohioans and the peoples around Illinois: it had, he said, "intirely broke up this great Confederacy and thrown the F-h [French] into confusion."[26]

Croghan's hope in divide and rule was widely shared in elite British circles, especially since Pontiac's War had raised the specter of intertribal cooperation. Gage urged his Indian agents to "raise up Jealousees" among Indian peoples and to "kindle those Suspicions so natural to every Indian"; otherwise, "if they are Friends, they will all join to cut our Throats." War among Indians might prevent the emergence of a much dreaded native confederacy, but it rarely made for easier imperial management. The colonies and the home government in Whitehall had no clear Indian policy. They drafted plans and failed to enact them. Management was instead a roughshod ride of quick decisions with unforeseen consequences. The tomahawk blow to Croghan's head was an example of the perils that accompanied efforts to check violence by raising armed allies and dividing Indians against one another.[27]

Kickapoos and Mascoutens claimed that French stories of a British-Cherokee plot to seize Illinois had inspired their assault. The flying report, that "the English would take their Country from them & bring the Cherokees there to settle and to enslave" the natives, had plausibility; the Cherokees were at war with Indians north of the Ohio, a war that British agents funded and which generated the kind of thick ambiguity upon which rumor flourishes.[28]

Southern Indian superintendent John Stuart worked to keep that war going. In January 1764 he wrote that he had "sent off Parties of Cherokees and Chickasaws" to intercept any boats from New Orleans carrying goods upriver which might enable "Pondiac and his Party" to "Carry on the War." In April he wrote further that some two hundred Cherokees intended to strike northward. The violence posed its own dangers, it turned out, to imperial management. When Gage learned that one Cherokee party had "killed five French-men on the Mississippi" and that another two parties had brought in three French scalps and a captive French boy, he was not sure he wanted to hear of dead Frenchmen, who were, even if in Illinois, technically British subjects, "sitting peaceably on their Habitations." The imperial policy of divide and rule suddenly appeared to be not just ineffective but dangerously beyond British control.[29]

Oconostota and Osteneco, two warriors of very high status in the Cherokee Overhills region, led a much smaller party northward in the winter of 1764–65. For some forty-six days they hovered about the Illinois Country. But they attacked no one until they discovered two bateaux ascending the Ohio, making for Shawnee country. The boats were laden with powder, ball, rum, flower, and salt and were powered by perhaps four French voyageurs. Assuming that the bateaux would rest at the abandoned Fort Massac, the Cherokees there planned their ambush. As one of the boats reached shore, the Indians struck. They captured the two French colonists alive and then made for their hidden canoes as they pursued the other craft and its bateaumen, fleeing across the Ohio. These bateaumen landed on the Kentucky side and wisely abandoned their boat, knowing it was the price for their lives. Content with their plunder and their two prisoners, the Cherokees gathered at the abandoned French post, opened a keg of rum, and insisted that the two captured voyageurs toast "King George's health." The next day, carrying all the plunder their small canoes could hold and destroying the rest, they journeyed homeward; the news lifted British hearts. Yet even in the wake of this almost ideal Cherokee raid, British officials saw the Cherokee case as "very unstable." And with good reason, the Cherokees had never been enthusiastic about this war. What's more, their northern enemies were effectively striking back.[30]

The chaos brought on by Cherokee incursions fertilized rumor. The Seneca Indian "little Getchy," a member of Croghan's attacked party who had escaped, brought word to Fort Pitt that a Shawnee "chief," presumably Charlot Kaské, had organized the assault. Kaské's speeches at Illinois, "in the name of the French," had so changed the Indians' "Dispositions" that those who had earlier assembled to meet Croghan instead dispersed to attack him. Other stories were more alarming. In mid-July, Detroit had "two very plausible Accounts of Colonel Croghan's being assassinated on the Ohio." He had been "burnt with his Retinue," including "Maisonville and the Wiandot" (Andrew the Huron), neither of whom had in fact been with Croghan. On such dangerous frontiers, all knew rumors had power; accurate news amounted to valuable currency. In a gesture toward the British, an Ottawa from Pontiac's village on the Maumee River informed Detroit, more or less accurately, of Croghan's capture, not death, and the confusion that had caused it.[31] At Fort de Chartres, St. Ange also had news of the attack, and he dispatched a messenger to accompany Maisonville to Ouiatenon, hoping to rescue Croghan and his party. Arriving at Ouiatenon on July 11, Maisonville and the messenger also carried word from Pontiac, who said that he looked forward to hearing Croghan, and that if Croghan's message was acceptable, "he would do everything in his power to Reconcile all Nations to the English."[32]

Released, Croghan was free to write letters to his superiors, hold several conferences with the peoples of the Wabash Valley, and resume his trip toward Illinois on July 18. Again, before getting very far and on that very day, he was stopped. Pontiac and the same delegation of Six Nations, Delawares, and Shawnees that had earlier accompanied Fraser now intercepted Croghan. They all returned to Ouiatenon, where Pontiac's War came to another ending. Croghan was dressed in clothing provided by his Indian hosts; he bore the marks of his misfortune on his head; he could be confined at any moment. Pontiac met him as an equal, if not as a superior. Pontiac explained that the Indians would not submit to British rule, though the British might garrison the French posts. He "desired that their Father the King of England might not look upon his taking possession of the Forts which the French had formerly possest as a title for his subjects to possess their Country." The Indians, Pontiac reminded Croghan, who would be reminded of this repeatedly over the next six weeks, "had never sold any part of it to the French."[33]

Pontiac, Croghan, Maisonville, and leading men from the Wea, Kickapoo, Mascouten, and Piankashaw peoples spent another week at Ouietanon, getting acquainted, recovering from already accomplished travels, and preparing for a journey of some three weeks to Detroit. They left on July 25 and passed through Miami, Wyandot, and Ottawa villages along the tributaries of the Maumee River. Croghan continued to note the qualities of the land for his business partners back east, and he took every opportunity to implicate *habitants* in the war. Pontiac, traveling with Croghan, remained highly cordial and "on extreme good Terms," while Croghan considered plans to "Ruin his Influence with his own people."[34]

WAR UNDER HEAVEN

Pontiac's Preliminary Peace, Detroit, 1765

Between August 23 and September 4, 1765, Croghan and Detroit's commander, John Campbell, held what amounted to five separate conferences with Indians from the region of the Wabash River and the western end of Lake Erie. During the first meeting, Croghan scolded leaders of the Miamis, Weas, Piankashaws, Kickapoos, and Mascoutens for having listened to the "Storys or idle reports of evil minded People," and they in turn begged to be pitied and given gifts by the commanders they now acknowledged as their "Fathers." They "promised to become the Children of the King of Great Britain." Furthermore, in Croghan's personal account, they "acknowledged that they had . . . given up the Sovereignty of their Country to [him] for His Majesty & promised to support his subjects in taking possession of all the Posts given up by the French." It should be noted that there exists from these conferences no signed treaty in which the Indians so surrendered sovereignty, but the proceedings do reveal the Indian displays of abject penitence so long desired by British commanders.[35]

Pontiac dominated the second conference with a characteristically careful performance. He spoke for the Ottawas, Potawatomis, Ojibwas, and Wyandots who had formerly inhabited the Detroit region. Campbell thought Pontiac "to be very penitent and . . . firmly attached to the English." Gracious and deferential, acknowledging the British as his fathers, Pontiac nonetheless began to propose terms, preparing the British for a harsher reality that the Indians would reveal only the next week. To Croghan's request that all the former inhabitants of Detroit return from the Maumee River to light their council "fire" on the Detroit River, Pontiac demurred: his people and British troops alike were better off living separately. British traders must, Pontiac insisted, extend credit to Indian hunters. Pontiac gave Croghan a pipe, requesting that Croghan take the pipe to Sir William Johnson as a sign of peace. Sir William was both to keep it and to care for it, and whenever a delegate came from the Anishinabeg, Sir William was to have it ready for a ceremonial smoke. As Pontiac spoke about this pipe, the Anishinabeg around him recalled Henry Gladwin's insulting treatment of an Ottawa sacred pipe in 1763. At last, Pontiac called for rum and merriment, to celebrate the peace.[36]

The third, fourth, and fifth conferences had a different tone entirely:

Indians insisted openly that British incivility was very much at issue, and they claimed their lands as their own. On August 30, the Wabash-area Indians announced to Croghan that as long as no English traders came to their villages, they would continue their trade with the merchants of Illinois, whose goods came up from New Orleans. Apparently reversing their surrender of sovereignty, if such they had ever made, they said plainly, "We tell you now the French never conquered us neither did they purchase a foot of our Country, nor have they a right to give it to you, we gave them liberty to settle for which they always rewarded us and treated us with great Civility." They demanded the same from the British. On September 2, in the fourth conference, Wyandots spoke in the same terms, and on September 4, in the fifth conference, so did Pontiac for the Anishinabeg. The Indians had never sold land to the French, he said, yet the French had settled it. Since the *habitants* were now British subjects, the British had to give the Indians "a proper satisfaction" for the lands on which the French-speaking British subjects dwelled. The Anishinabeg had a "very large" country, and "they were willing to give up such a part of it, as was necessary for their Father the English, to carry on Trade at, provided they were paid for it."[37]

The remarks led the pro-British Detroit residents Maisonville and George Anthon, along with Lieutenants Edward Abbot and John Carden, to violate grossly the terms of the Proclamation of 1763 forbidding the purchase of lands privately from Indians. These men obtained, in Croghan's presence, private deeds from Pontiac himself to some Detroit-area parcels of land. Pontiac turned over the lands in view of his regard for the men on September 17 and 18. Extending his gifts and his admiration to new British subjects, Frenchmen who understood the ways of the peoples of the Great Lakes, he was also asking them to help keep the British in line. Extending the gifts to British officers, he was establishing a bond.[38]

The peace conferences that Croghan began at Ouiatenon in July and which continued at Detroit in August and September can mark one end to the war. Croghan exulted that he had "been Lucky enough to Settle Matters with all those Nations, and reconcile them to his Majesty's Interest." Campbell assured William Johnson and Thomas Gage that "a General Peace [was] now Settled with all the Nations of Indians to the Westward." The Indians, and "Pondiac in particular," were "well pleased and satisfied." Pontiac would do "all the good actions in his power to ingratiate himself with the English," and that would be of great help, for "he certainly [had] great influence over the Indians." Campbell promised his betters that, to preserve the peace, he would strive to show the Indians and especially Pontiac "all the Civilities" in in his power, yet that, he added, would take presents.[39]

Croghan left Detroit for Niagara in a birch-bark canoe on September 26. Over the next two weeks, he had plenty of time to contemplate the peace. By November, he had come to several conclusions. Pontiac, he decided, was indeed "a shrewd sensible Indian of few words." The Ottawa leader commanded "more respect among those Nations, than any Indian [Croghan] ever saw could do amongst his own Tribe." But managing Pontiac alone was not managing Indians. Their relations with the British had not yet been formalized. "They are a rash, inconsiderate People, and don't look upon themselves under any obligations to us." They would not express the proper gratitude and deference superiors could expect from inferiors. Far from it, they instead thought that the empire was obliged to them for letting the British "reside in their country." Croghan, exploring what he called "their sentiments," understood that any posts the British intended to establish in order to run a fur trade would have to be paid for. Indians would not, as Amherst had once expected, simply be grateful for the opportunity to become lowly members of the British trading empire.[40]

British Illinois?

The Illinois Country still remained beyond British reach when Pontiac and Croghan finished their preliminary peace at Detroit in September 1765. Heavy August rains in Alleghenies had swollen the Ohio, causing it to rise a foot around Fort Pitt, suggesting to its commander, John Reid, that a force could rapidly descend the great river to Illinois. Reid dispatched Captain Thomas Sterling with a small detachment, a dozen Indians, and a mere 140 pounds worth of Indian presents to ride the high waters westward. From the other direction, toiling slowly against the current from Kaskaskias toward the Scioto, was Charlot Kaské, whose boatload of goods, "mostly ammunition," fell into British hands as the two parties met. Kaské had little choice but to return to the Illinois with Sterling. The British "came so unexpectedly and Suddenly upon" that country that "there was no time to form Plots, or to cabal against them," and Sterling was able to take possession of the garrison on October 10. But neither the Indians nor the local French were particularly submissive. Indians, noting the weakness of his force, "became very Insolent." Kaské stuck to his friends among the French, "who carress[ed] him very much." And, echoing Pontiac at Detroit and the Wabash-area Indians in between, the Indians of Illinois denied that the British could formally possess any lands but those on which the forts themselves stood.[41] Sterling's small force was relieved on December 2, 1765, by the arrival from New Orleans of Major Robert Farmar and the Thirty-fourth Regiment, accompanied by three Choctaw leaders, many of their followers, and fourteen Chickasaws. When it made land at Fort de Chartres (renamed officially Fort Cavendish but generally called Fort de Chartres), the joint Indian-British expedition was indeed impressive. But it did not portend effective British control of the region between the Illinois and Wabash Rivers.[42]

Fort de Chartres, once the most commanding in appearance of any garrison between Niagara and Louisiana, was likely to wash away in the spring, its mighty walls of no consequence to the eastward drift of the Mississippi River. Farmar was poorly provisioned; his Indian gifts were almost gone. Gage noted early in 1766 that none of the Illinois villages had yet made a formal peace with the British. The great hope for control over the Indians by regulating their trade was still a pipe dream: "[The] French People from Canada carry on an illicit trade to this Country whereby the Indians are supplied with ammunition." A larger trade would long continue with New Orleans. The very colony over which Farmar was to govern threatened, like the crumbling fort, to disappear beneath his feet as *habitants* and Indians moved across the Mississippi for St. Louis.[43]

At Sterling's arrival, Captain St. Ange led a French migration across the river to the Spanish side. "The Great Chief of the Illinois" and many of his people accompanied them. Sterling noted that the Kaskaskias' priest, "a former Jesuit, now a Suplician," crossed the river as well. The remaining French inhabitants in the Illinois region lived for the next decade under the threat of expulsion; indeed, Thomas Gage toyed with the idea. He had already considered the expulsion of Detroit's French in 1764, and he would seek to have the French people removed from Vincennes in the early 1770s. British correspondence about Pontiac's War was consistently hostile to the French Illinoisans.[44]

Mastery eluded the British in Illinois, and it always would. The colony remained in hot contention until the American Revolution. It had taken

"Very large Sums" to get possession of the Illinois Country, wrote Gage. It must have frustrated him that no American taxes would reimburse the Crown for its costly efforts, as the Stamp Act crisis, with riots then swirling about him even in New York, made all too plain. Before British administrators could seriously consider controlling Indians, they had to establish their own authority over the colonies themselves. As Gage told Johnson, Parliament would be busy with "too much other Business . . . respecting America, . . . to settle Matters concerning [his] particular Department."[45]

Imperial Confusion, 1765–1776

Gage had understated the case. Neither Parliament nor British officers and officials on the ground in America had much of an opportunity to "settle Matters" with Indians even as warriors gradually devoted more of their precious ammunition to hunting than to war. The most durable piece of high policy to come out of the war, the Royal Proclamation of 1763, testified far more to the inability of Indians, British officials, and colonial settlers to forge meaningful and enduring relationships than it did to an imperial decision to protect Indians from colonists. The proclamation foreshadowed Indian removal rather than sustained coexistence. The proclamation line, though never established with any precision in the north, was increasingly seen in the minds of imperial officials as a line that would admit no trespassing, would divide Indian from Briton, and would eventually shift westward to make room for new royal colonies.

The Proclamation of 1763, more than any other entity to emerge from Great Britain in the period, stands in recent interpretations as the best embodiment of the metropolitan government's decision to protect Indian lands in the wake of Pontiac's early successes in 1763. Yet as Fred Anderson has pointed out, the proclamation did less to protect Indian lands than it did to configure fights among His Majesty's subjects over who would get them. The proclamation was explicitly temporary and clearly "improvised." It provided for the generous granting to veterans and "reduced officers" of lands in "substantial amounts, more than enough to whet the appetite of speculators."[46] It established new colonial governments for Quebec and the Floridas, and in the latter places this clearly meant colonial expansion. The Proclamation of 1763 may have ordered a boundary, but the British government, determined by the late 1760s to establish its full authority over the colonies, had effectively decided not to enforce it. As a practical matter, the proclamation meant little to colonial hunters and squatters and less to the Indians who met them in the woods.

Some historians have argued very differently; they have made the case that Pontiac's War increased the metropolitan appreciation for Indian power. Pontiac and his Indian allies taught superintendents, officers, and privy councillors that Indian war cost more than it was worth; it was better to accommodate Indians through cordial, predictable relations—as Lord Hillsborough and the Board of Trade put it as early as 1763, "to reconcile their esteem and affections" by establishing a "well digested and general plan for the regulation of our Commercial and political concerns with them." Such a plan, it was hoped, would eliminate the causes of "this unhappy defection," which is how Whitehall termed Pontiac's War.[47] Indian militants, moreover, continued to organize after that war had ended, so the lesson of Indian power continued into the early 1770s. One scholar writes that as Shawnees especially called for a new, intertribal, anti-British alliance in the late 1760s, British privy councillors took note, and, hoping to avoid the cost of a renewed Indian war, they forbade colonial expansion. Thus the "natives' effort to preserve their Kentucky hunting territory helped to produce an imperial land policy that pro-tected their interests."[48] The protection of Indian nations, enshrined in the Proclamation of 1763, became British policy, at least to the degree that it gave Indians a claim on the empire. Whitehall and its representatives in America, according to this interpretation, stood in the late 1760s against both racist settlers on the move and racist speculators on the make.[49]

There is truth to the argument, too much so. But still, it is partial truth and dangerously misleading. It reckons without, for instance, the swirl of ministries that passed through Great Britain's high chambers in the 1760s. It reckons without the undulating numbers of British administrators and troops sent to enforce the supposed policy and without the chaotic condi-tion of authority in several of the western garrisons charged with imple-menting imperial designs. And it reckons without the frequent changes of British policy, including the ultimate abandonment of policy, in the areas of settler expansion, trade, and officially sanctioned colonization.

In the space of the six years between Pontiac's launching of the war and his death in 1769, the ministries of George Greenville (1763–65), the marquis of Rockingham (1765–66), the earl of Chatham (1766–68), and the duke of Grafton (1768–70) whirled through the offices at Whitehall.

WAR UNDER HEAVEN

Much as this instability at the official core of the empire was a factor in the chaotic relations of Great Britain and the American colonies, so too did it hinder stable relations with Indians. Each ministry brought to American affairs a different conception of the future of the North American interior. The Chatham administration's Indian policy was largely controlled by Lord Shelburne, who shared with many elite American colonists a desire to see the rapid demise of the Proclamation of 1763; if Shelburne did not have an enthusiasm for western expansion, he at least had a speculative interest in Indian lands. He even stoked a speculative boon, presiding over a period of bullish colonial investing and intensified trans-Appalachian surveying. He led many to believe that the king would revoke the proclamation, and he was on the verge of chartering new colonies across the Appalachians when, for political reasons unrelated to America, he lost control of American policy.[50]

Other ministries, such as that of the Rockinghamites, who preceded Chatham and Shelburne and among whom Lord Barrington took the lead in American affairs, wished the interior of the continent would simply go away. They sought to delay and reduce British obligations to protect either settlers or Indians until Parliament resolved its other conflicts with the colonies. They would maintain the proclamation line on paper, but they would leave no troops or any program to maintain it on the ground. If the Proclamation of 1763 "be right," mused Barrington, "the maintenance of forts to the westward of the line must be wrong. Why keep garrisons in a country professedly intended to be a desert?" The Rockinghamites' power was brief and had little influence on Indians or on western lands, but Barrington's policies, perhaps better described as nonpolicies, would find in Lord Hillsborough an agreeable minister. Hillsborough, who became the first secretary for American affairs in 1768 (the duke of Grafton headed the government), stood squarely against schemes for colonial expansion, both because he feared the cost and because he sought to ensure the subordination of the coastal colonies. But both Barrington and Hillsborough stood also squarely against the active protection of Indians and opposed Whitehall's tentative efforts to regulate the Indian trade. Barrington had seen no reason why the empire should shoulder the burden of regulating Indian affairs in order to protect colonists who, in the Stamp Act crisis, had shown what Gage called "scandalous behaviour and ingratitude" and what Barrington had scorned as "insolence."[51] Hillsborough entirely voided what plans for the regulation of Indian affairs had previously been drafted. Hardly a policy of establishing reciprocal, even unevenly reciprocal, relations with Indians, theirs was a policy of withdrawal, leaving the western region to colonial self-policing, claiming to protect Indians while eliminating the meager resources placed there ostensibly to do so.

Steady relations with the Indians of the Great Lakes and the Ohio Country, as Indian superintendents Johnson of the north and Stuart of the south well knew, would have required effort, not retreat. "Notice" would have to be taken of Indian leaders. British officers and troops would have to drive throngs of squatters off Indian lands, and this during a decade of unprecedented British migration to America. To be sure, the British could boast an effort or two to drive off squatters from Indian land in 1766 and 1767 (reminiscent of those Colonel Henry Bouquet had ordered in 1762—before Pontiac's War). But British authorities, never enthusiastic about the efforts to begin with, gave up the task, and the squatters returned—while speculators sent plans and agents to assemblies, to governors' councils, and to Whitehall itself.[52]

Steady relations with Indians would have meant funds adequate for the exigencies of Indian diplomacy: funds for presents, gunsmiths, interpreters, diplomats, and agents. Instead, Hillsborough cut the funding for the Indian departments and reduced the presence of the British military in the west, removing troops and closing posts. To some Indians this must have seemed like a triumph of decolonization, but it was nothing of the sort, for expansionists remained active in the colonies. It was rather the abandonment of promised good relations. The Crown promised protection, the protection was at best minimal, and even that flimsy shield was in the late 1760s withdrawn. In short, the argument that Whitehall embraced a paternal and hierarchical vision that allowed Indians a place and some claim on the government misrepresents what Whitehall was in the 1760s: a turbulent, shifting succession of ministries bent on either raising an American revenue or cutting American costs, beset by struggles at home and in the colonies.

Whitehall, of course, was far from Indian country; the British officers and superintendents on the ground in America might, in the manner of their French predecessors, have somehow turned their own material weaknesses into opportunities to forge strong and steady relations with Native Americans. They did not, however, do so, at least not until the Revolutionary War. The most important colonial and imperial officials responsible for Indian relations north of the Ohio were, to a man, failures as mediators after 1765. They were failures either because, like General Thomas Gage, they did not themselves negotiate with Indians or because, like Sir William Johnson and George Croghan, they were deeply interested, both economically and out of a sense of loyalty, in the outcomes of the negotiations they did conduct. The imperial drive for expansion and the prospects for personal gain combined too powerfully and too plausibly to allow the Indians a durable place on which to stand.

The instability at the core of the empire had its poor cousin in the chaos that engulfed the British posts in the west. At Forts de Chartres, Michilimackinac, and Pitt, the occupiers engaged in factional and self-interested competition, and sometimes in violence. In such settings, regular relations with Indians proved impossible, whatever the British ministry might order. In Illinois, competition among British trading companies, and between those companies and the ethnic French, was played out before a veritable stream of British officers whose tenures in command were but brief and generally disappointing opportunities for graft.[53] In the spring of 1768 Captain James Campbell at Fort de Chartres wrote words to Gage that Sir Jeffery Amherst might well have written five years earlier. He complained not only of the expense of the presents but also of their bad results. Presents made Indians "less contented," more "Effeminate," and convinced them that "their chief Dependance [rested] more upon His Majesty's Bounty than their own Industry." Most dangerous, in a resurrection of prewar sentiments, Campbell wrote that frequent presents served only to convince this "Dastardly Race of Cowards" that the bounty they received proceeded "from fear not of love." Gage, meanwhile, under orders from Whitehall, ordered severe retrenchment. In a replay of scenes from Detroit in 1762–63, the Illinois-area Indians saw presents dry up in the fall of 1768, and in the spring of 1769 the Indian agents, the Crown-subsidized gunsmith, and even the interpreter were all withdrawn from the region. The only thing that kept this from being a complete reprise of the eve of Pontiac's War was that the garrison itself was soon also withdrawn, and the once grand fort began to collapse into the insistent Mississippi. Though a small contingent of troops would remain at the town of Kaskaskia, it appeared that the Crown had chosen rather to abandon than to maintain direct relations with the Indians in Illinois.[54]

In Michilimackinac turmoil became the subject of wider discussion, for it involved the ambitions of the flamboyant Major Robert Rogers of the rangers. By the second week of December 1767, Rogers was in the garrison's jail; his keepers had charged him with "forming Conspiracies" with soldiers, Indians, and other friends "in order to take Detroit and Illinois, and go with the Plunder to Mississippi," where they would join Captain Joseph Hopkins. Hopkins, a ranger who had recently served at Detroit with great distinction, had nonetheless lost his commission and crossed the Mississippi to join the French under Spanish jurisdiction. A Rogers-Hopkins conspiracy was alarming enough, but Indian commissary Jehu Hay at Detroit added rumors that Rogers was trying to win over Pontiac. By May 1768, Michilimackinac was rife with rumors of an Indian war. The Ojibwas Minweweh, Mongamick, and Bonnair had thrown "away their English Colours in the Lake, and [they] invited the Ottawa Nation to feast with them and join in releasing Major Rogers." As Rogers was spirited away for trial (and eventual acquittal) in Montreal in 1769, there was no clear establishment of good relations at Michilimackinac. Minweweh, the Ojibwa who had taken the post in 1763, was again turning against the British.[55]

Of all the major posts in the trans-Appalachian west, only Fort Pitt oversaw a region seriously threatened by westering British colonists. Near here, by 1770, several small villages, each with hundreds of poor households, had illegally sprung up where Braddock's Road crossed the Youghiogheny and on two streams tributary to the Monongahela: Redstone Creek and Cheat River. That the settlers in the region came in illegally did not mean that they did not, after a fashion, have Indian permission; it meant only that they did not have the permission of the Crown. Settlers claimed the villages by living in them and, occasionally, by finding Indians to support their claims. Pennsylvania and Virginia both claimed the region on the basis of their charters. A fourth set of claimants drew increasing attention as the great Pennsylvania merchant Samuel Wharton roamed about England in 1770 seeking a charter for a new colony, eventually to be called "Vandalia," with a capital at Fort Pitt.

The stage was set for conflict by 1772, when the economizing Thomas Gage withdrew the British garrison from Fort Pitt. John Murray, the earl of Dunmore, had become the Royal governor of Virginia in 1771, and he had made it clear (by accepting shares in their ventures) that he favored the interests of Virginia speculators in the west. When Lord Dunmore dispatched a force to garrison the abandoned post, he did so not to maintain paternal relations with Indians but to maintain Virginia's claim against everyone else's. Virginia assumed the region within its Augusta County, and Dunmore appointed Dr. John Connolly as its justice of the peace. Pennsylvania responded by arresting Connolly, who in turn soon deployed fearful rumors about Shawnee hostilities in order to assert the need for immediate, prepared, and vigilant Virginia authority. A party of backcountry settlers obliged Connolly by murdering a peaceful group of Shawnee and Mingo Indians, and by 1774 the Old Dominion was at war with the Shawnees, a war spurred in large part by the actions of speculators and a doctor and fully endorsed by, and even named for, the colony's Royal governor.[56]

From the Straits of Mackinac to the Mississippi and Monongahela, officials in the British imperial service had done little to stabilize Indian relations. It was not entirely their fault, for their superiors in the Indian department, the army, and the cabinet had little concern for Indian affairs. The ministries' vacillating stands on the issues of the Indian boundary, the regulation of the Indian trade, and further British colonization of Indian lands betray the militant tendency of the muddling imperial state.

At the height of Pontiac's War in 1763 and 1764, the Board of Trade had decided both to establish, "for the present," an Indian boundary and to supervise, through the offices of the Indian superintendents, diplomacy with Indians who lived on the Crown's claimed lands. The Proclamation of 1763 established the boundary on paper; at the war's end it had yet to be surveyed. The Board of Trade initially expected that the posts lost to the Indians would be restored and that the French posts in the Illinois Country would be secured, so that from such places as Forts Niagara, Presque Isle, Venango, Le Boeuf, and Pitt soldiers would police the Indian country beyond the boundary. For this to work, there had to be British troops and commissaries in the west. Between 1768 and 1773, the British government drastically scaled back the Indian department's personnel and abandoned all the western posts save Forts Niagara, Detroit, and Michilmackinac. The withdrawal from Fort Pitt, where illegal settlers were thick on the ground, was only the clearest of many signs that Great Britain was abandoning its promise to protect Indians against colonial abuse.[57]

The decision to reduce the presence of British troops in the west was part of a larger decision to yield the management of Indian affairs to the colonies, a complete reversal of ideas and practices since 1764. An ambitious plan for Indian affairs, including especially the regulation of trade, had been drawn up that year by the Board of Trade. And though it was never formally adopted, the Indian superintendents, supported by Thomas Gage, put the plan haphazardly into effect. In Johnson's northern superintendency, which encompassed the Great Lakes, the Ohio Valley, and the Illinois regions that had been most involved in Pontiac's War, the superintendent and the general attempted to have the trade restricted to selected British posts, where an imperial commissary, backed by some soldiers, could oversee it.[58]

Johnson's insistence that trade be "prohibitted [sic] in the distant Indian Towns, or at the Small Posts, and Permits only granted for Detroit, Niagra and Osswego" meant real hardship to Indians, even when he expanded the list in another document to include Fort Pitt. The main beneficiaries of the trade as he would have had it were the Six Nations, who had the right to trade in all four places and in whose territory stood two of the posts (a third, Pitt, was in territory the Six Nations claimed). Johnson himself preposterously explained that Indians did not mind traveling over great distances to trade.[59] Even after Indians complained vigorously that they needed to have traders living among them, even after some commanders, such as William Howard at Michilimackinac, permitted licensed traders to trade well beyond their posts, Johnson continued to insist that his policy was for the best.[60] Perhaps, since his authority rested in large measure on his good relations with the Six Nations, it was best for him.

Croghan, traveling from Pennsylvania through Fort Pitt to Detroit, learned from Indians and others in the region that the trading restrictions were actually benefitting the French traders inhabiting Spanish Missouri. Andrew the Huron told him that the refusal to permit a British trading post at Vincennes had left the local Indians "Incensed against the English," and Alexander Maisonville told him a more alarming story from the Wabash. Indian leaders, returning to that valley from visits with British officials at both Chartres and Detroit, were much "dissatisfied" that the British would not give them a trader. In speeches reminiscent of those that opened Pontiac's War, these Indians declared "that the English despise[d] them."[61] Amherst had also restricted trade to the posts in 1761—but at that time the British had garrisoned posts more widely throughout the west than in 1765. Johnson's restrictions were, in that sense, even more restrictive than Amherst's had been. They were certainly more self-serving.

WAR UNDER HEAVEN

In the spring of 1768, a report by the Board of Trade itself properly called the northern policy "disadvantageous, inconvenient, and even dangerous." But its recommendations were equally disastrous: that all central regulations be dropped and that the colonies be given full control of the trade.[62] In 1769, under Lord Hillsborough, the empire did as much, passing the full "management as well as the Expense of the Indian Commerce" to the colonies.[63] Historian Clarence Alvord, writing long ago, noted that by 1769 "the management of the trade was turned over to the colonies, and the troops were no longer distributed throughout the west for the express purpose of promoting the imperial management" of Indian affairs. The troops instead were shifted eastward, to "overawe the colonies." "Nemesis," he noted, "did not overlook this carelessness."[64] Alvord exaggerated the effectiveness of the troops, but he and Nemesis each did better than those who portray British authorities in either Whitehall or the west as chastened and attentive paternalists. Pontiac's War may indeed have taught imperial authorities that they had to attend to Indian affairs, but in the years following the war, the distracted empire ignored the lesson.

Pontiac's War barely slowed down the speculation in western lands. Even during the war, many of the leading men of the middle colonies and Virginia and many of the leading officers and officials who had fought against or negotiated with Pontiac and his allies launched new projects that would establish a cordon of colonies along the Mississippi River from the Gulf of Mexico to the Great Lakes. Pontiac's War did little to shake the confidence of these men in the certainty of British landed expansion. Indeed, they used the war to argue that either their personal losses or their service to the king made them deserving of a piece of the western action. Some of their efforts made surprising headway, gradually advancing against the unpredictable winds of both British ministerial turmoil and colonial imperial crises.

During Pontiac's War, eastern gentlemen and merchants joined with new experts on the west to produce a series of schemes for colonization. Virginians, most famous for speculation, were not alone. Even British officers familiar with Indian fighting joined in the speculative enthusiasm. Thomas Hutchins appended a proposal for a military colony to his account of Colonel Henry Bouquet's expedition in 1764. Bouquet and Benjamin Franklin approved of the idea. Bouquet and Gage considered the establishment of military colonies at Niagara and Pitt, and Gage thought it might also be done in Illinois. Jeffery Amherst, Colonel John Bradstreet, and Lieutenant Thomas Mante advanced a rival plan to settle the Detroit region with roughly sixty officers heading well over six hundred families, each to be granted 150 acres. The plan, embodied in a memorial to the king in 1765, first encountered an unsympathetic Board of Trade, but its prospects soared in July 1766, when Lord Shelburne, Amherst's close friend, became secretary of state for the southern department (until 1768 the ministerial post that then oversaw North America).[65]

Joining the Virginia elite and the British officer corps in schemes for western colonization was the northern Indian department itself, whose officers were less interested in enduring relations with the Indians than in expansion with order, an order they meant to control. Sir William Johnson ensured his place in history as a defender of "Native rights and possessions" by writing frequent letters on the subject to his British superiors. He easily denounced colonial "Robberies and encroachments"; he condemned "the Frontier Inhabitants from Virginia to this Province" (New York) not only for wanton murders of Indians but also for the "avidity with which they pushed distant settlements." Yet he was as avid for lands and British expansion as any, after his own fashion. He argued that, following his methods, Britain would soon obtain from Indians "much more of their Country than [it would] do in a Century by the conduct now practiced."[66] During the war, he accepted gifts of land from the Six Nations, passing some of them on to the Crown and petitioning for royal confirmation of others, in spite of their dubious legitimacy.[67]

Johnson knew well where the planting of British subjects in Illinois and around Detroit might lead. When Gage asked him in 1766 if improvements might be made to Fort Schlosser, Johnson replied that the Senecas would care little, as long as no families settled near it: "Families, ... [the Senecas] know[,] will encrease [sic] when once a beginning is made." Still, he would have families settle elsewhere. As it became clear in 1767 that the western schemes in which he was most involved were clearing hurdles in London, Johnson grew worried that the proposed establishments might mean trouble with Indians, but he never withdrew his support for them.[68]

Most important was the Illinois Land Company, in which George Croghan was as involved as Johnson. Ultimately, Croghan also expected Indians to suffer conquest, dispossession, and servitude. Historian James Merrell is not convinced that Croghan shapes up well as the model for intercultural coexistence. To be sure, the British deputy was dead against the Paxton Boys and other frontier Indian killers. But this was not nascent humanitarianism or brotherhood: "Instead, Croghan argued, make such killing a part of a larger strategy. '[A]ll Indians have A Greatt Regard fer Each other,' he wrote on learning of the renewed attacks in 1763, and many natives still live among colonists. Lock these people up, he urged, then tell our foes if raids continue we will slay the hostages." Merrell says that "Croghan's cold-blooded calculations were a logical extension of his disdain for Indians." Croghan, moreover, was as hungry for Indian land as any stereotyped, hollow-cheeked, backcountry rifleman. In 1749 Croghan gobbled up two hundred thousand acres—or at least he tried to before the wars of 1754–65 prevented him from taking the land. But even those wars taught him only to restrict his diet: at the treaty of Fort Stanwix in 1768, he pecked at a mere one hundred thousand acres.[69]

The Illinois Company joined Croghan and Johnson to several great men of the middle colonies: Joseph Galloway, who headed the Quaker party in Pennsylvania; Benjamin Franklin, who represented the company in England; his son, New Jersey governor William Franklin; and others. It also joined them to two Philadelphia mercantile houses: Simons, Trent, and Franks and, especially, Wharton, Bayton, and Morgan (with this firm Johnson and Croghan had a deep financial relationship).[70] It is worth noting that Johnson and Croghan had Illinois Company "Shairs" as large as any other member: each stood to take an eighth of the profits. Thomas Gage, who had no shares, nonetheless worked closely with the great Philadelphia firm, and in the spring of 1766 he ordered the commander of Illinois to determine whether any Indians had legitimate claims to the region, something he doubted. Gage noted that the French farmers had never paid any Indians for their farms and that the Indians who inhabited Illinois had been refugees: driven from their former possessions, they "settled the Mississippi at the desire of the French, and . . . those lands did not belong to their Nation." The Indians of Illinois, in short, only "pretend[ed] the Lands [were] theirs."[71]

With Illinois under Crown control, the company anticipated the establishment of a civil government, the migration of settlers, and the Crown's purchase of vast lands from the few Indians who might claim, to Crown satisfaction, rightful ownership. The Illinois Company, in return for one hundred thousand acres, proposed to plant a Royal colony in a region that included much of what is now Indiana and Illinois, a large part of southern Wisconsin, and smaller parts of northwestern Ohio and southern Michigan. Benjamin Franklin, backed by careful letters from both Johnson and Croghan, presented the proposal to Lord Shelburne, who by November 1767 won the Privy Council's approval both for the Illinois colony and for Amherst's military colony in Detroit.[72]

The members of the Illinois Company became swept up, however, in a second scheme with much more immediate potential: to secure a large grant of land *east* of the Ohio, where settlers were likely to purchase lands sooner and at a higher price than in Illinois. Here, too, the necessity for purchase from local Indians was circumvented. Indians were instead freely to offer the land as a "recompense" for the harm they had done in the war years to a group of "suffering traders."

George Croghan presented the scheme as a Shawnee, Delaware, and Six Nations initiative, saying it was the "Desire of the Indians, to make the Traders [a grant] as satisfaction for their Robberys." For the Board of Trade and the Privy Council to accept the grant would amount to "indulging the Natives, in a scheme of Retaliation, that may Ever hereafter, be rendered inexpressibly subservient, to his Majesty's Service." As Shelburne radiated openness, the various company men focused on this new colony, to be called "Indiana," carved out from what is now western Pennsylvania and West Virginia, the very regions from which the army had only recently made its desultory attempts to drive out squatters.[73]

In 1768, with the advent of the duke of Grafton's ministry and the appointment of Lord Hillsborough as the first secretary of state for America, the speculators ran up against an apparent wall. Before any further colonies were to be established in the west, Hillsborough temporarily convinced the Privy Council, it would be better to gain control over the colonies already at hand, better at least to persuade them to pay taxes for the support of the army that had done so much to protect them. After several years of developing connections with powerful British ministers and lords, the colonial gentlemen-adventurers managed to overpower the lord. Samuel Wharton, actively advocating the plans in England, merged the Illinois and Indiana projects into yet another outfit, the Walpole Company (named for the prominent British supporter Thomas Walpole). Walpole placed a petition before the Privy Council's Committee for Plantation Affairs, which in the summer of 1772 approved the plan for a colony on the Ohio. Hillsborough promptly resigned. The queen, according to

WAR UNDER HEAVEN

the Board of Trade, was descended from the Vandals, and so to honor her the new colony was to be named not Indiana but "Vandalia." Had it been established, Indians would have undoubtedly approved of the name.[74]

During the late 1760s, official British policy turned away from desultory and largely paper-bound efforts to protect Indians or regulate their trade. Ruling Britons promoted the further colonization of lands around the Ohio, Detroit, and Wabash Rivers. A proposal for the Vandalia colony on the Ohio River had even cleared the Privy Council and had been drafted by the Board of Trade; the draft was again approved by a committee of the Privy Council and had been sent to the law officers for the final drafting by the end of October 1773. The project died not because London saw it as gross violation of Indian rights or because London had any interest in maintaining vaguely reciprocal relations with Indians but because in Boston colonists dressed as "Mohawks" hurled crates of tea into the harbor.[75] The British government became swept up in efforts to dominate the recalcitrant colonies, rather than to establish relations with the Indians.

Heading the southern Indian department was John Stuart, who comes off far better in recent works than his northern counterparts. His land quests were certainly more modest than Johnson's, but even he was not above seeking new land in such places as East Florida. His dealings with Indians raise another troubling issue. Stuart and his subordinates spent a good deal of time negotiating with Indians for the return of fugitive and stolen slaves. Eager for gifts with which to reward Indian man hunters, he asked his metropolitan lordships to imagine "the Danger which might arise to His Majesty's Southern Provinces by a Connection between the Indians and their Slaves, and the Latter finding an Azylum in the Indian Towns." Indeed, one of his associates and future Tory allies, Lachlan McGillivray (father of the future Creek leader Alexander McGillivray), was a partner in Georgia's largest slave-importing firm.[76]

Stuart understood that if Indians could secure the subordination of slaves through violence, they could also secure the subordination of other Indians. The Pax Britannica envisioned by Stuart meant intertribal war between the Choctaws and the Creeks, both of whom Stuart claimed as British dependents. Stuart did have a hierarchical vision, and he meant to impose it on the Creeks, "the most insolent Tribe in this District." Stuart wrote that there was "very little Subordination among them, and their young men [paid] little or no Regard to the Authority of their Seniors."

His method was to bring them to their knees through a war with the Choctaws, while claiming British sovereign protection over both. This was surgery with a rusty broadsword, highly damaging not only to both Indian peoples but, in the longer run, to British interests. Stuart's sub-agent David Taitt, in a letter informing Stuart that his "Steady friend," the Creek Emistisiguo, had been wounded in a firefight, nonetheless added: "I hope more [Creeks] will fall before the Winter is Over." Emistisiguo survived, but Stuart's staunch ally, Pya Houma, was not so lucky. Perhaps Stuart was more satisfied with the death of the Mortar, a Creek troublesome to the British. But it is hard to see how the killing of the Mortar compensated for the other losses. British settlers in the Mobile area lost cattle to passing war parties, and, like the Creeks themselves, they begged the Indian agents to broker an end to the conflict. When militant, anti-British Creeks demonstrated a willingness to come to terms with Stuart in 1774, he congratulated himself, but he did not try to end the war. Creeks, aware that Stuart had fanned the flames with gifts to the Choctaws, came to resent him. Indeed, part of the British failure to rally more effectively the numerous southern peoples against patriots during the Revolution was owing to the Creek-Choctaw war and the anti-British feeling it left among both peoples.[77]

Toward the Revolution

In 1774, as Whitehall refused to approve schemes for western expansion, some speculators saw the refusal as punitive. The Quebec Act of that year, which cut off many a venture from lands beyond the Ohio, was seen in the colonies as one of the Intolerable Acts, an effort to force the colonies to accept the unitary sovereignty of the king-in-Parliament. In an important way, this colonial perception was accurate; British ministers found it outrageous that Americans would not pay parliamentary taxes that were meant, in the first instance, to contribute to their own imperial defense. The British army, after all, had led the way in Pontiac's War. Henry Gladwin, Simeon Ecuyer, and Henry Bouquet—the men who were still seen by many to be the heroes of the war—had been British regulars. Though they had headed provincials and militia from the colonies as well as Royal forces, though those Royal forces also contained enlisted colonials, and though many colonial militiamen fought highly dangerous skirmishes near their homes, those facts tended to be forgotten in London. John Bradstreet had been born in the colonies, but from Gage to Bouquet to Johnson, Bradstreet's expenses and performance were disparaged in letters filed by the Board of Trade. As Whitehall saw it, Royal troops had defeated Pontiac. The colonists needed imperial protection, so they should pay the parliamentary taxes that supported that army. To ensure that they did so, the army had been shifted from the west to the troublesome ports.[78] In the meantime, as little money would be spent defending either the colonies or the Indians as was possible. British authorities came to believe that "an army of occupation was necessary for colonial security." Since the conquest of Canada, British authorities had occasionally floated the idea that the protection of Indians on the frontier might be a means of disciplining the colonies, but disciplining the colonies became the paramount objective of the army, and the Indians were largely forgotten until the empire erupted in revolution.[79]

The British struggle to impose hierarchy on North America in the years of imperial crises (1763–75) included two ideas: the supremacy of the king-in-Parliament over the colonies and the sovereignty of the Crown over temporary Indian protectorates. But the protectorates went undefined and unprotected. To be sure, Thomas Gage and Sir William Johnson kept the Board of Trade well informed both of the outrageous murders of allied Indians that were taking place on the frontier and of the squatters' settlements across the Alleghenies. Their reports were read in the light of the struggle over taxation as evidence that colonists had provoked Indians to violence while failing to contribute to their own defense.

This way of thinking would have dangerous consequences: it inaccurately and unfairly lumped all the colonies, and all settlers, together. The fact was that although Pennsylvania and New York may have shown a slowness to contribute to their defense during the war, by the campaigns of 1764 they were doing so, along with Massachusetts, New Jersey, Connecticut, and Virginia. Not surprisingly, Massachusetts, Connecticut, and Virginia, which had also contributed greatly to the British cause in the Seven Years' War, became terribly disappointed by Great Britain's failure to recognize their contributions. These colonies would be at the forefront of the movement for colonial rights and, later, for independence.[80]

Pontiac's War did not cause the American Revolution; neither did it convince Britain to favor Indians over colonists. It did not make rebels out of squatters or speculators; neither did it make French fathers out of

British officers, or Indian children out of the Anishinabeg, the Shawnees, and the Delawares. The relationship between Pontiac's War and the American Revolution nonetheless was intimate and is illuminating. Pontiac's War and the American Revolution were both expressions of Great Britain's struggle and failure to form stable, working relationships in the 1760s among the peoples within its suddenly acquired North American empire. As historian John M. Murrin has written of the American Revolution, Pontiac's War was a crisis of imperial integration. The crisis continued after the fighting had ended.[81]

CHAPTER EIGHT

Deaths and Legacies

Five known events, each revealed only through obscure sources, each surrounded by maddening silences or noisy confusion, orient us toward Pontiac in his elusive last years. First, in the spring of 1766, near the mouth of the Detroit River, Pontiac stabbed Black Dog, a "Principal Chief" of the Peoria Indians. Second, in midsummer, far to the east at Fort Ontario, where the Oswego River spills into Lake Ontario, Pontiac made his final and most formal peace with the British; never again would he rally warriors against the empire. Third, late in the summer of 1767, Pontiac asked imperial authorities at Detroit to close their investigation of Alexis Cuillerier, the primary suspect in a vicious wartime murder. Fourth, at Ouiatenon on May 10, 1768, Pontiac dictated a letter and had it delivered to Jehu Hay, explaining that the people of his own village on the Maumee River no longer recognized him as a chief. Finally, near Cahokia, on April 20, 1769, Pontiac, bludgeoned from behind, died on the knife blade of a young Peoria Indian. These events make up the last part of Pontiac's sketchy biography; they also, through him, lace together the themes of leadership, status, mastery, honor, and violence that played such a role in his people's relations with the emerging British empire.

Pontiac's Peace, 1766

In early 1766, British authorities invested great hope in Pontiac's planned treaty with Sir William Johnson. A captain mused, "Let Pontiac . . . hold up his Hand it is enough for a Mississippi Indian." Thomas Gage observed that the "gaining of Pondiac and his Friends" was "certainly worth [British] Attention." But Gage, ever cautious, did have his doubts. He understood that Pontiac's "power Alone was not Sufficient to gain [British] possession of Fort Chartres," so he was not certain that a peace with Pontiac would settle the war for good. In March and April, a fearful rumor further clouded British doubts about the reality of peace and the credibility of Pontiac: instead of coming to see Sir William, the rumor had it, Pontiac ("that Rogue") had crossed the Mississippi to visit Commandant St. Ange, who was by then in the Spanish service. There, at the formally Spanish but culturally French "new settlement," the Ottawa was "verry busy" and ready to "play his Tricks" on his British enemies. The rumor, Gage believed, could "be relied on." Fortunately for the British, it proved unreliable. A trickster he may have been, but Pontiac was in the spring of 1766 determined to board a British vessel for the first leg of his trip to treat with Indian superintendents.[1]

In June, Pontiac rendezvoused with Teata, the Wyandot who had broken with him three years earlier, at the mouth of the Detroit River. They joined some Illinois, Ojibwa, Potawatomi, Wyandot, and Ottawa leaders, and they met with Indian agent Hugh Crawford. It was here that Pontiac stabbed the Peoria, Black Dog. The blade went deep; as Black Dog's fellows carried him to Detroit, they thought his wound fatal. The documents tell us nothing of the cause of the quarrel or the circumstances. (The assumption by some historians that it occurred during a drunken affray is typical prejudice without evidentiary basis.)[2]

Having lost the Peoria and other Illinois delegates, Crawford urged the bloodied Pontiac and the remaining peace party to board the schooner *Victory*, the very vessel that had done so much to reinforce and resupply the Detroit garrison during the late war. By June 28 Pontiac was at Fort Erie, where he crossed paths, smoked a pipe, and drank a bottle of wine with Robert Rogers, himself en route from England to Michilimackinac. It is tempting to speculate that Rogers told him about his play, *Ponteach, or the Savages of America*, which he had already seen staged in London. Two days later, the western Indians were at Niagara, the garrison that had suffered the single greatest loss of the war at Devil's Hole. Here relations proved "a little troublesome," so the delegates hurried along the southern shore of Lake Ontario toward the meeting ground at Fort Ontario.[3]

Johnson grew "apprehensive" at the approach of the western Indians. He wished he could meet them farther from the Six Nations, many of whom were then grieving the loss of countrymen recently gunned down in a rash of colonial murders. Sir William feared an atmosphere poisoned by "many melancholy Tales, which might do [the British] prejudice." He was also worried because he had not yet received from New York the forty medals with which he had hoped to adorn the breasts of cooperative Indian leaders as marks of honor, commitment, and favor. Without medals, unsure of the Six Nations, and uncertain of the quantity of presents at Ontario, Johnson predicted that this would be "a Sad affair Indeed." To cap things off, Johnson was too sick to travel and had first to recover his strength.[4]

Weeks passed as Pontiac, Teata, and the other delegates awaited the superintendent, who at last arrived to open the ceremonies on July 23. The conference lasted only a week, not long by the standards of either Indian or European diplomacy. As the formal conclusion to a frightening war and as the forum for the establishment of a firm footing for good relations between Britons and the western Indians, it was a disappointment. Of sober, careful discussions by erstwhile enemies struggling to come to an understanding there is little evidence. The British record is all we have to go on, and in its rendition the main theme was Indian and British complaint, punctuated occasionally by both Sir William's lordly reprimands and Pontiac's lofty and ambiguous claims to vast authority over the interior of North America.

Johnson meticulously staged his welcoming address with all the formalities that might warm sentiments. He began by lighting the very pipe that Pontiac had delivered to Croghan the year before, mindful to show his respect for the Ottawa by cherishing this gift of peace. Soon, however, he grew didactic. He instructed the gathered Indians to consider the "Fruits of Peace": the traders who brought European goods into the interior, the good officers at the posts who would prevent all trade abuses, the good interpreters at the posts who would maintain smooth communication, the good smiths at the posts who would repair arms and implements. These good things, "attended with a great expense," were the work of "the Great King [their] Father as a proof of His Regard." Such evidence of good will from the king, their father, should cast "away all bad thoughts" and prevent the spread among Indians of ever-groundless rumors, those "flying idle reports of bad people." Johnson promised emptily that colonial murderers of Indians would be brought to justice, and he demanded that any Indian killers of colonists or soldiers be brought to the garrisons to be delivered to the courts of English justice "in order to have their Trial in like manner as His Majesty's English subjects." In return, Johnson insisted on demonstrations of "gratitude for this best of Princes."[5]

The western Indian response was delivered in small part by the Catholic Wyandot Teata, whose party had fought only very briefly at Detroit, and in large part by Pontiac, who had informally ended his part in the war the previous summer. It is puzzling that no other western Indians' speeches appear in the surprisingly brief record of this highly important conclusion to a war. That Teata spoke first is not surprising; the order suited, for different reasons, both the Anishinabeg and Johnson. The Anishinabeg acknowledged and honored the Wyandots as their predecessors in the region around western Lake Erie. Johnson had long advanced the superiority of such Iroquoian speakers as the Six Nations and the Wyandots over such Algonquian speakers as the Anishinabeg, the Delawares, and the Shawnees. So it made sense to all, if for different reasons, that Teata should have the first Indian word.[6]

And it made sense to the Anishinabeg that when Teata spoke, he should say little, offering the superintendent only high praise and complete equivocation. Although Teata glowingly told Johnson that the Indians loved everything that the superintendent had said, the Wyandot speaker would answer no particulars—would give no "minute answer" to Johnson's demands—until the western Indians had all fully discussed matters back in their own villages. Teata praised Hugh Crawford for his good care of the embassy as it had traveled eastward, and he requested that Crawford replace Jehu Hay as Detroit's Indian commissary. He told Sir William, in summary, that the Indians would maintain peace, would consider Johnson's words, and would like an important change in personnel at Detroit. This was hardly unconditional surrender; it was instead a prelude to Pontiac, who in the course of his more lengthy address also suggested that Crawford replace Hay. Johnson must somehow have registered disapproval, for Pontiac modified the request in midcourse, asking that Crawford at least be appointed to assist Hay. Johnson later said he would consider appointing Crawford, but he made no promises.[7]

And that was largely how the conference went; the Indians praised the British and then asked them to do better, only to have Johnson hedge or refuse. Johnson reminded the Indians to deliver up any remaining captives, and the Indians gave him in return good words but no captives. Someone among the Indians must at some point have requested that Johnson reconsider his policy of restricting the traders to the few British posts, because Johnson declared the policy essential to the prevention of abuse, adding, against hard facts, "[The posts are] so contiguous it can be no inconveniency to you to repair to them when you have anything to trade." Teata, who lived at Detroit, had no problem with this British policy; Pontiac, who lived farther away, said he could abide by it but wanted a trader posted at Fort Erie as well as at Niagara, a request Johnson refused. Teata expressed great pleasure at Johnson's arrangements, particularly the appointing of blacksmiths to mend their weapons and tools, but the Wyandot wondered if Johnson might not consider appointing to the post of smith at Detroit the *habitant* "Chauvin," who had pleased the Indians "for twenty or thirty years past." He begged Johnson not to refuse this request, but Johnson gave him no answer.[8]

If the council was weak in substance, it was less so in language and form. Few rhetorical flights grace the record, but one was Pontiac's: "It is the will of the Great Spirit that we should meet here today[,] and before him and all present I take you by the hand, . . . from this day I am resolved to hold your hand faster than ever, for I perceive that the Great Spirit who has made all these Lands about us will have it so." Unlike the honored Wyandot, Teata, Pontiac claimed early in the conference "to speak in the name of all the Nations to the Westward" that he commanded, all the "Nations," he said again (or so he is translated), of which he was "Master to the Northward." These phrases present another puzzle: Did Pontiac mean that he was "master" of all the nations to the west, or that he spoke in the name only of those groups whom he could lead? If his claim to mastery was ambiguous (and if we can trust the translations), Pontiac would retreat from it four days later. In concluding remarks on July 29, he promised that he would always remain at peace and that "all the Nations over whom [he had] any influence [would] do the same." Johnson then completed the ceremonies, distributing presents to the Indians as marks of his fatherly affection and noting the Indians' great pleasure. Before Johnson left for his home on July 31, Pontiac promised to maintain good personal relations with the superintendent and to visit him the following spring.[9]

What did not happen at the conference is as interesting as what did. No

lands were exchanged. No hostages were given for the return of prisoners, nor were any prisoners exchanged. Indians did not become British
subjects; their constitutional status was not addressed. The peace was
perfunctory. Johnson, who had himself expected little from it, gave it
mixed reviews. On the one hand, he wrote that transactions had been
concluded to his "Entire Satisfaction," and he thought that the British had
"great reason to rely on" the Indians' "Sincerity." Two weeks later, he
added that the proceedings were shrouded in danger: the Indians were "a
good deal discontented" both by French "artifices" and "by the Repeated
Misconduct" of the British. Johnson still worried that as long as Indians
faced murder, they would be "ready to take the alarm, and to unite in a
confederacy" against the British.[10]

Pontiac did not remain long at Fort Ontario, but before he left it on
August 4, he showed further regret at having become the main focus of
British attentions. Visiting the garrison, he explained that a "great war
Chief" known as "Mishilimakina Man," perhaps Minweweh, the "Grand
Saulteur," had taken offense at not having been given due regard at the
conference. Norman Macleod, the Indian department commissary at Ontario, gave the overlooked Ojibwa a silver gorget, and he gave gifts of
brown sugar, toddy, and a bottle of Madeira to Pontiac, which apparently
pleased both men and their followers. But the concentration of attention
on Pontiac as a great chief had clearly been an error; how great an error
Pontiac himself would soon learn.[11]

Pontiac's Status

The treaty council at Fort Ontario hardly touched on the question of the
status of Indian nations within British imperial claims. In imperial circles
the position that the Crown reigned sovereign over protected, dependent
nations whose members were not subjects became more firmly embedded
in practice, but neither Pontiac nor many of his allies had explicitly
yielded such dominion to the Crown. The question of the Indians' status
faced Pontiac squarely a year later, during one of the few British inves-
tigations of crimes committed in the course of the war. The case, obscure
in its details, involved the murder of a British child, Elizabeth Fisher.
Standing accused was a French-speaking "new subject," Alexis Cuillerier,
son of Pontiac's friend Antoine Cuillerier, *dit* Beaubien, one of the leaders
of the French community of Detroit. Young Cuillerier was a nephew, too,

of the former French commander François-Marie Picoté de Belestre, who, as luck had it, happened to be visiting Detroit in the summer of 1767 to settle certain matters of family property. British officials saw in the investigation an opportunity to assert the majesty and authority of British law over Detroit's ethnic French, but it did not work out that way. In the long course of the inquiry, Detroit's British officers strove to drive a constitutional wedge between the French speakers and the Indians, calling the Euro-Americans "subjects" and the Indians "children." In the case of young Cuillerier, the wedge shattered.[12]

Alexis Cuillerier had spent the war years among Pontiac's Ottawas, first near Detroit and later near the rapids of the Maumee River, a place beyond British authority after the Indian capture of Forts Miami and Sandusky. Not only had Cuillerier lived with these enemies of the king, but he had "assisted them in fighting against the English at Detroit." After four years, with peace settling in, he risked a summertime visit to Detroit, where British troops promptly placed him in jail to await trial for the murder of Betty Fisher. The testimony secured against Cuillerier, particularly that given by his friend Jean Maiet on August 4, was "clear and point blank," according to Indian commissary and British officer Jehu Hay. But it was also highly troubling, for it implicated Pontiac, who was then Great Britain's very best hope for a lasting peace in a region still swept by rumors of war.[13]

Betty Fisher's late father had been a retired sergeant, one of the very few Britons to stake out a farm near Detroit before Pontiac's War. In one of the war's opening raids, Ottawas captured Betty and one or two of her siblings, killing the rest of her household. When Pontiac's Ottawas retreated from Detroit to the Maumee River in late 1763, they carried the girl with them. Cuillerier and Maiet joined them, too, and, according to Maiet, they shared a cabin with Pontiac, Betty Fisher, and others during that winter. Maiet testified that on a particularly bitter night, the little girl, sick with "a flux," "beshit the blanket she lay on." The woman who cared for her washed the blanket, but before it could dry, the shivering and sick child approached Pontiac's fire for warmth, only to be seized roughly by the great man, carried out, and thrown into shallow, freezing Maumee waters. Turning to Cuillerier and Maiet, Pontiac ordered them to "Drown the Child." Both initially refused, but Pontiac insisted. Cuillerier went to the river and submerged the child in its shallows until she was still.[14] Maiet added the otherworldly detail that as he and Cuillerier buried the child, her legs began to shake. He did not say that this indicated that the child was still alive; he seems instead to have seen it as a cosmic rebuke to the guilty living.

A deeply troubled Maiet left Pontiac in the spring of 1765 and reported the murder to Lieutenant George McDougall and two prominent French supporters of the British. Nothing was done until the summer of 1767, when Cuillerier came to Detroit and was imprisoned. On August 17, Cuillerier "made his escape." One might speculate that members of the garrison, the community, or both, having considered the social marginality of the dead Fisher family against the local importance of the living Cuilleriers, sprang the young man from the jail. But the escape infuriated some British officials, notably the commissary Hay, who wrote that the guards "did not do their duty" and that "The Commanding Officer [was] much distress'd at [Cuillerier's] getting away." The investigation of Cuillerier, moreover, continued.[15]

This was a difficult summer for Pontiac. At home on the Maumee, he faced among his people a "Strong party" that inclined toward a Shawnee-led effort to revive the intertribal movement against Great Britain. To the southwest, the Peorias, partially Catholic and never supportive of his earlier movement, now held him responsible for the stabbing of Black Dog. To the west, many St. Joseph River Potawatomis objected to his peace, and to the south, many in the lower Wabash and Ohio Valleys wondered at its wisdom, given the continued raids by Cherokees, rumored to be spirited on by the British. With so many opponents, he was not anxious to go north to Detroit in response to a summons from Detroit's commander, George Turnbull.[16]

Nonetheless, on August 29 he presented himself to the officers. Over the next two weeks, members of his own family, an unnamed nephew and a "Brother in Law" named Oskkigoisin, confirmed Maiet's story, at least in rough outline. Detroit's interpreter, Elleopolle (nicknamed "Meni") Chesne, further testified on September 4 that Pontiac had once, "in his liqor [sic]," told him the same story, adding two details: at the time of her murder the girl was already dying, and she had infuriated Pontiac by soiling his clothes. When the officers told Pontiac of these allegations in mid-September, he neither affirmed nor denied them; he simply refused to hear such things. And he asked the British to drop the case against Alexis, the son of his old friend Antoine Cuillerier.[17]

By the summer of 1767, Pontiac's high standing among the British and his refusal to cooperate with a new militantly anti-British movement coming out of the Shawnees' Scioto Valley were gaining him enough enemies, even among his relations, to cast some doubt on the two Ottawas' testimony against him. As for Jean Maiet, there is the possibility that he had meant to complicate the case against Cuillerier by linking it to Pontiac, on whom British authorities felt peace depended. Pontiac never denied the accusations, but he never admitted to them, either. Maddening as it is, though the case against him would seem to be strong, we cannot firmly establish Pontiac's guilt or innocence in the murder of this child. The affair does, however, clarify another matter, one of lesser biographical interest, perhaps, but of greater historical consequence. It illuminates the emerging, yet still confused, British official perspective on the Indians' status in the empire.

The investigation of young Cuillerier demonstrates yet again that the British understood Indians to occupy a status apart—a status unlike that held by old British colonists, His Majesty's old subjects, and unlike that held by the newly conquered French of the region, the king's new subjects. After hearing repeated testimony from Frenchmen and Indians that Pontiac had ordered Betty Fisher's death, British authorities showed not the least interest in prosecuting him. This was not simply because they needed to support his struggles against the renewed pan-Indian efforts against the empire. The fact was that Pontiac, though he lived within the king's claimed realm and under the Crown's claimed sovereignty and protection, was not, in anyone's view, a Crown subject. He was not a "new subject," he was not an old one, he was not one at all. He was instead the leading member of a separate nation, a nation that, however subordinate, had just made a peace with Great Britain, a peace that obliterated the acts of war.

Lieutenant Hay explained this to Pontiac himself. Pontiac had come to Detroit to plead for a pardon for Cuillerier, should he be recaptured: "I Should be glad this man could be pardon'd if caught again." Hay insisted that this was impossible. Detroit's French had, since 1760, taken oaths of allegiance to the king, thus becoming subjects, and now they "must be ruled by the same Laws" as the old British subjects. As for Pontiac and "Other Indians," Hay said that the peace so recently formalized with the British had buried all "that had happen'd dureing [sic] the war, . . . and that the Belt of friendship which he carried was a Witness of it." Hay noted that Pontiac "seem'd to understand" the distinctions Hay was drawing between new subjects and Indian nations, but the Ottawa also manifested such "affections . . . for the french in General, and particularly" for the Cuillerier-Belestre family, that these "biass'd him a good deal."[18]

Hay could define the legal distinction between French new subjects and nonsubject Indians, but Pontiac would not allow the definition to work against his friends. Pontiac requested that Hay allow Chesne, the interpreter whose testimony had, along with others, vilified both Pontiac and Cuillerier, to winter with him on the Maumee River. This would prevent Chesne from participating in any trial of Cuillerier that might occur should the fugitive be recaptured. Chesne, meanwhile, now not only cooperated with Pontiac but filled Detroit with so many different versions of his own story that Hay felt compelled to defend the validity of Chesne's sworn affidavit against Chesne's later rumors. What's more, Chesne absconded with Pontiac to the Maumee River; the two later moved to a village south of Ouiatenon on the Wabash. Hay declared Chesne "a deserter from his Majesty's service," and Hay was even finally forced to undercut Chesne's credibility: "He is Capable of saying or doing almost anything." The case against Cuillerier, collapsing rapidly, weakened further when Maiet took a similarly unauthorized leave amid rumors of renewed Indian war, going to trade illegally that winter with the still turbulent St. Joseph Potawatomis. Detroit's commander, George Turnbull, would that spring again refer to the distinction between the ethnic French and the Native Americans when he promised to "treat both the New Subjects and Indians with the greatest Lenity," but the Cuillerier affair had cast doubt on the garrison's ability to make such distinctions good, and as for lenity, the affair had shown that Turnbull had little choice.[19] If "Pontiac's Rebellion" had indeed been a rebellion, hangman's nooses might have decorated its conclusion; instead, no Great Lakes, Illinois, or Ohio-area Indian was ever brought to trial for turning against the Crown.

Pontiac's Repudiation

In the summer of 1766, that summer of Pontiac's final peace, Sir William Johnson received disturbing word that the Detroit Indians were furious with Pontiac and suspicious that the British made "to [sic] much of him." Johnson's sources were good: a Montreal-based British trader and an eminent Detroit merchant. Both said they had heard of rumors spread by Pontiac's Indian enemies that the imperial authorities paid him "ten Shillings sterling a day." Detroit's Philip Dejean, a betting man, placed odds that "Pondiac would be killed in less than a year, if the English took so much notice of him." Great Britain's earlier failure to "take notice" of Indian leaders had done much to bring on Pontiac's War; now the empire was concentrating far too much "notice" on a single man. As for Dejean's bet, he would have lost, but only because his sense of timing was slightly off.[20]

That winter, Pontiac reminded Johnson that he intended to visit John-son Manor on the Mohawk River in the coming spring. Still asserting Pontiac's great power, Johnson expected that the meeting would have "a verry good Effect." The superintendent must have been disappointed when Pontiac failed to appear. Johnson remained confident that Pontiac still had "extensive influence," but he grew increasingly doubtful that the 1766 peace would long hold. By winter, persuaded that Pontiac would not come east, Johnson notified his superiors that the Indians of the west were busily patching up old differences—even the Dakotas and the Ojib-was were making peace—all signs of danger, the superintendent thought, to British interests. Some rumored that Pontiac himself was contemplat-ing another anti-British war.[21]

In fact, Pontiac was contemplating his own political collapse. Ejected from his village on the Maumee River, he had moved to the neighborhood of Ouiatenon on the Wabash, where he was hunting in an effort to pay off his debts. In the presence of Alexander Maisonville and other French-speaking men on May 10, 1768, he dictated a message to Jehu Hay, who had recently invited him to Detroit. Calling Hay "My Father," he com-plained that he had been "shamed" [chagriné] by the young men of his village, who had insulted him repeatedly, saying that he "never was chief." Where William Johnson had portrayed Pontiac as a "master" of many tribes in the west, Pontiac had left his alienated villagers with this cutting remark: "You are chiefs like me[;] prepare to command the village." To remain a leader, he needed followers. To become leaders, they needed access to European goods. As things stood, they were chiefs like him, which was to say: not at all.

Pontiac went on to assure the British of his loyalty and to explain why he would not soon visit Detroit. He said that he and Johnson remained bound together and had rejected all "bad affairs," that he was still faithful, that he did not listen to the "bad birds" of rumor and hostility. He notified the British that he would soon travel to Illinois on personal business: he planned to seek out his wife's brothers and to obtain a few charges of powder. He closed by assuring Hay that he had accepted the Indian agent's belt and gift of tobacco, proof that he was not involved in any trouble, and that he would hold Hay's hand always. George Turnbull, commanding at Detroit, read the message in the light of other news. Over the two winters past, Pontiac's "own tribe" had "given him several severe beatings." No longer was the Ottawa of the same "consequence as formerly."[22]

Pontiac's Death

In the retelling, Pontiac has suffered many murders: killed in a drunken affray; killed by his wife's lover; killed in woods; killed at Fort de Chartres; and, in the most authoritative accounts, killed in the streets of Cahokia, after soberly trading with a merchant, by a young Peoria seeking vengeance. Many reports, which found voice in Illinois at the time of his death and in Detroit generations later, blamed the British for convincing the Peoria youth to assassinate the Ottawa. Immediately after Pontiac's death, the rumor of British culpability "spread like lightening through the country." With it went the false news that "great numbers" of Indians immediately descended upon and "destroyed all the Peorias except about thirty families," who fled to the protection of Fort de Chartres. According to the story, the wretched Peoria survivors later moved to a village on the Wabash, where northern Indians surprised them one winter night "and killed the whole." So recalled Charles Gouin at Detroit in the 1820s. That terrifying retaliation made it from legend into fact in Francis Parkman's history, but as Howard Peckham demonstrated, it never happened. It is easy to see how in the nineteenth century a Gouin or a Parkman might desire such a dark and bloody savage past to justify what each saw as a better-ordered, civilized present. But Gouin did not dream up the legend; it began as a rumor in the year of Pontiac's death.[23]

Daniel Blouin and William Clajon, Illinois inhabitants and traders, did not claim to know all the details of Pontiac's murder when they wrote of it in 1770 and 1771. What they did know was this: on April 20, 1769, a young unnamed Peoria man who was nephew to the Illinois leader Makachinga had joined Pontiac peacefully at a trading post in the Cahokia Indians' village, adjacent to but separate from the French-speaking hamlet, Cahokia. In full daylight and without warning, the Peoria smashed his war club into the back of Pontiac's head and then sunk a blade deep into the

Ottawa's body. The British knew the killer's uncle, Makachinga, as Black Dog—the very man Pontiac had stabbed and badly wounded in 1766. By this April day, Black Dog had for months been beseeching the British at Fort de Chartres for assistance against an expected Ottawa attack; his nephew's assassination of Pontiac only intensified his pleas.

Recently scholars have put the killing in the French town of Cahokia, but it appears that it actually took place in the adjacent Indian village. Blouïn put the killing "au Millieu du Village des Kahoquias," by which he meant the Cahokia Indians' village, not in French Cahokia. That Indian village was served by the resident Jesuit priest Father S. L. Maurin, who also said the killing took place there. Father Pierre Gibault, who served at Kaskaskia and who may well have gotten his news from Maurin, said the same thing, and he called the village "Tamaroa." A 1744 map of the Illinois Country shows the "Cáquias et Tamarouas" as inhabiting the same village, in the neighborhood of what would become French Cahokia.[24]

It is likely that the Peoria killer was at some level avenging the insult done to his uncle, but further underlying foundations of animosity between Pontiac and the Peorias are uncertain. No one in Illinois believed that the assassination settled the conflict; instead, panic rode on rumors of war. "It is feared," Father Gibault warned, "that his death will kindle a great war among the Indian tribes." Rumors were circulating that many Ottawas and their allies intended to avenge Pontiac's murder. Peorias, as Gouin much later recalled, had indeed fled to the gates of Fort de Chartres, but the commander, Lieutenant Colonel John Wilkins, had refused them admittance. Nonetheless, the Peorias camped under his guns, spreading word, meanwhile, that Wilkins had authorized Pontiac's assassination. That accusation the Ottawas and others readily believed, for by his "bearing" Wilkins had already demonstrated his domineering character.[25] Leading French traders accused Wilkins of favoring the Peorias, even of arming them, despite the fact that their assassination of Pontiac had threatened the colony with a vast northern invasion. And there was truth to the charge. Wilkins did organize scouting parties made up of Peoria warriors. It is true, too, that a Peoria was captured by Shawnees and Potawatomis the summer following Pontiac's death. And what generated the most alarm was that Minweweh, the great Ojibwa who had captured Michilimackinac and who (it was now widely reported) was a kinsmen of the murdered Pontiac, had come to Cahokia to punish the British commissary there; not finding him, Minweweh had killed and scalped two or three of his servants. British authorities had not only imposed martial law in Illinois but had also ordered unwilling former French subjects into the militia, where they would be under military discipline. Fear spread throughout the French-speaking population that it was to be enveloped in violence it had done nothing to create; Blouin protested against Wilkins' authoritarian orders and saw the rumored Ottawa attack as a mere pretext for Wilkins to expand his authority. In a formal, written protest peppered with exclamation points, he accused Wilkins of discrediting the British by both failing to investigate Pontiac's murder and sheltering the (in Blouin's view) guilty and treacherous Peorias. Worse, Wilkins had dishonored Great Britain by convincing Indians that the empire had resorted to an assassin to vanquish a foe who had already made peace. Panic, Blouin said, was everywhere.[26]

Gage knew of the French complaints, and he knew that Pontiac's murder by an Illinois Indian was "beleived [*sic*] to have been excited by the English." He also feared that the rumor was drawing "many of the Ottawas and other northern" Indians to the Illinois Country "to revenge his death." Now it was the British commander of Illinois who was rumored to have instigated Indian violence; once it had been the French commander who had been so vilified. The irony was not lost on Gage, who continued to see events as the result of French conspiracy. The *habitants*, he wrote, "are turning the Tables upon us by way of answering our complaints against their own intrigues."[27] In the wheeling world that had swept Pontiac away, rumor still turned against rumor, unsettling hopes for peace; depriving Indians, old subjects, and new subjects of firm ground on which to stand, it drew their attention instead to the groundless world of flying reports, of words, and of the word.

Spoken Legacies

The achievements of Indian militants in cooperating with one another over vast distances, eliminating British posts, and preventing definitive British punishment impressed their British opponents. Colonists had worried about intertribal union almost since they first came ashore, and with good reason: Indians knew as well as anyone else that power could reside in numbers. Identifying intertribal cooperation as a possible threat to colonial security was much easier, though, than preventing it. Throughout 1766, as peace seemed to settle on the region, the British struggled to find some plan that would prevent "Attempts to form a Confederacy between the great Nations" of the interior. All they could come up with was an unoriginal policy of divide and rule, with all its glaring dangers.[28]

Even John Stuart, who had worked hard to have Cherokees launch attacks against northern Indians and who continued to promote intertribal war in the south, worried about divide and rule. Of a Choctaw-Creek war, Stuart thought it "an Event rather advantageous" to the British, though he feared that if the British were seen to be the "Instruments of bringing it about," they would "infallibly lose the confidence of all the Indian Nations." Of the Cherokees' war with "Northward" Indians Stuart was receiving horrifying reports, including notice that a British trader had been killed in a northward attack, which caused "the Traders with one Voice" to call for British mediation to end the conflict. Stuart was torn; on the one hand, he thought that militant Creek efforts to draw the Cherokees away from the British meant that the Cherokees' war with the northwards should continue; on the other hand, he did not wish the Cherokees to be so weakened that the Creeks, among whom the militants might gain too much influence, would come to command the southeast.[29]

Sir William Johnson, who had long argued that intertribal warfare drained off bad Indian humors, recognized that the violence also imperiled Britons. He had come to the conclusion by March 1766 that an intertribal war between the Shawnees and the Illinois Indians would "obstruct the Communications, and render [Britons] liable to much Danger." So he instead ordered his agents to perform condolence ceremonies, replete with gifts, to prevent the Shawnees from retaliating against the Kickapoos and Mascoutens for Shawnee losses in the 1765 attack on Croghan's ill-fated Illinois expedition.[30] Reluctantly, Johnson agreed to work as well for a peace between the Six Nations and the Cherokees, a peace that Virginia demanded, both because the colony hoped to keep warriors from traveling through its backcountry and because it sought better relations with the Cherokees in the wake of its failure to bring colonial killers of Cherokees to justice. Virginia governor Francis Fauquier knew that the Cherokee nation would appreciate Virginia's role in mediating a peace with the Six Nations. When Oconostota, a leading Cherokee ally of the British, lost his brother's son to an attack by northern Indians, Fauquier pushed for a British-mediated peace, and Johnson, encouraged by Gage and Stuart, fell into line. By March 1768 Johnson had made the arrangements; indeed, he had never seen "the Six Nations so hearty in anything."[31]

As the Shawnees revived interest in pan-Indian action over the next two years, Gage and Johnson began dreaming of orchestrating a general Cherokee–Six Nations war against them and other western Indians. Gage put it bluntly in a Christmas letter to Sir William: "It is a shocking alternative to let these savages destroy each other or by mediating peace turn their hatchets against our own heads. In such an extremity there is no doubt which to prefer, but humanity must make us regret that our affairs are in such a situation." From 1768 into the 1770s, while Stuart encouraged intertribal war in the south, Cherokees and Chickasaws attacked northern Indians, particularly in the lower Ohio Valley. There, Kaskaskias, Cahokias, Peorias and French-speaking inhabitants rumored that the invaders had "whites" among them, that men among the invaders had the "beard and the hair" of the English, that the English were therefore spurring on the assaults.[32] Once again, Gage's hope for imposing British order by divide and rule only spread the kind of destabilizing chaos that prevented good relations. Against divide and rule Shawnees raised the loudest voices.

A Legacy of Intertribal Organization

Something big was afoot in Shawnee country, two Shawnees told George Croghan at Fort Pitt in 1766. Twenty Shawnees, they said, had just returned from Illinois carrying French and Indian speeches to a council to be held at Scioto, a major Shawnee town on the broad plains that lay along the river of that name. The intention, it was clear to Croghan, was to drive "the English out of the Country."[33] The Scioto Valley Shawnees' struggle to form an intertribal alliance crested in the fall and winter of 1767–68 and again in 1769.[34] Croghan took credit for disrupting the first wave, diverting Indians to a large council that he held at Fort Pitt in the spring of 1768. He settled all the issues, he said, except encroachments, for the Indians still insisted on the people "being Removed."[35]

To Gage, who rarely left New York City, the frontier settlers bore the heaviest responsibility for the turbulence in the Ohio Valley. Gage had ordered the garrison of Fort Pitt to clear out the "huts" of the settlers on the Cheat River and Redstone Creek, and the governments of Virginia and Pennsylvania had sent word to the intruders that they should leave. Yet even after British troops had burned their crude houses, the settlers returned and were "joined by some hundreds more." Gage wrote to his superiors that he kept trying to push the various civil authorities into greater action, and he asked them at least to give him permission to act, but he was always ignored. Insofar as the Indians had any real grievances against the British, Gage insisted, the American colonists were clearly to blame.[36]

For the Upper Ohio Country, Gage had a point. But when he blamed colonial squatters for a Saginaw Bay Ojibwa and Maumee Valley Ottawa attack on British traders, something was amiss. These Anishinabeg were not threatened by squatters; nor were colonial murderers killing their relatives. Ottawas and Ojibwas made excuses and pled for pardon, saying that the evil spirit provoked the assault, that young hotheaded men were responsible, or that the two merchant craft had been mistaken for attacking Cherokees. Never did these Anishinabeg blame ordinary colonists from Virginia or Pennsylvania for encroachments on their lands.[37] They knew well the complaints of Shawnees, Mingos, and Delawares, and they undoubtedly knew of the encroachments in the Upper Ohio Country, but their hostility to the British had sources even farther away, well to the east in the governors' chambers and across the Atlantic in London itself.

That squatters and murderers were not mostly to blame for the renewed militancy among western Indians became even clearer in 1769, as news spread through the Ohio Country of the previous year's Treaty of Fort Stanwix and its vast cessions of lands south of the Ohio River to the British. There had been some Delawares at Fort Stanwix, but for the most part it was the work of the Six Nations Iroquois, Sir William Johnson, and various land speculators connected with him. Many Delawares, and even some Six Nations—particularly the Genesee Senecas—later expressed outrage that Iroquois League councillors had ceded lands to which the Six Nations had no good claim and on which Cherokees, Shawnees, Mingos, and Delawares regularly hunted. Although Johnson maintained that the cession was valid, militant Indians organized against it, and "Apprehensions of danger" spread among the Virginians, Marylanders, and Pennsylvanians who had settled illegally across the Appalachians and who feared Indian war.[38]

British agent Alexander McKee, whose mother was a Shawnee, learned that the Shawnees had built a "very large Council House at Scioto" and had in the spring of 1769 sent invitations in all directions, inviting Indians to join them for a great meeting. The Shawnees deplored the Six Nations' conduct in "giving up so much of the Country to the English without asking their Consent." Already groups of Ohioans had met with southern Indians to discuss a possible response to the cessions. Now that Shawnees were at peace with the Cherokees, they could advance the intertribal plan that had "been on foot" for several "years past." Only a faction among the Shawnees supported the measure, but with support from militant factions from throughout the region between the Mississippi and the Appalachians, the idea of renewed pan-Indian action against the English revived. Rumors of it spread eastward, and in the country of the Six Nations, British agents heard that many Ohioans, "determined . . . to begin a Warr," were "making ready their death Hammers."[39] The Shawnees' Scioto movement coincided with the death of Pontiac and the consequent fears of an outbreak of war in Illinois. Stable peace eluded the Great Lakes and the Ohio Valley regions.

A Legacy in Rumor

The war named Pontiac's dissipated in a haze of rumor, and rumor long survived it. Despite France's complete withdrawal from the continent by 1765, rumors of French mischief still periodically blew across the great valleys and along the freshwater shores. From 1766 through the end of the decade officers and agents such as Jehu Hay, William Johnson, Robert Rogers, Guy Johnson, and Alexander McKee wrote of French and Spanish belts, ammunition, and dangerous reports circulating in the west from New Orleans or from somewhere in Spanish Louisiana. In the spring of 1766, both Croghan and Farmar reported that former French subjects within the British claims were spreading nasty, anti-British rumors. Major Robert Farmar noted that the Shawnee Charlot Kaské had implored St. Ange to help him cut off the bad English weeds.[40] Gage remained convinced in 1769 that French traders and inhabitants circulated "idle stories" among the "credulous" Indians, but he admitted that he had "never been able to discover" official French sanction for such evil speech.[41]

The genuine recession of France from America, accomplished by 1765, was obvious: Spanish flags flew over its scattered former and new forts in the Louisiana Territory, and British flags flew over its scattered garrisons in the Illinois, Great Lakes, and Ohio regions. France's withdrawal, however, made little impression on the rumormongers; most of the colonists in these regions remained French speaking, even commanders of nominally Spanish garrisons. The idea of the French king's return with armies and munitions survived Pontiac's War and would resurface sporadically among the Indians for another thirty years. That Indians continued to speak of the French king's revival suggests that the idea was more than the contrivance of French *habitants*, even if that is how it began, which is uncertain. The power of the idea, moreover, grew not from its nostalgic character—although it clearly did appeal to nostalgia—but rather from the hope it gave to opponents of both Great Britain and, very soon, the United States. The rumor, and its strength, powerfully remind us that Great Britain never successfully replaced France as the mediator of heartfelt alliances in the Great Lakes region and the trans-Appalachian west.

As the American Revolution erupted in the Atlantic colonies, James Wood, a Pittsburgh Committee of Safety member who had been sent out "to investigate among the nations how matters stood," reported the presence of the notion among the Wyandots and Delawares. Wood had learned that the idea had been propagated, oddly enough, by the very targets of its first expression. Wood was told that Detroit's British officers and Duperont Baby, a Frenchman who had joined Detroit's British garrison during Pontiac's siege, had announced the imminent French return: "Tho' their fathers the French were thrown down the last War by the English they were now got up again and much Stronger than ever and would Assist their Children [the Indians] as they formerly did."[42] Almost a year later, in the late spring or early summer of 1776, as Ottawas and Shawnees visited the Cherokees with messages of intertribal unity, they spoke simultaneously of alliance with the French and of a war against the American settlers. The leading Ottawa deputy promised that "the French in Canada had found the means to supply them and would assist them." A Shawnee spokesman (probably Charlot Kaské, for he was described as a renowned "French partisan") displayed a nine-foot belt of dark wampum, covered with red paint, and he unleashed a stream of arguments calling for a united Indian war against the Anglo-Americans. This speaker claimed that "the French, who seemed long dead, were now alive again, that they had supplied them plentifully with ammunition, arms and provisions, and that they promised to assist them against the Virginians."[43] Such talk of the French, after a decade of officially peaceful relations with Great Britain that had followed Pontiac's War, demonstrates how little Great Britain had done to establish its good leadership among the Indians of the west.

In the end, it was neither the French king nor his armies that the Indians truly sought. They sought instead the support that the French could give them in their efforts to meet with strength threats to their way of life. What would ultimately destroy nostalgia for New France was not the French failure to arrive but French arrival. During the American Revolution, the French king did "wake up," but for most Great Lakes and upper Ohio Indians, he did so on the wrong side of the war. The patriots at Pittsburgh received word of the Franco-American alliance on May 26, 1778. In July, Colonel George Morgan sent the news from Pittsburgh to the still neutral factions among the Delawares and Shawnees that French ships were "more than three times the force of the British": "You may be sure the French will not lose so fine an opportunity of conquering the English."[44] A month earlier, from Valley Forge, George Washington had ordered a French lieutenant colonel in the Continental Line, Phillippe-Louis Chevalier de Failly, to Fort Pitt, where "the affection which the Indians in general" had for France might enable him "to render great service."[45] Two *habitants* in George Rogers Clark's service delivered rebel belts to the Indians of the Wabash Valley with encouragement to "turn out [their British] father" at Detroit: "For now your late Father the King of France is come to life and will recover the country he has lost to the English."[46]

Following the news was the greatest series of rebel victories in the western war: Clark's reconquest of Vincennes (February 25, 1779), Evan Shelby and John Montgomery's destruction of the Chickamauga Cherokee towns (April 1779), John Bowman's destruction of the Shawnee towns (June 1779), and Daniel Brodhead's and John Sullivan's separate invasions of the Seneca country (August and September 1779). The raids left thousands of Indians homeless, and as famine set in, so did Indian alienation from the British. This was especially true among peoples who, like the Ottawas, Ojibwas, Wyandots, Delawares, and Potawatomis, had avoided destruction.[47] Their alliances with Britain wavered as news of both the American victories and the French alliance spread west.

As Indians along the Great Lakes and in the Illinois Country—precisely those Indians who had been most attached to the notion of the French king's revival—expressed doubt about the value of the British alliance, the British worried, throughout 1779 and 1780, about the effect of the rebels' French coup. The Indians' friendship with Great Britain, General Frederick Haldimand wrote his superiors, was "every day declining, particularly since the American alliance with the French," to whom they had "an old and a very firm attachment."[48]

But in the hands of the United States, the news of the French return to North America proved to be of little value. The notion had not been fundamentally nostalgic to begin with—it had been fundamentally defensive; as its nostalgic temper collided with its defensive raison d'être, the dream vanished. The American inability to gain from the notion is summed up in the western career of Colonel Augustin Mottin de La Balme, an unofficial envoy working with the acknowledgment of, but without any real support from, George Washington, the marquis de La-Fayette, and the French minister in Philadelphia. As La Balme worked to rally Indians and *habitants* of the Ohio and Illinois regions to the white Bourbon flag, he became disgusted by his allies' treatment of Indians in the Pittsburgh region. In one instance, a gang of whites tried to murder a group of Delawares with whom the Frenchman was attempting to discuss an alliance. Farther to the west, in American-occupied Illinois Country, La Balme had some success in raising a small Indian and French force for a raid on Detroit. The *habitants* who threw their support to him, it is clear, did so in part out of desperation; they had never gotten on well with the British officers, but they had just faced extreme mistreatment at the hands of the Virginia occupying forces. They truly sought the return of France. In joining La Balme, they made it clear that they were joining France, not the United States. Under the *drapeau blanc* and without American colors, the eighty-odd gunmen moved north in 1780 and captured the recently reestablished British Fort Miami, but they were quickly counterattacked and annihilated by Little Turtle and Miami Indians unconvinced of the advantages to be gained by working with a French king who allied with the United States.[49] Indian victories over the Americans late in 1779 and throughout the rest of the Revolutionary War also undermined American efforts to deploy the French revival. No further French troops, moreover, appeared on the frontier. By the war's final years, very few of the Indian villages that had once been allies of the French remained at peace with the United States, despite its French alliance. From the Creeks in Alabama to the Ojibwas in Ontario, the overwhelming majority of Native Americans within fighting range of the United States continued their struggle against the Anglo-American threat to their autonomy.

Talk of a French revival would surface again after Great Britain conclusively abandoned its Great Lakes and Ohio Indian allies in the mid-1790s. Abandoned by the British and defeated by the Americans, the Indians may have wanted to believe the rumor. Alexander McKee, then still a British agent working among the Miamis, reported that a Frenchman in Michigan had promised the Shawnees that "the time for their French Father to shew himself was drawing very near and he would support and protect them."[50] By that time, however, the memory of France had grown dim, France had itself beheaded its own king, and Indians, defeated by General Anthony Wayne and intimidated by his legion, took steps toward making peace with the United States.

The demise of the French monarchy in 1792 and of the dethroned king the following year precipitated events that, paradoxically, came closest to bringing about the promise of France's return to America in the years following the fall of Canada. According to the French Revolutionary calendar, on the twenty-ninth day of Fructidor in the Year IX (September 16, 1801), a Louisiana Creole presented a document to Napoleon's government supporting the retrocession of the Louisiana Territory from Spain to France. Among other arguments, Joseph Pontalba pointed out that the "old men" among the Indians recalled "French domination" with "grateful remembrance, and those people [would] see the return of their former protectors with a satisfaction equal to the umbrage which the United States [would] take at it."[51] Two weeks later, a nominally republican France under First Consul Napoleon took official, short-lived, and only formal possession of Louisiana. This revival of French power on paper meant little, at first, to the Indians. Indians of the Great Lakes area knew little or nothing of it; at least they said nothing. For the brief one and a half years that France retained the claim, Louisiana remained largely in the hands of its Spanish-speaking authorities. The revival's main importance lies less in the French return than in its precipitation of the Louisiana Purchase, in which France passed its Louisiana claim to the United States, an event pregnant with terrible consequences for Indians on both sides of the Mississippi River.

The Indians and the few *habitants* who had fought beside Pontiac and who had believed that they could bring the French king and his forces back to recapture New France were mistaken. The British traders and officers who argued that Pontiac's War was a product, "at bottom," of French machinations were also mistaken. The misconception they shared with their enemies, that French power was on the rise in North America, lived a brief active life—long enough for the American Revolutionaries, and later Napoleon, to repeat the error. Among historians, however, the notion that Indians responded readily to active French intrigue has endured. Much like the notion of the French revival itself, the historians' notion is a fantasy, one springing more from the fears of Britons who left records and from the behavioral assumptions of historians than from the evidence. The French and even France have been assigned a control over events that they no longer had. Although France and the French themselves had decisively lost power in North America with their massive defeat in the Seven Years' War, the idea that French king would return blossomed in the long shadow of that war, before fading, with the fleur-de-lis itself, in the Age of Democratic Revolutions.

An Otherworldly Legacy

Pontiac's War had raised issues of the spirit that sent many a warrior to fight for a transformed world. The indecisive conclusion of the war neither fulfilled nor debunked the prophecies of Neolin and others. The Delaware Prophet retained enough respect among other Delawares that he joined in the negotiations that brought the Delawares out of the war. Into the early 1770s, he welcomed visitors and sometimes discussed religion with them. Although he no longer preached on his visions to inspire intertribal multitudes, the message he had once advanced found other voices, and well into the nineteenth century Indians from the Genesee Senecas west to the Ojibwas would attend to other prophets seeking a similar Indian destiny in a ritually remade world.

Far from abandoning sacred efforts in the wake of Pontiac's War, Indians in the upper Ohio Valley saw intensified spiritual contests among their own visionaries and Moravian Christian missionaries. Well into the 1770s, influential Delaware prophets who had encountered the Master of Life in visions preached on the evils of witchcraft, on the intentions of Christians to enslave them, and on the separate path of Indians to a separate Indian salvation. Mary Jemison, one of the captives who willfully remained among the Indians in spite of the British demands, later remembered that in the years immediately following Pontiac's War, among her own Genesee Senecas, the people "observed the religious rites of their progenitors, by attending with the most scrupulous exactness and a great degree of enthusiasm."[52]

From among the Ottawas would come one of the most remarkable Indian prophecies. In 1807, near Michilimackinac, alarmed American agents learned of the speech of one Le Maigois, or the Trout, an Ottawa who claimed only to be reciting the visions of "the first man whom God created, said to be now in the Shawanese country." In all likelihood, the "first man" was Tecumseh's brother, Tenskwatawa, the Shawnee Prophet, who had his first visions while living among the Delawares in 1805. Thus the Delaware-Ottawa connection, so crucial to the origins of Pontiac's War, persisted into the great early-nineteenth-century intertribal movements of the Shawnees Tecumseh and Tenskwatawa.[53]

The first man had been sleeping "the sleep of the Dead" when the Great Spirit—like a Mide raising an initiate, or like Nanabush breathing life back into the nostrils of the muskrat—restored him to life. The Great Spirit told the first man that he would soon "Destroy the Earth." The first man begged for a chance, for a little more time, to "reclaim" his "*Red Children*" (emphasis in original), and his request was granted. So the first man preached to the Indians, insisting that they follow his "counsel" and "instructions for Four Years," at the end of which there would be a transforming "two Days of darkness" and the animals would "come forth out of the Earth" as God had formerly created them. The first man then repeated the Great Spirit's commands.

"I am your Father," the Great Spirit had said; "you are to have very little intercourse with the whites. They are not your Father, as you call them, but your brethren." There was no more talk here of the resurrection of the French king or of the French father; instead the Anishinabeg listening to the Trout were not to call American, British, Spanish, or even French officers "Father." But as with the visions of Pontiac's day, those of the early nineteenth century distinguished among the Euro-Americans, singling out in this case the citizens of the United States for special condemnation. These, unlike the French, Spanish, and now the British Canadians, were "not [the Great Spirit's] children" but came from "the scum of the Great Water, when it was troubled by the Evil Spirit"—troubled by the evil, underwater beings who had flooded the world, the world later rescued by

Nanabush and the muskrat. The Americans' evil was clearest in their increasing theft of Indian lands, "which were not made for them."

But if Americans of the Trout's day were worse than the British, the French, and the Spanish, with none of these peoples were the Indians to grow too close. They were to abandon the domesticated European animals; they were not to shake hands with whites or sell corn or maple sugar to them. Hats, that great symbol even to Neolin of the Euro-American man, were expressly prohibited. Indians might drink a little alcohol purchased from Canadian traders, but they were never to sell it to other Indians. The Great Spirit would permit "lawful" marriage between Indians and whites, but he disapproved of it, for his "white and red children were thus marked with different colours, that they might be a separate people."

He insisted on kindness to dogs and even to trees. He forbade a new, rival spiritual movement, called the Wabano, but he permitted other forms of worship that he saw as traditional, such as the Midewiwin ceremony, as long as it was performed with newly gathered, pure medicine. He asked the men to carry war clubs with them, and he asked all people to play that game favored as well by Nanabush, lacrosse: "For I made you to amuse yourselves and I am delighted when I see you happy." Counterposing lacrosse to war, however, he immediately ordered that Indians were "never to go to war against each other. But to cultivate peace between [their] different Tribes, that they [might] become one great people."

After their war with the United States had broken out in 1811, Tecumseh, Tenskwatawa, the Trout, and others readily allied with the British against the United States, much as Pontiac had sought to gain assistance from France. But it is a mark of their historically unsatisfactory relations with British officers and with the empire itself that they never called for a revival of the British king south of the Great Lakes. Ever since the American Revolution had made the British their convenient allies, Indians had met British officers with fresh and discouraging memories. At the Battle of the Thames in 1813, British troops would once again abandon their Indian allies as American forces advanced. In the stories that surrounded his last act, Tecumseh took off his British uniform and exchanged it for buckskin before he turned his guns and led his men against the United States. Indian memory shrouded the British Empire, like the United States, with powerful feelings of betrayal.

War under Heaven

Thomas Gage could be satisfied at the end of Pontiac's War that his troops and the Indian department had preserved several important western posts, had taken formal possession of the Illinois Country, and had gained important cessions of land in the Seneca country. John Penn could be satisfied that Indian life in the Susquehanna Valley had become so disrupted that Indians would soon yield those lands to settlers. British officers could count it as a victory that hundreds of the king's subjects and several African slaves who had been captured since the Seven Years' War had recently been returned to the east. For their part, the Indians who challenged the British Empire could look to certain achievements. They had successfully preserved most of their lands, they had substantially reduced the British presence in the west (and that presence would be further reduced in the late 1760s), they had prevented the British from punishing them, and they had retained the company of some "white Indians." Most important, they had convinced the British to regard them as nations, as peoples exercising a collective power that could not be ignored. Beyond that, however, much remained unsettled.

The war raised more issues than it had resolved, which is itself a reflection on war. But amid all the high thinking about constitutional status and native spirituality, it should not be forgotten that the war also raised terrors, terrors that would inflame for centuries the issue of the Indians' status. It is better to remember the humanity of Indian families who lost children to smallpox; colonial households murdered in a fiery night; elderly settlement Indians clobbered to death by mounted, armed colonial bands; Enoch Brown and his schoolchildren surprised and destroyed at their lessons; Papunhank and his dying fellows in the infested Philadelphia barracks; sick seven-year-old Elizabeth Fisher, who saw both of her parents killed and who, months later, died herself beneath the surface of a shallow, frigid Maumee River; every Indian warrior captured alive by British troops only to receive, perhaps after an interrogation, his "Quietus"; every ordinary regimental soldier trapped in a tiny, besieged stockade; "Crooked Mouth" and the many other returned captives leaving the only world they could remember for unpredictable and unrecorded fate. Howard Peckham has reliably estimated that the British lost more than 450 regular and provincial soldiers, and we can probably accept the *Pennsylvania Gazette*'s figures from the summer of 1763 alone that the war made refugees out of some 4,000 Virginians and Pennsylvanians; but beyond that, the casualties cannot be quantified, for we have no good figures for the backcountry folk or the Indians.[54]

Even if we callously ignore these casualties as small in scale and unimportant by the standards of our own time, even if we recognize that Pontiac's War neither paved the way for an Anglo-Saxon triumph nor turned self-styled British conquerors into reliable guardians, we still can attend to the lessons of the war. In its origins, in its unfolding, in its many endings and turbulent aftermath, it revealed spiritual yearnings that led Indians to seek intertribal unity against a British menace. It exposed passionate disagreements that set British officers determined to rule against Indians, and in some cases against settlers, who were determined to rule themselves. It raised issues about the constitutional status of Indians and Britons in this rapidly changing colonial world. It did not resolve these issues, but it forced even the highest levels of the British government to consider, if only briefly and inconclusively, the place of Indians in the empire.

Abbreviations

Amherst Papers

Jeffery Amherst Papers, American Series, William C. Clements Library, University of Michigan, Ann Arbor.

"Aspinwall Papers"

Thomas Aspinwall, George E. Ellis, William S. Bartlet, and John Langdon Sibley, eds., "Aspinwall Papers," in *Collections of the Massachusetts Historical Society*, ser. 4, vols. 9–10 (Boston, 1871).

BHC

Burton Historical Collection, Detroit Public Library, Detroit, Mich.

"Bouquet Papers"

Michael Shoemaker, John H. Forster, Henry Holt, and Frederick Carlisle, eds., "Bouquet Papers," in *Collections of the Michigan Pioneer and Historical Society*, vol. 19 (Lansing, 1892).

CISHL 2

Clarence Walworth Alvord, ed., *Cahokia Records, 1778–1790*, Virginia Series, vol. 1 of 2, Collections of the Illinois State Historical Library, vol. 2 of 35 (Springfield, 1907).

CISHL 5

Clarence Walworth Alvord, ed., *Kaskaskia Records, 1778–1790*, Virginia Series, vol. 2 of 2, Collections of the Illinois State Historical Library, vol. 5 of 35 (Springfield, 1909).

CISHL 10

Clarence Walworth Alvord and Clarence Edwin Carter, eds., *The Critical Period, 1763–1765*, British

	Series, vol. 1 of 3, Collections of the Illinois State Historical Library, vol. 10 of 35 (Springfield, 1915).
CISHL 11	Clarence Walworth Alvord and Clarence Edwin Carter, eds., *The New Regime, 1765–1767*, British Series, vol. 2 of 3, Collections of the Illinois State Historical Library, vol. 11 of 35 (Springfield, 1916).
CISHL 16	Clarence Walworth Alvord and Clarence Edwin Carter, eds., *Trade and Politics, 1767–1769*, British Series, vol. 3 of 3, Collections of the Illinois State Historical Library, vol. 16 (Springfield, 1921).
CO [series] / [volume]	Colonial Office Papers (e.g., CO 5/67), [British] Public Record Office, Kew, England.
DCB	*Dictionary of Canadian Biography* (Toronto, 1996–).
Draper MSS	Lyman Copland Draper Manuscripts, State Historical Society of Wisconsin, microfilm at the Newberry Library, Chicago.
Ethnohistory Archive	Great Lakes Ethnohistory Archive, Glenn A. Black Archaeological Laboratory, Indiana University, Bloomington.
Gage Papers	Thomas Gage Papers, American Series, William C. Clements Library, University of Michigan, Ann Arbor.
"Gladwin Manuscripts"	Charles Moore, ed., "Gladwin Manuscripts," in *Collections of the Michigan Pioneer and Historical Society*, vol. 27 (Lansing, 1897).
HSP	Historical Society of Pennsylvania, Philadelphia, Pa.
JR	Reuben Gold Thwaites, ed., *Jesuit Relations and Allied Documents: Travel and Explorations of the Jesuit Missionaries in New France*, 73 vols. (Cleveland, 1896–1901).
Michigan Pioneer	*Collections of the Michigan Pioneer and Historical Society*, Lansing.
Navarre/Burton, *Pontiac Journal*	C. M. Burton and M. Agnes Burton, eds., R. Clyde Ford, trans., *The Journal of Pontiac's Conspiracy, 1763* (Detroit, 1912). This edition contains the original French as well as the English translation.

Navarre/Quaife, *Journal of Pontiac's Conspiracy*	Milo Milton Quaife, ed., R. Clyde Ford, trans., "Journal of Pontiac's Conspiracy," in *The Siege of Detroit in 1763: The Journal of Pontiac's Conspiracy and John Rutherfurd's Narrative of a Captivity* (Chicago, 1958).
NYCD	Edmund B. O'Callaghan and B. Fernow, eds., *Documents Relative to the Colonial History of the State of New York*, 15 vols. (Albany, 1853–87).
PCHB	Sylvester K. Stevens and Donald H. Kent, eds., *The Papers of Col. Henry Bouquet*, 16 vols. [enumerated by British Library "Additional Manuscript" series numbers] (Harrisburg, Pa., 1940–43). Copies in the Newberry Library, Chicago, and the Firestone Library, Princeton University, Princeton, N.J.
Pennsylvania Archives, 1st ser.	Samuel Hazard, ed., *Pennsylvania Archives*, 1st ser., 12 vols. (Philadelphia, 1852–56).
Pennsylvania Archives, 2nd ser.	William Egle, ed., *Pennsylvania Archives*, 2nd ser., 19 vols. (Harrisburg, 1874–93).
Pennsylvania Archives, 8th ser.	Charles F. Hoban, ed., *Pennsylvania Archives*, 8th ser., 8 vols. (Harrisburg, 1931–35).
Pennsylvania Colonial Records	State of Pennsylvania, *Minutes of the Provincial Council of Pennsylvania from the Organization to the Termination of the Proprietary Government*, 16 vols. (Harrisburg, 1838–53).
Pennsylvania Gazette	*Accessible Archives: Pennsylvania Gazette*, 4 discs or "folios" (Provo, Utah, 1990–).
PHB	Sylvester K. Stevens, Donald H. Kent, Autumn Leonard, Louis M. Waddell, and John L. Tottenham, eds., *Papers of Henry Bouquet*, 6 vols. (Harrisburg, Pa., 1951–94).
PMHB	*Pennsylvania Magazine of History and Biography*
WCL	William Clements Library, University of Michigan, Ann Arbor.
Westward Expansion	Randolph Boehm, ed., *British Public Record Office, Colonial Office, Class 5 Files: Westward Expansion, 1700–1783, The Board of Trade, the French and Indian War*, 12 microfilm reels (Frederick, Md., 1972).

WJP	Milton Wheaton Hamilton et al., eds., *The Papers of Sir William Johnson*, 13 vols. (Albany, N.Y., 1921–62).
WMQ	*William and Mary Quarterly*, 3rd ser.

Notes

INTRODUCTION Heroes of History, Heaven, and Earth

1. Robert Rogers, *Journals of Major Robert Rogers*, ed. Howard Peckham (1765; New York, 1961), 165. Throughout this volume I will employ the spelling "Ottawa," because it is far more common in scholarship. Ottawas increasingly employ the spelling "Odawa," though both spellings are still used.

2. Wilbur Jacobs, "Was the Pontiac Uprising a Conspiracy?" *Ohio State Archaeological and Historical Quarterly* 51 (1950): 26–37; Francis Jennings, *Empire of Fortune: Crowns, Colonies, and Tribes in the Seven Years' War in America* (New York, 1988); Howard Peckham, *Pontiac and the Indian Uprising* (1947; New York, 1970); Anthony F. C. Wallace, *The Death and Rebirth of the Seneca* (New York, 1969); Gregory Evans Dowd, *A Spirited Resistance: The North American Indian Struggle for Unity, 1745–1815* (Baltimore, 1992); Michael N. McConnell, *A Country Between: The Upper Ohio Valley and Its Peoples, 1724–1774* (Lincoln, Nebr., 1992); Richard White, *The Middle Ground: Indians, Empires, and Republics in the Great Lakes Region, 1650–1815* (New York, 1991); William R. Nester, *"Haughty Conquerors": Amherst and the Great Indian Uprising of 1763* (Westport, Conn., 2000).

3. The quotation is from Nester, *Haughty Conquerors*, 197.

4. For the "Journal of a Conspiracy," see editor's introduction and translator's preface in Milo Milton Quaife, ed., *The Siege of Detroit in 1763: The Journal of Pontiac's Conspiracy and John Rutherfurd's Narrative of a Captivity* (Chicago, 1958), xiii–lv. One can compare Navarre's known handwriting with that of the journal in the best published edition, on which the Quaife edition is based but which also transcribes the original French: C. M. Burton and M. Agnes Burton, eds., R. Clyde Ford, trans., *The Journal of Pontiac's Conspiracy, 1763* (Detroit, 1912), images facing 188 and 204. Or one can go to Detroit, to the Burton Historical Collection at the Detroit Public Library. Well maintained but once badly damaged, the manuscript has been leaf-pressed to preserve its fragmented

seventy-two pages. The paper, ink, and handwriting seem authentic enough, though one could hope for a serious chemical and handwriting analysis. The handwriting, to this eye, could be Navarre's; the angle is about the same, and the letters *S*, *d*, and *t* are similarly and distinctively rendered. See "Journal ou dictation d'une conspiration, faite par les sauvages contre les Anglais, et du siège du fort de Detroix par quatre nations différentes le 7 mai, 1763" (the manuscript is rebound, and the title on the binding is "Journal of Pontiac's Conspiracy, 1763"); Navarre Manuscript, September 26, 1755; Potawatomi Deed, 1772; and Navarre to François Navarre, Detroit, May 1, 1790, all in the BHC.

Jehu Hay, stationed at Detroit during the same period, writes on July 2 and July 26 of Navarre being outside the garrison, sending intelligence into the garrison. Navarre secured letters brought from the Illinois Country, which he sent into the garrison. See Jehu Hay, "Diary of the Siege of Detroit," 133, 169, WCL. Given the few persons who would have been literate and who would have spoken the already colloquial (and Algonquian-influenced) French of the upcountry in Detroit in the later part of the seventeenth century, Navarre does seem to be the most likely author. Navarre's likely authorship is accepted by Peckham, *Pontiac and the Indian Uprising*, 123; Jennings, *Empire of Fortune*, 444; and Nester, *Haughty Conquerors*, 103. White, *Middle Ground*, 58, employs the journal sparingly. Henry Rowe Schoolcraft, in *Personal Memoirs of a Residence of Thirty Years with the Indian Tribes on the American Frontiers* (1851; New York, 1978), 680 (entry for February 10, 1840), reports receiving a translated copy of the manuscript, which had recently been "found in the garret of one of the French *habitants*, . . . partly torn, and much soiled by rains and the effects of time."

5. On Robert Rogers, see John R. Cuneo, *Robert Rogers of the Rangers* (New York, 1959), 13–15. On George Croghan, see Francis Jennings, *Empire of Fortune*, 44, 59, 342 (Penn's quotation), 431; or, for a friendlier view, see Nicholas B. Wainwright, *George Croghan: Wilderness Diplomat* (Chapel Hill, N.C., 1959), "devious" quotation, 212, 28, 276, 277, 288, 299, 301.

6. Richard D. Brown, "Where Have All the Great Men Gone," in Brown, ed., *Major Problems in the Era of the American Revolution* (Lexington, Mass., 1992), 618; for Parkman's racism and elitism and attitudes toward Lincoln, see Howard Doughty, *Francis Parkman* (Cambridge, Mass., 1982), 382, 400–401 and passim; Francis Parkman, *The Conspiracy of Pontiac and the Indian War after the Conquest of Canada*, 6th ed., 2 vols. (1851; Boston, 1870), 1:183, 185, 186.

7. David Hume, "Of Suicide," in Alasdair MacIntyre, ed., *Hume's Ethical Writings: Selections from David Hume* (London, 1965), 299–300; Gordon Wood, *The Radicalism of the American Revolution* (New York, 1992), 61.

8. General Thomas Gage to the earl of Halifax, New York, April 14, 1764, *NYCD* 7:619–20; Thomas Gage to William Johnson, New York, July 2, 1764, *WJP* 11:250; Parkman, *Conspiracy of Pontiac*, 1:166.

9. Parkman, *Conspiracy of Pontiac*, 1:228. Peckham, *Pontiac and the Indian Rising*, 22. Nester, *Haughty Conquerors* (xii), criticizes Peckham for putting too much emphasis on Pontiac, but Peckham's focus was the siege of Detroit, which Pontiac did lead, and his thesis was that Pontiac led little else. I will show that Pontiac was also very influential in lower Illinois. Nester's work focuses on English personalities and blames the war

squarely on Jeffery Amherst, failing to recognize how typical Amherst was. There is much fine discussion of the progress of the war, but Nester pays little attention to archival sources, sources in French, ethnography, and the past two decades of scholarship on Native American history. For other works that have a blundering Amherst stumble into the war, see Randolph Downes, *Council Fires on the Upper Ohio* (Pittsburgh, 1949), 106–14; Wilbur Jacobs, *Dispossessing the American Indian* (New York, 1972), 75–81. Fred Anderson also focuses largely on Amherst, but he places Amherst more squarely within the context of the officer class; see Fred Anderson, *The Crucible of War: The Seven Years' War and the Fate of Empire in British North America, 1754–1766* (New York, 2000), 535–46.

10. Richard White, *Middle Ground*, 37.

11. James McClurken, "We Wish to Be Civilized: Ottawa-American Political Contests on the Michigan Frontier" (Ph.D. diss., Michigan State University, 1988), 15–16; W. Vernon Kinietz, *The Indians of the Western Great Lakes, 1615–1760*, Occasional Papers from the Museum of Anthropology of the University of Michigan 10 (Ann Arbor, 1940), 246–48.

12. Frederic Baraga, *A Dictionary of the Otchipwe Language* (Cincinnati, 1853), 332, 636. Baraga's dictionary has the two words as fully distinct. In the original French, the Ottawas appear even more real as a people, since the others are called not "Outaouacs" but "Doutaoüacs"; see *JR* 51:20–21. For contrasting views, see McClurken, "We Wish to Be Civilized," 14; White, *Middle Ground*, 105–6.

13. White, *Middle Ground*, is the best work on the role of mediation in Indian societies and between those societies and Europeans. For Ottawas in particular, see Beverly Ann Smith, "Systems of Subsistence and Networks of Exchange in the Terminal Woodland and Early Historic Periods in the Upper Great Lakes" (Ph.D. diss., Michigan State University, 1996), 95–96, 278. William James Newbigging, "The History of the French-Ottawa Alliance, 1613–1763" (Ph.D. diss., University of Toronto, 1995), places the Ottawa effort to control Lake Huron at the analytical center; see 2, 26, 47, 83, 95, 102.

14. McClurken, "We Wish to Be Civilized," 14, 23, ("most respected") 24, ("no authority") 28, 33–38. I rely on McClurken for this discussion of the relationship between trade and leadership. Nicolas Perrot, "Memoir on the Manners, Customs, and Religion of the Savages of North America," in Emma Helen Blair, ed., *The Indian Tribes of the Upper Mississippi Valley and Region of the Great Lakes*, 2 vols. (Cleveland, 1911), 1:188–89.

15. Alethea Helbig, "Manabozho of the Great Lakes Indians: As He Was, As He Is," *Michigan Academician* 11 (1978): 49–58, compares narratives of the figure collected in the early nineteenth century with those collected more than a century later and finds much continuity. See commentaries by Karl Kerenyi and C. G. Jung in Paul Radin, *The Trickster: A Study in American Indian Mythology* (London, 1956), 173 ff.; for St. Blaise, see Emmanuel Le Roy Ladurie, *Carnival in Romans*, trans. Mary Feeney (New York, 1979), 99. For an interesting essay on the Jesuit perception that Great Lakes Indians engaged in carnivalesque acts, see Martin W. Walsh, "The Condemnation of Carnival in the Jesuit Relations," *Michigan Academician* 15 (1982): 13–23. Thanks to Professor Norman

Risjord of the University of Wisconsin for pointing out in an early draft the similarity to "Puck." The Catholic missionary to the Ojibwas, Frederic Baraga, believed in 1847 that Nanabush was a Jesus figure directly borrowed from Christian traders. Frederic Baraga, *Chippewa Indians, As Recorded by Rev. Frederick Baraga in 1847*, Studia Slovenica 10 (New York and Washington, D.C., 1976): 34.

16. Andrew J. Blackbird, *History of the Ottawa and Chippewa Indians of Michigan: A Grammar of Their Language, and Personal and Family History of the Author* (Ypsilanti, Mich., 1887), 72; Perrot, "Memoir," 1:31–42, 48; Radin, *Trickster*, 212–13.

Alexander Henry, living among the Ojibwas and Ottawas in the 1760s, not only describes a flood and a re-creation of the world but also identifies "Nanibojou" with "Michabou" and "The Great Hare," in *Travels and Adventures in Canada and the Indian Territories between the Years 1760 and 1776*, March of America Facsimile Series No. 43 (1809; Ann Arbor, Mich., 1966), 212–13. Theresa Smith proposes that the end of his name, "-abush" or "-abozo," is kin to the Ojibwa word for rabbit, *wabooz*; see Theresa S. Smith, *The Island of the Anishnaabeg: Thunderers and Water Monsters in the Traditional Ojibwe Life World* (Moscow, Idaho, 1995), 171–72.

17. Radin, *Trickster*, 135, 140, 151; Stith Thompson, ed., *Tales of the North American Indians* (Bloomington, Ind., 1929), 55, 296; Thomas W. Overholt and J. Baird Callicott, eds., *Clothed-in-Fur and Other Tales: An Introduction to an Ojibwe World View, with Ojibwe Texts by William Jones and Forward by Mary B. Black-Rogers* (Washington, D.C., 1982), 131–33. There is nothing uniquely Indian about the flatulent hero; see the discussion of St. Blaise in Ladurie, *Carnival in Romans*, 99; Sam D. Gill, "Religious Forms and Themes," in Alvin M. Josephy Jr., ed., *America in 1492: The World of the Indian Peoples before the Arrival of Columbus* (New York, 1993), 283. In 2001, one finds a Nanaboozhoo story on the Internet with a link from the Waganakising Odawa (or Little Traverse Bay Ottawa) Education page. Posted in the late 1990s by the education director Fred Harrington Jr., it is located at odawa.com/fred/edu.html.

18. Blackbird, *History of the Ottawa and Chippewa Indians*, 75–77; Helbig, "Manabozho of the Great Lakes," 52. Compare the Menominee version in Thompson, *Tales*, 11–14, and Nicolas Perrot's rendition of the Ottawa creation story in "Memoir," 1:31–36; D. Peter MacLeod, "The Anishinabeg Point of View: The History of the Great Lakes Region to 1800 in Nineteenth-Century Mississauga, Odawa, and Ojibwa Historiography," *Canadian Historical Review* 73 (1992): 195–210. Elements of this story can be found in colonial French documents. Father Claude Jean Allouez, working among the Ottawas, wrote in the late 1660s of "Michabous," the "Great Hare," and of "Michibizi," who may well be a rendition of the same being, as he displays human and supernatural characteristics, alters and defines the world, and teaches his people. See *JR* 54:199–201; *JR* 50:289. Pierre François Xavier de Charlevoix, reflecting on the Indians of Michigan while at Fort St. Joseph (Niles) in 1721, writes of the Great Hare, Michabou, who created the earth "of a grain of sand, which he took from the bottom of the ocean," and of a "god of the waters," a "great Tyger," who "opposed the designs of the great Hare," in his *Journal of a Voyage to North America*, ed. Louise Phelps Kellogg, 2 vols. (1761; Chicago, 1923), 2:131. Henry Rowe Schoolcraft refers to this story in his

Information Respecting the History, Condition, and Prospects of the Indian Tribes of the United States, 6 vols. (Philadelphia, 1860), 6:659.

19. Basil Johnston notes that "Nana'b'oozoo behaved more like a human being than a manitou," in *The Manitous: The Spiritual World of the Ojibway* (New York, 1965), 52, 94–95.

20. Joel W. Martin, *Sacred Revolt: The Muskogees' Struggle for a New World* (Boston, 1991), 22.

21. Melissa A. Pflug, "Contemporary Revitalization Movements Among the Northern Great Lakes Ottawa (Odawa) Indians: Motives and Accomplishments" (Ph.D. diss., Wayne State University, 1990), 89–90, 91; Assikinack, "Social and Warlike Customs of the Odahwah Indians," *Canadian Journal of Industry, Science and Art* 3 (1858): 304–5. Christopher Vescey, *Traditional Ojibwa Religion and Its Historical Changes* (Philadelphia, 1983), 74–75, 78; Thomas Vennum, "Ojibwa Origin-Migration Songs of the *Mitewiwin*," *Journal of American Folklore* 91 (1978): 755; also see 771, 775, for Nanabush at the origins of Anishinabe ceremonialism. Michael R. Angel, "Discordant Voices, Conflicting Visions: Ojibwa and Euro-American Perspectives on the Midewiwin" (Ph.D. diss., University of Manitoba, 1997), i, 39–42.

22. Thomas McKenney, *Sketches of a Tour to the Lakes, of the Character and Customs of the Chippway, and of the Incidents Connected with the Treaty of Fond du Lac* (1827; Minneapolis, 1959), 487 (ceremony); Baraga, *Chippewa Indians*, 41 (religion); I take the spelling of *jaasakid* from Angel, "Discordant Voices," 17; Schoolcraft, *Personal Memoirs*, 105, 511, 572.

23. Father Gabriel Sagard, *The Long Journey to the Country of the Hurons* (Toronto, 1939), 208–9; Charles C. Trowbridge, *Meeameer Traditions*, in Vernon Kinietz, ed., University of Michigan Museum of Anthropology, Occasional Contributions 7 (Ann Arbor, Mich., 1938): 34–35; *JR* 55:137; Perrot, "Memoir," 1:83–84; Charlevoix, *Journal of a Voyage to North America*, 353.

24. William Smith to Horatio Gates, November 22, 1763, quoted in Peckham, *Pontiac and the Indian Uprising*, 109 n. 12. Interestingly, the leading Cherokee diplomat of the 1750s and 1760s, Attakullakulla (Little Carpenter), had been an Ottawa captive for six years in the 1740s. See South Carolina Council Minutes, October 19, 1754, CO 5/471, fols. 27b–29.

25. Newbigging, "History of the French-Ottawa Alliance," 97–98; Theresa Marie Shenk, "Continuity and Change in the Sociopolitical Organization of the Lake Superior Ojibwa" (Ph.D. diss., Rutgers, The State University of New Jersey, 1995), 58.

26. Pflug, "Contemporary Revitalization Movements," 10, 58, 91, 95; Weston La Barre calls Pontiac "the celebrated Ottawa chief and shaman of the Midewiwin Grand Medicine Society," in *The Ghost Dance: The Origins of Religion* (London, 1972), 208; both claims seem to be based on Parkman, *Conspiracy of Pontiac*, 1:183 n. 1. For the rituals at Detroit, see some of their components described in John Porteous to James Porteous, Detroit, n.d. 1762, in Porteous Papers, BHC. For Nanabush, muskrats, otters, and shamans, see Schoolcraft, *Personal Memoirs*, 572; Vennum, "Ojibwa Origin-Migration Songs," 753–91.

27. Angel, "Discordant Voices, Conflicting Visions," 17.

28. Charles Cleland, *Rites of Conquest: The History and Culture of Michigan's Native Americans* (Ann Arbor, Mich., 1992), 96–97; *JR* 50:285.

29. Ake Hultkrantz, *The Religions of the American Indians*, trans. Monica Setterwall (Berkeley, 1979), 27; Henry, *Travels and Adventures*, 130–31.

30. Schoolcraft, *Information Respecting the History*, 6:661; Edwin James, ed., *A Narrative of the Captivity and Adventures of John Tanner during Thirty Years Residence among the Indians in the Interior of America* (New York, 1830), 34, 39–40.

31. James, *Captivity and Adventures of John Tanner*, 47–48, see also 32–34; Henry, *Travels and Adventures*, 153; *JR* 50:287.

32. A. Irving Hallowell, "Ojibwa World View," in *The North American Indians: A Sourcebook*, ed. R. C. Owen, J. F. Deetz, and A. D. Fisher (New York, 1967), 211; Pflug, "Contemporary Revitalization Movements," 88; Robin Ridington, "Northern Hunters," in Josephy, *America in 1492*, 45; Vescey, *Traditional Ojibwa Religion*, 63–64.

33. Vescey, *Traditional Ojibwa Religion*, 177; Vernon Kinietz, *Indians of the Western Great Lakes*, 373.

34. James Axtell, *The Invasion Within: The Contest of Cultures in Colonial North America* (New York, 1985), 75–77.

35. C. J. Jung, Commentary, in Radin, *Trickster*, 197; Walsh, "Condemnation of Carnival," 13–23; *JR* 51:31, 291; Allouez quoted in François Mercier, "Relation of What Occurred in New France in the Years 1666 and 1667," Quebec, November 10, 1667, *JR* 50:285.

36. Quoted in Kenneth Morrison, "Montagnais Missionization in Early New France: The Syncretic Imperative," *American Indian Culture and Research Journal* 10 (1986): 1–23.

37. *JR* 54:171; *JR* 50:291.

38. McClurken, "We Wish to Be Civilized," 32–33; Cleland, *Rites of Conquest*, 88–101; Susan Sleeper-Smith, "Silent Tongues, Black Robes: Potawatomi, Europeans, and Settlers in the Southern Great Lakes, 1640–1850" (Ph.D. diss., University of Michigan, 1994).

39. Harold Hickerson, *The Chippewa and Their Neighbors: A Study in Ethnohistory* (New York, 1970), 57–59; Angel, "Discordant Voices, Conflicting Visions," 10, summarizes the dispute. He concludes that the Midewiwin, despite its historical changes, is of aboriginal origin.

CHAPTER 1 Ottawas, Delawares, and the Colonial World, 1615–1760

1. Beverly Ann Smith, "Systems of Subsistence and Networks of Exchange in the Terminal Woodland and Early Historic Periods in the Upper Great Lakes" (Ph.D. diss., Michigan State University, 1996), 37–38, 86–87; William James Newbigging, "The History of the French-Ottawa Alliance, 1615–1763" (Ph.D. diss., University of Toronto, 1995), 29, 39–49.

2. Bruce Trigger, *The Huron: Farmers of the North* (New York, 1969), 1–3, 20; James McClurken, "We Wish to Be Civilized: Ottawa-American Political Contests on the Michigan Frontier" (Ph.D. diss., Michigan State University, 1988), 5–14; Richard

White, *The Middle Ground: Indians, Empires, and Republics in the Great Lakes Region, 1650–1815* (New York, 1991), 106; Charles Cleland, *Rites of Conquest: The History and Culture of Michigan's Native Americans* (Ann Arbor, Mich., 1992), 86; Smith, "Systems of Subsistence," 244, 249–52, 277, 278; Newbigging, "History of the French-Ottawa Alliance," 64–69.

3. For an eighteenth-century description of blackflies, see Alexander Henry, *Travels and Adventures in Canada and the Indian Territories between the Years 1760 and 1776,* March of America Facsimile Series No. 43 (1809; Ann Arbor, Mich., 1966), 29.

4. Cleland, *Rites of Conquest,* 88.

5. Daniel K. Richter, "War and Culture: The Iroquois Experience," *WMQ* 40 (1983): 528–59.

6. McClurken, "We Wish to Be Civilized," 28–30; Newbigging, "History of the French-Ottawa Alliance," 117–40, 159; Smith, "Systems of Subsistence," 104; Helen Hornbeck Tanner, ed., *Atlas of Great Lakes Indian History* (Norman, Okla., 1986), 13–35.

7. McClurken, "We Wish to Be Civilized," 15, 33; Nicolas Perrot, "Memoir on the Manners, Customs, and Religion of the Savages of North America," in Emma Helen Blair, ed., *The Indian Tribes of the Upper Mississippi Valley and Region of the Great Lakes,* 2 vols. (Cleveland, 1911), 1:173–74; White, *Middle Ground,* 98; Gary Clayton Anderson, *Kinsmen of Another Kind: Dakota-White Relations in the Upper Mississippi Valley, 1650– 1862* (Lincoln, Nebr., 1984), 29.

8. Claude Charles Le Roy, Bacqueville de la Potherie, "History of the Savage Peoples Who Are Allies of New France," in Blair, *Indian Tribes of the Upper Mississippi Valley,* 1:282–83.

9. White, *Middle Ground,* 175–85; W. J. Eccles, "Sovereignty-Association, 1500– 1783," *Canadian Historical Review* 65 (1984): 475–510. W. J. Eccles, "The Fur Trade and Eighteenth-Century Imperialism," *WMQ* 40 (1983): 341–62.

10. Peter N. Moogk, "Reluctant Exiles: The Problems of Colonization in French North America," *WMQ* 46 (1989): 464, 481.

11. Ibid., 487. There was nothing Gallic about such relationships. There is abundant evidence that colonial Britons and Anglo-Americans intermarried with Indians, especially in the southern, northern, and western reaches of British North America and the United States, at various times over the next two centuries. That Britons and Anglo-Americans formed more-than-fleeting sexual relationships with Native Americans is evident in Sylvia Van Kirk, "The Role of Native Women in the Fur Trade Society of Western Canada, 1670–1830," *Frontiers* 7 (1984): 9–13, and in Edward J. Cashin, *Lachlan McGillivray, Indian Trader: The Shaping of the Southern Colonial Frontier* (Athens, Ga., 1992); Albert Hurtado, "Hardly a Farm House—a Kitchen without Them: Indian and White Households on the California Borderland Frontier in 1860," *Western Historical Quarterly* 13 (1982): 245–70. Even French official efforts to promote Indian-European marriage had counterparts in Anglo-American societies (in neither case, it must be said, did those efforts have much influence). John Marshall wrote to James Monroe of a piece of such "advantageous" legislation that failed in the House of Burgesses, "the bill for encouraging intermarriages with Indians": "Our prejudices however opposes themselves to our interests and operate too powerfully for them." Herbert A. Johnson,

Charles T. Cullen, Nancy G. Harris, eds., *The Papers of John Marshall* (Chapel Hill, N.C., 1974–), 1:131. I thank R. Kent Newmeyer and Charles T. Cullen for their help in locating this.

On the Métis, see Baron de Lahonton, *New Voyages to North America*, ed. Reuben Gold Thwaites, 2 vols. (1905; New York, 1970), 2:455; White, *Middle Ground*, 69–70, 214–15. But for a discussion of the complexities of French views, see Cornelius J. Jaenen, *Friend and Foe: Aspects of French-Amerindian Contact in the Sixteenth and Seventeenth Centuries* (New York, 1976), 161–65. For godparents, see Susan Sleeper-Smith, "Silent Tongues, Black Robes: Potawatomi, Europeans, and Settlers in the Southern Great Lakes, 1640–1850" (Ph.D. diss., University of Michigan, 1994).

12. This widely held view is currently under critical scrutiny by Matthew R. Laird, who delivered a paper challenging the view, "The Price of Empire: Anglo-French Competition for the Great Lakes–Ohio Valley Fur Trade, 1715–1760," at the First Annual Conference of the Institute of Early American History and Culture, Ann Arbor, Mich., 1995. Daniel Richter's response as the session's commentator, however, renders Laird's view moot, at least for the moment.

13. M. Du Chesneau's [Jacques Duchesneau] "Memoir on the Western Indians," November 13, 1681, *NYCD* 9:161–62; White, *Middle Ground*, 36, 181.

14. [Sieur de] Noyan, "State of Canada in 1730," *Michigan Pioneer*, vol. 34 (1905), 84.

15. White, *Middle Ground*, 119–22.

16. For critics, see, for example, W. J. Eccles, *The Canadian Frontier, 1534–1760* (Albuquerque, 1969), 136–37. For Ottawa initiative, see Newbigging, "History of the French-Ottawa Alliance," 226, 229, 242–43, 258–59.

17. Cleland, *Rites of Conquest*, 114–15; Tanner, *Atlas of Great Lakes Indian History*, 39; Harlan Hatcher, *The Great Lakes* (New York, 1944), 124–25.

18. Richard White has gone the furthest to cast doubt on the extent of Indian dependence. First, in a wide-ranging and provocative discussion of the phenomenon as it developed among the Choctaws, Pawnees, and Navajos, he suggests that the demand for European goods was limited, particularly in the early years, by the durability of those goods. Guns, metal goods, and even cloth could last years, so the demand was not constant. The political arrangements of a people could inhibit (as among the Pawnees) or welcome (as among the Choctaws) such dependency. He later expanded the argument, suggesting that "traditional" forms of manufacturing—bonework, stonework, woodwork, and pottery—persisted well into the colonial period. The old skills did not disappear; Indians did not grow rapidly and absolutely dependent on the European trade. The flow of goods into Indian villages, limited as it was by the carrying capacity of canoes and bateaux, was simply too thin for those goods utterly to replace native manufactures among entire populations. Archaeological evidence suggests, he argues, that the traditional pattern of subsistence continued beside the new engagement in the market. Moreover, when cut off from access to Europeans, Indians sometimes obtained European goods from other Indians. White, *Middle Ground*, 140. Indeed, White doubts that it makes sense to speak of Great Lakes Indian dependency at any time in the history of New France.

In his study of the Five Nations Iroquois, just to the southeast of the *pays d'en haut* and also around the Great Lakes, Daniel K. Richter, examining much the same archaeological and documentary evidence as White, concludes that as early as the middle of the seventeenth century, the "Five Nations were literally dependent." Daniel K. Richter, *Ordeal of the Longhouse: The Peoples of the Iroquois League in the Era of European Colonization* (Chapel Hill, N.C., 1992), 87. Grave sites in Iroquoia show a marked decline in traditional goods, which were almost entirely replaced by European items. Traditional manufactures declined, he argues, and were replaced by European trade. George Quimby's classic archaeological work on the upper Great Lakes, like Richter's, suggests considerable material dependence on European goods by the middle of the eighteenth century. George Quimby, *Indian Culture and European Trade Goods* (Madison, Wisc., 1966), 158. Although the subsistence economy may have remained the same, the material culture had changed profoundly. A strong and persuasive argument for dependency in the Northeast is Denys Delâge, *Bitter Feast: Amerindians and European in Northeastern North America, 1600–1664,* trans. Jane Brierley (Vancouver, 1992), first published as *Le Pays Renversé: Amérindians et Européens en Amérique du Nord-est, 1600–1664* (Quebec, 1985).

Another kind of dependence, a personal rather than societal dependence, was particularly pernicious from the early years onward: dependence on alcohol, "since it was consumed quickly and the English discovered that Indian appetites for it could be constantly stimulated." For guns and alcohol, see Richard White, *The Roots of Dependency: Subsistence, Environment, and Social Change among the Choctaws, Pawnees, and Navajos* (Lincoln, Nebr., 1983), 46–47, 58. W. J. Eccles agrees: "The appetite for *eau de vie* was virtually insatiable, driving the Indians to produce furs in ever larger quantities." Eccles, "Fur Trade and Eighteenth-Century Imperialism," 350; see also Thomas Elliot Norton, *The Fur Trade in Colonial New York, 1686–1776* (Madison, Wisc., 1974), 32. Alcohol was indeed an important trade item, and attempts by both Indians and colonial officials to prevent its sale to Indians proved fruitless. Peter C. Mancall, *Deadly Medicine: Indians and Alcohol in Early America* (Ithaca, N.Y., 1995), 12–14; Richter, *Ordeal of the Longhouse,* 263–68.

19. Francis Jennings, *The Ambiguous Iroquois Empire: The Covenant Chain Confederation of Indian Tribes with the English Colonies* (New York, 1984), 80–81; Patrick M. Malone, *the Skulking Way of War: Technology and Tactics among the New England Indians* (Baltimore, 1991), 96. During the American Revolution, American citizens would depend on Europe for almost two-thirds of their gunpowder supplies (even without including imported saltpeter). David L. Salay, "The Production of Gunpowder in Pennsylvania during the American Revolution," *Pennsylvania Magazine of History and Biography* 99 (1975): 421–42.

20. McClurken, "We Wish to Be Civilized," 50–52; Claude T. Hamilton takes note of the importance of Langlade and of the Indians in "Western Michigan History (Colonial Period)," *Michigan History Magazine* 13 (1929): 211–15; Ian K. Steele, *Betrayals: Fort William Henry and the "Massacre"* (New York, 1990), 24; White, *Middle Ground,* 122.

21. McClurken, "We Wish to Be Civilized," White, *Middle Ground,* 94–185; 41–42; W. J. Eccles, "The Fur Trade in the Colonial Northeast," in Wilcomb E. Washburn, ed., *History of Indian-White Relations,* vol. 4 of *Handbook of North American Indians,* William

C. Sturtevant, gen. ed., 15 vols. (Washington, D.C., 1978–), 327–28; Cleland, *Rites of Conquest*, 114–15; Eccles, *Canadian Frontier*, 137–56; Delâge, *Bitter Feast*.

22. McClurken, "We Wish to Be Civilized,"149.

23. Tanner, *Atlas of Great Lakes Indian History*, map 9; Charles Hanna, *The Wilderness Trail, or, the Ventures and Adventures of the Pennsylvania Traders on the Allegheny Path* (New York, 1911), 321.

24. Helen Hornbeck Tanner, "The Location of Indian Tribes in Southeastern Michigan and Northern Ohio," in Tanner and Ermine Wheeler-Vogelin, eds., *Indians of Northern Ohio and Southeastern Michigan: An Ethnohistorical Report*, Garland American Indian Ethnohistory Series, David Agee Horr, gen. ed. (New York, 1974), 9. I thank Colin G. Calloway for the caution on the Openango; they may have been Pennacooks.

25. Ives Goddard, "Delaware," in Bruce Trigger, ed., *Northeast*, vol. 15 of *Handbook of North American Indians*, William C. Sturtevant, gen. ed., 15 vols. (New York, 1978–), 213–16; Ives Goddard, "Eastern Algonquian Languages," in ibid., 72, 73; and Ives Goddard, "The Delaware Language, Past and Present," in Herbert C. Kraft, ed., *A Delaware Indian Symposium* (Harrisburg, Pa., 1974), 103–11. The terms *Munsee* and *Unami* do not appear in the historical record until the middle quarters of the eighteenth century; hence, there seems little likelihood that the languages bore any strict political correlation. See Herbert C. Kraft, *The Lenape: Archaeology, History, and Ethnography* (Newark, 1986), xvii–xviii.

26. For "Lenni Lenape," see Kraft, *Lenape*, xvii–xviii; Melissa A. Pflug, "Contemporary Revitalization Movements among the Northern Great Lakes Ottawa (Odawa) Indians: Motives and Accomplishments" (Ph.D. diss., Wayne State University, 1990), 1–2. Today Ojibwas who wish to assert ethnic identity might greet one another with the term "'nishna."

27. Today people who descend from both Munsee- and Unami-speaking peoples employ the terms *Delaware* and *Lenape;* each term usefully covers both Unamis and Munsees, as "Delaware" did in Pontiac's day. The foremost archaeologist of these peoples, Herbert C. Kraft, has chosen to denominate them the "Lenape." Kraft, *Lenape*. The term first was noted by Thomas Campanius Holm, *A Short Description of the Province of New Sweden, Now Called, by the English, Pennsylvania*, trans. Peter S. Du Ponceau, in *Memoirs of the Historical Society of Pennsylvania* 3 (1834): 144.

28. For various, early renderings of the story, see David Zeisberger, "History of the North American Indians," ed. Archer Butler Hulbert, trans. William Nathaniel Schwarze, in *Ohio Archaeological and Historical Society Publications* 19 (1910): 132; Holm, *Short Description*, 112–13; Jasper Dankers and Peter Sluyter, "Journal of a Voyage to New York, 1679–1680," trans. Henry C. Murphy, *Memoirs of the Long Island Historical Society* 1 (1867): 151; John Ettwein, "Some Remarks and Annotations Concerning the Traditions, Customs, Languages &c. of the Indians in North America . . . Sent to General Washington . . . Bethlehem, [Pa.] March 28, 1788," 26, manuscript in Historical and Philosophical Society of Ohio, Cincinnati, microfilm in the Ethnohistory Archive; Adriaen Van Der Donk, *A Description of the New Netherlands (1656)* (Syracuse, N.Y., 1968), 107–9. For a modern rendering, see Paul Wallace, *Indians in Pennsylvania*,

2nd ed., ed. William A. Hunter (Harrisburg, Pa., 1981), 74–75, and Daniel G. Brinton, *The Lenape and Their Legends* (1884; New York, 1969), 134–35.

29. "Hare" is rendered as Tschimammus in David Zeisberger [1721–1808], "History of the Indians," ed. Archer Butler Hulbert, trans. William Nathaniel Shwarze, *Ohio Archaeological and Historical Society Publications* 19 (1910): 140. For Delaware religion, see Kraft, *Lenape*, 161–73; Mark Harrington, *Religion and Ceremonies of the Lenape* (New York, 1921), 17–18, 29, 31–35, 49; William Newcombe Jr., "The Culture and Acculturation of the Delaware Indians," *Anthropological Papers: Museum of Anthropology, University of Michigan* 10 (1956): 73; Waubuno, *The Traditions of the Delaware* (London, 1875), 10–12 (photocopy in the Ayer Collection, Newberry Library, Chicago), and, especially, John Bierhorst, *Mythology of the Lenape: Guide and Texts* (Tuscon, 1995), 30–31; Hìtakonanulaxk, *The Grandfathers Speak: Native American Folk Tales of the Lenapé People* (New York, 1994), expressly lays Lenape claim to "Nanapush."

30. Quotation: John E. Pomfret, *The Province of West New Jersey, 1609–1702* (Princeton, N.J., 1956), 59. Indian population: guesswork based on figures in Goddard, "Delaware," 216, and Charles Wolley, *A Two Years' Journal in New York (1701)*, Edward Gaylord Borne, ed. (Cleveland, 1902), 61 ff.; European and African figures are from the United States Bureau of the Census, *Historical Statistics of the United States, Colonial Times to 1970*, 2 vols. (Washington, D.C., 1975), 2:1168.

31. Contrast Elizabeth Tooker, "The Demise of the Susquehannocks: A 17th Century Mystery," *Pennsylvania Archaeologist* 54, no. 3 (1984): 1–10, with Francis Jennings, "Glory, Death and Transfiguration: The Susquehannock Indians in the Seventeenth Century," *Proceedings of the American Philosophical Society* 112 (1968): 15–53.

32. Jennings, *Ambiguous Iroquois Empire*, 155–56; 215, 263–89, 297.

33. The Indians did recall a deed in 1686, but they did not recall such an extensive cession. Neither the original deed of 1686 nor the copy produced by Logan at Pennsbury has survived; thus it is impossible to verify them. Other purported copies of these deeds have survived, but they do not correspond with other available data surrounding William Penn's purchases in the 1680s. Jennings has studied the events most closely in ibid., 325–46. But see also, for exampe, Richter, *Ordeal of the Longhouse*, 273–75; Anthony F. C. Wallace, *King of the Delawares: Teedyuscung, 1700–1763* (Philadelphia, 1949), 18–30; Francis Parkman, *The Conspiracy of Pontiac and the Indian War after the Conquest of Canada*, 6th ed., 2 vols. (Boston, 1870), 1:83–87.

34. Matthew Dennis's observations of Iroquois goals still apply, in some measure, to the early eighteenth century. See his *Cultivating a Landscape of Peace: Iroquois-European Encounters in Seventeenth-Century America* (Ithaca and Cooperstown, N.Y., 1993), 268.

35. For this and the next two paragraphs see Peter Mancall, *Valley of Opportunity: Economic Culture along the Upper Susquehanna, 1700–1800* (Ithaca, N.Y., 1991), 29–46.

36. Richter, *Ordeal of the Longhouse*, 275–76; Richard Aquilla, *The Iroquois Restoration: Iroquois Diplomacy on the Colonial Frontier, 1701–1754* (Detroit, 1983); Barbara Graymont, *The Iroquois in the American Revolution* (Syracuse, N.Y., 1972), 26–47.

37. David Brainerd, *The Life of David Brainerd*, ed. Jonathan Edwards and Philip E. Howard Jr. (1749; Chicago, 1949), 233–35.

38. This man, generally regarded as a Delaware, was more likely a Conoy. Conoys,

and this is the important point, shared much with Delawares; they mingled with them, and they would be scattered among them as they lost their town in the 1750s to British imperial expansion. Ibid., 233–38; Mark Harrington, *Religion among the Lenape: Indian Notes and Monographs*, Museum of the American Indian, Heye Foundation 3 (New York, 1921), 41–42; 151–52; Charles Hunter, "The Delaware Nativist Revival of the Mid-Eighteenth Century," *Ethnohistory* 18 (1971): 39–49; Anthony F. C. Wallace, "New Religions among the Delaware," *Southwestern Journal of Anthropology* 12 (1956): 1–21; Gregory Evans Dowd, *A Spirited Resistance: The North American Indian Struggle for Unity, 1745–1815* (Baltimore, 1992), 29; Christian F. Feest, "Nanticoke and Neighboring Tribes," in Trigger, *Northeast*, 15:246.

39. As recently as 1995 floods in the region made national headlines. Francis Jennings, "Pennsylvania Indians," in Daniel K. Richter and James H. Merrell, eds., *Beyond the Covenant Chain: The Iroquois and Their Neighbors in Indian North America, 1600–1800* (Syracuse, N.Y., 1987), 89–91.

40. Thomas Brainerd, ed., *Life of John Brainerd* (Philadelphia, 1865), 234–37, 239.

41. Tanner, "Location of Indian Tribes in Southeastern Michigan," 15.

42. This and the following paragraph are based on ibid., 3–4, 7, 10–13; Michael N. McConnell, "The Search for Security: Indian-English Relations in the Trans-Appalachian Region, 1758–1763" (Ph.D. diss., College of William and Mary, 1983), 31–32, 45, 49; and Michael McConnell, *A Country Between: The Upper Ohio Valley and Its Peoples, 1724–1774* (Lincoln, Nebr., 1992), 217; Richter, *Ordeal of the Longhouse*, 257–62.

43. For the conspiracy of Orontony, see Tanner, "Location of Indian Tribes in Southeastern Michigan," 17–20; R. David Edmunds, *The Potawatomis: Keepers of the Fire* (Norman, Okla., 1978), 42–43; and White, *Middle Ground*, 192–203. For Mississauga, see Ian K. Steele, *Warpaths: Invasions of North America* (New York, 1994), 173.

44. Mary Carson Darlington, "Journal of the Campaign," in *Fort Pitt and Letters from the Frontier* (Pittsburgh, 1892), 9–62. The report of Virginian Christopher Gist in 1751 also reveals that Ohio Indians initially opposed both the French and British designs on the region: "An Indian, who spoke good English, came to Me & . . . desired to know where the Indian's Land lay, for that the French claimed all the Land on one Side the River Ohio & the English on the other Side . . . to which I had made him no Answer"; see "Christopher Gist's First and Second Journals," in Lois Mulkearn, ed., *George Mercer Papers Relating to the Ohio Company of Virginia* (Pittsburgh, 1954), 39.

45. "Pécaudy de Contrecoeur, Claude-Pierre," *DCB* 4:617; Fernand Grenier, ed., *Papiers Contrecoeur et autres documents concernant le conflit Anglo-Français sur l'Ohio de 1755 à 1756* (Quebec, 1952), 1:418; "Christopher Gist's First and Second Journals," 13.

46. "Pécaudy de Contrecoeur, Claude-Pierre," 4:617; Paul Kopperman, *Braddock at the Monongahela* (Pittsburgh, 1977), 21–22; Charles Morse Stotz, "Defense in the Wilderness," in James Alfred Procter, ed., *Drums in the Forest* (Pittsburgh, 1958), 128–37; Walter O'Meara, *Guns at the Forks* (Englewood Cliffs, N.J., 1965), 60–71.

47. Duquesne's design and weaknesses: O'Meara, *Guns at the Forks*, 60–71; Ian K. Steele, *Betrayals: Fort William Henry and the "Massacre"* (New York, 1990), 7; Stotz, "Defense in the Wilderness," 126–40.

48. As with so much else, uncertainty surrounds this first reference to Pontiac. It is

found in an English-language abstract in Richard E. Day, *Calendar of the Sir William Johnson Manuscripts*, New York State Library History Bulletin 8 (Albany, 1909), 92. The abstract reads "1757 Speech of Pondiague [Pontiac] Outava [Ottawa] chief at Fort Duquenne, reporting efforts of Gorge Craane [George Croghan] to influence Indians by false story of the fall of Quebec, reminding of promise to the Indians of advantage from French alliance, and describing his superiority to evil suggestions." The New York State Library acquired the original French-language fragment from which this English abstract is taken as part of William L. Stone's large collection of Sir William Johnson Papers. Stone's father, also William L. Stone, had obtained that collection from a variety of sources, so the true origin of the original fragment is obscure. The original fragment was since lost in the fire that destroyed many items of value at the New York State Library. Why copies of the destroyed fragment and why other references to Pontiac before 1760 have not turned up in Canadian or French collections is a mystery that casts doubt on the authenticity of the abstract, which misspells the single French name it contains. Howard Peckham, *Pontiac and the Indian Uprising* (1947; New York, 1970), 47–48; O'Meara, *Guns at the Forks*, 68–69.

49. Joseph L. Peyser, trans. and ed., *Letters from New France: The Upper Country, 1686–1763* (Urbana, 1992), 198–99; Fred Anderson, *The Crucible of War: The Seven Years' War and the Fate of Empire in British North America, 1754–1766* (New York, 2000), 52–53.

50. Quotation: Peyser, *Letters from New France*, 201–3, also 199; also Kopperman, *Braddock at the Monongahela*, 103–4; Lawrence Henry Gipson, *The Great War for the Empire: The Years of Defeat, 1754–1757*, vol. 6 of *The British Empire before the American Revolution*, 15 vols. (Caldwell, Idaho, 1936–70), 35–43; Francis Jennings, *Empire of Fortune: Crowns, Colonies, and Tribes in the Seven Years' War in America* (New York, 1988), 47–70.

51. Kopperman, *Braddock at the Monongahela*, 18.

52. Ibid., 6.

53. Contrecoeur to Vaudreuil, June 21, 1755, in Grenier, *Papiers Contrecoeur*, 1:365.

54. On Langlade, see the memoir by Augustin Grignon in Lyman C. Draper, ed., "Seventy-Two Years' Recollections of Wisconsin," *Wisconsin Historical Society Collections* 3 (1857): 212–15. This memoir, written a century after the battle, nonetheless commands some respect in that it accurately relates such matters as numbers. For Braddock's defeat more generally, see "Etat des morts et blesses a la Bataille de la Monongahela," n.d., Contrecoeur to the minister, July 20, 1755, and Contrecoeur to Vaudreuil, July 26, 1755, in Grenier, *Papiers Contrecoeur*, 390–91, 397–400; Kopperman, *Braddock at the Monongahela*; Gipson, *Great War for the Empire: The Years of Defeat*, 63–97; Jennings, *Empire of Fortune*, 157–60.

55. "John M'Kinney's Description of Fort Duquesne," in Grenier, *Papiers Contrecoeur*, 231.

56. Wallace, *King of the Delawares*, 72 (quotation); Joseph Mortimer Levering, *History of Bethlehem, Pennsylvania, 1741–1892* (Bethlehem, Pa., 1903), 316–18; C. Hale Sipe, *The Indian Wars of Pennsylvania* (Harrisburg, Pa., 1929), 204–43; C. Hale Sipe, *The Indian Chiefs of Pennsylvania* (Butler, Pa., 1927), 232–33.

57. Weiser to Hamilton, May 2, 1754, in Julian P. Boyd, ed. *The Susquehanna Company Papers*, 11 vols. (Wilkes-Barre, Penn., 1930), 1:90; Weiser to Richard Peters, October 12, 1754, in ibid., 136–37; Daniel Claus to Peters [October 1754], in ibid., 131; see also Speech of Governor to Scarrooyady, December 24, 1754, *Pennsylvania Colonial Records*, 6:217.

58. Jennings, *Empire of Fortune*, 262–74; Wallace, *King of the Delawares*.

59. For various views on the Ohio Indians' coming to terms with the British, see Christian Frederick Post, "The Journal of Christian Frederick Post, from Philadelphia to the Ohio . . . ," in Reuben Gold Thwaites, ed., *Early Western Travels, 1748–1846* (Cleveland, 1904), 1:230; McConnell, *Country Between*, 126–34; Stephen F. Auth, *The Ten Years' War: Indian-White Relations in Pennsylvania* (New York, 1989), 106; Edward P. Hamilton, ed. and trans., *Adventure in the Wilderness: The American Journals of Louis Antoine de Bougainville, 1756–1760* (Norman, Okla., 1964), 196; Jennings, *Empire of Fortune*, 365–67, 395.

60. Bouquet to Burd, August 26, 1758; Forbes to Bouquet, August 28, 1758; Bouquet to Washington, August 30, 1758, *PHB* 2:419, 439, 446–47; Hamilton, *Adventure in the Wilderness*, 169, 193.

61. Bouquet to Forbes, September 11, 1758 (trans. Donald Kent); Bouquet to Forbes (trans. Kent), September 17, 1758, *PHB* 2:489–95, 517–22. Catawbas (Siouan speakers) were a Carolinian people. Tuscaroras, formerly of North Carolina, and Nottaways, formerly of Virginia (both speakers of Iroquoian languages), shared villages on the Susquehanna River at the time of the war.

62. Lawrence Henry Gipson, *The Great War for the Empire: The Victorious Years: 1758–1760*, vol. 7 of *The British Empire before the American Revolution*, 15 vols. (Caldwell, Idaho, 1936–70), 268–70; Hamilton, *Adventure in the Wilderness*, 294–95; Grant to Forbes, September 14, 1758, *PHB* 2:499–505.

63. Ottawas: O'Meara, *Guns at the Forks*, 156; Miamis: Indian and Quaker intelligence, January 29, 1758, *WJP* 2: 774–75; McConnell, "Search for Security," 157–58.

64. Gipson, *Great War for the Empire: The Victorious Years*, 282–83; *Pennsylvania Gazette*, fol. 2, item 9997, November 30, 1758; George Washington to Francis Fauquier, November 28, 1758, in John C. Fitzpatrick, ed., *The Writings of George Washington from the Original Manuscript Sources, 1745–1799*, 39 vols. (Washington, D.C., 1931), 2:299.

65. Forbes to Beaver and Shingas, in Alfred Proctor James, ed., *The Writings of General John Forbes* (Menasha, Wisc., 1938), 251–52.

66. Comparing two "substantially discrepant reports" of these discussions, historian Francis Jennings has raised concerns about their actual content. One report, by the French officer at Fort Machault [Venago], who got his information from the anti-British Delaware warrior Custaloga, "noted that the Indians (Delawares and Iroquois alike) had asked the English to withdraw from the smoking ruins." The other report, the official English minutes, contains no such demand, but, as Jennings argues, "it seems apparent from Colonel Bouquet's speech to the Indians that he was responding defensively to Indian suggestions. 'I return you hearty Thanks for the Speech you made,'. . . . 'We are not come here to take Possession of your hunting Country in a hostile manner, as the French did. . . . but to open a large and extensive Trade with you

and all the other nations of Indians to the Westward who chose to live in friendship with us.'" Francis Jennings, "The Indians' Revolution," in Alfred Young, ed., *The American Revolution: Explorations in the History of American Radicalism* (De Kalb, Ill., 1976), 333–34.

67. Tamaqua quoted in "Minutes of a Conference Held by Croghan," August 7, 1759, *PHB* 3:510. For the full conference, see Nicholas Wainwright, ed., "George Croghan's Journal, 1759–1763," *PMHB* 71 (1947): 316–17, and "Minutes of a Conference held at Pittsburgh in July, 1759 . . . ," Mercer to Denny, August 6, 1759, "Intelligence enclosed in the foregoing letter," August 4, 1759, *Pennsylvania Colonial Records*, 8: 382–93. For analysis, see McConnell, *Country Between*, 143. Pitt quoted in O'Meara, *Guns at the Forks*, 218; Indian reaction: James Kenny, "Journal of James Kenny, 1761–1763," ed. John W. Jordan, *PMHB* 37 (1913): 433.

68. Croghan: O'Meara, *Guns at the Forks*, 219–23; Croghan to William Johnson, December 22, 1759, *WJP* 10:131. Delawares: Paul A. Wallace, ed., *Thirty Thousand Miles with John Heckewelder* (Pittsburgh, 1958), 41, 42, 64. Horsetheft: William Walters to Johnson, April 5, 1762, *WJP* 10:427; Kenny, "Journal of James Kenny," 173; Archibald Blane to Bouquet, April 25, 1762, *PCHB*, ser. 21648, pt. 1:85; Livestock killed: Kenney, "Journal of James Kenny," 38; Shawnees kill Virginia hunters at Redstone: Angus McDonald to Bouquet, April 8, 1762, *PHB* 6:74; Bouquet to Amherst, March 7, 1762, *PCHB*, ser. 21634:75–76; Bouquet to Amherst, May 24, 1762, *PCHB*, ser. 21653:133–34; Wainwright, "George Croghan's Journal," 419–20, 423; Kenny, "Journal of James Kenny," 158.

69. Henry Balfour's Conference with Indians, September 29, 1761, *WJP* 3:542–43; McConnell, "Search for Security," 54. See also John Heckewelder, *History, Manners, and Customs of the Indian Nations Who Once Inhabited Pennsylvania* [1819], Memoirs of the Historical Society of Pennsylvania 12 (Philadelphia, 1876), 291; Tanner, *Atlas of Great Lakes Indian History*, maps 9 and 11.

CHAPTER 2 A Worldly War

1. Lawrence Henry Gipson, *The Great War for the Empire: The Victorious Years: 1758–1760*, vol. 7 of *The British Empire before the American Revolution*, 15 vols. (Caldwell, Idaho, 1936–70), 465–66.

2. Robert Rogers, *Journals of Major Robert Rogers*, ed. Howard Peckham (1765; New York, 1961), 140, 143–44; Gipson, *Great War for the Empire: The Victorious Years*, 7:465–66; George Croghan to William Johnson, January 25, 1760, *WJP* 10:134–35; Nicholas B. Wainwright, ed., "George Croghan's Journal, 1759–1763," *PMHB* 71 (1947): 387.

3. Rogers, *Journals*, 155–56; John R. Cuneo, *Robert Rogers of the Rangers* (New York, 1959), 133; Howard Peckham, *Pontiac and the Indian Uprising* (1947; New York, 1970), 59–63 n. 3; Robert Rogers, *A Concise Account of North America* (1765; New York, 1966).

4. The two principal companions had met with Croghan in 1759 at Pittsburgh to discuss the possibility of peace. It is possible that one of these was Pontiac, but he is not listed by that name among the named Ottawas—Misseaghge, Oulamey—in the records of the 1759 negotiations at Pittsburgh. Pontiac might have been one of the twenty-two

unnamed Ottawa warriors mentioned in the records. George Croghan, "Journal," in "Aspinwall Papers," 9:363–64. For 1759, see "Minutes of a Conference Held by Croghan," August 7, 1759, *PHB* 3:507.

5. Rogers, *Journals*, 157–65; Donald Campbell to [Henry Bouquet?], December 2, 1760, in Robert Rogers' Correspondence, 1760–71, 1:1, BHC.

6. William Renwick Riddell, trans., "The Last Indian Council of the French at Detroit," *Transactions of the Royal Society of Canada* 25 (1931): 165–68; Bouquet to Monckton, July 29, 1760, in "Aspinwall Papers," 9:282.

7. Michael N. McConnell, "The Search for Security: Indian-English Relations in the Trans-Appalachian Region, 1758–1763" (Ph.D. diss., College of William and Mary, 1983), 385; Riddell, "Last Indian Council," 165–67; Court of Enquiry, Detroit, April 6, 1765, in Gage Papers; copy of an embassy sent to the Illinois by the Indians at Detroit, by the courier Godfrey and Chene, in "Gladwin Manuscripts," 27:644.

8. Riddell, "Last Indian Council," 166.

9. George Croghan, "Croghan's Journal, October 21, 1760–January 7, 1761," in Reuben Gold Thwaites, ed., *Early Western Travels, 1748–1846* (Cleveland, 1904), 1:114–22; Detroit Council, "A True Copy from the Original by Alexander McKee," December 3–5, 1760, *WJP* 10:203, 205; Campbell to Bouquet, received at Presque Isle, December 24, 1760, in "Aspinwall Papers," 9:357–58. Major Henry Gladwin, who suffered episodic malarial fevers, attempted to take command from Campbell in the fall of 1761 but was too ill to take true charge, and he returned to the St. Lawrence Valley until the summer of 1762. See William R. Nester, *"Haughty Conquerors": Amherst and the Great Indian Uprising of 1763* (Westport, Conn., 2000), 57.

10. Rogers, *Journals*, 166–67; Campbell to Bouquet, November 21, 1760, "Bouquet Papers," 19:45; Peckham, *Pontiac and the Indian Uprising*, 63–65; ("pleasant") George Croghan, "Croghan's Journal, May 15–September 26, 1765," in Thwaites, *Early Western Travels*, 1:152; Bouquet to Monckton, Presque Isle, August 6, 1760, in "Aspinwall Papers," 9:294–95.

11. Francis Jennings, *Empire of Fortune: Crowns, Colonies, and Tribes in the Seven Years' War in America* (New York, 1988), 445.

12. Croghan, "Croghan's Journal, May 15–September 26, 1765," in Thwaites, *Early Western Travels*, 1:152–53; Bouquet to Monckton, Presque Isle, August 6, 1760, in "Aspinwall Papers," 9:294–95.

13. Amherst, September 22, 1760, *The Journal of Jeffery Amherst*, ed. J. Clarence Webster (Toronto, 1931), 254; (quotation) George Croghan to Horatio Gates, enclosure, dated May 22, 1760, in "Aspinwall Papers," 9:250; Amherst's circular letter, September 9, 1760, in "Aspinwall Papers," 9:318–19; Richard Peters to Robert Monckton, September 11, 1760, in "Aspinwall Papers," 9:318–19.

14. George Croghan to Horatio Gates, enclosure, dated May 22, 1760, Donald Campbell to Bouquet, December 2, 1760, in "Aspinwall Papers," 9:250, 358. One inhabitant later claimed that the garrison's taxes were "almost unsupportable." Anon. to Lt. Col. John Campbell, August 7, 1766, "Bouquet Papers," 19:462–63.

15. Wainwright, "George Croghan's Journal, 1759–1763," 360; Campbell to Bouquet, December 24, 1760, *PCHB*, ser. 21645:259; Croghan, "Croghan's Journal," Octo-

ber 21, 1760–January 7, 1761, in Thwaites, *Early Western Travels*, 1:114–15, 118; Dr. Christian Anthony to Bouquet, November 7, 1761, "Bouquet Papers," 19:119.

16. McConnell, "Search for Security," 15; Croghan, "Croghan's Journal," October 21, 1760–January 7, 1761," in Thwaites, *Early Western Travels*, 1:118.

17. Campbell to Bouquet, March 10, 1761, *PCHB*, ser. 21646:61–62. Bouquet left the remarks about men and women out of the copy he sent to his superiors; see "Aspinwall Papers," 9:399–400.

18. ("Slaves") Captain Daniel Claus to William Johnson, September 8, 1764, *WJP* 11:352–54; ("indifferently") Jean Baptiste de Couagne to William Johnson, Niagara, May 26, 1763, *WJP* 10:684; ("As soon as") Indian Conference, May 10, 1765, *WJP* 11:730–31; John Campbell to William Johnson, Detroit, August 17, 1765, *WJP* 11:898–99; ("The English . . .") copy of an embassy sent to the Illinois by the Indians at Detroit, by the courier Godfrey and Chene, in "Gladwin Manuscripts," 27:644; Navarre/Burton, *Pontiac Journal*, 17. R. Clyde Ford's translation is on the even pages, the original French on the odd pages. In this case, I risk my own translation. Ford adds the adjective "fancied" to the word "insult." Robert Rogers, *Ponteach: or the Savages of America* (London, 1765), 13–17, 28, copy in the Ayer Collection, Newberry Library, Chicago.

19. Hugh Mercer to Governor Denny, August 12, 1759, in Sylvester K. Stevens and Donald H. Kent, eds., *The Wilderness Chronicles of Northwestern Pennsylvania* (Harrisburg, Pa., 1941), 166; speech of the Shawnees to Mons. De Neyon, interpr. Mes Bobe, December 11, 1763 [French original, translation mine], Gage Papers. The phrase "bad discourse" brings to mind Greg Dening's *Mr. Bligh's Bad Language: Passion, Power and Theatre on the Bounty* (New York, 1992); much as Bligh's self-consciously modern efforts to control his ship offended his men, so British officers offended Indians, largely through acts—spoken and performed—that manifested British intentions to mastery more than they caused immediate physical pain or loss of land. For *mauvais discours*, see Arlette Farge, *Dire et mal dire: L'Opinion publique au xviii*^e*siècle* (Paris, 1992), 92, 187; I thank Janine Lanza for alerting me to this work.

20. Jeffery Amherst to William Johnson, July 9, 1763, *WJP* 4:166–67; John Porteous to James Porteous, 1762, BHC.

21. Nester is typically admiring in *Haughty Conquerors*, 57.

22. Court of Inquiry, August 9, 1763; Court of Inquiry, September 8, 1763, Major Gladwin to Col. Bouquet, November 1, 1763, in "Gladwin Manuscripts," 642, 647 (that this is Manning Fisher is clear on 649), 680; Gladwin to Croghan, August 6, 1763, *WJP* 4:181. For Indian complaints about the gunsmith's work, see William Johnson to Croghan, October 1762, *WJP* 10:561; Gladwin to Amherst, July 26, 1763, Amherst Papers, vol. 2, no. 7; Gladwin to Gage, January 9, 1764, Gage Papers.

23. Gladwin to Amherst, April 20, 1763, *WJP* 4:95; Amherst to Gladwin, September 15, 1762, in "Gladwin Manuscripts," 675; Amherst to Johnson, May 29, 1763, *WJP* 10:689.

24. Edward P. Hamilton, ed. and trans., *Adventure in the Wilderness: The American Journals of Louis Antoine de Bougainville, 1756–1760*, fwd. Colin G. Calloway (Norman, Okla., 1990), 105.

25. August 30, 1760, *Journal of Jeffery Amherst*, 222–23; Indian Conference, Septem-

ber 25–October 3, 1761, *WJP* 10:1761; Ecuyer to Bouquet, February 8, 1763, *PCHB*, ser. 21649:42–45; Bouquet to Monckton, July 27, 1761, in "Aspinwall Papers," 9:437; Wainwright,"George Croghan's Journal," November 24, 1761, 417–18.

26. McConnell, "Search for Security," 227; Alexander McKee's Journal, October 12, 1762, *WJP* 10:578; Croghan to Johnson, July 25, 1761, *WJP* 10:317; see also Johnson to Lords of Trade, August 30, 1764, in CISHL 10:307.

27. Testimony of Mr. Fisher, September 8, 1763, in "Gladwin Manuscripts," 647; William Johnson to Gage, July 6, 1765, *WJP* 11:831–32; Board of Trade to the earl of Halifax, March 6, 1765, in CO 5/66, fol. 25; extract of a minute of the House of Lords, March 6, 1765, CO 5/66, fol. 27.

28. Ecuyer to Bouquet, November 20, 1763, in *PHB* 6:463. Oddly, the translation of the document offered by the editors (465) omits the anti-Semitic language. The original reads: "mais quand on et Juif, on est Juif, et on reste tel." Albert T. Volwiller, ed., "William Trent's Journal at Fort Pitt, 1763," *Mississippi Valley Historical Review* 11 (1924–25): 400, 408. In an apotheosis of disdain, Ecuyer and Trent presented a visiting Delaware delegation with two blankets and a handkerchief from the fort's smallpox ward. In his journal, Trent hoped the gifts would "have the desired effect," and he saw them as a precise token of "our regard." This act, as a form of indiscriminate warfare, will be treated later.

29. John Porteous, "A Short Journal of the Siege of Detroit," 1763, 2:5, 17, and John Porteous to his parents, November 20, 1763, both in BHC; Lt. John Montresor to Basset, November 2, 1763, CISHL 10:535–36; *Pennsylvania Gazette*, fol. 2, item 18816, August 11, 1763; item 18849, August 18, 1763; item 18967, September 1, 1763; item 24382, October 17, 1765; Jehu Hay to George Croghan, August 28, 1767, *WJP* 5:643; Lt. James McDonald to Croghan, July 12, 1763, *WJP* 10:740; William Eyre to Johnson, January 7, 1764, and Michael Byrne to Johnson, January 22, 1765, *WJP* 11:6, 547; Bradstreet to Gage, August 5, 1764, and Turnbull to Gage, Detroit, May 12, 1768, Gage Papers; Bouquet to Amherst, June 25, 1763, "Bouquet Papers," 19:200.

30. Gage to Bradstreet, October 15, 1764, and Aubry to minister, February 25, 1765, CISHL 10:343–46, 457; C. C. Trowbridge [interviewer], "Mr. Gabriel St. Aubin's Account," *Michigan Pioneer*, vol. 8 (1885), 356–57.

31. Thomas Mante, *History of the Late War in America and the Islands of the West-Indies* (London, 1772), 481, in Ayer Collection, Newberry Library, Chicago; "Extract of a Letter from Fort Ontario," August 7, 1764, *Pennsylvania Gazette*, fol. 2, item 21522, August 30, 1764.

32. Copy of letter from St. Ange, commandant at the Illinois, to D'Abbadie, director general, August 12, 1764, CISHL 10:294–95; testimony of Thomas King, Sandusky, October 3, 1764, *WJP* 11:372.

33. Wilbur Jacobs, "Gift-Giving and Pontiac's Uprising," in *Dispossessing the American Indian* (New York, 1972), 75–82; Wilbur Jacobs, *Wilderness Politics and Indian Gifts: The Northern Colonial Frontier, 1748–1763* (1950; Lincoln, Nebr., 1966), 11–28, 180–85; Randolph Downes, *Council Fires on the Upper Ohio* (Pittsburgh, 1949), 106–14.

34. Thomas Hobbes, *Three Discourses: A Critical Modern Edition of New Identified*

Work of the Young Hobbes, ed. Noel B. Reynolds and Arlene W. Saxonhouse (Chicago, 1995), 51; Sterling to Loring, August 19, 1762, Sterling to Syme, June 8, 1762, and Sterling to Syme, July 20, 1762, in James Sterling Letter Book, WCL; Croghan to Johnson, March 12, 1765, *WJP* 11:633; Johnson to Croghan, April 20, 1766, *WJP* 12:80; S. B. Hertel to William Johnson, August 16, 1764, and Croghan to Johnson, January 17, 1767, in Richard E. Day, *Calendar of the Sir William Johnson Manuscripts*, New York State Library History Bulletin 8 (Albany, 1909), 233, 342.

35. Edmund Atkin to the Board of Trade, June 1756, CO 323/13, fol. 304; Johnson to Lords of Trade, July 1, 1763, *NYCD* 7:525; Croghan to Bouquet, Fort Pitt, December 10, 1762, *WJP* 10:596–97; Daniel K. Richter finds similar expressions in the seventeenth century. Richter, *Ordeal of the Longhouse: The Peoples of the Iroquois League in the Era of European Colonization* (Chapel Hill, N.C., 1992), 47; George Croghan to Henry Bouquet, March 27, 1762, *PCHB*, ser. 21655:183; William Johnson to Amherst, January 21, 1763, *WJP*10: 612.

36. Testimony before James Grant, April 5, 1764, in "Gladwin Manuscripts," 27: 663; Bouquet to Monkton, July 9, 1760, in "Aspinwall Papers," 9:265; Gregory Evans Dowd, "'Insidious Friends': Gift-Giving and the Cherokee-British Alliance in the Seven Years' War," in Andrew R. L. Cayton and Fredrika J. Teute, eds., *Contact Points: American Frontiers from the Mohawk Valley to the Mississippi, 1750–1830* (Chapel Hill, N.C., 1998), 114–50.

37. John Lewis Gage to William Johnson, December 4, 1763, *WJP* 4:259.

38. "Capt. Croghan's Journal to Presque Isle," entry for July 13, 1760, in "Aspinwall Papers," 9:287; Amherst to Johnson, September 30, 1763, *WJP* 10:856–57; Amherst to Gladwin, June 22, 1763, Amherst Papers, vol. 2, no. 2; Indian Conference, Detroit, May 7–10, 1764, *WJP* 11:177; "A Montreal Letter," November 1, 1763, *WJP* 4:225. Indians were not alone. Conquered Canadiens were to be grateful, as were Jamaican slaves, at least according to Pennsylvania's Indian agent, Richard Peters. Richard Peters to Gen. Monckton, Philadelphia, June 10, 1760, in "Aspinwall Papers," 9:258. After the war, George Croghan at Fort Pitt and Jehu Hay at Detroit would exhort Ottawas, Shawnees, and Delawares to "behave with Gratitude," and not to show "a want of gratitude," for "His Majesty's Pity for, and generous disposition, towards them"; Jehu Hay to George Croghan, October 15, 1767, *WJP* 5:728–29; Howard H. Peckham, ed., *George Croghan's Journal of His Trip to Detroit in 1767* (Ann Arbor, Mich., 1939), 47; Amherst to Johnson, July 16, 1763, *WJP* 4:172.

39. Croghan, "Croghan's Journal, October 21, 1760–January 7, 1761," in Thwaites, *Early Western Travels*, 1:116–17; Wainwright, "George Croghan's Journal," January 7, 1761, 398; Robert Monckton to Bouquet, February 12, 1761, and Donald Campbell to Henry Bouquet, June 1, 1761, in "Bouquet Papers," 19:61, 71; Bouquet to Monckton, January 26, 1761, in "Aspinwall Papers," 9:390–91; Croghan to Johnson, February 1761, and Johnson to Lords of Trade, July 1761, *WJP* 3:337, 349.

40. Amherst to Johnson, February 2, 1759, *WJP* 10:96; August 1, 1760, *Journal of Jeffery Amherst*, 223; Patrick Frazier, *The Mohicans of Stockbridge* (Lincoln, Nebr., 1992), 127; Amherst to Lt. Gov. Bull, CO 5/58, fol. 387; General Amherst's talk to the several

Indian tribes, April 28, 1760; ("misunderstood") Gov. James Hamilton to Monckton, July 24, 1760; and Amherst to Monckton, August 2, 1760, in "Aspinwall Papers" 9:240–41, 280, 292.

41. Amherst to Johnson, September 20, 1760; Amherst to Johnson, June 11, 1761; Amherst to Johnson, December 26, 1761; Amherst to Johnson, January 16, 1762; Amherst to Johnson, September 12, 1762, *WJP* 10:187–88, 284–85, 348, 354–55; 508–9; Amherst to Bouquet, May 2, 1762, and Bouquet to Amherst, October 5, 1762, in "Bouquet Papers," 19:141, 168; Wainright, "George Croghan's Journal," March and April 1762, 421–25; George Croghan, "Report of an Indian Conference at Fort Pitt, December 8, 1762," *PCHB* 16:192–94; [Ensign Robert] Holmes, March 30, 1763: Copy of Speech of Miami Chiefs, *PHB* 6:171.

42. Francis Gordon to Bouquet, August 18, 1762, September 19, 1762, in Stevens and Kent, *Wilderness Chronicles*, 240–41; Gawahe to Johnson, July 9, 1763, *WJP* 10:768–69.

43. Johnson to Gage, January 27, 1764, *WJP* 4:308–9; Wainwright, "George Croghan's Journal," September and October 1762, 428, 432–33; Lieutenant Thomas Hutchins, "Journal," 1762, *PCHB*, ser. 21655:167–74; Lieutenant Thomas Hutchins, "Journal and Report of Thomas Hutchins," [April 4–September 24, 1762], *WJP* 10:523–29; Ecuyer to Bouquet, January 8, 1763, and Ecuyer to Bouquet, April 23, 1763, *PHB* 6:140–42, 176–79.

44. Wainwright, "George Croghan's Journal," 388, 392; Croghan, "Croghan's Journal, October 21, 1760–January 7, 1761," in Thwaites, *Early Western Travels*, 1:119–20.

45. Amherst to Johnson, February 22, 1761, *WJP* 3:345; Peckham, *Pontiac and the Indian Uprising*, 71–72. For the diplomatic uses of the Indian trade, see Tom Hatley, *The Dividing Paths: Cherokees and South Carolinians through the Revolutionary Era* (Oxford, 1995), 68–71. For examples in the early 1760s, see Bouquet to Monckton, July 10, 1761, and July 24, 1761, and Amherst to Bouquet, July 25, 1762, in "Bouquet Papers," 19:91, 96–97, 157; Niagara Conference, July 13, 1764, *WJP* 4:473–74.

46. James Sterling to James Syme, June 17, 1762; Sterling to Syme, August 19, 1762; and Sterling to John Duncan, October 25, 1762, in James Sterling Letter Book, WCL; Donald Campbell to Bouquet, May 21, 1761; Campbell to Bouquet, October 16, 1761; and Campbell to Bouquet, November 28, 1761, in "Bouquet Papers," 19:67, 116–17, 121; Hutchins, "Journal and Report," November 12, 1762, *WJP* 10:529; "Indian Council," *WJP* 3:453–56; "Conference . . . at . . . Pittsburgh," August 12, 1760, *Pennsylvania Archives*, 1st ser., 3:744–52; Bouquet to Monckton, March 23, 1761, in "Aspinwall Papers" 9:401; Council with Shawnees, April 16, 1763, Wainwright, "George Croghan's Journal," 441–42; Amherst to William Johnson, April 3, 1763, *WJP* 10:648–49.

47. Johnson to Amherst, July 11, 1763, *PCHB*, ser. 21634:212–13; for Sandusky and Ohio, see Paul A. Wallace, ed., *Thirty Thousand Miles with John Heckewelder* (Pittsburgh, 1958), 67–68.

48. Croghan to Johnson, January 25, 1760; Daniel Claus to Johnson, May 1, 1761; James Gorrell to Johnson, May 7, 1762; Johnson to earl of Egremont, May 1762; Croghan to Bouquet, December 10, 1762; and Johnson to Amherst, January 21, 1763, *WJP* 10:134–35, 259–62, 450, 461, 596–97, 612; Johnson to Lt. Dan. Claus, March 10,

1761, Claus Papers, M. G. 19 F1/1, reel 1, microfilm in Princeton University Library, Princeton, N.J.; Donald Campbell to Monckton, June 1, 1761, in "Aspinwall Papers," 9:416; Campbell to Bouquet, April 26, 1762, *PCHB*, ser. 21643:87. Donald Campbell at Detroit ceased to complain by the late spring of 1762 and even began to inform his superiors that Amherst's policies were showing the kind of "good effects" the general had hoped for: "Tho' the Indians grumbled and even threatened at first, they begin to hunt & mind their corn and I have not half some much Trouble with them as last year." His sudden change of heart is unconvincing: he still gave them "trifles." Campbell to Bouquet, June 8, 1762, *PCHB*, ser. 21643:139–40; Ecuyer to Bouquet, November 20, 1763, *PHB* 6:463, 464–65. For new critics, see Mante, *History of the Late War in America*, 478–79; "A Montreal Letter" enclosed in John Welles to Johnson, February 27, 1764, in *WJP* 4:224–25; Gavin Cochran, chap. 2, "Treatise on the Indians of North America and present state of affairs there, the beginning of the year, 1764," Ayer MSS, Newberry Library, Chicago. Various critical remarks—direct and implied—by Croghan or Johnson can be sampled in *WJP* 4:170–71, 216, 249–50, 276, 398; *WJP* 10:549, 717, 880; CISHL 10:259, 260–61, 262–63, 307, 331. Nester, in *Haughty Conquerors*, ix, 65, places blame for the war squarely on Amherst.

49. Clarence Walworth Alvord, *The Mississippi Valley in British Politics*, 2 vols. (Cleveland, 1917), 1:186; Francis Parkman, *The Conspiracy of Pontiac and the Indian War after the Conquest of Canada*, 6th ed., 2 vols. (1851; Boston, 1870), 1:176; Thomas Gage to John Penn, July 2, 1766, Ayer MSS, Newberry Library, Chicago; Speech of the Chippewas, sent to Illinois, 1763, in "Gladwin Manuscripts," 645; Croghan, "Croghan's Journal, October 21, 1760–January 7, 1761," in Thwaites, *Early Western Travels*, 1:120; Croghan, "Croghan's Journal," May 15–September 26, 1765," in Thwaites, *Early Western Travels*, 1:148, 159.

50. Jack Stagg, *Anglo-Indian Relations in North America to 1763 and an Analysis of the Royal Proclamation of 7 October 1763* (Ottawa, 1981), 259, in Newberry Library, Chicago; "Draft of Instruction for the Governors . . . ," Whitehall, December 2, 1761, and Lords of Trade to Lt. Gov. Colden, Whitehall, December 11, 1761, *NYCD* 7:478–79, 480–81; and "Royal Instructions to Governor Monckton," December 9, 1761, *WJP* 10:340–42; Henry Bouquet to Jeffery Amherst, April 1, 1762, *PHB* 6:72; Bouquet to Monckton, March 20, 1761, and April 22, 1761, in "Aspinwall Papers," 9:397, 406.

51. Volwiller, "Trent's Journal," 398; Amherst's instructions to Henry Gladwin, Albany, June 22, 1761; Johnson to Amherst, July 29, 1761; and Six Nations to Amherst, May 1763, *WJP* 10:293–96, 321–22, 680; Bouquet's Orders, October 18, 1762, *PCHB*, ser. 21655:180; Bouquet to Monckton, March 20, 1761, and Bouquet to Gates, April 22, 1761, in "Aspinwall Papers," 9:396, 408; Ensign Pauli to Henry Bouquet, February 19, 1762, *PCHB*, ser. 21648:33.

52. Bouquet's Orders and Regulations, February 21, 1761–May 13, 1761, Bouquet Papers, Additional MSS, 21655, fols. 175–78, British Museum, London; Bouquet to Monckton, May 22, 1761, "Bouquet Papers," 19:69; Gavin Cochrane to Bouquet, Presque Isle, June 1, 1761, and T. Guy to Bouquet, June 1, 1761, in Stevens and Kent, *Wilderness Chronicles*, 210–13, 214–15; Wainwright, "George Croghan's Journal," 400, 407; Bouquet to Monckton, May 4, 1761; Bouquet to Monckton, May 15, 1761; and

Bouquet to Monckton, June 12, 1761, in "Aspinwall Papers," 9:411, 413, 419; copy of Major Ward's speech, June 28, 1761, and Col. H. Bouquet: speech to the Indians, June 29, 1761, *PCHB*, ser. 21655:115, 118–20; McConnell, "Search for Security," 341; T. Guy to Bouquet, June 25, 1761, *PCHB*, ser. 21646:237.

53. Walter Rutherfurd to Johnson, May 12, 1761; Johnson to Daniel Claus, May 20, 1761; and Croghan to Johnson, April 24, 1763, *WJP* 10:265, 270, 660; McConnell, "Search for Security," 96.

54. Wainwright, "George Croghan's Journal," 375–76; Croghan to William Johnson, London, March 10, 1764, and Johnson to Colden, April 6, 1764, *WJP* 4:363, 388; editors' note, CISHL 10:374.

55. James Hamilton to William Johnson, February 10, 1761, and Richard Peters to William Johnson, February 12, 1761, *WJP* 10:210–15.

56. Richard Peters to Johnson, May 18, 1761, Amherst to Johnson, July 18, 1762, and Report of Daniel Brodhead, September 27, 1762, *WJP* 10:266–68; 473, 530–31.

57. McConnell, "Search for Security," 414; Francis Jennings, William N. Fenton, Mary A. Druke, and David R. Miller, eds., *The History and Culture of Iroquois Diplomacy* (Syracuse, N.Y., 1985), 194; James Hamilton to Johnson, October 17, 1762, *WJP* 10 551–53.

58. James Hamilton to Johnson, April 16, 1763; Indian Journal, May 1763; Hamilton to Johnson, May 18, 1763; and Journal of Indian Affairs, June 1763, *WJP* 10:656, 664–66, 671, 772–73; Thomas McKee to Johnson, June 2, 1763, and Eliphalet Dyer to Susquehanna and Delaware Company, May 25, 1764, *WJP* 4:132, 428–29; Paul Wallace, *Thirty Thousand Miles*, 70.

59. Croghan, "Croghan's Journal, October 21, 1760–January 7, 1761," in Thwaites, *Early Western Travels*, 1:115–16; [Christian] Frederick Post, "Two Journals of Western Tours," in Thwaites, *Early Western Travels* 1:199, 243.

60. Bouquet to Monckton, December 25, 1760, Croghan, "Journal," in "Aspinwall Papers" 9:359–60, 369–70; Indian Conference, September 25–October 3, 1761, *WJP* 10:327–29.

61. James McColloch to Bouquet, *PCHB*, ser. 21655:111.

62. Croghan, "Croghan's Journal," October 21, 1760–January 7, 1761, in Thwaites, *Early Western Travels*, 1:119; "Council held at the State House in Philadelphia, Friday, July 11, 1760," Pennsylvania Council Minutes, Huntington MS 8249, Huntington Library, San Marino, Calif.; Colonel Hugh Mercer to Bouquet, Pittsburgh, February 7, 1759, *PHB* 3:107–8.

63. Wainwright, "George Croghan's Journal," 432; Alexander McKee's Journal, October 12–November 27, 1762, *WJP* 10:577; John Baird to Bouquet, Wackatomica, June 8, 1762, *PCHB*, ser. 21648, pt. 1:137; "Conference . . . held at Lancaster," August 16, 1762, *Pennsylvania Colonial Records*, 8:734–41.

64. Bouquet to James Pemberton, September 1, 1759, *PCHB*, ser. 21652:235–36; Hugh Mercer to Henry Bouquet, December 19, 1758, and Hugh Mercer to Bouquet, December 23, 1758, *PHB* 2:636, 640; Mercer to Governor Denny, January 8, 1759, *Pennsylvania Colonial Records*, 8:292–93; James Kenny, "Journal of James Kenny, 1761–1763," ed. John W. Jordan, *PMHB* 37 (1913): 152, 162. For an examination of the

relationship between hunting, manhood, and politics among the Cherokees in the same era, see Nathaniel Sheidley, "Hunting and the Politics of Masculinity in Cherokee Treaty-Making, 1763–1775," in Martin Daunton and Rick Halpern, eds., *Empire and Others: British Encounters with Indigenous Peoples, 1600–1850* (Philadelphia, 1999), 167–85.

65. Sgt. Angus McDonald to Bouquet, October 25, 1761, in Bouquet Papers, Additional MSS, 21647, fol. 217–217v, British Museum, London; Bouquet to Major Levingston, February 6, 1762, Bouquet Papers, Additional MSS, 21634, fol. 94–94v, British Museum, London; Wainwright, "George Croghan's Journal," 405–6, 442–43; Croghan, "Report of an Indian Conference at Fort Pitt, December 8, 1762," *PCHB* 16:193–94.

66. Donald Campbell to Henry Bouquet, February 10, 1762; Bouquet to Amherst, March 7, 1762; and Bouquet to Amherst, May 24, 1762, in "Bouquet Papers," 19:130, 132, 144; Croghan to Amherst, May 10, 1762, *WJP* 10:452.

67. Forrest McDonald and Grady McWhiney, "The Antebellum Southern Herdsman: A Reinterpretation," *Journal of Southern History* 61 (1975): 147, 156, 158–59; Forrest McDonald and Grady McWhiney, "The South from Self-Sufficiency to Peonage: An Interpretation," *American Historical Review* 85 (1980): 1095–1163; Sam Bowers Hilliard, *Hog Meat and Hoecake: Food Supply in the Old South, 1840–1860* (Carbondale, Ill., 1972), 94, 96–97; Richard White, *The Roots of Dependency: Subsistence, Environment, and Social Chage among the Choctaws, Pawnees, and Navajos* (Lincoln, Nebr., 1983), 99.

Thomas R. McCabe and Richard E. McCabe estimate that as colonization began, the continent boasted some 24 million to 36 million deer. By 1900, there were only half a million left. The numbers soared during the twentieth century and now stand at close to their early colonial levels. See Tom Horton, "Deer on your Doorstep," *New York Times Magazine*, April 28, 1991, 38.

68. Navarre/Quaife, *Journal of Pontiac's Conspiracy*, 15.

69. Bouquet to Monckton, July 24, 1761, in "Aspinwall Papers," 9:434–35; Robert Callendar to Bouquet, May 23, 1761, *PCHB*, ser. 21646:168; McConnell, "Search for Security," 346–47; Eric Hinderaker, *Elusive Empires: Constructing Colonialism in the Ohio Valley, 1673–1800* (New York, 1997), 148–49; Kenny, "Journal of James Kenny," 28; Sylvia Van Kirk, "The Role of Native Women in the Fur Trade Society of Western Canada, 1670–1830," *Frontiers* 7 (1984): 156–62; Susan Sleeper-Smith, "Silent Tongues, Black Robes: Potawatomi, Europeans, and Settlers in the Southern Great Lakes, 1640–1850" (Ph.D. diss., University of Michigan, 1994), 109–17, 206–8; and Gary Clayton Anderson, *Kinsmen of Another Kind: Dakota-White Relations in the Upper Mississippi Valley, 1650–1862* (Lincoln, Nebr., 1984), 58–76.

70. Bouquet to Gavin Cochrane, July 12, 1761, *PCHB*, ser. 21653:70–71; McConnell, "Search for Security," 229; Ecuyer to Bouquet, January 8, 1763; Ecuyer to Bouquet, April 23, 1763; Ecuyer to Bouquet, June 18, 1763; and W. Grant to Bouquet, September 4, 1764, *PHB* 6:140–42, 177, 179, 236, 238, 627.

71. Dulcinea is the stout, ordinary girl mistaken in Cervantes' *Don Quixote* for a golden-haired lady: "her neck is alabaster, her hands are polished ivory, and her bosom whiter than new-fallen snow." Philip Ward, *The Oxford Companion to Spanish Literature*

(Oxford, 1978), 174. The term *Dulcinea* was well understood in eighteenth-century English to be associated with outsiders or the poor. Milo Milton Quaife, ed., "John Rutherfurd's [*sic*] Captivity Narrative," in Quaife, ed., *The Siege of Detroit in 1763: The Journal of Pontiac's Conspiracy and John Rutherfurd's Narrative of a Captivity* (Chicago, 1958), 225–26; McDonald to Croghan, July 12, 1763, *WJP* 10:738; Court of Inquiry, Detroit, July 6, 1763, James Burns (Beems?) testifying, in both *WJP* 10:731 and "Gladwin Manuscripts," 27:637; Jehu Hay, "Diary of the Siege of Detroit," 109, 114, WCL; Amherst, *Journal of Jeffery Amherst*, 316; Court of Inquiry, Detroit, December 20, 1763, and Court of Inquiry, Detroit, February 21, 1764, Captain John McCoy testifying, in "Gladwin Manuscripts," 27:657–58, 660.

72. Anon., "Some Account of a Visit divers Friends made to the Indians at the time of the treaty at Easton," MSS, in WCL.

73. Indian Conference, July 1763, *WJP* 10:770.

CHAPTER 3 An Otherworldly War

1. Navarre/Quaife, *Journal of Pontiac's Conspiracy*, 8.

2. Richard E. Day, *Calendar of the Sir William Johnson Manuscripts*, New York State Library History Bulletin 8 (Albany, 1909), 92, Joseph-Gaspard, Chaussegros de Léry, "Journal of the Winter Campaign, 1754–1755," trans. L. Oughtred Woltz, typescript, 110, BHC, microfilm at Ethnohistory Archive; James Grant, testimony at Detroit, April 5, 1764, *Michigan Pioneer*, vol. 27 (1897), 663; Ensign Holmes to Major Gladwin, Fort Miami, March 30, 1763, Gladwin to Amherst, April 20, 1763, and copy of a speech made by the chiefs of the Miami Indians, March 30, 1763, *WJP* 4:95–97.

3. Copy of an embassy sent to the Illinois by the Indians at Detroit, in Gladwin to Gage, March 24, 1764, Gage Papers; also in "Gladwin Manuscripts," 27:644. Croghan: Croghan to Bouquet, "Bouquet Papers," 19:192; Louis Chevalier to Major Gladwin, St. Joseph, November, 24, 1763, in Joseph Peyser, ed., *Letters from New France: The Upper Country, 1686–1763* (Champaign-Urbana, 1992), 215–16.

4. De Léry, "Journal of the Winter Campaign," 141–42; Christian Frederick Post, August 18, 1758, "The Journal of Christian Frederick Post, from Philadelphia to the Ohio . . . ," in Reuben Gold Thwaites, ed., *Early Western Travels, 1748–1846* (Cleveland, 1904), vol. 1; Sir William Johnson, "Review," September 1767, *NYCD* 7:960.

5. James Howard, *Shawnee!: The Ceremonialism of a Native Indian Tribe and Its Cultural Background* (Athens, Ohio, 1981), 185–87; Frank Speck, "The Wapanachki Delawares and the English," *PMHB* 69 (1943): 319–44; for the revivals, see Gregory Evans Dowd, *A Spirited Resistance: The North American Indian Struggle for Unity, 1745–1815* (Baltimore, 1992), 23–46.

6. Edward P. Hamilton, ed. and trans., *Adventure in the Wilderness: The American Journals of Louis Antoine de Bougainville, 1756–1760*, fwd. Colin G. Calloway (Norman, Okla., 1990), 55, 112, 123, 126, 133, 134; Navarre/Quaife, *Journal of Pontiac's Conspiracy*, 67–68; Milo Milton Quaife, ed., "John Rutherfurd's [*sic*] Captivity Narrative," in Quaife, ed., *The Siege of Detroit in 1763: The Journal of Pontiac's Conspiracy and John Rutherfurd's Narrative of a Captivity* (Chicago, 1958), 234; Thomas Morris, "Journal of

Captain Thomas Morris of His Majesty's XVII Regiment of Infantry," in Thwaites, *Early Western Travels, 1748–1846*, 1:306, 309–10, compare with Pierre de Charlevoix, *Journal of a Voyage to North America*, 2 vols., March of America Facsimile Series, no. 36 (1761; Ann Arbor, Mich., 1966) 1:338–39; Michael N. McConnell, "The Search for Security: Indian-English Relations in the Trans-Appalachian Region, 1758–1763" (Ph.D. diss., College of William and Mary, 1983), 38. See Alexander Henry, *Travels and Adventures in Canada and the Indian Territories between the Years 1760 and 1776*, March of America Facsimile Series No. 43 (1809; Ann Arbor, Mich., 1966), 108, 127, 150, 178, for dog sacrifices.

7. John Porteous to James Porteous, Detroit, n.d. 1762, in Porteous Papers, BHC; Bougainville reported shaking tent rituals among the Potawatomis during the Seven Years' War, in Hamilton, *Adventure in the Wilderness*, 55; Sam D. Gill, "Religious Forms and Themes," in Alvin M. Josephy Jr., ed., *America in 1492: The World of the Indian Peoples before the Arrival of Columbus* (New York, 1993), 295.

8. Lacrosse: "Porteous Journal," Detroit Public Library, entry for May 8; divine deception: Henry, *Travels and Adventures*, 116; examination of two Mohawks, Detroit, June 10, 1764, in Gladwin to Gage, June 11, 1764, Gage Papers; William Johnson to Lords of Trade, September 25, 1763, *NYCD* 7:561. For the ethnohistory of lacrosse, see Eugene McCluny, "Lacrosse: The Combat of the Spirits," *American Indian Quarterly* 1 (1974): 34–42; Thomas Vennum, *American Indian Lacrosse: Little Brother of War* (Washington, D.C., 1994); Dane Lanken, "'Little Brother of War,' the Indians Called It," *Canadian Geographic* 104 (1984): 36–43; Roger Wolf, "Lacrosse among the Seneca," *Indian History* 10 (1977): 16–22. Individuals in the 1760s carried the name "Na, ne, banjou," Norman Macleod to William Johnson, *WJP* 5:662; Alexander Henry, *Travels and Adventures*, 212.

9. Ermine Wheeler-Vogelin, ed., "John Heckewelder to Peter S. Du Ponceau, Bethlehem, 12th August, 1818," *Ethnohistory* 6 (1959): 73–74; John Bierhorst, ed., *Mythology of the Lenape: Guide and Texts* (Tuscon, 1995), 7–8, 9, 11, 28, 30, 80, 81, 84, 86, 91; Henry, *Travels and Adventures*, 143–44; 152, 168–69, 212–13; John Heckewelder, *History, Manners, and Customs of the Indian Nations Who Once Inhabited Pennsylvania and the Neighboring States* (1819), Memoirs of the Historical Society of Pennsylvania 12 (Philadelphia, 1876), 252; William Warren, *History of the Ojibway Nation* (Minneapolis, 1957), 72; Hamilton, *Adventure in the Wilderness*, 133; John M'Cullough, "A Narrative of the Captivity of John M'Cullough," in Archibald Loudon, ed., *A Selection of Some of the Most Interesting Narratives of Outrages Committed by the Indians in Their Wars with the White People*, 2 vols. in 1 (1808; New York, 1971) 1:287, 289; Charlevoix, *Journal of a Voyage to North America*, 2:142; David Zeisberger, "History of the Northern American Indians," ed. and trans. Archer Butler Hulbert and Nathaniel Schwarze, *Ohio Archaeological and Historical Society Publications* 19 (1910): 132, 140, 147.

10. "Porteous Journal," Detroit Public Library, 2; Porteous to his parents, Detroit, November 20, 1763, BHC, Detroit; examination of Cornelius Vanslyke, July 21, 1767, Native American Collection, WCL, 655; John Heckewelder writes of the Delawares' "incredible . . . belief in witchcraft" in *History, Manners, and Customs*, 239; M'Cullough, "Narrative," 1:299–300.

11. James Kenny, "Journal of James Kenny, 1761–1763," ed. John W. Jordan, *PMHB* 37 (1913): 171–72, 175. Beatty's journal corroborates the use of the emetic; Charles Beatty, *Journal of a Two Months' Tour with a View of Promoting Religion* (Edinburgh, 1798), 30.

12. Charles E. Hunter, "The Delaware Nativist Revival of the Mid-Eighteenth Century," *Ethnohistory* 18 (1971): 43, 46; Anthony F. C. Wallace, "New Religions among the Delaware Indians, 1600–1900," *Southwestern Journal of Anthropology* 12 (1956): 9; Anthony F. C. Wallace, *The Death and Rebirth of the Seneca* (New York, 1969), 114–22; Melvin Delano Thurman, "The Delaware Indians: A Study in Ethnohistory" (Ph.D. diss., University of California, Santa Barbara, 1973), 160; Howard Peckham, *Pontiac and the Indian Uprising* (1947; New York, 1970), 116.

13. For *Schwonack* and *Choanshikan*, see the Draper MSS, 1 D 399. For *Pelaciman*, see Frank G. Speck, *A Study of the Delaware Indian Big House Ceremony* (Harrisburg, Pa., 1931), 43.

14. C. M. Burton, preface to Navarre/Quaife, *Journal of Pontiac's Conspiracy*, xlii; Jehu Hay, "Diary of the Siege of Detroit," 133, 169, WCL.

15. Navarre/Quaife, *Journal of Pontiac's Conspiracy*, 8, 17; Navarre/Burton, *Pontiac Journal*, 28–30.

16. Navarre/Burton, *Pontiac Journal*, 174–76. Navarre's rhetorical strategy is to demonstrate that the French suffered during the siege as well as the English. But he willingly relates information that is potentially damaging to this purpose. For example, he portrays Ojibwas and Delawares as seeking, like Pontiac, the return of the French king: a curious strategy for one wishing to exculpate the French. See also Francis Jennings, *Empire of Fortune: Crowns, Colonies, and Tribes in the Seven Years War' in America* (New York, 1988), 441–44.

17. De Neyon to Dabaddie, December 1, 1763, CISHL 10:51–52. De Beaujeu used the term *Abnaki* as the Potawatomis would: "Wapanachki," or "easterners," the same word that encompasses the "Abenakis" of northern New England as well as the Delawares and other coastal Algonquians.

18. De Neyon to Dabaddie, December 1, 1763, CISHL 10:51–52; "A council in Illinois," April 15–17, 1764, in Major Robert Farmar to Gage, December 21, 1764, Gage Papers.

19. De Neyon to Dabaddie, December 1, 1763, CISHL 10:51; "A council in Illinois," April 15–17, 1764, in Farmar to Gage, December 21, 1764, Gage Papers; Navarre/Quaife, *Journal of the Conspiracy of Pontiac*, 14; Morris, "Journal of Captain Thomas Morris," 306, 309–10; M'Cullough, "Narrative," 273. For a balanced examination of the syncretic nature of Neolin's message, see Alfred Cave, "The Delaware Prophet, Neolin: A Reappraisal," *Ethnohistory* 46 (1999): 265–90. Cave argues convincingly that the message, threaded as it was with such Christian elements as the devil, a hell, and a jealous, omnipotent, and accessible God, nonetheless was shot through with traditional ideas and was preached for Indian purposes.

20. Excerpts from Beatty's 1767 journal are in Thomas Brainerd, ed., *The Life of John Brainerd, Brother of David Brainerd and His Successor as Missionary to the Indians of New Jersey* (Philadelphia, 1865), 367. For popularity of the text among Presbyterian

missionaries to Indians, see Mary Young, "The Cherokee Nation: Mirror of the Republic," *American Quarterly* 33 (1981): 502–24.

21. Vaudreuil to minister, February 13, 1758, in Sylvester K. Stevens and Donald H. Kent, eds., *Wilderness Chronicles of Northwestern Pennsylvania* (Harrisburg, Pa., 1941), 110; Pierre Pouchot, *Memoirs on the Late War in North America between France and England* (1781), trans. Michael Cardy and ed. Brian Leigh Dunnigan (Youngstown, N.Y., 1994), 122–24 nn. 378, 379; John Heckewelder, *Narrative of the Mission of the United Brethren* (1820; New York, 1971), 59–66; Hamilton, *Adventure in the Wilderness*, 180–81, 196.

22. "Indian Conference," Johnson Hall, September 8–10, 1762, *WJP* 10:505–6, 511; J. Clarence Webster, *The Journal of Jeffery Amherst* (Chicago, 1931), 325; Hay, "Diary," entry for July 18, 1763; Robert Rogers, *A Concise Account of North America* . . . (London, 1765), quotation 217, also 194–219; copy in the Newberry Library, Chicago.

23. Bouquet to Lt. Francis and Col. Cayton, September 23, 1764, *PCHB*, ser. 21650:142; Howard, *Shawnee*, 174.

24. Dowd, *Spirited Resistance;* Kenny, "Journal of James Kenny," 177.

25. Charles Beatty, *Journals of Charles Beatty, 1762–1769,* ed. Guy Soulliard Klett (University Park, Pa., 1962), 29–30, 65; M'Cullough, "Narrative," 275; the source mentioned is Heckewelder, *History, Manners, and Customs,* 291.

26. Journal of an Indian Council, January 31, 1764, *WJP* 11:34–35; Navarre/Quaife, *Journal of the Conspiracy of Pontiac,* 17

27. This and the following paragraphs discussing Neolin's vision, as related by Pontiac, are based on Navarre/Quaife, *Journal of the Conspiracy of Pontiac,* 8–17.

28. See Carl Van Doren, ed., *Indian Treaties Printed by Benjamin Franklin, 1736–1762* (Philadelphia, 1938), and Witham Marshe's "Journal of the Treaty held with the Six Nations by the Commissioners of Maryland, and other Provinces, at Lancaster, in Pennsylvania, June, 1744" (first published in 1841), *Collections of the Massachusetts Historical Society,* 1st ser., 7 (Boston, 1846), 171–201; Francis Jennings, *The Ambiguous Iroquois Empire: The Covenant Chain Confederation of Indian Tribes with the English Colonies* (New York, 1984), 356–63; Edmund A. DeSchweinitz, *The Life and Times of David Zeisberger* (Philadelphia, 1871), 276–77.

29. George Croghan to Major Gates, May 23, 1760; Henry Bouquet to Major General Robert Monckton, March 20, 1761; Bouquet to Monckton, March 28, 1761; and Campbell to Monckton, June 1, 1761, in "Aspinwall Papers," 9:252, 397, 402, 416; James Sterling to anon., September 7, 1761; Sterling to J. Syme, June 8, 1762; Sterling to John Sterling, August 19, 1762; Sterling to John Sterling, August 26, 1762; Sterling to John Sterling, September 4, 1762; and Sterling to Livingston and Rutherfurd, January 25, 1763, in James Sterling Letter Book, WCL.

30. Gladwin to Amherst, November 1, 1763, in "Gladwin Manuscripts," 27:676; William Johnson to Gage, May 11, 1764, *WJP* 11:190; William Johnson on the organization of the Indian department, October 1764, CISHL 10:335; James Sterling to Magill Wallace, May 29, 1765, in James Sterling Letter Book, WCL.

31. Gage to Hillsborough, April 1, 1769, CO 5/87, fol. 86; address of D'Abbadie to the Tunica Indians, July 14, 1764, CISHL 10:285–86; George Croghan, "Croghan's

Journal," May 15–September 26, 1765," entry for August 28, 1765, in Thwaites, *Early Western Travels*, 1:157.

32. Campbell to Bouquet, June 16, 1761, in Stevens and Kent, *Wilderness Chronicles*, 216; Bouquet to Monckton, June 30, 1761, in "Bouquet Papers," 19:81. The role of the Senecas in the rebellion has been suggested since before Parkman. In 1843, A. W. Patterson noted in his *History of the Backwoods* that "Pontiac's war" had also been called the "Kiyasuta and Pontiac war"; quoted in Peckham, *Pontiac and the Indian Uprising*, 106 n–107 n. Two recent works pointing to a Seneca origin are Jennings, *Empire of Fortune*, 440, and William R. Nester, *"Haughty Conquerors": Amherst and the Great Indian Uprising of 1763* (Westport, Conn., 2000), 36.

33. William Renwick Riddell, "The Last Indian Council of the French at Detroit," *Royal Society of Canada, Transactions* 25 (1931): 166; Peckham, *Pontiac and the Indian Uprising*, 60–67; "Croghan's Journal," and "Copy of an Indian Council, 18 June, 1761," in "Aspinwall Papers," 9:375, 427–29.

34. Contrast Jennings, *Empire of Fortune*, 432, 438, 440, with McConnell, "Search for Security," 362–73, and with Michael N. McConnell, "Peoples in Between: The Iroquois and the Ohio Indians," in Daniel K. Richter and James H. Merrell, eds., *Beyond the Covenant Chain: The Iroquois and Their Neighbors in Indian North America* (Syracuse, N.Y., 1987), 108–9. See also Richard White, *The Middle Ground: Indians, Empires, and Republics in the Great Lakes Region, 1650–1815* (New York, 1991), 272. Adding weight to Six Nations protests of innocence is the "Seneca Plan" itself, which did not name British posts anywhere east of Seneca country as projected objects of destruction but which did single out all posts from the Seneca country to the west. See Campbell to William Walters, Detroit, June 17, 1761, and Campbell to Bouquet, June 16, 17, and 21, 1761, *WJP*, 3:405–6, 450–53; "Bouquet Papers," 19:76–79. For Six Nations denials, see Sir William Johnson, "Niagara and Detroit Proceedings, July–September, 1761," *WJP* 3:428–503, esp. 459–60; 463, 465, 467, and Johnson to Amherst, Little Niagara, August 19, 1761, *WJP* 3:521. For Tahaiado'ris, see *WJP* 3:460. For Kiashuta, see C. Hale Sipe, *The Indian Chiefs of Pennsylvania* (New York: Arno and New York Times, 1971 [facsimile of Butler, Pa., 1927]), 370–408.

35. Francis Parkman, *The Conspiracy of Pontiac and the Indian War after the Conquest of Canada*, 4th ed., 2 vols. (1851; Boston, 1905), 1:184–86; Peckham, *Pontiac and the Indian Uprising*, 95–96; 105–6. For recent assertions see, for example, Helen Hornbeck Tanner, ed., *Atlas of Great Lakes Indian History* (Norman, 1986), 48. Here the "encouragement of local French residents of Detroit as well as the French in the Illinois country" is listed as one of "three outside influences." Also see Wallace, *Death and Rebirth*, 115; Dwight L. Smith, "Mutual Dependency and Mutual Distrust: Indian-White Relations in British North America, 1701–1763," in Philip Weeks, ed., *The American Indian Experience: A Profile, 1524 to the Present* (Arlington Heights, Ill., 1988), 61.

36. Parkman, *Conspiracy of Pontiac*, 1:184–86; Lieut. Jenkins to Gladwin, Ouiatenon, March 28, 1763, in "Gladwin Manuscripts," 27:634.

37. Edmund Moran revealed the possible ulterior motives of the group when he wrote, "I am sure it will never be worth any English trader's while to follow this trade

unless the French are prohibited to come here." Edmund Moran to Joseph Spear, and Company, Merchants at Detroit, May 16, 1763, in "Gladwin Manuscripts," 27:635; McKee to William Johnson, December 3, 1763, *WJP* 11:482; George Croghan to Henry Bouquet, Fort Bedford, June 17, 1763, *PHB* 6:233–35; Croghan to Gage, May 16, 1765, CO 5/83, fol. 697 (transcript in Shawnee File, 1765, in Ethnohistory Archive); Croghan, "Croghan's Journal," May 15–September 26, 1765," in Thwaites, *Early Western Travels*, 1:144, 150, 152; William Johnson to Robert Leake, July 18, 1765, *WJP* 4:793. William Johnson to Sir Jeffery Amherst, Johnson Hall, July 8, 1763, and William Johnson to Lords of Trade, Johnson Hall, October 8, 1766, *NYCD* 7:531, 871; Bouquet to Thomas Gage, November 30, 1764, *PHB* 6:714.

38. Peckham, *Pontiac and the Indian Uprising*, 95–96, 105–6. Reports of such French promises intensified with the French departure from the upper Ohio in 1758 and 1759. See, for example, Hugh Mercer to Governor Denny, Pittsburgh, August 12, 1759, in Stevens and Kent, *Wilderness Chronicles*, 165. For promises in 1761 and 1762, see Nicholas B. Wainwright, ed., "George Croghan's Journal, 1759–1763," *PMHB* 71 (1947): 397. For other renditions of the rumor, see McConnell, "Search for Security," 368.

39. Abstracted in Richard D. Brown, ed., *Major Problems in the Era of the American Revolution, 1760–1791* (Lexington, Mass., 1992), 49.

40. Hay, "Diary," 93–95, 100; "Answer . . . made by the Hurons . . . ," May 10, 1764; Mohawk's Intelligence at Detroit, June 10, 1764; and Gladwin to Johnson, June 9, 1764, *WJP* 11:178–80, 227, 228; John Porteous to James Porteous, August 16, 1767, BHC; Croghan, "Croghan's Journal, May 15–September 26, 1765," in Thwaites, *Early Western Travels*, 1:153.

41. Rev. George Paré and M. M. Quaife, eds. and trans., "The St. Joseph Baptismal Register," *Mississippi Valley Historical Review* 13 (1926): 201–39; for a view of the register as revealing Catholic vitality, see Susan Sleeper-Smith, "Silent Tongues, Black Robes: Potawatomi, Europeans, and Settlers in the Southern Great Lakes, 1640–1850" (Ph.D. diss., University of Michigan, 1994). Sleeper-Smith emphasizes the fact that Indians and Métis did meet the Jesuits' high standards and were baptized, accepting French godparents and forming a religious community. This is plausible. Most of the Indians who took the sacrament in good health, however, were not Potawatomis but Miamis, Ottawas, and "Panis." Potawatomis, with at most a handful of exceptions in the entire period before 1765, did not receive the sacrament.

42. Thomas Gage to Mons. Langlade, Montreal, July 17, 1763 (French); Capt. George Etherington to Charles Langlade, Instructions, [L'Arbre Croche], June 10, 1765 (French); Etherington to Langlade, June 18, 1763 (two letters, French); Etherington to Langlade, L'Arbre Croche, June 21, 1763 (French); Etherington to Langlade, L'Arbre Croche, June 21, 1763 (French), all in Ayer MSS, Newberry Library, Chicago; Hay, "Diary," 177, August 5, 1763; Alexander Henry, *Travels and Adventures*, 95–140.

43. Henry, *Travels and Adventures*, 47, 96–97, 106; Claus to Johnson, August 6, 1763; "Indian Conference," August 9–11, 1764; and Amherst to Johnson, September 30, 1763, *WJP* 10:777–78; 779–86; 857–58; Bradstreet to Gage, August 4, 1765, Gage Papers; Johnson to Amherst, September 30, 1763, and "A Conference with Foreign Nations,"

Niagara, July 9–14, *WJP* 4:209, 466–80; Indian Congress, July 9–11, July 15, July 17–August 4, 1763, *WJP* 11:262–69, 273–74, 279–85.

44. Gladwin to Gage, January 9, 1764, Gage Papers; abstract of Claus to Johnson, April 10, 1764, *WJP* 4:395; *Pennsylvania Gazette*, fol. 2, items 19010, 20865, September 8, 1763, May 31, 1764. A small body of Kahnawakes who had resided for some decades in the Ohio Valley allied with Pontiac, but these were not then Christian. See "At a Conference held with the Shawanese, Muskingum,November 12, 1764," *WJP* 11:461; James Smith, *An Account of the Remarkable Occurrences in the Life and Travels of Col. James Smith during His Captivity with the Indians in the Years, 1755, '56, '57, '58, and '59*, ed. William M. Darlington (Cincinnati, 1870), 20, 25–29; Smith lived as a captive among Kahnawakes south of Lake Erie.

45. Croghan to Johnson, April 24, 1763, *WJP* 10:1763; Croghan to Amherst, April 30, 1763, *Michigan Pioneer*, vol. 19 (1892), 183–84; Kenny, "Journal of James Kenny," February 21, 1763, 187; The lower Shawnee towns, about a third of the way downstream from Fort Pitt to Fort de Chartres, had the news by late February; it is very likely that France's Illinois garrisons had received word from the Indians by March or April. The official French dispatch did not reach Louisiana until early April—not enough time for word to have reached Illinois before the outbreak. The English, moreover, apparently dispatched no messengers to Illinois bearing official tidings. In September 1763, when de Neyon published the news of the *final* peace, he noted that the cession was drawn "comfortable to the Article in the Preliminaries concerning this Quarter," which suggests that he had received the news, in some form, earlier. See Wainwright, "George Croghan's Journal," 436–38; Marc de Villiers du Terrage, *Les dernières années de la Louisiane Française* (Paris, 1903), 149; Neyon de Villiers to D'Abbadie, Fort de Chartres, December 1, 1763, *Collections of State Historical Society of Wisconsin*, ed. Rueben Gold Thwaites (Madison, 1908), 18:259; "Villiers to Inhabitants of Fort Chartres," *WJP* 10:821; McConnell, "Peoples in Between," 110. See also Parkman, *Conspiracy of Pontiac*, 1:189–90; Bernard Knollenberg, *Origin of the American Revolution* (New York, 1960), 113–14; Jennings, *Empire of Fortune*, 442.

46. Jeffery Amherst to George Croghan, Bouquet Papers, Additional MSS, 21634, fols. 244–45, British Museum, London.

47. Court of Enquiry, Detroit, April 6, 1765, Gage Papers. I agree with McConnell that, while some Indians defined "resistance in terms of re-establishing the pre-war system," this was not "primarily the result of outside agitation." McConnell, "Search for Security," 417–18, 421; W. J. Eccles, "Sovereignty—Association, 1500–1783," *Canadian Historical Review* 65 (1984): 504–7.

CHAPTER 4 Besieging Britons, 1763

1. William Eyre to William Johnson, October 3, 1763, in Eyre Manuscripts, BHC; Simeon Ecuyer, "Orderly Book," entry for August 11, 1763, in Mary C. Darlington, *Fort Pitt and Letters from the Frontier* (New York, 1971), 170; James Sterling to John Sterling, October 6, 1763, in James Sterling Letter Book, WCL; Jeffery Amherst to William Johnson, July 7, 1763, *WJP* 10:733.

2. William Johnson, "Memorandum on Six Nations and Other Confederacies," November 18, 1763, *WJP* 4:240–46. The Dakotas are excluded from these figures. Johnson reaffirmed his estimate, this time referring to hunters rather than fighting men, in a letter to the Board of Trade, October 8, 1764, *WJP* 4:558; John Shy, *Toward Lexington: The Role of the British Army in the Coming of the American Revolution* (Princeton, N.J., 1965), 114.

3. Navarre/Quaife, *Journal of Pontiac's Conspiracy*, 3–28. This document alone takes us into the Indian councils. Unfortunately, it displays inconsistencies. Discussing the meeting of May 5, for example, it reports that "no women should be allowed to attend for fear of betraying their plans" (21). Yet that meeting decided, the journal states, that Ottawa women would participate in the assault on Detroit by entering the fort with sawed-off guns hidden beneath their blankets (25). How they could participate without being previously informed is undisclosed. Moreover, in the discussion of the May 7 attempt, women are not mentioned.

4. Navarre/Quaife, *Journal of Pontiac's Conspiracy*, 19–20, 28–30; Jehu Hay, "Diary of the Seige of Detroit," 82, WCL; Gladwin to Amherst, May 14, 1763, Amherst Papers, vol. 2, no. 1; "Extract of a Letter from Lieut. McDonald to George Croghan Esquire giving an Account of all Transactions at Detroit from the 6th of May to the 12th July 1763," *WJP* 10:736–37; John Porteous, "A Short Journal of the Siege of Detroit," 1763, 5–8, BHC ; *The Journal of Jeffery Amherst*, ed. J. Clarence Webster (Toronto, 1931), entry for June 21, 1763, 308; Dateline: Detroit, July 9, 1763, *Pennsylvania Gazette*, fol. 2, item 18849, August 18, 1763; account of Mrs. Meloche, taken in 1825 by C. C.Trowbridge, *Michigan Pioneer*, vol. 8 (1885), 340. Meloche was a young woman during the siege and spent the entire time outside the walls of the fort. Her memoir contains many descriptions of Pontiac's kindness to the French. She appears to confuse May 7 with May 9.

5. "some Indians": Extract of McDonald to Croghan, July 12, 1763, *WJP* 10:737; Gladwin to Amherst, May 14, 1763, Amherst Papers, vol. 2, no. 1; *Journal of Jeffery Amherst*, June 21, 1763, 308; Howard Peckham compiles a "roster" of nine individuals— Ottawa, Ojibwa, French, and English—credited with betraying the Indians' plan. "What is highly probable," he writes, is that "more than one person brought the dread news to Detroit," in *Pontiac and the Indian Uprising* (1947; New York, 1970), 121–24. A tenth individual is "One *Robee*, a Frenchman," though perhaps this refers to Jacques Duperont Baby, whom Peckham names; see Croghan to William Johnson, Fort Bedford, July 2, 1763, *WJP* 10:728. An Ottawa Indian, "Mahiganne," is named in Navarre/ Quaife, *Journal of Pontiac's Conspiracy*, 27; Peckham, *Pontiac and the Indian Uprising*, 122 n. 3. The "old woman": Porteous, "Short Journal," 6–8, BHC; McDonald to Croghan, July 12, 1763, *WJP* 10:737; the account of Mrs. Meloche, the account of Mr. Jacques Parent, and the account of Mr. Pettier, January 15, 1825, *Michigan Pioneer*, vol. 8 (1885), 340, 358–60; Frederic W. Gleach points to the similarities in legends surrounding Jamestown and Dublin in his *Powhatan's World and Colonial Virginia: A Conflict of Cultures* (Lincoln, 1997), 151.

6. Hay and Lieutenant James McDonald agree that Campbell did the talking on May 8. Hay, "Diary," 82. McDonald to Croghan, July 12, 1763, *WJP* 10:738. Gladwin

led Amherst to believe that he had conducted the negotiations. Gladwin to Amherst, May 14, 1763, Amherst Papers, vol. 2, no. 1; *Journal of Jeffery Amherst*, 308.

7. Porteus, "Short Journal," May 9, 1763, 10, BHC.

8. Hay, "Diary," 82–84; Porteus, "Short Journal," May 9, 1763, 10–12, BHC; McDonald to Croghan, July 12, 1763, *WJP* 10:738–9; Account of Mr. Gabriel St.Aubin, collected by C. C. Trowbridge, *Michigan Pioneer*, vol. 8 (1885), 352; *Journal of Jeffery Amherst*, 308; Peckham, *Pontiac and the Indian Uprising*, 135–36.

9. Gladwin to Amherst, May 14, 1763, Amherst Papers, vol. 2, no. 1; Hay, "Diary"; McDonald to Croghan, July 12, 1763, *WJP* 10:739–41; *Journal of Jeffery Amherst*, 308–9; Porteous, May 10, May 11, 1763, "Short Journal," 15–17, BHC ; Francis Jennings, *Empire of Fortune: Crowns, Colonies, and Empires in the Seven Years' War in America* (New York, 1988), 441–44.

10. "Proceedings of a Court of Enquiry Held by Order of Major Henry Gladwin, Commanding at Detroit, 9th August, 1763," in "Gladwin Manuscripts," 641. The story was corroborated by one Monsieur La Bute, Indian interpreter, in ibid., 643. Jehu Hay confirms the story, saying that Mr. Cuillerier "accepted of their offer of being made Commandant." See his "Diary," January 14, 1764, 17–18. Cuillerier continued to be connected to Bellestre, who still owned property in Detroit. Cuillerier was the former commandant's legal representative. John Campbell to Gage, Detroit, June 30, 1765, Gage Papers.

11. For adoption rituals, see Ake Hultkrantz, *Conceptions of the Soul among North American Indians: A Study in Religious Ethnology*, Ethnographical Museum of Sweden, Monograph Series, No. 1 (Stockholm, 1953), 326; Nicolas Perrot, "Memoir on the Manners, Customs, and Religion of the Savages of North America," in Emma Helen Blair, ed., *The Indian Tribes of the Upper Mississippi Valley and Region of the Great Lakes*, 2 vols. (Cleveland, 1911), 1:184–85; Father Gabriel Sagard, *The Long Journey to the Country of the Hurons*, ed. George M. Wrong, trans. H. H. Langton (New York, 1968 [facsimile of Toronto, 1939]), 208–9; Charles C. Trowbridge, *Meeameer Traditions*, in Vernon Kinietz, ed., University of Michigan Museum of Anthropology, Occasional Contributions, 7 (Ann Arbor, Mich., 1938): 34–35; Claude Dablon, "Relation of 1670–1671," *JR* 55:137.

12. That Pontiac was angry at the killing is suggested by Hay, "Diary," 140, who records that the Ojibwas took Campbell after an argument with Pontiac, and by Gabriel St. Aubin, in C. C. Trowbridge, ed., "Mr. Gabriel St. Aubin's Account" (1825), *Michigan Pioneer*, vol. 8 (1885), 355. St. Aubin states that Campbell was killed quickly, as does the author of the Navarre/Quaife, *Journal of Pontiac's Conspiracy*, 174. Hay reports nothing of the execution, only of ritual dismemberment and cannibalism of the body. The same is true of John Rutherford, a captive among the Ottawas; see Quaife, ed., "John Rutherfurd's [*sic*] Captivity Narrative," in Quaife, ed., *The Siege of Detroit in 1763: The Journal of Pontiac's Conspiracy and John Rutherfurd's Narrative of a Captivity* (Chicago, 1958), 248. Lieutenant James McDonald, no eyewitness, says he was killed in the "most cruel Manner," but he does not elaborate; McDonald to Croghan, July 12, 1763, *WJP* 10:745. Charles Gouin speaks at length of Campbell's death by torture, but he does not claim to have been present; "Mr. Charles Gouin's Account" (1824), *Michigan Pioneer*, vol. 8 (1885), 348.

13. Hay, "Diary," June 10, June 13, June 14, 108–9, 111–13. Amherst issued the order informally in a letter and formally in instructions. See Amherst to Gladwin, June 22, 1763, and By His Excellency Sir Jeffery Amherst Instructions to Major Gladwin of H. M. 80th Regim't of Foot, vol. 2, no. 3, Amherst Papers, vol. 2, no. 2.

14. McDonald reported twelve wounded and one killed within the fort; see Lt. McDonald to Croghan, July 12, 1763, *WJP* 10:745. For expanding forces, see Hay, "Diary," June 10, 110; Navarre/Quaife, *Journal of Pontiac's Conspiracy*, 91, 103–4, 121, 128; Gladwin to Amherst, June 26, 1763, Amherst Papers, vol. 2, no. 7.

15. Amherst to Monckton, Albany, November 3, 1760, in "Aspinwall Papers," 9:347.

16. Court of Inquiry, Detroit, July 6, 1763, Ensign Paulie, Ensign Schlosser testifying, in both "Gladwin Manuscripts," 636–37, and *WJP* 10:730–31. See also Lieutenant Edward Jenkins to Major Henry Gladwin, Ouiatenon, June 1, 1763, *WJP* 10:691; Richard Winston to Detroit Merchants, St. Joseph, June 19, 1763, *WJP* 10:715; McDonald to Croghan, July 12, 1763, *WJP* 10:743–44; see, too, *Journal of Jeffery Amherst*, 316; *Pennsylvania Gazette*, fol. 2, item 18569, June 30, 1763.

17. Court of Inquiry, Detroit, July 6, 1763, James Burns (Beems?) testifying, in both *WJP* 10:731 and "Gladwin Manuscripts," 27:637. Hay, "Diary," 109, 114; *Journal of Jeffery Amherst*, 316; Court of Inquiry, Detroit, December 20, 1763, and Court of Inquiry, Detroit, February 21, 1764, Captain John McCoy testifying, in "Gladwin Manuscripts," 27:657–58, 660.

18. On the size of the garrison and the extent of its casualties: Alexander Henry in his memoir puts the garrison at ninety and claims that the Indians slaughtered more than seventy, but contemporary documents challenge this; Alexander Henry, *Travels and Adventures in Canada and the Indian Territories between the Years 1760 and 1776*, March of America Facsimile Series No. 43 (1809; Ann Arbor, Mich., 1966), 91, see also 39–40. *Journal of Jeffery Amherst*, 315, puts the garrison at thirty, fifteen of whom were killed. McDonald puts the garrison at thirty-seven, twenty-two of whom were killed; McDonald to Croghan, Detroit, July 12, 1763, *WJP* 10:744. The commander, Captain George Etherington, put the number of men killed in the assault and its immediate aftermath at twenty-two, one of whom was a trader, in Etherington to Gladwin, June 12, 1763, in "Gladwin Manuscripts," 27:631.

19. Henry, *Travels and Adventures*, 71–72, 77.

20. Ibid., 77, 105. Henry states that Sauks participated in the game and the attack. It is possible that he meant Saginaw Ojibwas, since *Saginaw* derives from the Ojibwa word for Sauk. For more on the attack, see McDonald to Croghan, July 12, 1763, *WJP* 10:744; Gladwin to Amherst, Detroit, July 8, 1763, Amherst Papers, vol. 2, no. 6; Captain George Etherington to Gladwin, Michilimackinac, June 12, 1763, in both "Gladwin Manuscripts," 27:631, and *WJP* 10:695.

21. Croghan to William Johnson, Fort Pitt, September 6, 1760, *WJP* 10:179. R. Peters to Monckton, Philadelphia, July 24, 1760, in "Aspinwall Papers," 9:277.

22. Albert T. Volwiller, ed., "William Trent's Journal at Fort Pitt, 1763," *Mississippi Valley Historical Review* 11 (1924–25): 401–2; *Journal of Jeffery Amherst*, 93–94.

23. Bouquet to Gladwin, Fort Pitt, August 28, 1763, in "Gladwin Manuscripts," 27:678–79; Garrison size: Bouquet to Monckton, Presque Isle, November 4, 1760, in

"Aspinwall Papers," 9:344–45; Attack on Presque Isle: Volwiller, "Trent's Journal," 402; Ecuyer to Bouquet, June 26, 1763, *PHB* 6:258–63; George Croghan to William Johnson, Fort Bedford, July 2, 1763, *WJP* 10:727; Amherst to William Johnson, New York, July 7, 1763, *WJP* 10:733; Court of Inquiry, Detroit, July 6, 1763, Lieutenant Cornelius Cuyler testifying, and Court of Inquiry, Detroit, July 10, 1763, Ensign John Christie testifying, in both *WJP* 10:732, 733, 735, and "Gladwin Manuscripts," 637, 638–39; *Journal of Jeffery Amherst*, 310. For an example of Indians using trenches, see Edward P. Hamilton, ed. and trans., *Adventure in the Wilderness: The American Journals of Louis Antoine de Bougainville, 1756–1760*, fwd. Colin G. Calloway (Norman, Okla, 1990), 163.

24. Hay, "Diary," entry June 6, 1763, 105; Etherington to Major Henry Gladwin, July 18, 1763, in "Gladwin Manuscripts," 27:639.

25. Volwiller, "Trent's Journal," 393, 394; *Journal of Jeffery Amherst*, 305–3; *Pennsylvania Gazette*, fol. 2, item 18444, June 9, 1763; Ecuyer to Bouquet, May 30, 1763, *PHB* 6:194–96. Ecuyer wrote to Bouquet in French; the translations are from the *PHB* edition—but in this instance, despite the general superiority of *PHB* over Mary Darlington's edition of some of the Ecuyer-Bouquet correspondence, Darlington's translation "head breaker" is equally appropriate (note, however, that she gets the date of the document wrong). See *Fort Pitt and Letters from the Frontier*, 126.

26. Volwiller, "Trent's Journal," 394–95; Ecuyer to Bouquet, May 30, 1763, *PHB* 6:194–96.

27. Volwiller, "Trent's Journal," 395–97; Alexander McKee's Report, Fort Pitt, June 1, 1763, *WJP* 10:685–88. Louis Waddell, editor of *PHB* volume 6, identifies Daniel here as an elderly leader, which would mean that he should not be confused with Shamokin Daniel, of whom we will see more, below. *PHB* 6:197–99.

28. Volwiller, "Trent's Journal," 399.

29. Ibid., 397–400; and Ecuyer to Bouquet, June 2, 1763, *PHB* 6:200–203.

30. "Discourse between Delawares and Ecuyer," June 24, 1763, *PHB* 6:261–63; Volwiller, "Trent's Journal," 400, 407.

31. Volwiller, "Trent's Journal," 408–9; Ecuyer to Bouquet, June 26, 1763, and August 2, 1763, and Bouquet to Amherst, August 11, 1763, *PHB* 6:258–60, 330–33, 361–62. Orderly Book in Darlington, *Fort Pitt and Letters from the Frontier*, 152, 162, 196; *Journal of Jeffery Amherst*, August 26, 1763, 318.

32. On Forts Ligonier and Bedford, see Croghan to William Johnson, Fort Bedford, July 12, 1763, *WJP* 10:728; *Pennsylvania Gazette*, fol. 2, item 18474, June 16, 1763. On Forts Burd, Bushy Run, and Red Stone, see Bouquet to Gladwin, August 28, 1763, *PCHB*, ser. 21649, pt. 2:27.

33. Court of Inquiry, Detroit, July 6, 1763, *WJP* 10:732; *Navarre / Quaife, Journal of Pontiac's Conspiracy*, 124.

34. *Navarre / Quaife, Journal of Pontiac's Conspiracy*, 94; Hay, "Diary," 158, e.g.; Campbell to Monckton, May 22, 1761, in "Aspinwall Papers," 9:414; James Smith, *An Account of the Remarkable Occurrences in the Life and Travels of Col. James Smith during his Captivity with the Indians, in the Years 1755, '56, '57, '58, and '59*, ed. William M. Darlington (Cincinnatti, 1870), 55.

35. Amherst to Monckton, August 31, 1760; Amherst to Monckton, Albany, Novem-

ber 3, 1760; Campbell to Monckton, Detroit, June 1, 1761; and Bouquet to Monckton, Fort Pitt, June 30, 1760, all in "Aspinwall Papers," 9:309–10, 346, 417, 430; James Sterling to John Duncan, July 8, 1761, and Sterling to J. Syme, August 2, 1762, in James Sterling Letter Book, WCL; Jeffery Amherst to William Johnson, Albany, May 30, 1761, *WJP* 10:274; Amherst's instructions to Henry Gladwin, Albany, June 22, 1761, *WJP* 10:293; Porteous, "Short Journal," 3, BHC.

36. Hamilton, *Adventure in the Wilderness*, 247, 245. Hay, "Diary," 88, 92, 93; Porteous, "Short Journal," 19, BHC; Navarre/Quaife, *Journal of Pontiac's Conspiracy*, 73–74; McDonald to Croghan, July 13, 1763, *WJP* 10:741.

37. Hay, "Diary," 102; Navarre/Quaife, *Journal of Pontiac's Conspiracy*, 111–12, *Journal of Jeffery Amherst*, 306–7; McDonald to Croghan, July 12, 1763, *WJP* 10:742–43; Jean Baptiste De Cougne to William Johnson, June 5, 1763, *WJP* 4:135; Volwiller, "Trent's Journal," 398. It is impossible to reconcile the various reports of the British casualties in the battle and in the Detroit villages. Trent heard at the time that fifty-eight were killed in the battle, including one woman and one child. Charles Gouin reported in the 1820s that sixty-four captives were executed in the villages. "Gouin's Account," 347. Both figures are probably too high, the latter much too high.

38. Navarre/Quaife, *Journal of Pontiac's Conspiracy*, 121; Jean Baptiste de Couagne to William Johnson, June 5, 1763, Niagara, *WJP* 4:134; *Journal of Jeffery Amherst*, 307; *Pennsylvania Gazette*, fol. 2, item 18527, June 23, 1763.

39. Navarre/Quaife, *Journal of Pontiac's Conspiracy*, 157; Hay, "Diary," 141.

40. Hay, "Diary," 130, 154, 158, 177, 197; McDonald to Croghan, July 12, 1763, *WJP* 10:744; *Journal of Jeffery Amherst*, 307, 309, 317; compare William R. Nester, *"Haughty Conquerors": Amherst and the Great Indian Uprising of 1763* (Westport, Conn., 2000), 100, with Joseph Hopkins, Court of Inquiry, July 6, 1763, *WJP* 10:732, to see that Nester confuses the two vessels.

41. Navarre/Quaife, *Journal of Pontiac's Conspiracy*, 104–5, 150–52; Hay, "Diary," 88, 93 106, 128.

42. Navarre/Quaife, *Journal of Pontiac's Conspiracy*, 177, 184, 189; Court of Inquiry, John Severings testifying, Detroit, October 1, 1763, in "Gladwin Manuscripts," 27:650; "Gouin's Account, 350.

43. "Row Galleys": James Sterling to John Duncan, October 6, 1763, in James Sterling Letter Book, WCL; *Journal of Jeffery Amherst*, 326; Hay, "Diary," 169; Navarre/Quaife, *Journal of Pontiac's Conspiracy*, 200–201.

44. Major Duncan to William Johnson, n.d., *WJP* 10:762; *Journal of Jeffery Amherst*, 319–20; Peckham, *Pontiac and the Indian Uprising*, 200–202.

45. Major John Duncan to William Johnson, n.d., *WJP* 10:762–66; James Sterling to William MacAdams, August 7, 1763, and James Sterling to Duncan and Co., August 7, 1763, in James Sterling Letter Book, WCL; *Journal of Jeffery Amherst*, 319–20; Thomas Mante, *History of the Late War in America and the Islands of the West-Indies* (London, 1772), 489. Amherst, who could be harsh in his criticism of his subordinates for their failures, was very forgiving of Dalyell. Howard Peckham convincingly treats the two men as unjustifiably contemptuous of Indian military prowess. Peckham, *Pontiac and the Indian Uprising*, 202. None of the enumerations of Indian casualties is credible.

46. Quotations: Sterling to Duncan and Co., August 7, 1763, and Sterling to William MacAdams, August 7, 1763, in James Sterling Letter Book, WCL; Gladwin to Amherst, August 8, 1763, and Gladwin to Amherst, August 11, 1763, Amherst Papers, vol. 2, nos. 8–9; Gage to Bradstreet, December 25, 1763, Gage Papers; News: Volwiller, "Trent's Journal," August 25, 1763, 411. Results: Mante, *History of the Late War in America*, 489; abstract of William Johnson to John Stuart, September 2, 1763, *WJP* 4:199; Gladwin to William Johnson, Detroit, October 7, 1763, *WJP* 10:873; Gladwin to Amherst, Detroit, November 1, 1763, in "Gladwin Manuscripts," 27:675–76.

47. *Journal of Jeffery Amherst*, 320–21; Hay, "Diary," 197; Jean Baptiste de Couagne to William Johnson, Niagara, September 8, 1763; *WJP* 10:812; Collin Andrews to William Johnson, Niagara, September 9, 1763, *WJP* 10:812; Gage to Gladwin, December 22, 1763, and Gladwin to Gage, January 9, 1764, Gage Papers.

48. Sterling to John Duncan, September 8, 1763, and October 9, 1763, in James Sterling Letter Book, WCL; *Journal of Jeffery Amherst*, 323; John Stoughton to William Johnson, September 16, 1763, and Alexander Duncan to Johnson, Fort Ontario, October 1, 1763, *WJP* 10:814, 864; Gladwin to Amherst, October 7, 1763, Amherst Papers, vol. 2, p. 18; Browning to Gage, Niagara, September 4, 1764, Gage Papers.

49. Jean Baptiste de Couagne to William Johnson, Niagara, September 16, 1763, *WJP* 10:815, and Michael N. McConnell, "The Search for Security: Indian-English Relations in the Trans-Appalachian Region, 1758–1763" (Ph.D. diss., College of William and Mary, 1983), 5.

50. *Journal of Jeffery Amherst*, 322; Amherst to Bouquet, New York, October 3, 1763, in "Bouquet Papers," 237; Jean Baptiste de Couagne to William Johnson, Niagara, September 16, 1763; George Etherington to William Johnson, Niagara, September 17, 1763; William Browning to William Johnson, Niagara, September 17, 1763; Alexander Duncan to William Johnson, Fort Ontario, October 1, 1763; and Journal of Indian Affairs, October 4–17, 1763, *WJP* 10:815, 816, 817–18, 863, 893. The Seneca leaders were reported to be "Oghnawaisse, Korihonti, Tagadareghesera, Adungat, C——ga, Oguaghquanda, Ouaqudecka, and Kayenquerego"; in *WJP* 10:893. De Neyon (de Villiers) to D'Abbadie, Fort de Chartres, April 20, 1764, CISHL 10:242–43.

51. Edward Cole to Henry Vanshaack, Detroit, November 19, 1763; editors' note, *WJP* 4:247, 453–54; William Eyre to William Johnson, New York, October 3, 1763; Jean Baptiste de Couagne, Niagara, October 17, 1763; Jean Baptiste de Couagne, Niagara, November 11, 1763: and Indian Conference, *WJP* 10:866, 884, 921, 962; William Browning to William Johnson, Niagara, April 10, 1764, *WJP* 11:124; *Pennsylvania Gazette*, fol. 2, item 21199, July 19, 1764.

52. Thomas Gage to Bouquet, December 23, 1763, and Gage to Wilkins, December 28, 1763, in Gage Papers; Howard H. Peckham, ed., "Lieut. Jehu Hay's Diary, 1763," in *Narratives of Colonial America, 1704–1765* (Chicago, 1971), 224–25; William Johnson to Amherst, October 6, 1763, Rogers to Johnson, Detroit, October 7, 1763, William Browning to William Johnson, Niagara, October 22, 1763, Gavin Cochrane to William Johnson, Fort Johnson, November 5, 1763, Loring to Johnson, Oswego, November 9, 1763, Jean Baptiste de Couagne to William Johnson, Niagara, December 15, 1763, and

Indian Council, December, 1763, *WJP* 10:869, 871, 906, 919, 920, 955, 962; Gage to Johnson, January 12, 1764, and Gage to Johnson, May 28, 1764, *WJP* 4:293, 432.

53. Peckham, *Pontiac and the Indian Uprising*, 158, 236–37; Navarre / Quaife, *Journal of Pontiac's Conspiracy*, 123–24; *Journal of Jeffery Amherst*, 300; Hay, "Diary," May 16, p. 90; Court of Inquiry, Detroit, July 6, 1763; De Villiers [De Neyon] to Indian Nations, Fort de Chartres, September 27, 1763; and William Edgar to William Johnson, Detroit, November 1, 1763, *WJP* 10:732, 819–21, 914–15.

54. Gage to William Johnson, New York, January 12, 1764, and Gage to Johnson, April 25, 1764, *WJP* 4:292, 408; Gladwin to Amherst, Detroit, November 1, 1763, in "Gladwin Mansucripts," 27:675–76; Montresor to Bassett, November 2, 1763, CISHL 10:534–35; Gage to Gladwin, March 23, 1764, *WJP* 11:115; Hay, "Diary," entries for October 19, October 30, November 2, November 3, and November 7, 1763, 1; Peckham, *Pontiac and the Indian Rising*, 236–37.

55. Helen Hornbeck Tanner, ed., *Atlas of Great Lakes Indian History* (Norman, 1986), 50; Gladwin to Amherst, Detroit, November 1, 1763, in "Gladwin Manuscripts," 27:675–76; Indian Intelligence from James Grant, Detroit, June 4, 1764, and "Intelligence from [Detroit]," June 11, 1764, *WJP* 11:218–19, 229.

56. *Pennsylvania Gazette*, fol. 2, item 21199, July 19, 1764; item 23583, June 27, 1765. James Sterling to Duncan, Detroit, September 16, 1764, in James Sterling Letter Book, WCL; Loring to Gage, September 2, 1764, and Gage to Loring, August 28, 1764, Gage Papers.

57. Lt. Samuel Hunter, entry for July 29, 1763, "Journal kept at Fort Augusta, 1763," in John B. Linn and William H. Egle, eds., *Pennsylvania Archives*, 2nd ser., 7 (1878): 439; C. Hale Sipe, *The Indian Wars of Pennsylvania* (1929; New York, 1971), 430–32; *Pennsylvania Gazette*, fol. 2, item 18714, July 21, 1763. A year later, Daniel denied that he had taken a part in the war, which he blamed on unnamed French agents. Thomas Smallman to Alexander McKee, November 8, 1764, *WJP* 11:404; Jennings, *Empire of Fortune*, 396; Christian Frederick Post, "The Journal of Christian Frederick Post, from Philadelphia to the Ohio . . . ," in Rueben Gold Thwaites, ed., *Early Western Travels, 1748–1846* (Cleveland, 1904), 1: 209, 212–13, 223–24; Randolph C. Downes, *Council Fires on the Upper Ohio: A Narrative of Indian Affairs in the Upper Ohio Valley until 1795* (Pittsburgh, 1940), 84–89.

58. For green powder, see *Pennsylvania Gazette*, fol. 2, item 20800, May 24, 1764; Colonel James Burd of the Susquehanna had word of the over-mountain attacks by June 10. See "Speech of Colonel Bird to the Delawares . . . ," June 10, 1763, Native American Collection, WCL.

59. See Croghan to the Lords of Trade, June 8, 1764, in CISHL 10:256; *Pennsylvania Gazette*, fol. 2, item 18714, July 21, 1763; item 18772, August 4, 1763; item 18895, August 25, 1763,.

60. *Pennsylvania Gazette*, fol. 2, item 18808, August 11, 1763; William Richardson to Governor, August 31, 1763, extract, South Carolina Council Journal, CO 5/447, fol. 208; Johnson to Colden, October 24, 1763, and abstract of John Duncan to Johnson, March 10, 1764, *WJP* 4:274; 363; Johnson to Gage, December 23, 1763, *WJP* 10:975;

Eleazer Wheelock to Johnson, April 17, 1764, and Eleazar Wheelock to Johnson, ca. March 15, 1764, *WJP* 11:102, 133; Gage to Gov. Murray, January 1, 1764, Gage Papers.

61. *Pennsylvania Gazette*, fol. 2, item 18736, July 28, 1756.

62. Paul Wallace, *Indian Paths of Pennsylvania* (Harrisburg, Pa., 1961), end papers; James Truslow Adams, *Atlas of Early American History* (New York, 1943).

63. The *Pennsylvania Gazette* contains some thirty-six reports of Indian attacks in the neighborhood of that triangle during the war. It reported fifteen elsewhere. In the triangle: *Pennsylvania Gazette*, fol. 2, items 18474 (reports of attacks: 2), June 16, 1763; 18569 (3), June 30, 1763; 18616 (1), July 7, 1763; 18769 (1), August 4, 1763; 18772 (2), August 4, 1763; 18733 (3), July 28, 1763; 18736 (2), July 28, 1763; 19012 (4), September 8, 1763; 19280 (1), October 13, 1767; 20400 (2), April 5, 1764; 20947 (5), June 14, 1764; 21076 (2), June 28, 1764; 21077 (1), June 28, 1764; 21522 (2), August 30, 1764; 21578 (2), September 6, 1764; 21623 (2), September 13, 1764. Outside the triangle: *Pennsylvania Gazette*, fol. 2, items 18736 (2), July 28, 1763; 19375 (4), October 27, 1763; 19062 (2), September 15, 1762; 19280 (1), October 13, 1763; 20076 (1), February 16, 1764; 22091 (1), November 15, 1764; 20645 (2), May 3, 1764; 20567 (1), April 26, 1764; 20947 (1), (June 14, 1764).

64. Pattern one: *Pennsylvania Gazette*, fol. 2, item 18736, July 28, 1763; see also items 19375, October 21, 1763; 19316, October 20, 1763; 20567, April 26, 1764; 20645, May 3, 1764; and 22091, November 15, 1764. Prisoners delivered by Shawnees at Fort Pitt, May 10, 1765, *WJP* 10:720–21. Pattern two: *Pennsylvania Gazette*, fol. 2, items 19062, September 15, 1763; 19280, October 13, 1763; 19375, October 27, 1763; and 20076, February 16, 1764.

65. "Indian Intelligence," July 22, 1764, *WJP* 4:495; David Van der Heyden to Johnson, October 19, 1763, *WJP* 10:880; Johnson to Robert Elliot, April 28, 1764, *WJP* 11:165–66; *Pennsylvania Gazette*, fol. 2, item 20747, May 17, 1764; Gage to Lt. Gov. Colden, July 18, 1765, and Colden to Gage, July 22, 1765, Gage Papers.

66. Quotation: William Eyre to Johnson, January 7, 1764, *WJP* 11:6; for convoys, see *Pennsylvania Gazette*, fol. 2, item 21578, September 6, 1764; Ecuyer to Bouquet, Bedford, November 13, 1763, *PCHB*, ser. 21649, pt. 2:146–47. A small raid could temporarily halt a convoy, as in Bouquet to Johnson, March 26, 1764, *WJP* 4:377–79; Mante, *History of the Late War in America*, 493.

67. Bouquet to Gladwin, August 28, 1763, *PCHB*, ser. 21649, pt. 2:27; Mante, *History of the Late War in America*, 490, 494.

68. "Considerable": Bouquet to Gladwin, Fort Pitt, August 28, 1763, *PCHB*, ser. 21649, pt. 2:28 (fol. 313); "Bravery,": *Pennsylvania Gazette*, fol. 2, item 18966, September 1, 1763; *Journal of Jeffery Amherst*, 316–18. Mante, *History of the Late War*, 497, says the Indian losses could not be known, and Bouquet, in his letter to Gladwin, agreed, though Captain Basset, in a letter published in the September 1 issue of the *Pennsylvania Gazette*, guessed that their losses were at least sixty men. But no one had counted bodies.

69. Bouquet to Amherst, August 26, 1763 (quotations), and October 24, 1764, in "Bouquet Papers," 19:226–27, 239; Amherst to Bouquet, New York, September 10, 1763, *WJP* 4:201; Mante, *History of the Late War*, 498; Bouquet to Gladwin, Fort Pitt, August

28, 1763, *PCHB*, ser. 21649, pt. 2:27; Volwiller, "Trent's Journal," 410; *Journal of Jeffery Amherst*, August 26, 1763, 318; Peckham, *Pontiac and the Indian Rising*, 213.

70. According to lists of captives returned after peace was restored, seventeen were taken from Virginia in 1763 and sixteen in 1764. For Pennsylvania the figures are three for 1763 and five for 1764. See Bouquet, List of Captives, Fort Pitt, November 1764, *WJP* 11:484–90; *Pennsylvania Gazette*, fol. 2, item 24194, September 19, 1765; prisoners delivered by Shawnees at Fort Pitt, May 10, 1765, *WJP* 11:720–21. Public reports of raiding do not slack off in Virginia in 1764, though they do in Pennsylvania. The *Pennsylvania Gazette* does not say much about killings in Virginia and Maryland in 1763, but it does suggest that entire settlements on the Greenbriar and Jacksons' Rivers were "cut off." The *Pennsylvania Gazette* identifies eleven Virginians killed in 1764, besides six to seven families "cut off." Other reports add sixteen. A reasonable guess for the total would be forty Virginians. See *Pennsylvania Gazette*, fol. 2, item 20567, April 26, 1764; item 21076, June 28, 1764; item 21522, August 30, 1764; item 21623, September 13, 1764; item 22091, November 15, 1764; also, Gage to Halifax, CISHL 10:284; Bouquet to Bradstreet, Bedford, September 5, 1764, Gage Papers, vol. 24; and Bouquet to William Johnson, Tuscarawas, October 20, 1764, *WJP* 11:445. In Pennsylvania, the *Pennsylvania Gazette* puts the 1763 dead at perhaps 140; see item 18569, June 30, 1763; item 18616, July 7, 1763; item 18714, July 21, 1763; item 18736, July 28, 1763. In 1764 the numbers drop, amounting to some eight. See item 20254, March 8, 1763; item 20400, April 15, 1764; item 21077, June 28, 1764. The total figures of forty-one captured and perhaps two hundred killed on the frontier are serious underestimates based on inadequate sources. But they do suggest that Croghan's guess is too high. Quotation: *Pennsylvania Gazette*, fol. 2, item 18714, July 21, 1763.

CHAPTER 5 Defending the Villages, 1764

1. Gladwin to Amherst, May 28, 1763, Amherst Papers, vol. 2, no. 5; "Journal of Indian Affairs," June 2, 1764, *WJP* 11:233; Jehu Hay, "Diary of the Siege of Detroit," 165–66, WCL; Gladwin to William Johnson, Detroit, October 7, 1763, and Gavin Cochrane to William Johnson, November 5, 1763, *WJP* 10:873, 918.

2. Johnson to Amherst, Johnson Hall, July 24, 1763; Amherst to Johnson, New York, July 28, 1763; and Croghan to Johnson, New York, September 28, 1763, *WJP* 10:757; Amherst to Johnson, New York, July 16, 1763; William Johnson to Cadwalader Colden, October 13, 1763; and "Memoranda Concerning Indians," November 10, 1763, *WJP* 4:172, 216, 235; Johnson to Amherst, August 4, 1763, *NYCD* 7:534–35; Johnson to Lords of Trade, September 25, 1763, CISHL 10:31; Amherst to Bouquet, September 25, 1763, *PHB* 6:398. For the Stockbridges in the Seven Years' and Pontiac's War, as well as for more on Amherst's contempt for them, see Patrick Frazier, *The Mahicans of Stockbridge* (Lincoln, Nebr., 1992), 105–45.

3. Johnson to Gage, November 23, 1763, *WJP* 4:252–53; Johnson to Gage, December 5, 1763, and Gage to Johnson, December 12, 1763 (quotation), *WJP* 10:944, 953; Johnson to the Stockbridge Indians, February 17, 1764, *WJP* 11:68.

4. [Thomas Pownall], "Memorial Stating the Nature of the Service in America

1755" (1758), CO 5/18, fols. 298–319; Johnson to Gage, November 23, 1763, *WJP* 4:252; Johnson to Gage, December 30, 1763, Gage Papers; an Indian congress, March 5, 1764, and an Indian congress, March 31, 1764, *WJP* 11:95, 150.

5. Johnson to Gage, August 25, 1763, *WJP* 10:802; Johnson to Gage, November 23, 1763, and Gage to Johnson, December 26, 1763, *WJP* 4:252, 279; instructions to Daniel Claus, February 10, 1764, *WJP* 11:52–53; Johnson to Gage, January 12, 1764, Gage Papers.

6. Johnson to William Eyre, Johnson Hall, January 26–29, 1764, and Indian Journal, January 29, 1764, *WJP* 11:23, 32–33; Johnson to Henry Montour, February, 21, 1764, address to Indians, [ca. February 21, 1764], and Johnson to Colden, March 16, 1764, *WJP* 4:336–37, 338, 365; Johnson to Lords of Trade, May 11, 1764, *NYCD* 7:624.

7. Henry Montour, John Johnson, and William Hare to Johnson, Auqvauge, February 28, 1764, *WJP* 4:349; Johnson to John Bradstreet, Johnson Hall, March 2, 1764, *WJP* 4:349; Johnson to John Stuart, Johnson Hall, March 18, 1764, and "Indian Proceedings," March 16, 1764, *WJP* 11:103, 110; Gage to Halifax, March 10, 1764, in Clarence Edwin Carter, ed., *The Correspondence of General Thomas Gage with the Secretaries of State, 1763–1775* (New Haven, 1931), 18.

8. Cadwallader Colden to the earl of Halifax, March 10, 1764; Johnson to Gage, March 16, 1764; and Gage to Johnson, March 26, 1764, *WJP* 4:361, 368–69, 377–79; Witham Marsh to Johnson, April 2, 1764, *WJP* 11:119–20.

9. Johnson to Gage, February 3, April 14, and April 16, 1764, *WJP* 11:36, 128–29, 132; "Intelligence from Johnson Hall" and "Information Concerning White Prisoners," *WJP* 4:405–6, 495–98; *Pennsylvania Gazette*, fol. 2, item 20577, April 26, 1764.

10. Court of Enquiry, Detroit, July 10, 1764, in "Gladwin Manuscripts," 27:666; "Journal of Indian Affairs," April 24–May 11, 1764, and June 7, 1764, *WJP* 11:182, 234–35.

11. "A Conference with the Chenussios," August 3, 1764; Johnson to Gage, August 22, 1764; Johnson to Gage, September 30, 1764; and Johnson to Gage, December 21, 1765, *WJP* 11:316–24, 336–37, 365, 983; Johnson to Cadwalader Colden, August 23, 1764, *WJP* 4:512–13; Johnson to Lords of Trade, August 30, 1764, CISHL 10:306.

12. "Conference with Indians," Niagara, July 9–14, and Johnson to Gage, Niagara, August 5, 1764, *WJP* 11:268–69, 272, 326; Indian Journal, Niagara, July 13 and July 22, 1764, *WJP* 4:474–77, 492.

13. Johnson to Bouquet, June 18, 1764, and "Indian Conference," July 21, 1764, *WJP* 4:451–52, 493; Henry Montour and John Johnson to Johnson, May 23, 1764; Johnson to Gage, Oswego, June 29, 1764; and Johnson to Gage, September 30, 1764, *WJP* 11:197–98, 245–47, 365–66; Alexander Henry, *Travels and Adventures in Canada and the Indian Territories between the Years 1760 and 1776*, March of America Facsimile Series No. 43 (1809; Ann Arbor, Mich., 1966), 182–85.

14. Gladwin to Bradstreet, July 12, 1764, and Bradstreet to Gage, August 5, 1764, Gage Papers; Gage to Johnson, August 15, 1764, *WJP* 4:508–9; Gage to Bouquet, August 18, 1764, in "Bouquet Papers," 19:276; Thomas Mante, *History of the Late War in America and the Islands of the West-Indies* (London, 1772), 507.

15. For a defense of Bradstreet, see Mante, *History of the Late War in America*, 511–30.

For the treaty, see Lake Erie Camp, August 12, 1764, *WJP* 11:330–33, also *WJP* 4:503–8, also enclosure in Bradstreet to Gage, Presque Isle, August 14, 1764, Gage Papers.

16. William Johnson to Bradstreet, May 5, 1764, *WJP* 4:416; Bouquet to Gage, August 27, 1764, and Bradstreet to Gage, Sandusky, September 29, 1764, Gage Papers; Gage to Bradstreet, October 15, 1764, CISHL 10:343–46.

17. For Johnson's antipathy toward Bradstreet, see James Abercromby to Johnson, October 13, 1758, and William Johnson to Abercromby, Albany, November 10, 1758, *WJP* 10:41, 54. Gage to Johnson, New York, September 2, 1764, *WJP* 4:521–22; Gage to William Johnson, New York, August 16, 1764, *WJP* 11:333–34.

18. For Croghan and the boundary, see Croghan to the Lords of Trade, June 8, 1764, CO 323/17, fol. 305; Gage to Johnson, September 4, 1764; Gage to William Johnson, May 16, 1764; and Johnson to Gage, September 11, 1764, *WJP* 4:425, 534, 535; Johnson to Gage, November 20, 1764, *WJP* 11:472; Gage to Bradstreet, September 2 and September 15, 1764, Gage Papers; Gage to Halifax, October 12, 1764, and Gage to Bradstreet, October 15, 1764, CISHL 10:343–46. For Delaware and Shawnee failure: Gage to William Johnson, September 4, 1764, and William Johnson to Gage, September 11, 1764, *WJP* 4:524; 534–36; Michael McConnell, *A Country Between: The Upper Ohio Valley and Its Peoples, 1724–1774* (Lincoln, Nebr., 1992), 197–205.

19. Journal of Indian Affairs, April 30, 1764, *WJP* 11:184; Johnson to Gage, September 21, 1764, *WJP* 4:543–44.

20. Howard Peckham, ed., "The Journal of Captain Thomas Morris, 1764," *Old Fort News* 6 (1941): 3–11: the early version of the journal. The later version: Thomas Morris, *Journal of Captain Thomas Morris from Miscellanies in Prose and Verse* (Ann Arbor, 1966 [facsimile of London, 1791]). The quotations in the following paragraphs from each journal are from portions dated August 27. See also testimony of Thomas King, Sandusky, October 3, 1764, *WJP* 11:369–72; St. Ange to D'Abbadie, November 9, 1764, CISHL 10:355.

21. John Campbell to Gage, Detroit, May 21, 1765, Gage Papers; testimony of Thomas King, Sandusky, October 3, 1764, *WJP* 11:369–72.

22. French warships and regiments flew flags with white fields. During the Seven Years' War, Indians, Canadians, and Britons would have understood the white flag as symbolic of France. See Gustave Desjardins, *Recherches sur les drapeaux français. Oriflamme, bannière de France, marques nationales, couleurs du roi, drapeau de l'armée, pavillons de la marine* (Paris, 1874), 84, 95, 114, and plates xvii–xxxiii, copy at the New York Public Library; Frank Earle Schermerhorn, *American and French Flags of the Revolution* (Philadelphia, 1948), 107, 109, 141–42; quotation: William Renwick Riddell, trans., "The Last Indian Council of the French at Detroit," *Transactions of the Royal Society of Canada* 25 (1931): 167.

23. For a similar effort among seventeenth-century Anishinabeg, see Claude Dablon, "Relation of 1670 and 1671," *JR* 55:187–89. The longing for the return of French armies and supplies, and the effort to bring the event about through the apparent imitation of French military forms, resemble the Pacific attempts in the nineteenth through mid-twentieth centuries to bring in a Western cargo through the use of ceremonies. See Kenelm Burridge, *Mambu: A Melanesian Millennium* (London, 1960),

xvi, xxi; Peter Lawrence, *Road Belong Cargo: A Study of the Cargo Movement in the Southern Mandang District, New Guinea* (Manchester, U.K., 1964), 224. Both in Oceana and in the Great Lakes, the movements played what Peter Worsley has called an "integratory role," that is, they welded "previously hostile and separate groups together"; see *The Trumpet Shall Sound: A Study of "Cargo" Cults in Melanesia* (London, 1957), 227. The millennialism of the Great Lakes Indians can hardly, of course, be reduced to a desire for Western goods; that this has also been true in the Pacific is made strikingly clear in a topical special issue, "Millennial Countdown in New Guinea," *Ethnohistory* 47 (2000). See, esp., Jan Bieniek and Garry W. Trompf, "The Millennium, Not the Cargo?" 113, 120, 126–27.

24. Peckham, "Journal of Captain Thomas Morris, 1764," 3–11; Morris, *Journal of Captain Thomas Morris*, 305, 313–14; congress with western nations, Detroit, September 7–10, 1764, and testimony of Thomas King, Sandusky, October 3, 1764, both in *WJP*, 4:528, 552–55 (King's testimony is also in *WJP* 11:369–72 and the Gage Papers; Morris to Lt. Mante, Rochedebout village of the Ottawas, August 31, 1764, Gage Papers; St. Ange to D'Abbadie, November 9, 1764, CISHL 10:354–57.

25. "Transactions of a Congress held with the Chiefs of the Ottawas and Chippewas Nations, with several others," September 7, 1764, and Bradstreet to Gage, September 12, 1764 (enclosure), Gage Papers; Mante, *History of the Late War in America*, 514–21; Gage to Bouquet, October 15, 1764, and Johnson to Lords of Trade, December 26, 1764, CISHL 10:347–48, 388; congress with the western nations, Detroit, September 7–10, *WJP* 4:526–27; Bradstreet to Johnson, August 28, 1764, *WJP* 11:340.

26. John Campbell to Gage, February 25, 1765, Gage Papers; Indian Conference, Sandusky, October 5, 1764; Gage to Johnson, October 26, 1764; and Indian Journal, December 14, 1764, December 16, 1764, January 17, 1765, February 6, 1765, and April 27, 1765, *WJP* 11:373, 392, 503–4 506–8, 553, 593–94, 704; Gage to Bouquet, October 15, 1764; Gage to Johnson, October 26, 1764; Johnson to the Lords of Trade, December 12, 1764; and Johnson to Lords of Trade, December 26, 1765, CISHL 10:347–48, 349; 389; 390–91; examination by Israel Putnam, September 29, 1764, *WJP* 4:549.

27. "A Conference between Bradstreet and the Wendots," September 29, 1764, *WJP* 4:547–48; see also vol. 25, Gage Papers; Col. Bradstreet's Thoughts on Indian Trade, Necessary posts, etc., December 4, 1764, CO 5/65, pt. 1: fols. 135–41; Bradstreet to Gage, December 12, 1764, Gage Papers; see also Mante, *History of the Late War in America*, 516.

28. Alexander Henry to Captain William Howard, May 22, 1765, enclosed in John Campbell to Gage, June 30, 1765, and John Campbell to Gage, September 15, 1765, Gage Papers; extracts of a letter from Capt. William Howard, May 17, 1765, and William Johnson to William Howard, July 2, 1765, *WJP* 11:739, 815.

29. Bouquet to Gage, Carlisle, May 2, 1764, Sylvester K. Stevens and Donald H. Kent, eds., *The Wilderness Chronicles of Northwestern Pennsylvania* (Harrisburg, Pa., 1941), 268–69; Gage to Johnson, May 16, 1764, *WJP* 4:425; Gage to Bouquet, September 2, 1764, Gage Papers.

30. Bouquet to Gage, Fort Loudon, August 15, 1764; Bouquet to Gage, Bushy Run, September 16, 1764; and Bouquet to Gage, October 2, 1764, Gage Papers; Gage to

Johnson, July 13, 1764, *WJP* 4:483; *Pennsylvania Gazette*, fol. 2, item 21938, October 25, 1764.

31. Indian Journal, September 22, 1764; Gage to Johnson, October 10, 1764; and Johnson to Gage, December 6, 1764, *WJP* 11:361, 376, 492; Bouquet to Gage, Fort Pitt, November 30, 1764, in "Bouquet Papers," 19:283–94; Bouquet to Gage, October 2, 1764, Gage Papers.

32. Alexander McKee to Johnson, October 21, 1764, *WJP* 11:386; Indian proceedings, camp near Tuskarowas, October 16–20, *WJP* 11:436–37, 440–41, 445–47; see also messages between Bouquet and Indians in *PCHB*, ser. 21655, 16: 232–35.

33. On the murder, see Indian proceedings, November 7, 1764 *WJP* 11:451; for the key ingredient, see Gage to Johnson, January 12, 1764, *WJP* 4:291–92; Gage to Johnson, September 2, 1764, *WJP* 11:344, Gage to Bradstreet, September 2, 1764; Gage to Bouquet, September 2, 1764; and Bouquet to Gage, November 15, 1764, Gage Papers.

34. Delaware hostages included Mondeaticker, or William Davis; Noondias, or Andrew Trump; Killackchcker, or Simon Girty; Katepakomin, or John Compass; Possqetonckmy, or Custalogas's Son, Steel; Waylsckonowias; the deputies were Killbuck; Weyweyaughing; Lahalapowkeg, or Hutchins; Tilipawiska; Luquet, or Flour. "Private Conference," November 11, 1764, *WJP* 11:459. For the Shawnees, see "conference," November 14, 1764, *WJP* 11:465. Two of the Shawnee men, Red Hawk and Corn Stalk, would become hostages to American Patriots in 1777, only to be killed by the Revolutionaries.

35. Bouquet to John Penn, November 15, 1764, in Stevens and Kent, *Wilderness Chronicles*, 289; Gage to Johnson, December 6, 1764, CISHL 10:367–69; Johnson to Bouquet, December 17, 1764, *WJP* 4:620; also "A List of Recovered Captives," July 4, 1765, *WJP* 4:783–84; *Pennsylvania Gazette*, fol. 2, item 22434, January 17, 1765, and 22650, February 21, 1765.

36. *Pennsylvania Gazette*, fol. 2, item 24100, September 5, 1765.

37. John M. M'Cullough, "A Narrative of the Captivity of John M'Cullough," in Archibald Loudon, ed. *A Selection of Some of the Most Interesting Narratives of Outrages Committed by the Indians in Their Wars with the White People*, 2 vols. in 1 (1808; New York, 1971), 284; Bouquet to Gage, November 30, 1764, CISHL 10:365–66; Mante, *History of the Late War in America*, 541; McKee to Johnson, December 3, 1764, Bouquet to Custaloga, December 3, 1764, and Bouquet to Six Nations, December 22, 1764, *WJP*, 11:482, 484, 510; Bouquet to Johnson, November 30, 1764, and December 3, 1764, *WJP* 4:607, 683.

38. S. Wharton to B. Franklin, December 19, 1764, CISHL 10:376; Johnson to Penn, June 18, 1764, and John Penn to William Johnson, June 9, 1764, *WJP* 11:224–25, 241.

39. *Pennsylvania Gazette*, fol. 2, item 20520, April 19, 1764; Johnson to Lords of Trade, October, 1764, CISHL 10:334 and *NYCD* 7:665; Johnson to Gage, December 6, 1764, and Alexander McKee to William Johnson, January 14, 1765, *WJP* 11:495, 531. Bernhard Knollenberg, *Origin of the American Revolution, 1759–1766* (New York, 1960), chap. 9, sees the campaign as a failure. He is criticized by John Shy in *Toward Lexington: The Role of the British Army in the Coming of the American Revolution* (Princeton, N.J., 1965), 137, 175, who cites praise bestowed on Bouquet by the people of Lancaster

County, Pennsylvania (as related through the encomium of a subordinate), as evidence of his success. To the west of Lancaster, however, the people of the Conococheague Valley in Cumberland County were not fooled. James Smith, a prominent young man who had spent years as a captive, served in the campaign as an interpreter. He later pointed out that Bouquet got only "a small part" of the Indians' captives, that Bouquet achieved only a "cessation of arms for six months," and that the hostages Bouquet took escaped. James Smith, *A Treatise on the Mode and Manner of Indian War* (1812; Chicago, 1948), 49–50.

40. See Winstanley Briggs, "Le Pays des Illinois," *WMQ* 47 (1990): 30–46; Aubry's account of the Illinois Country, 1763; D'Abbadie to minister, January 10, 1764; and ("destitute") St. Ange to D'Abbadie, April 7, 1765, all in CISHL 10:4, 209, 471; Donald Campbell to Bouquet, Detroit, March 10, 1761, in "Aspinwall Papers," 9:400; (wine and beer) Howard Peckham, ed., *George Croghan's Journal of His Trip to Detroit in 1767* (Ann Arbor, Mich., 1939), 37.

41. Journal of D'Abbadie, April, August, and September 1764, CISHL 10:182–83, 196, 199; ("very large Convoy") Gage to Penn, June 16, 1765, CISHL 10:518; ("Channel") John Stuart to John Pownall (copy), January 24, 1764, CO 5/66, fol. 342.

42. Journal of D'Abbadie, January and February 1764; report from Roberston, March 8, 1764; and accounts given by Loftus to D'Abbadie, June 29, 1764, all in CISHL 10:168, 170–71, 217, 227–29.

43. Accounts given by Loftus to D'Abbadie, June 29, 1764, CISHL 10:225–31; extract, M. Desmazellieres to D'Abbadie, March 14 [*sic*], 1764, CISHL 10:234–36; Loftus to Gage, April 9, 1764, CISHL 10:237–38; Gage to Halifax, November 9, 1764, CISHL 10:352; see also Robert R. Rea, "Assault on the Mississippi—The Loftus Expedition, 1764," *Alabama Review* 26 (1973): 173–93.

44. *Pennsylvania Gazette*, fol. 2, item 22614, February 14, 1765; Journal of D'Abbadie, April and September 1764, and D'Abbadie to the minister, September 30, 1764, CISHL 10:182–83, 198, 315–17; Gage to Secretary Conway, June 24, 1766, CO 5/84, fol. 157.

45. Gage to William Johnson, January 23, 1764, *WJP* 4:303; report from Robertson, March 8, 1764; Gage to Halifax, July 13, 1764; and Gage to Bouquet, November 11, 1764, CISHL 10:220, 284, 361–62.

46. Council in Illinois, April 15 and April 17, in Farmar to Gage, December 21, 1764, Gage Papers; Howard Peckham, *Pontiac and the Indian Uprising* (1947; New York, 1970), 246–51; De Villiers [de Neyon] to D'Abbadie, March 13, 1764, and De Villiers [de Neyon] to D'Abbadie, April 20, 1764, CISHL 10:224–25; 242–43.

47. Journal of D'Abbadie, July 1764; "Extract of a letter from M. de St. Ange . . . to M. Dabbadie . . . July 15, 1764"; St. Ange to D'Abbadie, November 9, 1764; and [Charles Philippe] Aubry to [John] Stuart, all in CISHL 10:190, 289–91, 354–60; 384–87.

48. "Indian Intelligence," June 9–11, 1764; Johnson to Gage, June 29, 1764; Gage to William Johnson, July 2, 1764; Gage to William Johnson, October 19, 1764; and Gage to Johnson, December 6, 1764, all in *WJP* 11:226; 247, 249–50, 376, 497; Gage to Bradstreet, July 15, 1764, CISHL 10:286–88. See also Gage to Major Loftus, July 30, 1764, Gage Papers, and Gage to Bouquet, December 7, 1764, in "Bouquet Papers," 19:288.

49. Journal of D'Abbadie, June and August 1764; "copy of the discourse held . . . by

M. Pittman, . . . August 12, 1764"; D'Abbadie to Gage, August 16, 1764; and Gage to Halifax, November 9, 1764, all in CISHL 10:186, 189–90, 191–93, 194–95, 297, 302–3, 351.

50. D'Abbadie to Famar, n.d. Gage Papers; Farmar to secretary at war, November 20, 1764; Gage to Bouquet, December 20, 1764; and Aubry to the minister, February 25, 1765, *all in CISHL* 10:364, 378–79, 455.

CHAPTER 6 Mobs, Germs, and the Status of American Indians

1. Richard White, *The Middle Ground: Indians, Empires, and Republics in the Great Lakes Region, 1650–1815* (New York, 1991), 248, 256, 268, has convincingly and best established that in Pontiac's War Indians rejected British "mastery." I disagree with what for White's book is an incidental point but for this one is central—that the British saw the supposedly conquered Indians as "subjects." This, true in an abstract sense, obscures the eighteenth-century British legal connotations of the word *subject*. In the 1760s, while British administrators applied the term *subject* systematically and legally to the French in Canada and Illinois, they generally avoided applying that word to Indians. At the end of the war, Sir William Johnson did not, as White paraphrases it, tell Delawares, Shawnees, and Mingos "they were now subjects of the king of Great Britain." Johnson said they were "children of the Great King of England . . . closer linked to the British Crown to whom they [would] pay all due submission and subjection." Subjection did not make one His Majesty's subject. Indeed, in this very document, the subjected Indians are clearly distinguished from His Majesty's subjects. See "Treaty with the Ohio Indians," July 13, 1765, *NYCD* 7:754; articles 3, 7, 8, 10, *NYCD* 7:739–40, and "Articles of a Treaty of Peace between English and Delawares, Shawnees and Mingos," July 13, 1765, HSP, microfilm copy in Francis Jennings, William N. Fenton, Mary A. Druke, and David R. Miller, *Iroquois Indians: A Documentary History*, 50 microfilm reels (Woodbridge, Conn., 1984), reel 28, Newberry Library, Chicago.

2. Linda Colley, *Britons: Forging the Nation, 1707–1837* (New Haven, 1992), 48 and throughout. While there exists a growing literature on citizenship, there is not yet a comparable interest in the topic of British subjects. Catherine Hall makes a start with "William Knibb and the Constitution of the New Black Subject," in Martin Daunton and Rick Halpern, eds., *Empire and Others: British Encounters with Indigenous Peoples, 1600–1850* (Philadelphia, 1999), 303–24. C. A. Bayly, whose essay "The British and Indigenous Peoples: Power, Perception, and Identity, 1760–1860," is in the same volume (p. 20), states that even the Eurasians of British India were denied the status of British subjects, despite a campaign that reached Parliament. Interesting sidelong glances at the topic are also taken up in new work on the status both of women, whom some saw as properly subject to men as well as to the sovereign, and of foreigners or strangers who lived in England but were not British subjects. On women, see, for example, Steven Rappaport, *Worlds within Worlds: Structures of Life in Sixteenth-Century London* (Cambridge, 1989), 36–42; Bridget Hill, introduction to Hill, ed., *Reflections upon Marriage and Other Writings by Mary Astell* (New York, 1986), 39–43; and Ruth Perry, *The Celebrated Mary Astell: An Early English Feminist* (Chicago, 1986), esp. 164. On

strangers and foreigners, see, generally, Laura Hunt Yungblut, *Strangers Settled Here amongst Us* (London, 1996), 11, 63–4, 66, 78, and Rappaport, *Worlds within Worlds*, 29–30, 42–47. I thank Frances Dolan and Amy Froide for recommending these volumes to me.

3. For the phrase "riot and murder," see Carl Van Doren, *Benjamin Franklin* (New York, 1938), 308. For interpretations that tend to view the backcountry as out of the control of a more enlightened, if flawed, administration in the 1760s, see Alden Vaughan, "Frontier Banditti and the Indians: The Paxton Boys' Legacy, 1763–1775," *Pennsylvania History* 51 (1984): 21–22. Eric Hinderaker, *Elusive Empires: Constructing Colonialism in the Ohio Valley, 1673–1800* (New York, 1997), 175, recognizes imperial duplicity while viewing settlers as the main problem. In White's *Middle Ground* and Edward Countryman's "Indians, the Colonial Order, and the Social Significance of the American Revolution," *WMQ* 53 (1996): 342–62, esp. 354, and his *Americans: A Collision of Histories* (New York, 1996), 57–58, frontier "Indian haters" challenged and undid fragile imperial accommodations for Indians from 1765.

4. Howard Peckham, *Pontiac and the Indian Uprising* (1947; Chicago, 1961), 179; L. C. Green, "Claims to Territory in Colonial America," in L. C. Green and Olive P. Dickason, eds., *The Law of Nations and the New World* (Calgary, Alberta, 1989), 103; Lords of Trade to Indian superintendents, October 10, 1763, *WJP* 4:214; Jack Sosin, *Whitehall and the Wilderness: The Middle West in British Colonial Policy, 1760–1775* (Lincoln, Nebr., 1961), 39, 52–65. Wilcomb E. Washburn, *Red Man's Land / White Man's Law* (New York, 1971), 49–50, observes that Indian rights to land "were less formal and less fundamental in European eyes than European claims." Sovereignty, as understood in the period, was fundamental. As Grotius put it, "That power is called sovereign whose actions are not subject to the legal control of another, so that they cannot be rendered void by the operation of another human will." Hugo Grotius, *The Law of War and Peace*, trans. Francis W. Kelsey, ed. James Brown Scott et al., *The Classics of International Law*, vol. 3 (Oxford, 1925), bk. 1, chap. 3:102. In the proclamation, the Crown claimed the sovereign right to render void all unapproved sales of lands that the Crown reserved for the Indian tribes.

5. Gage to Johnson, *WJP* 4:290–91; R. A. Humphreys, "Lord Shelburne and the Proclamation of 1763," *English Historical Review* 49 (1934): 241–64.

6. Dorothy Jones, *License for Empire: Colonialism by Treaty in Early America* (Chicago, 1982), 101–94. Contrast Woody Holton, "Ohio Indians and the American Revolution," *Journal of Southern History* 40 (1994): 453–78, with Eugene M. Del Papa, "The Royal Proclamation of 1763: Its Effect upon Virginia Land Companies," *Virginia Magazine of History and Biography* 83 (1975): 406–7, and Thad Tate, "The Coming of the Revolution in Virginia: Britain's Challenge to Virginia's Ruling Class, 1763–1776," *WMQ* 29 (1962): 338. Holton expands his thesis in *Forced Founders: Indians, Debtors, Slaves, and the Making of the American Revolution in Virginia* (Chapel Hill, N.C., 1999), chap. 1. For Canada, see Green, "Claims to Territory," 96–124.

7. Lords of Trade to Johnson, August 5, 1763, and Proclamation of 1763, October 7, 1763, CISHL 10:17–18, 43. While Indian peoples understood that they possessed what we can justly call sovereignty, the British fairly consistently denied that any but the

Crown was sovereign. As Jack Sosin puts it, "For reasons of expediency the British government had to acknowledge native ownership in the soil to the North American Indians, but vis-à-vis British subjects and foreign powers, the British King, of course, had the dominion as well as the ownership of the lands by virtue of the Peace of Paris"; see his *Whitehall and the Wilderness*, 231. Wilbur Jacobs suggests that the proclamation had as much to do with racism against Indians as with protection of them, and he sees it as foreshadowing Indian "removal," in *Dispossessing the American Indian* (New York, 1972), 102–3.

8. Johnson to Gage, January 12, 1764, and Johnson to Gage, January 23, 1764, *WJP* 4:296, 304; conference held with the [Mingo] Senecas, November 9, 1764, *WJP* 11:455.

9. Plan for the Future Management of Indian Affairs, [July 10], 1764, and commissioners of trade to John Stuart, Whitehall, July 10, 1764, *Pennsylvania Archives*, 1st ser., 4:182–83, 189.

10. George Croghan, "Croghan's Journal, October 21, 1760–January 7, 1761," in Reuben Gold Thwaites, ed., *Early Western Travels, 1748–1846* (Cleveland, 1904), 1:116–17; George Croghan, "Journal," December 4, 1760, in "Aspinwall Papers," 9:370; Thomas Mante, *History of the Late War in America and the Islands of the West-Indies* (London, 1772), 519, Ayer Collection, Newberry Library, Chicago; congress with the western nations, Detroit, September 7–10, 1764, *WJP*, 4:528–29, 532–33; Lieutenant Colonel John Campbell, speech to Potawatomis, January 27, 1765, *WJP* 11:550–51; Thomas Morris to Lt. Thomas Mante, Rochebedout village of the Ottawas, August 31, 1764, Gage Papers. J. Russell Snapp, *John Stuart and the Struggle for Empire on the Southern Frontier* (Baton Rouge, La., 1996), suggests that when Stuart, in a note on a 1771 map, contrasted Indians with "white Subjects," he was "implying that Indians qualified fully as subjects" (59). Although this is unconvincing, Snapp's earlier suggestion that Stuart thought Indians should be eventually integrated "as full members of the empire and subjects of the King" is plausible. But Stuart did not think that the Indians were ready yet. He argued, in the passage Snapp quotes, that the empire, through just treatment, might "from Savage Barbarians render them rational people, industrious and Good Subjects: Ends never to be ordained by Force and restraint." Harsh treatment, however, would "be the sure means of their continuing in their present state of Barbarity" and would deprive the king and the empire "of 80,000 Subjects" (58).

11. Proclamation of Gage to the inhabitants of the Illinois, December 30, 1764, CISHL, 10:395–96; Plan of Forts and Garrisons proposed for North America, Jeffery Amherst, 1763, CISHL 10:5–7; message of Gen. Amherst to the Indians, 1761, *Pennsylvania Archives*, 1st ser., 4:48–49; report of Roberts, March 8, 1764, CISHL, 10:218. Although the term *subject* did imply access to courts, the British penal laws did exclude British and Irish Catholics from juries, from serving as attorneys, and from taking certain types of cases to court. The capitulation of Canada, which promised French Canadians freedom of religion, presented British rulers with a dilemma, resolved only in 1766 when the British cabinet quietly ordered that such legal privileges and protections be extended even to French-speaking Catholics in the newly conquered territories. Clarence Walworth Alvord, *The Mississippi Valley in British Politics: A Study of the*

Trade, Land Speculation, and Experiments in Imperialism Culminating in the American Revolution, 2 vols. (Cleveland, 1917), 2:253–59.

12. Amherst to William Johnson, August 14, 1763, *WJP* 4: 189.

13. Johnson to Lords of Trade, September 25, 1763, *NYCD* 7:561; Johnson to Gage, October 31, 1764, *WJP* 10:395; Johnson to Gage, December 6, 1764, *WJP* 11:493; Johnson to Lords of Trade, December 26, 1764, CISHL 10:391.

14. Johnson to Gage, October 31, 1764, Gage Papers; "Copy of Petition . . . by Silas Charles in Behalf of the Montawk Indians to the Honorable Charles Cadwallader Colden," n.d., Native American Collection, 742, WCL.

15. Snapp, *John Stuart*, 63–66.

16. Johnson paid little attention to New England, where, he acknowledged, many Indians were living "under the Laws, and reconciled to them." But from the colony of New York westward, he had little confidence in the extension of British law to Indians. "Plan for the Future Management," July 10, 1764, and Sir William Johnson, "Sentiments, Remarks, and additions humbly offered," October 8, 1764, *NYCD* 7:638, 663; CISHL 10:276; Yungblut, *Strangers Settled Here amongst Us*, 63–64, 78. Snapp, *John Stuart*, 66.

17. Edward Ward to Johnson, May 2, 1764, and Alexander McKee to Johnson, October 21, 1764, *WJP* 11:169–70, 385; William Grant to Gage, April 26, 1764, and Gage to Bouquet, May 14, 1764, *PHB* 6:522–26, 539–540; Bouquet to Gage, September 26, 1764, Gage Papers; Gage to Bouquet, October 15, 1764, CISHL 10:348–49; Col. Henry Bouquet to Lieut. Col. Asher Clayton, Fort Pitt, December 1, 1764, *PCHB*, ser. 21653: 338.

18. Gage to Johnson, January 31, 1764; Johnson to Gage, February 19, 1764; and Gage to Johnson, May 16, 1764, and June 3, 1764, *WJP* 4:314, 329, 424, 439–40; Johnson to Robert Elliot, April 28, 1764; Johnson to Gage, May 3, 1764; Johnson Calendar, May 3, 1764; and Johnson to Gage, May 26, 1764, all in *WJP* 11:165–66, 174–75, 201; *Pennsylvania Gazette*, fol. 2, item 20747, May 17, 1764.

19. Ensign John Christie to Gage, July 10, 1765; Gage to Lt. Gov. Colden, July 18, 1765; and Colden to Gage, July 22, 1765, Gage Papers.

20. Croghan to Lords of Trade, June 8, 1764, CISHL 10:257–58; Johnson to Gage, December 1, 1763, *WJP* 4:256; Johnson to Lords of Trade, September 25, 1763, CISHL 10:33.

21. Johnson to Board of Trade, September 25, 1763, CISHL 10:33; South Carolina Journal of the Upper House of Assembly, June 2, 1742, CO 5/443, fols. 21b–25; charges against John Thomas, Esq., April 10, 1772, CO 5/73, fol. 223; John Stuart to John Thomas, Pensacola, April 10, 1772, CO 5/73, fol. 226. In 1730, after negotiations in London resulted in a treaty between Cherokees and Britons, the Board of Trade suggested that, because this treaty was to be "only with Savages," His Majesty need not bother with formal procedures for approval; Board of Trade to duke of Newcastle, August 20, 1730, Co 5/4, fol. 198.

22. Croghan, "Croghan's Journal, October 21, 1760–January 7, 1761," in Thwaites, *Early Western Travels*, 1:119; Croghan's 1760 Journal, in "Aspinwall Papers," 9 (1871), 374–76; Gage to William Johnson, *WJP* 12:238. Jon William Parmenter, "Pontiac's

War: Forging New Links in the Anglo-Iroquois Covenant Chain, 1758–1766," *Ethno-history* 44 (1997): 617–54, explores the British and Iroquois League efforts to extend the Covenant Chain westward in the period. For a concise statement of Iroquois authority over the Shawnees in the west, see Gage to Hillsborough, January 6, 1770, CO 5/88, fol. 26. For recent statements on the so-called subordination of the Delawares to the Six Nations, see Parmenter, "Pontiac's War," 630; James H. Merrell, "Shamokin: 'The Very Seat of the Prince of Darkness': Unsettling the Early American Frontier," in Fredrika Teute and Andrew R. L. Cayton, eds., *Contact Points: American Frontiers from the Mohawk Valley to the Mississippi, 1710–1850* (Chapel Hill, N.C., 1998), 25. George Croghan made a list of the tribes in the Northern District in 1765; the Delawares and Shawnees he listed as "Dependent on the Six Nations, and connected with Pennsylvania," in "Croghan's Journal, May 15–September 26, 1765," in Thwaites, *Early Western Travels*, 1:167–68.

23. Edward P. Hamilton, ed. and trans., *Adventure in the Wilderness: The American Journals of Louis Antoine de Bougainville, 1756–1760*, fwd. Colin G. Calloway (Norman, Okla., 1990), 103–6. For recent analyses of the status of the Delawares, see Daniel Maltz and JoAllyn Archamhault, "Gender and Power in Native North America: Con-cluding Remarks," in Nancy Shoemaker, ed., *Women and Power in Native North America* (Norman, Okla., 1995), 248–49, and Jane T. Merritt, "Metaphor, Meaning, and Misun-derstanding: Language and Power on the Pennsylvania Frontier," in Teute and Cayton, *Contact Points*, 77–78. Merritt writes that the Iroquois and "whites perhaps used their knowledge of the other's gender constructs to infuse this metaphor with new meaning." Nancy Shoemaker convincingly emphasizes the plastic qualities of gender metaphors in "An Alliance between Men: Gender Metaphors in Eighteenth-Century American In-dian Diplomacy East of the Mississippi," *Ethnohistory* 46 (1999): esp. 241–46. See also Francis Jennings, *The Ambiguous Iroquois Empire: The Covenant Chain Confederation of Indian Tribes with the English Colonies* (New York, 1984), 159–62. Contrast with the older interpretation in Clinton A. Weslager, *The Delaware Indians* (New Brunswick, 1972), 103.

24. *Pennsylvania Gazette*, fol. 2, item 6870, April 15, 1756, and item 21148, July 12, 1764; *The Journal of Jeffery Amherst*, ed. J. Clarence Webster (Toronto, 1931), October 24, 1763, 325; Peters to Monckton, August 15, 1761, in "Aspinwall Papers," 9:440; Bouquet's negotiations of October 2–November 14, 1764, are recorded, among other places, in the *Pennsylvania Colonial Records*, 9:207–33; Johnson's, of May 2, May 7, May 8, and May 10, 1765, are in *NYCD* 7:723, 731–32, 733–41, 736–37, see esp. article 10 of the treaty, 740; Gage to Bradstreet, September 15, 1764, Gage Papers.

25. Patricia Galloway, "'The Chief Who Is Your Father': Choctaw and French Views of the Diplomatic Relation," in Peter H. Wood, Gregory A. Waselkov, and M. Thomas Hatley, eds., *Powhatan's Mantle: Indians in the Colonial Southeast* (Lincoln, Nebr., 1989), 254–78; White, *Middle Ground*, 33–40, emphasizes mediation; Croghan, "Croghan's Journal, May 15–September 26, 1765," entry for August 23, 1765, in Twaites, *Early Western Travels* 1:155; Croghan, Pittsburgh Conference, May 9 and 10, 1765, and William Howard to Johnson, June 24, 1765, *WJP* 11:727, 805; Benjamin Roberts to Johnson, July 7, 1766, *WJP* 5:312–13.

26. "Domiciled": Daniel Claus to Johnson, August 30, 1764, abstracted in *WJP*

4:516; "Domesticated" and "Domestic": Gage to Halifax, June 7, 1764, in Clarence Carter, ed., *The Correspondence of General Thomas Gage*, 2 vols. (New Haven, 1931), 1: 8; William Johnson to Roger Morris, August 26, 1765, *WJP* 11:912.

27. Johnson to Gage, January 27, 1764, and Gage to Johnson, February 6, 1764, *WJP* 4:307–8, 318; Land fraud: William Johnson to Roger Morris, August 26, 1765, *WJP* 11:912; Indian conference, March 10, 1763, *WJP* 4:58; "Indenture of an Indian Woman," June 15, 1763, *WJP* 4:147. Arne's "Rule Britannia" became the unofficial national anthem.

28. Ecuyer to Bouquet, June 16, 1763, *PHB* 6:228–33; Amherst to Bouquet, June 29, 1763, and Bouquet to Gage, June 7, 1764, in "Bouquet Papers," 19:203, 261; Amherst to Gladwin, June 29, 1763, Amherst Papers, vol. 2, no. 3; William Johnson to John Penn, February 9, 1764, *Pennsylvania Archives*, 1st ser., 4:163; *Pennsylvania Gazette*, fol. 2, item 18966, September 1, 1763. Stephen Brumwell, *Redcoats: The British Soldier and War in the Americas, 1755–1763* (Cambridge, 2002), 162, opens an authoritative chapter on the British army and Native Americans with a rare mention of an Indian captive taken near Quebec in 1759. This Ottawa lived long enough to escape from the ship that was to carry him into slavery.

29. Donald H. Kent and Bernard Knollenberg, "Communications," and Bernard Knollenberg, "General Amherst and Germ Warfare," *Mississippi Valley Historical Review* 41: (1954–55), 762–63, 489–64; Albert T. Volwiller, "William Trent's Journal at Fort Pitt, 1763," *Mississippi Valley Historical Review* 11 (1924): 400; Ecuyer to Bouquet, June 16, 1763, *PHB* 6:232; "Orderly Book," August 31, 1763, in Darlington, *Fort Pitt and Letters from the Frontier*, 182; Bouquet to Amherst, June 23, 1763, in "Bouquet Papers," 19:195; Peckham, *Pontiac and the Indian Uprising*, 226–27. On smallpox in 1764, see, for example, documents in CISHL 10:236, 397, *WJP* 4:640, *WJP* 11:51, 537, 618, 660; Col. Lewis to Col. Henry Bouquet, September 10, 1764, *PCHB*, ser. 21650, pt. 1:127; deposition of Gershom Hicks, April 14, 1764, in "Bouquet Papers," 19:254; examination of Gershom Hicks, April 15, 1764, Gage Papers. For European convention, see Grotius, *Law of War and Peace*, bk. 3, chap. 4:651–52. Elizabeth A. Fenn, *Pox Americana: The Great Smallpox Epidemic of 1775–82* (New York, 2001), finds evidence that British officers considered deploying smallpox against American rebels during the Revolutionary War and that Americans rumored that the British had done just that (88–92, 131–33).

30. *Pennsylvania Gazette*, fol. 2, item 6773, March 18, 1756; Edward Shippen to Gov. Morris, Lancaster, Pa., April 19, 1756, *Pennsylvania Archives*, 1st ser., 2:634–35. For Shickellamy, see James Merrell, *Into the American Woods: Negotiators on the Pennsylvania Frontier* (New York, 1999), 167.

31. John Heckewelder, *Narrative of the Mission of the United Brethren* (1820; New York, 1971), 67–68, 76–77; *Pennsylvania Gazette*, fol. 2, item 18808, August 11, 1763, and item 19062, September 15, 1763.

32. Heckewelder, *Narrative of the Mission*, 69–70; "A Conference," December 1, 1763, *Pennsylvania Colonial Records*, 9:77–79; 1:166–69; Indian Council, September 13, 1763, Johnson Hall; William Johnson to Amherst, October 6, 1763; and Indian Council, Johnson Hall, October 8, 1763, *WJP* 10:848–51, 868, 893.

33. Thomas McKee to Johnson, Lancaster, February 15, 1764, *WJP* 11:56; Barry C. Kent, *Susquehanna's Indians* (Harrisburg, Pa., 1984), 13–69; Francis Jennings, "Susquehannock," in Bruce Trigger, ed., *Northeast*, vol. 15 of *Handbook of North American Indians*, William C. Sturtevant, gen. ed., 15 vols. (Washington, D.C, 1978–), 366. For Conestogas and their neighbors, see Robert F. Ulle, "Pacifists, Paxton, and Politics: Colonial Pennsylvania, 1763–1768," *Pennsylvania Mennonite Heritage* 1 (October 1978): 19. I was guided to this source and well informed of the religious context by Steven Nolt, "A Spirit of Exclusivity: The Progress of Religious Intolerance in Colonial Pennsylvania" (graduate seminar paper, University of Notre Dame, 1995).

34. For Elder and the "Ham" quotation, see Patrick Griffin, "The People with No Name: Ulster's Migrants and Identity Formation in Eighteenth-Century Pennsylvania," *WMQ* 58 (2001): 612; John Dunbar, introduction to Dunbar, ed., *The Paxton Papers* (The Hague, 1957), 22; "Instructions to Col. Armstrong, 11 July, 1763" and "Recruiting Instructions to Armstrong, Elder &c., 1763" *Pennsylvania Archives*, 1st. ser., 4:114–17.

35. Dunbar, introduction to Dunbar, *Paxton Papers*, 21–22 (John Penn to Thomas Penn, November 15, 1763, quoted 22 n. 2); Rev. John Elder to Gov. Hamilton, October 25, 1763, *Pennsylvania Archives*, 1st ser., 4: 127; Votes of Assembly, October, 21, 1763, and December 24, 1763, *Pennsylvania Archives*, 8th ser., 6: 5482–83, 5497; Heckewelder, *Narrative of the Mission*, 73; John Penn to Gage, December 31, 1763, Gage Papers.

36. Dunbar, *Paxton Papers*, 23, 27; Humbertis M. Cummings, "The Paxton Killings," *Journal of Presbyterian History* 44 (1966): 219–30; Minutes of the Provincial Council, December 19–22, 1763, *Pennsylvania Colonial Records*, 9:88–96.

37. John Shy, *Toward Lexington: The Role of the British Army in the Coming of the American Revolution* (Princeton, N.J., 1965), 205, points to the ill health of the soldiers at Lancaster. John Penn issued a pass to "Michael, and Mary, his wife," whom he certified as "friendly Indians of the Delaware Tribe." But when Moravian missionary Bernhard Adam Grube and his wife met Mary on a chance encounter in 1767, Grube called her a Conestoga (meaning a Susquehanna), and he was surprised at how poorly she understood the Delaware language. As an authority on Indian peoples, Grube surpasses Penn. Penn's certificate and Grube's diary are quoted in C. H. Martin, "Two Delaware Indians who Lived on Farm [*sic*] of Christian Hershey," *Historical Papers and Addresses of the Lancaster County Historical Society* 34 (1930): 217–20. Steven Nolt's "Spirit of Exclusivity" guided me to this source. Heckewelder, *Narrative of the Mission*, 78–79; John Penn to William Johnson, December 31, 1763, *WJP* 4:284; Thomas McKee to William Johnson, Lancaster, February 15, 1764, *WJP* 11:55.

38. "Indian Conference," March 24–April 23, 1764, *WJP* 11:135–36, 138, 143, 145; Penn to Gage, December 31, 1763, Gage Papers; *Pennsylvania Gazette*, fol. 2, item 19822, December 29, 1763; item 19871, January 5, 1764; item 19906, January 12, 1764; Rev. John Elder to Penn, December 16, 1763, and Penn to Elder, December 29, 1763, *Pennsylvania Archives*, 1st ser., 4:148–49, 153.

39. Anon. [Anthony Benezet?], "Some Account of a Visit divers Friends made to the Indians at the time of the Treaty of Easton [1760]," taken by one of the company as follows," n.d., 13, 14, WCL; entries by James Burd and Samuel Hunter, "Journal Kept at Fort Augusta," *Pennsylvania Archives*, 2nd ser., 7:439, 446; Heckewelder, *Narrative of the*

Mission, 73, 77; Penn to assembly, Votes of Assembly, December 20, 1763, *Pennsylvania Archives*, 8th ser., 6:5492; Col. James Irvine to Gov. Penn, November 23, 1763, and Asher Clayton to provincial commissioners, November 26, 1763, *Pennsylvania Archives* 1st ser., 4:138–39, 142; council, December 10 and December 21, 1763, *Pennsylvania Colonial Records* 9:85–88, 93–94.

40. Petition by Lewis Weiss, January 3, 1764, *Pennsylvania Archives*, 8th ser., 6:5502; John Penn to Thomas Gage, December 31, 1763, Gage Papers; Heckewelder, *Narrative of the Mission*, 81–82.

41. Heckewelder, *Narrative of the Mission*, 81–82; Penn to Gage, January 5, 1764, Gage Papers.

42. Gage to Penn, January 6, 1764, and January 10, 1764, and Schlosser to Gage, January 20, 1764, Gage Papers; also Schlosser to Penn, January 20, 1764, *Pennsylvania Archives* 1st ser., 4:158; Gage to Johnson, January 12, 1763; Johnson to Colden, January 27, 1764; and Johnson to Gage, March 8, 1764, *WJP*, 4:293, 306, 357–58; Cadwallader Colden to Johnson, January 9, 1764, *WJP* 11:12–13; Colden to John Penn, January 10, 1764, and copy of minutes of New York Council, January 9, 1764, in Votes of Assembly, January 16, 1764, *Pennsylvania Archives* 8th ser., 7:5515–17; Gage to Halifax, January 7, 1764, in Carter, *Correspondence of General Thomas Gage*, 1:8.

43. Thomas McKee to Johnson, February 15, 1764, *WJP* 11:56; John Penn to Johnson, February 17, 1764, *WJP* 4:327; *Pennsylvania Gazette*, fol. 2, item 20067, February 9, 1764; Heckewelder, *Narrative of the Mission*, 85–86; governor to the assembly, February 2, 1764; Council Minutes, February 3–4, 1764; and remonstrance, February 13, 1764, *Pennsylvania Colonial Records*, 9:129, 131–33, 138–42. For more on John Elder and Matthew Smith, see Frank J. Cavaioli, "A Profile of the Paxton Boys: Murderers of the Conestoga Indians," *Journal of the Lancaster County Historical Society* 87 (1983): 89; Gage to Halifax, May 12, 1764, in Carter, *Correspondence of General Thomas Gage*, 1:26; Votes of Assembly, February 3, 1764, *Pennsylvania Archives*, 8th ser., 7:5536–37; instructions of governor to Capt. Schlosser, February 4, 1764, *Pennsylvania Archives* 1st ser., 4:161.

44. Nicole Gothelf, whose emphases and interests lie elsewhere, identifies Indian status as a debating point among Pennsylvanians in "Persecution, Identity, and Politics: The English Protestant Martyr Narrative and Oppositional Politics in Early New England and Pennsylvania" (Ph.D. diss., University of Notre Dame, 2001), chap. 5. My reading suggests that, of the anti-Paxtonians' terms, only the rarely used term *subject* extended any stable legal protections to Indians. The term *denizen* would also have granted such protection, but it was not used. For denizens, see Yungblut, *Strangers Settled Here amongst Us*, 66, 78.

45. Thomas McKee to Johnson, Lancaster, February 15, 1764, *WJP* 11:56–57; *Pennsylvania Gazette*, fol. 2, item 19906, January 12, 1764; Penn to assembly, Votes of Assembly, December 20, 1763, *Pennsylvania Archives*, 8th ser., 6:5493; [Benjamin Franklin], "A Narrative of the Late Massacres, in Lancaster County, of a Number of Indians, Friends of this Province, by Persons unknown"; Charles Read, "Copy of a Letter from Charles Read, Esq: To the Hon: John Ladd, Esq: And his Associates, Justices of the Peace for the County of Gloucester"; "A Serious Address, to Such of the Inhabitants of Pennsylvania, As have connived at, or do approve of, the late Massacre of the Indians at Lancaster; or

the Design of Killing those who are now in the Barracks at Philadelphia"; "A Dialogue, Containing some Reflections on the late Declaration and Remonstrance, Of the Back-Inhabitants of the Province of Pennsylvania"; and "The Quakers Assisting. To Preserve the Lives of the Indians in the Barracks, Vindicated And proved to be consistent with Reason, agreeable to our Law, hath an inseparable Connection with the Law of God, and exactly agreeable with the Principles of the People call'd Quakers," all in Dunbar, *Paxton Papers*, 64, 65, 80, 93–95, 115, 119, 356. Carter, *Correspondence of General Thomas Gage*, 1:8.

46. "A Declaration And Remonstrance Of the distressed and bleeding Frontier Inhabitants Of the Province of Pennsylvania, Presented by them to the Honourable the Governor and Assembly of the Province, Shewing the Causes Of their late Discontent and Uneasiness and the Grievances Under which they have laboured, and which they humbly pray to have redress'd"; "An Historical Account, of the late Disturbance, between the Inhabitants of the Back Settlements; of Pennsylvania, and the Philadelphians, &."; "The Apology of the Paxton Volunteers addressed to the candid & impartial World"; and [Thomas Barton?], "The Conduct of the Paxton-Men, impartially represented: with some Remarks on the Narrative," all in Dunbar, *Paxton Papers*, 101, 102, 105 (quotation); 128, 193 (quotation), 194 (quotation), 202–3, 273–74, 282 (quotation), 293.

47. Votes of Assembly, February 29, 1764, *Pennsylvania Archives*, 8th ser., 7:5559; for earlier rejections of petitions, see ibid., 6:5437, 5440; Heckewelder, *Narrative of the Mission*, 89–95; Johnson to Penn, February 9, 1764, *WJP* 4:324; George Croghan to Johnson, September 25, 1767, *WJP* 5:701; *Pennsylvania Gazette*, fol. 2, item 21148, July 12, 1764; Johnson to Penn, June 18, 1764, *WJP* 11:241.

48. "Declaration and Remonstrance Of the distressed and bleeding Frontier Inhabitants" and "An Historical Account, of the late Disturbance, Between the Inhabitants of the Back Settlements; of Pennsylvania, and the Philadelphians, &.," both in Dunbar, *Paxton Papers*, 108, 129; "A Petition from the County of *Cumberland*" in Votes of Assembly, *Pennsylvania Archives*, 8th ser., 7:5581. For raids in Cumberland County, see *Pennsylvania Gazette*, fol. 2, items 18569, June 30, 1763; 18714, July 21, 1763; 18736, July 28, 1763; 20400, April 5, 1764; 20693, May 10, 1764; 20947, June 14, 1764; 21522, August 30, 1764; 21623, September 13, 1764; John Armstrong to Penn, November 21, 1763, *Pennsylvania Archives*, 1st ser, 4:138. For Penn's acquiescence to and discussion of Indian removal from the province, see Penn to Johnson, February 17, 1764, and Johnson to Penn, February 27, 1764, *WJP* 4:327, 343; Gov. Colden to Gov. Penn, March 5, 1764, and minute of a council at Fort George, March 5, 1764, *Pennsylvania Archives*, 1st ser., 4:167–68; Heckewelder, *Narrative of the Mission*, 90–95; Papunhank had been hoping to move north since December—see "A Conference," December 1, 1763, *Pennsylvania Colonial Records* 9:77–79.

49. Charles Read, "Copy of a Letter from Charles Read, Esq: To the Hon: John Ladd, Esq: And his Associates, Justices of the Peace for the County of Gloucester," in Dunbar, *Paxton Papers*, 80; Gage to Johnson, April 22, 1764, and May 16, 1764, and Johnson to Gage, *WJP* 4:403, 423; Johnson to Gage, May 26, 1764; Penn to Johnson, May 23, 1765; and Johnson to Penn, June 7, 1765, *WJP* 11:201, 747, 778. For Johnson's efforts to find a

place for Pennsylvania's Indians with the Iroquois, see his "Journal of Indian Affairs," December 23, 1766, *WJP* 12:242–43.

50. Heckewelder, *Narrative of the Mission*, 95–96.

51. Lt. Gov. [Francis] Fauquier to upper Cherokee chiefs, May 16, 1765, Williamsburg; "Proclamation, by . . . Fauquier," May 13, 1765; Fauquier to Board of Trade, June 14, 1765; Col. Lewis to Lt. Gov. Fauquier, June 3, 1765; and "A Proclamation," Augusta County, CO 5/1331, fols. 13, 15, 16, 18, 27; Fauquier to Penn, July 6, 1765, Gage Papers; *Pennsylvania Gazette*, fol. 2, item 23414, June 6, 1765; item 23468, June 13, 1765; Albert Tillson Jr. *Gentry and Common Folk: Political Culture on a Virginia Frontier, 1740–1785* (Lexington, Ky., 1991), 49; Stuart to Gov. Tryon, May 28, 1765, CO 323/23, fol. 281.

52. Thomas Wharton to Benjamin Franklin, August 14, 1765, CISHL 11:73–74; Bouquet to Gage, May 19, 1765; Croghan to Gage, March 16, 1766; and William Murray to Gage, April 24, 1766, Gage Papers; deposition of Lemuel Barrit, March 6, 1766; Croghan to Johnson, March 10, 1766; Johnson to Croghan, March 28, 1766; John Brodhead and Samuel Gonsales to Johnson, April 6, 1766; testimony of Johnathan Coburn and John Davis, February 15, 1767 (abstract); and Gage to Johnson, June 28, 1767, *WJP* 5:53, 70, 119, 150–51, 492, 573–74; Alexander McKee to Johnson, June 18, 1765, and Johnson to Gage, December 21, 1765, *WJP* 11:796, 982–83; John Penn to Johnson, March 11, 1766; Johnson to Gage, April 17, 1766; and Gage to Johnson, May 19, 1766, *WJP* 12:41, 74, 92; Howard H. Peckham, ed., *George Croghan's Journal of His Trip to Detroit in 1767* (Ann Arbor, Mich., 1939), 16, 33–34; Gage to Conway, June 24, 1766, CO 5/84, fol. 157; Gage to Shelburne, April 7, 1767, CO 5/85, fol. 91; Johnson to Lords of Trade, June 28, 1766, *NYCD* 7:837; John Brainerd to Eleazar Wheelock, February 12, 1768, in Thomas Brainerd, ed., *The Life of John Brainerd, the Brother of David Brainerd* (Philadelphia, 1865), 377; Heckewelder, *Narrative of the Mission*, 98; Merrell, *Into the American Woods*, 320–15; John Armstrong to Penn, January 24, 1768; William Patterson to the secretary, Carlisle, January 23, 1768; Armstrong to Penn, January 7, 1768; Armstrong to Penn, January 29, 1768; testimony of James Cunningham, February 2, 1768; and Penn to William Johnson and Armstrong to Penn, February 26, 1768, *Pennsylvania Colonial Records*, 9:444, 447, 448–49, 450–51, 453, 462, 468–70, 485–86; John Penn to Johnson, January 21, 1768; Penn to Johnson, February 18, 1768; and Johnson to Croghan, March 5, 1768, *WJP* 12:419–20, 432, 462–64.

53. See *Pennsylvania Gazette*, fol. 3, item 527, April 17, 1766; item 566, April 24, 1766; item 1108, July 10, 1766; item 1156, July 17, 1766; item 1274, August 7, 1766; item 2240, January 1, 1767; item 3294, June 10, 1767. Also see Alden Vaughan, "Frontier Banditti and the Indians: The Paxton Boys' Legacy," *Pennsylvania History* 51 (1984): 14–16. Willard Sterne Randall mentions the killings in *A Little Revenge: Benjamin Franklin and His Son* (Boston, 1984), 190–91, as does Sheila L. Skemp, *William Franklin: Son of a Patriot, Servant of a King* (New York, 1990), 102–4, who puts Franklin's response in the context of his western-lands speculation.

54. Skemp, *William Franklin*, 104–5.

55. *Pennsylvania Gazette*, fol. 3, item 1274, August 7, 1766; item 2240, January 1, 1767; Vaughan, "Frontier Banditti," 14–17; W. Franklin to the earl of Shelburne, Burlington, N.J., December 23, 1766, in William A. Whitehead, ed., *Documents Relating to*

the Colonial History of the State of New Jersey (Newark, 1880–86), 9:578–79; William Franklin to Benjamin Franklin, [July 13, 1766], in Leonard W. Labaree and Whitfield J. Bell Jr., eds., *The Papers of Benjamin Franklin* (New Haven, 1959–), 13: 333 and editors' note; Samuel Wharton, George Morgan, and John Baynton to William Johnson, December 28, 1766, CISHL 11:464–66; "Papers Relative to the Murder of an Oneida Indian . . ." April 3–15, 1766, New Jersey Council Proceedings, November 8–December 11, 1766, *WJP* 5:169–72, 418–21; W. Franklin to Johnson, April 15, 1766, and Gage to Johnson and Johnson to the magistrates of Minisink, September 8, 1766, *WJP* 12:72–73, 134, 170; Johnson to Lords of Trade, August 8, 1766, *NYCD* 7:852.

56. William Franklin to William Johnson, April 15, 1766, *WJP* 12:73. Johnson, Croghan, and Franklin were at this very time active participants in western speculation; see Alvord, *Mississippi Valley in British Politics*, 1:320, 2: 67, 142; Croghan to Johnson, March 30, 1766, and Johnson to Benjamin Franklin, July 18, 1766, *WJP* 5:128, 336; Johnson to William Franklin, June 20, 1766, *WJP* 12:107.

57. His condemnation of such murder is in James Smith, *An Account of the Remarkable Occurrences in the Life and Travels of Col. James Smith during his Captivity with the Indians, in the Years 1755, '56, '57, '58, and '59*, ed. William M. Darlington (Cincinnati, 1870), 50, 160. For the Black Boys' mistaken identification with the Paxton Boys, see Francis Parkman, *The Conspiracy of Pontiac*, 3:151; John Penn to William Johnson, March 21, 1765; Nathaniel McCullough to George Croghan, March 12, 1765; John Watts to Johnson, March 26, 1764; and William Johnson to Tomas Gage, April 3, 1765, *WJP* 11:636, 644–45, 663–64, 664–65. For Smith's mission: James Smith to Israel Ludlow, December 21, 1801, in Historical and Philosophical Society of Ohio, photocopy in Ethnohistory Archive; Col. James Smith, *A Treatise on the Mode and Manner of Indian War* (1812; Chicago, 1948), 10; Wilbur. S. Nye, *James Smith: Early Cumberland Valley Patriot* (Carlisle, Pa., 1969), 29; Willard Rouse Jillson, *A Bibliography of the Life and Writings of Col. James Smith* (Frankfort, Ky., 1947), 23–24.

58. "Petition from the Inhabitants of the Great Cove," in Votes of Assembly, *Pennsylvania Archives*, 8th ser., 6:5437–38.

59. Testimony of Elias Davidson before James Maxwell, justice of the peace for Cumberland County, March 11, 1765, and deposition of Herman Alick, March 11, 1765, Gage Papers.

60. Deposition of Herman Alick, March 11, 1765; Lieut. Grant to Bouquet (copy), March 9, 1765; and Lt. Col. John Reid to Gage, June 4, 1765, Gage Papers; John Armstrong to John Penn, November 21, 1763, *Pennsylvania Archives*, 1st ser., 4:138; Votes of Assembly, *Pennsylvania Archives* 8th ser., 6:5437, 5440; Johnson to Lords of Trade, May 24, 1765, CISHL 10:509; Croghan to Johnson, March 12, 1765; Nathaniel McCullogh to George Croghan, March 12, 1765; and John Penn to Johnson, March 21, 1765, *WJP*, 11:634, 635, 643; John Penn to Gage, March 22, 1765, Gage Papers.

61. Wharton to his partners, March 19, 1765, Ayer MSS, Newberry Library, Chicago; Croghan to Gage, March 12, 1765; Bouquet to Gage, March 29, 1765; and Croghan to Gage, May 12, 1765, Gage Papers; Gage to Johnson, April 15, 1765, and Johnson to Gage, April 27, 1765, *WJP* 4:718, 732; Penn to Johnson, March 21, 1765; Johnson to Penn, April 3, 1765; Johnson to Croghan, April 8, 1765; Johnson to Gage, April 27,

1765; Johnson to Penn, June 7, 1765; and Croghan to Johnson, December 21, 1765, *WJP* 11:644–45, 666, 681, 704, 767–77, 968; Johnson to Lords of Trade, July 1765, CISHL 10:522–23.

62. Affidavit of Richard Brownson, April 3, 1765, Gage Papers.

63. Grant to Bouquet (copy), March 9, 1765; Thomas Barnsely to Gage, Carlisle, March 11, 1765; John Reid to Gage, June 4, 1765, June 7, 1765, and June 9, 1765, Gage Papers; "Extract of a Letter from Lt. Colonel Reid to General Gage," June 1, 1765, and another, June 4, 1765; memorandum, January 15, 1766; Penn to Gage, February 10, 1766; and Council Minutes, March 6, 1766, *Pennsylvania Colonial Records*, 9:268–70; 293; 302–3; copies of passes given by William and James Smith, 1765; deposition of Lt. Charles Grant, 1765; and warrant to arrest Leonard McGlasken, 1765, *Pennsylvania Archives*, 1st ser., 4:219–22, 224.

64. Smith, *Remarkable Occurrences*, 106; Lt. Charles Grant to Gage, April 25, 1765, Gage Papers; extract, Lt. Charles Grant to Col. John Reid, November 22, 1765, and extract, Capt. William Grant to Col. John Reid, November 25, 1765, *Pennsylvania Archives*, 1st ser., 4:246–48,

65. Wharton, Bayton, and Morgan to Gage, March 7, 1766; John Penn to Gage, March 6, 1766; and Robert Calender to William Trent, March 2, 1766, Gage Papers; Gage to Conway, May 6, 1766, in Carter, *Correspondence of General Thomas Gage*, 91.

66. The only full-length work on the Black Boys is Neil H. Swanson's imaginative *The First Rebel* (New York, 1937). For renewed fears and the packhorse train, see *Pennsylvania Gazette*, fol. 3, item 7932, August 17, 1769. For the taking of Fort Bedford and the springing of the prisoners, one must rely on Smith's autobiography, which Swanson accepts, as does Sherman Day, *Historical Collections of the State of Pennsylvania* (1843; Port Washington, N.Y., 1969), 121. Corroboration, however, may appear in an act passed by Pennsylvania against the Black Boys, which mentions their having "once broke one of his Majesty's Goals, and rescued thereout Prisoners committed for capital Offences, and since attempted to do the like," for which, see the next paragraph. "An Act for punishing wicked and evil disposed Persons . . . ," *Pennsylvania Gazette*, Supplement, fol. 3, item 9068, March 8, 1770; "Minutes of the Provinicial Council," January 15, 1770, *Pennsylvania Colonial Records* 9:646–47; it is doubtful that this act refers to the Stump affair, almost two years old. Smith had been only just released by this time, and the wording of the act is clearly more concerned with attacks on property than with murdering Indians; it does not mention Indians at all.

67. *Pennsylvania Gazette*, fol. 3, item 8180, September 28, 1769; item 8225, October 5, 1769; item 8396, November 2, 1769; item 8397, November 2, 1769.

68. The Black Boys once merited enough notice to be included without explanation in one of the several decorative drawings accompanying maps in James Truslow Adams, ed., *Atlas of American History* (New York, 1943), 47. No other illustration accompanies that map of Pontiac's War. For the Black Boys as Paxton Boys, see Francis Parkman, *Conspiracy of Pontiac*, chap. 30:293; Peter Marshall, "Imperial Regulation of American Indian Affairs, 1763–1774" (Ph.D. diss., Yale University, 1959), 67; Shy, *Toward Lexington*, 207. The list of persons who rescued Stump and Ironcutter is found in Oyer and Terminer Papers, Cumberland County, Supreme Court Papers, Record Group

33, Pennsylvania State Archives, Harrisburg; I am grateful to Linda A. Reis of the Pennsylvania State Archives for obtaining a copy of the document for me.

69. The document is copied in Col. John Reed to Gage, June 1, 1765, Gage Papers. See also "Advertisement," *Pennsylvania Colonial Records* 9:271; Smith, *Remarkable Occurrences*, 149; "James Smith's Account (1766–1767)," in Samuel Cole Williams, ed., *Early Travels in the Tennessee Country* (Johnson City, Tenn., 1928), 204–7. James Merrell writes that Smith's captivity narrative, with all its apparent respect and affection for his captors, was published only after Smith was "was well out of the woods and Indians, long since removed from Pennsylvania, were solely of antiquarian interest." He adds that Smith never after his captivity served "as a go-between." These two points underestimate James Smith, who published the work after moving to Kentucky (where he also wrote diatribes against the Shakers). Indians were not of solely antiquarian interest to Kentuckians in the 1790s; nor were they so in 1812, when, in the last year of his life, Smith published a tract on how to fight them. In between, Smith spent time as a missionary to the Wyandots. See Merrell, *Into the American Woods*, 94, 165; Nye, *James Smith*, and Jillson, *Bibliography of the Life and Writings of Col. James Smith*.

70. Robert Calendar to William Trent, March 2, 1766, Gage Papers.

CHAPTER 7 Uneasy Conclusions

1. Gage to Halifax, December 13, 1764, CISHL 10:373; Gage to Johnson, December 6, 1764, *WJP* 11:497–98; Gage to Campbell, June 5, 1765, Gage Papers.

2. Witham Marsh to William Johnson, April 2, 1764; Indian Proceedings, April 12, 1765; and Johnson to Lieut. Col. John Vaughan, May 7, 1765, *WJP* 11:119, 708, 716; "Proceedings . . . with the Indians," April 29, 1765; council with Delawares, May 7, 1765; Johnson to Lords of Trade, May 24, 1765; and treaty with Delawares, May 1765, *NYCD* 7:720, 711, 731, 739; Johnson to Capt. William Murray, May 25, 1765, Native American Collection, 631, WCL; Croghan to Gage, May 12, 1765, and William Murray to Gage, May 12, 1765, Gage Papers; George Croghan, "Croghan's Journal, May 15–September 26, 1765," in Reuben Gold Thwaites, ed., *Early Western Travels, 1748–1846* (Cleveland, 1904), 1:252–54; Johnson to Daniel Claus, July 21, 1762, *WJP* 10:474.

3. Indian Council, December 30, 1764; Gage to Johnson, January 18, 1765; and Croghan to Johnson, May 13, 1765, *WJP* 11:515, 540, 737; Gage to Halifax, January 23, 1765, and Johnson to Lords of Trade, May 24, 1765, CISHL 10:420–21, 500–501; Bouquet to Gage, January 25, 1765, *WJP* 4:642. Bouquet to Gage, December 22, 1764, *PCHB*, ser, 21653: 343; Alexander McKee to Bouquet, December 3, 1764; Sharpe to Bouquet, January 11, 1765; condolence with Shawnese, Fort Pitt, February 10, 1766; and William Murray to Gage, February 17, 1766, Gage Papers.

4. Croghan, Meeting with Shawnees, Fort Pitt, May 9, 1765; William Murray to Gage, May 12, 1765; list of prisoners delivered up by Shawnees, May 10, 1765; and Croghan to Gage, May 12, 1765, Gage Papers; Croghan to Johnson, May 12, 1765; Croghan to Johnson, May 13, 1765; "At a Meeting of the Shawanese, Delawares, . . . Fort Pitt," May 9, 1765; and "Journal of Indian Affairs," May 29, 1765, *WJP* 11:723–24, 736, 737–38, 768.

5. George Croghan, minutes of a conference held at Fort Pitt, April and May 1768 (HSP), in Francis Jennings, William N. Fenton, Mary A. Druke, and David R. Miller, *Iroquois Indians: A Documentary History*, 50 microfilm reels (Woodbridge, Conn., 1984), reel 29, Newberry Library, Chicago.

6. Mingos also signed this treaty, but Johnson—who saw these people as members of the Six Nations—demanded that they withdraw from their western homes and return to their "respective Nations [among the Six Nations] to whom they belong[ed]," a promise few kept. "[July 13, 1765], Copy of Articles subscribed to by the Shawanese, Mingoes, &c annexed to the treaty subscribed by the Delawares in May, 1765," in Johnson to Gage, July 25, 1765, Gage Papers.

7. Articles of treaty of peace between English and Delawares, Shawnees and Mingos, July 13, 1765 (HSP), Jennings et al., *Iroquois Indians*, reel 28. For the role of the Six Nations in this treaty, see Michael J. Mullin, "Sir William Johnson's Reliance on the Six Nations at the Conclusion of the Anglo-Indian War of 1763–1765," *American Indian Culture and Research Journal* 17 (1993): 72–74.

8. Johnson to Lords of Trade, July 1765, CISHL 10:522–23.

9. D. Campbell to Bouquet, Detroit, March 10, 1761, in "Aspinwall Papers," 9:400; Croghan to Gage, Fort Pitt, March 2, 1765, Gage Papers; Johnson to Gage, April 3, 1765, CISHL 10:467.

10. Fraser to Gage, Kaskaskia, May 15, 1765, Gage Papers.

11. De Neyon to D'Abbadie, December 1, 1763, CISHL 10:52–55; speech of the Shawnees to Mons. de Neyon, December 21, 1763, Gage Papers.

12. St. Ange to D'Abbadie, August 12, 1764, and St. Ange to D'Abbadie, November 9, 1764, in CISHL 10:295, 354–57; "Intelligence . . . from Kyashuta," May 9, 1765, and Fraser to Gage, March 21, 1765, Gage Papers.

13. Journal of D'Abbadie, December, 1764; "Copy of a Speech made by the Shawnee Indian. . . .", CISHL 10:204, 444; "Discours fait par le sauvage Chawanon," in Stuart to Gage, March 19 1765, Gage Papers.

14. Aubry to Gage, June 21, 1765, Gage Papers; "Speeches made by the Shawnee Chief . . . ," February 24, 1765, and reply of M. Aubry, February 24, 1765, CISHL 10:448, 452–53.

15. Robert Farmar to Gage, June 1, 1765, in Gage Papers, microfilm copy of selected documents at the Ethnohistory Archive.

16. Ross to Farmar, copy, February 21, 1765; Court of Enquiry, Detroit, March 16, 1765; Court of Enquiry, Detroit, February 21, 1765' Campbell to Gage, February 27, 1765; and Fraser to Gage, March 21, 1765, Gage Papers. See editor's note, CISHL 10:487 and the correction in CISHL 11:660.

17. Clarence Walworth Alvord and Clarence Edwin Carter, "Introduction: The British Occupation of the Illinois Country," in CISHL 10:xlix–l; Ross to Major Farmar, March 24, 1765; St. Ange to D'Abbadie, February 21, 1765; St. Ange to D'Abbadie, April 7, 1765; Ross to Farmar, May 25, 1765; and Crawford's statement, July 22, 1765, CISHL 10:441, 442–43, 468–77, 481–83, 483–84; Harry Gordon to Johnson, August 10, 1765, *WJP* 11:881; Fraser to Gage, April 27, 1765, Gage Papers.

18. Bouquet to Gage, February 22, 1765; Fraser to Gage, March 4, 1765; Fraser to

Gage, March 21, 1765; and Croghan to Gage, March 22, 1765, Gage Papers; Gage to Bouquet, December 30, 1764, CISHL 10:395.

19. This and the foregoing paragraphs are based on Fraser to Gage, April 27, 1765, May 15, 1765, Gage Papers. On Massac (sometimes rendered Massiac), see C. J. Balesi, *The Time of the French in the Heart of North America*, rev. ed. (Chicago, 1991), 270.

20. Gage to Johnson, June 17, 1765; Johnson to Gage, June 19, 1765; Gage to Johnson, June 22, 1765; Johnson to Campbell, June 26, 1765; and Indian Journal, ca. June 26, 1765, *WJP* 11:795, 798, 803–4, 810–11, 818; intelligence received from Neoland, July 15, 1765; intelligence received from White Mingo, July 21, 1765; and Reid to Gage, July 24, 1765, Gage Papers; *Pennsylvania Gazette*, fol. 2, item 23583, June 27, 1765; item 23871, August 8, 1765; item 23897, August 15, 1765.

21. Fraser to Gage, May 15, 1765; Fraser to Campbell, May 17, 1765; and Fraser to Campbell, May 20, 1765, CISHL 10:492, 493, 495–97; Fraser to Gage, May 18, 1765, Gage Papers, also in *WJP* 11:743.

22. Fraser to Campbell, May 17, 1765, and Fraser to Gage, May 18, 1765, CISHL 10:494, 495; Fraser to Johnson, May 18, 1765, and Gage to Johnson, August 12, 1765, *WJP* 11:743, 882–83.

23. Fraser to Johnson, May 18, 1765, *WJP* 11:743; Fraser to Gage, May 18, 1765; Fraser to Gage, May 26, 1765; Robert Famar to Gage, May 31, 1765; and Fraser to Farmar enclosed in Reid to Gage, Aug, 2, 1765, Gage Papers; Fraser to Campbell, May 20, 1765, CISHL 10:496.

24. John Richard Alden, *John Stuart and the Southern Colonial Frontier: A Study of Indian Relations, War, Trade, and Land Problems in the Southern Wilderness, 1754–1775* (Ann Arbor, Mich., 1944), 203; Sinnott to Gage, March 2, 1765; copy of J. Capucin to Baptiste Campeau, June 7, 1765; copy of Sinnott to Croghan, June 14, 1765; and Croghan to Gage, August 17, 1765, Gage Papers.

25. Gage to Reid, August 13, 1765, and Gage to Johnson, August 12, 1765, *WJP* 11:882–83; James Campbell to Gage, August 16, 1765, Gage Papers.

26. Croghan, "Croghan's Journal, May 15–September 26, 1765," in Thwaites, *Early Western Travels*, 1:133, 136, 138–39, 141–46; Croghan to Johnson, July 12, 1765, and George Croghan to Alexander McKee, July 13, 1765, *WJP* 11:837–38, 846; Croghan to William Murray, July 12, 1765, Gage Papers.

27. Gage to Johnson, December 26, 1763, January 12, 1764, and January 23, 1764, *WJP* 4:279–80, 296, 304.

28. Croghan, "Croghan's Journal, May 15–September 26, 1765," in Thwaites, *Early Western Travels*, 1:171.

29. Stuart to John Pownall, January 24, 1764, CO 5/66, fol. 343; Stuart to Johnson, April 12, 1764, abstract, Richard E. Day, *Calendar of the Sir William Johnson Manuscripts; New York State Library History Bulletin* 8 (Albany, 1909), 217; South Carolina General Assembly Minutes, August 24, 1764, August 25, 1764, CO 5/482, fol. 131b–136; Gage to Halifax, July 13, 1764, CISHL 10:282; Gage to Stuart, August 10, 1764, Gage Papers.

30. Alexander Cameron to John Stuart, February 3, 1765, CO 323/23, fol. 234; Croghan to Gage, April 26 and June 3, 1765, Gage Papers; *Pennsylvania Gazette*, fol. 2, item 23116, April 25, 1765.

31. Croghan, "Croghan's Journal, May 15–September 26, 1765," in Thwaites, *Early Western Travels*, 1:145–46; John Campbell to Gage, July 15, 1765, and Reid to Gage, Pitt, August 11, 1765, Gage Papers; Alexander McKee to Johnson, Fort Pitt, August 12, 1765, *WJP* 11:884; Richard Shuckburgh to Johnson, July 14, 1765, CISHL 10:520–21.

32. Croghan to Johnson, July 12, 1765, *WJP* 11:839

33. Croghan, "Croghan's Journal, May 15–September 26, 1765," in Thwaites, *Early Western Travels*, 1:146–48; Croghan to Johnson, August 17, 1765, *WJP* 11:899–901.

34. Croghan, "Croghan's Journal, May 15–September 26, 1765," in Thwaites, *Early Western Travels*, 1:150–52; Croghan to Alexander McKee, Miami, August 3, 1765, Gage Papers.

35. Croghan, "Croghan's Journal, May 15–September 26, 1765," in Thwaites, *Early Western Travels*, 1:154–56.

36. John Campbell to Gage, Detroit, August 25, 1765, Gage Papers; Croghan, "Croghan's Journal, May 15–September 26, 1765," in Thwaites, *Early Western Travels*, 1:156–59.

37. Croghan, "Croghan's Journal, May 15–September 26, 1765," in Thwaites, *Early Western Travels*, 1:159–60.

38. George C. Anthon, deed, September 17, 1765, in Anthon Family Papers, BHC. Copies of deeds Lt. Abbot, September 17, 1765, and Alexis Maisonville, September 18, 1765 (in French), marked (apparently) by Oquichioinon and Pontiac, in Labadie Family Papers, BHC.

39. Croghan to Johnson, August 17, 1765, and Campbell to Johnson, September 16, 1765, *WJP* 11:899–901, 938; Campbell to Gage, September 11, 1765, Gage Papers.

40. Croghan, "Croghan's Journal, May 15–September 26, 1765," in Thwaites, *Early Western Travels*, 1:161–62; Croghan to Johnson, November 1765, in Thwaites, *Early Western Travels*, 1: 170–72.

41. Reid to Gage, August 24, 1765; Sterling to Gage, December 15, 1765; and Fraser to Gage, December 16, 1765, Gage Papers; Gage to Johnson, December 30, 1765, *WJP* 11:988.

42. Farmar to Gage, August 12, 1765; Farmar to Gage, December 19, 1765; and Stuart to Gage, January 21, 1766, Gage Papers; Stuart to Johnson, March 30, 1765, *WJP* 12:54–55.

43. Farmar to Gage, December 19, 1765, and Frazier to Gage, December 16, 1765, Gage Papers; Gage to Johnson, February 10, 1766, *WJP* 12:25–26.

44. Sterling to Gage, December 15, 1765; Croghan to Gage, August 17, 1765; and Fraser to Gage, December 16, 1765, Gage Papers; Jack Sosin, *Whitehall and the Wilderness: The Middle West in British Colonial Policy, 1760–1775* (Lincoln, Nebr., 1961), 235.

45. Gage to Johnson, February 10, 1766, *WJP* 12:16.

46. Fred Anderson, *The Crucible of War: The Seven Years' War and the Fate of Empire in British North America, 1754–1766* (New York, 2000), 566, 568, 569, 740.

47. Lords of Trade to Johnson, September 29, 1763, *NYCD* 7:567.

48. Woody Holton, *Forced Founders: Indians, Debtors, Slaves and the Making of the American Revolution in Virginia* (Chapel Hill, N.C., 1999), 5, 13–38.

49. Richard White, *The Middle Ground: Indians, Empires, and Republics in the Great*

Lakes Region, 1650–1815 (New York, 1991), 314, observes that the emerging British relationship with Great Lakes Indians "was the French system reborn, but . . . a Frankenstein monster," with a "missing soul." Fred Anderson, in a chapter titled "The Lessons of Pontiac's War," agrees that the British never equaled their French predecessors as successful mediators, but that, he argues, could not have been known in 1765; see his *Crucible of War*, 633–37. Other historians emphasize a degree of imperial responsibility toward Indians. See Edward Countryman, "Indians, the Colonial Order, and the Social Significance of the American Revolution," *WMQ* 53 (1996): 342–62, esp. 354; Countryman, *Americans: A Collision of Histories* (New York, 1996), 57–58; Eric Hinderaker, *Elusive Empires: Constructing Colonialism in the Ohio Valley* (New York, 1997), 185 and passim; Russell Snapp, *John Stuart and the Struggle for Empire on the Southern Frontier* (Baton Rouge, La.,, 1996), 3–4.

50. Clarence Alvord, *The Mississippi Valley in British Politics: A Study of the Trade, Land Speculation, and Experiments in Imperialism Culminating in the American Revolution*, 2 vols. (Cleveland, 1917), 1:345–47, 358; Sosin, *Whitehall and the Wilderness*, 138–63.

51. Lord Barrington to Gage, October 10, 1765, quoted in Peter Marshall, "Imperial Regulation of American Indian Affairs, 1763–1774" (Ph.D. diss., Yale University, 1959), 118, 119–20; report on the forts in North America, enclosed in Gage to Barrington, December 18, 1765, in Clarence Carter, *Correspondence of General Thomas Gage*, (New Haven, 1933), 2:321.

52. Bernard Baylin, with Barbara De Wolfe, assist., *Voyagers to the West: A Passage in the Peopling of America on the Eve of the Revolution* (New York, 1986), 1–28, esp. 26, finds that between 1760 and 1775, the number of immigrants (including slaves) to North America formed close to 10 percent of the total colonial population in 1775. They came at a rate "triple the average of the years before 1760." For British efforts to drive off squatters, see Sosin, *Whitehall and the Wilderness*, 108–9; John Penn to Gage, December 7, 1767, *Pennsylvania Colonial Records* 9:403; White, *Middle Ground*, 319–20; Solon J. Buck and Elizabeth Hawthorn Buck, *The Planting of Civilization in Western Pennsylvania* (Pittsburgh, 1939), 142; Johnson to Gage, July 11, 1767, and Gage to Shelburne, August 24, 1767, CISHL 11:582, 595; John Shy, *Toward Lexington: The Role of the British Army in the Coming of the American Revolution* (Princeton, N.J., 1965), 228–29.

53. Robert Farmar to Gage, March 18, 1766, and Captain Gordon Forbes to Gage, April 15, 1768, Gage Papers; Gage to Hillsborough, June 18, 1768, CISHL 16:321–22, and editor's note 1, on 322.

54. Capt. James Campbell to Gage, April 23, 1768, Gage Papers; Max Savelle, *George Morgan: Colony Builder* (New York, 1932), 51–54.

55. Benjamin Roberts to Fred. Christopher Spiesmacher, August 20, 1767, *WJP* 5:629; Frederick Christopher Spiesmacher to Johnson, February 25, 1768, and Jehu Hay to Johnson, April 25, 1768, *WJP* 12:449, 479–80; Capt. Spiesmacher to Gage, May 26, 1768, Gage Papers. For the trial of Rogers, see David Armour, ed., *Treason? at Michilimackinac: The Proceedings of a General Court Martial Held at Montreal in October 1768 for the Trial of Major Robert Rogers* (Mackinac Island, Mich., 1967); William R. Nester, *"Haughty Conquerors": Amherst and the Great Indian Uprising of 1763* (Westport, Conn., 2000), 129, 261–62.

56. Randolph C. Downes, *Council Fires on the Upper Ohio* (Pittsburgh, 1940), 154–68; Marshall, "Imperial Regulation," 251–54; Buck and Buck, *Planting of Civilization in Western Pennsylvania*, 143–44, 163–67.

57. Marshall, "Imperial Regulation," 36; Johnson to Gage, July 11, 1767, and Gage to Shelburne, August 24, 1767, CISHL 11:582, 595; Shy, *Toward Lexington*, 112, 228–229, 238, 328 (maps), and throughout; Alvord, *Mississppi Valley in British Politics*, 2:44, 52–53; Jack Sosin, *The Revolutionary Frontier, 1763–1783* (New York, 1967), 15; transcribed extract from *Pennsylvania Chronicle*, November 14, 1772, in Draper MSS, 13 J 158.

58. Gage to Johnson, October 14, 1764, *WJP* 11:376; "Plan for the future Management of Indian Affairs," enclosed in Lords of Trade to Johnson, July 10, 1764, and enclosure, October 8, 1764, *NYCD* 7:637–41, 657–667; Lords of Trade to Johnson, August 5, 1763, and William Johnson on the organization of the Indian department, October 1764, CISHL 10:274, 328. See also William Franklin, "Remarks on the Plan for the Future Management of Indian Affairs," October 27, 1764, in CO 323/20, fol. 59; Marshall, "Imperial Regulation," 54–55; "Extracts of Orders Given by . . . Gage" January 17, 1765, Gage Papers. The Southern District had no posts among the major Indian nations except Fort Prince George on the eastern edge of the Cherokee Nation. There, specific towns were fixed for the traders' residences. See John Stuart to Johnson, March 30, 1766, *WJP* 12:55–56.

59. Johnson to Cadwallader Colden, June 9, 1764, *WJP* 4:443; William Johnson on the organization of the Indian department, October 1764, CISHL 10:328.

60. Johnson to William Howard, July 2, 1765, and Johnson to Gage, August 28, 1765, *WJP* 11:815, 915; Alexander Henry, *Alexander Henry's Travels and Adventures in the Years 1760–1776*, ed. Milo Milton Quaife (Chicago, 1922), 192–93; Sosin, *Revolutionary Frontier*, 12; William L. Clements, ed., "Rogers' Michilimackinac Journal," in *American Antiquarian Society Proceedings* 28 (1918): 53; message from a Delaware chief, extract, September 24, 1766, and Johnson to Lords of Trade, January 15, 1767, *NYCD* 7:895; Guy Carleton to Johnson, March 27, 1767; Henry Van Schaak and other traders to Jehu Hay, September 4, 1767; and Gage to Johnson, October 20, 1766, *WJP* 5:381, 399–400, 521–22, 654. Marshall, "Imperial Regulation," 53, 72, 105, 106, 115.

61. Howard Peckham, ed., *George Croghan's Journal of His Trip to Detroit in 1767* (Ann Arbor, Mich., 1939), 32, 37.

62. "Report from the English Board of Trade and Plantations to the King of England, concerning Indian war in North America," March 1768, CO 5/6, fols. 60–88, Jennings et al., *Iroquois Indians*, reel 29.

63. Hillsborough to Gage, July 15, 1769, CO 5/87, fol. 119.

64. Alvord, *Mississippi Valley in British Politics*, 2:32, 61.

65. Ibid., 1:94–95, 244, 315–16; Sosin, *Whitehall and the Wilderness*, 72, 105–6, 112; "General Bradstreet's Statement upon Indian Affairs," December 17, 1765, in Franklin B. Hough, ed., *Diary of the Siege of Detroit in the War with Pontiac. Also a Narrative of the Principal Events of the Siege, by Major Robert Rogers; A Plan for Conducting Indian Affairs, by Colonel Bradstreet; and other Authentic Documents, Never Before Printed* (Albany, 1860), 156–57, facsimile at the Newberry Library; Merrill Jensen, *The Founding of a Nation: A*

History of the American Revolution, 1763–1776 (New York, 1968), 384; Holton, *Forced Founders*, 71–73; Thomas Perkins Abernathy, *Western Lands and the American Revolution* (New York, 1937), 4–13.

66. Johnson to Secretary Conway, June 28, 1766, *NYCD* 7:835–36.

67. Laurence Hauptman, *Conspiracy of Interests: Iroquois Dispossession and the Rise of New York State* (Syracuse, N.Y., 1999), 131; "Articles of Peace between Sir William Johnson and the Genessee Indians," August 6, 1764, *NYCD* 7:652–53; Eric Hinderaker puts it well: "Private temptations were too great for Johnson to resist (as they were also for his assistant, George Croghan)"; see *Elusive Empires*: 163; "Intelligence received from Kyashuta," May 9, 1765, Gage Papers; Holton, *Forced Founders*, 10.

68. Johnson to Gage, April 5, 1766, Gage Papers; Alvord, *Mississippi Valley in British Politics*, 2:23.

69. James Merrell, *Into the American Woods*, 291; Merrell writes, "No one was more enamored of Indian lands than George Croghan" (295). Anderson says that "at the 1768 Fort Stanwix sweepstakes and land lottery, he was among the biggest winners, making off with more than 100,000 acres," in *Crucible of War*, 30, 327.

70. Abernathy, *Western Lands*, 22–25; Jensen, *Founding of a Nation*, 233–34.

71. Gage to Farmar, April 14, 1766, Gage Papers; Croghan to Johnson, March 30, 1766, *WJP* 5:128.

72. Croghan to Johnson, March 30, 1766; Johnson, "Advantages of an Illinois Colony," enclosed in Johnson to Henry Seymour Conway, July 10, 1766; and Johnson to Benjamin Franklin, July 18, 1766, *WJP* 5:128, 319–28, 336; Croghan to Lords of Trade, June 8, 1764, CISHL 10:260–61; Savelle, *George Morgan*, 57–58; Jensen, *Founding of a Nation*, 233–34; Alvord, *Mississippi Valley in British Politics*, 1:345–53.

73. Croghan to Franklin, February 25, 1766, *WJP* 5:37–38; Alvord, *Mississippi Valley in British Politics*, 1:354–55, 2:67; Abernathy, *Western Lands*, 31–33; Jensen, *Founding of a Nation*, 233–36; Savelle, *George Morgan*, 59.

74. Marshall, "Imperial Regulation," 246; Sosin, *Whitehall and the Wilderness*, 181–92, 200–207.

75. Marshall, "Imperial Regulation," 262; Sosin, *Whitehall and the Wilderness*, 209–10; Abernathy, *Western Lands*, 45–57.

76. John Stuart to the Board of Trade, Charleston, September 23, 1766, CO 5/67, fol. 179, in *Westward Expansion*, reel 4:565; John Stuart's abstracts of letters from David Taitt, commissary to the Creeks, Hickory Ground, October 25, 1773, and Stuart to Dartmouth, October 6, 1774, Savannah, CO 5/75, fols. 38, 459; Stuart to Lord George Germain, September 15, 1777, CO 5/79, fols. 13–16, in *Westward Expansion*, reel 7:21, 194, 721–23; Edward J. Cashin, *Lachlan McGillivray, Indian Trader: The Shaping of the Southern Colonial Frontier* (Athens, Ga., 1992), 258–63; Claudio Saunt, *A New Order of Things: Property, Power, and the Transformation of the Creek Indians* (New York, 2000), 67.

77. Land: John Stuart to the Board of Trade, Charleston, September 23, 1766, CO 5/67, fol. 179, in *Westward Expansion*, reel 4: 565. War: Stuart to Shelburne, Charleston, May 7, 1768, CO 5/69, fols. 381–86, in *Westward Expansion*, reel 5:76–81; David Taitt to Stuart Little Tallassies, January 3 and 12, 1774 (abstracts), and James Wright to John

Stuart, Savannah, January 27, 1774, CO 5/75, fol. 104; abstract of a letter from His Excellency Josiah Martin Governor of North Carolina, New Bern, July 21, 1774; Stuart to Dartmouth, *Savannah*, October 6, 1774; and Charles Stuart to John Stuart, Mobile, December 12, 1774, CO 5/75, fols. 89, 93, 389, 459, CO 5/76, fols. 69–73, in *Westward Expansion*, reel 7:33, 37, 47, 159, 194, 220–21.

78. See Chapter 5 for criticisms of Bradstreet's performance. For his expenses, see Johnson to Cadwallader Colden, October 10, 1763, *WJP* 4:273. For provincials, see William Pencak, "Warfare and Political Change in Mid-Eighteenth-Century Massachusetts," in Peter Marshall and Glyn Williams, eds., *The British Atlantic Empire before the American Revolution* (London, 1980), 65; Shy, *Toward Lexington*, 135, 174–81. For complaints about the colonists' unwillingness to pay for their own defense, see Gage to Johnson, June 3, 1764, *WJP* 4:439; Gage to Bradstreet, July 15, 1764, and Gage to Bouquet, December 20, 1764, CISHL 10:288, 380.

79. Francis Jennings makes this argument in his *Empire of Fortune: Crowns, Colonies, and Tribes in the Seven Years' War in America* (New York, 1988), 460. See also Bernard Knollenberg, *Origin of the American Revolution, 1759–1766* (New York, 1960), 93–94, 319 n. 22.

80. Pencak,"Warfare and Political Change," 51–73; John M. Murrin, "The French and Indian War, the American Revolution, and the Counterfactual Hypothesis: Reflections on Lawrence Henry Gipson and John Shy," *Reviews in American History* 1(1973): 307–18; Jack Greene, "'A Posture of Hostility': A Reconsideration of Some Aspects of the Origins of the American Revolution," *Proceedings of the American Antiquarian Society* 87 (1977): 27–68; Knollenberg, *Origin of the American Revolution*, 122, 124.

81. John M. Murrin, "A Roof without Walls: The Dilemma of American National Identity," in Richard Beeman, Stephen Botein, and Edward Carter II, eds., *Beyond Confederation: Origins of the Constitution and American National Identity* (Chapel Hill, N.C., 1987), 340.

CHAPTER 8 Deaths and Legacies

1. Harry Gordon to Mr. Thornton, May 20, 1766, BHC; Gage to Johnson, March 9, 1766, CISHL 11:178–79; Johnson to Croghan, March 28, 1766, *WJP* 5:119–20; Gage to Johnson, April 20, 1766; Croghan to Gage, April 20, 1766; and Gage to Croghan, April 24, 1766, Gage Papers; Gage to Johnson, February 10, 1766; Gage to Johnson, April 7, 1766; and Johnson to Gage, June 27, 1766, *WJP* 12:15–15, 67, 116–17.

2. Edward Cole to Johnson, June 23, 1766, *WJP* 5:278–79; Howard Peckham, *Pontiac and the Indian Uprising* (1947; New York, 1970), 289; "Journal" in John Wilkins to Gage, June 1, 1772, Gage Papers (this uncataloged item can be found in volume 138).

3. Croghan to Johnson, March 26, 1766, *WJP* 5:108; Rogers to Johnson, June 28, 1766, and Thomas Morris to Johnson, July 1, 1766, *WJP* 12:120, 128. The *Victory* had been deemed unseaworthy the previous year, but carpenters had kept it sailing until it burned to the waterline in an accidental fire in the fall. Lieutenant Colonel John Vaughan to Gage, August 31, 1765, Gage Papers; Lieutenant Benjamin Roberts to Johnson, December 3, 1766, Native American Collection, WCL.

4. Croghan to Gage, June 17, 1766, Ayer MSS, Newberry Library, Chicago; Johnson to Gage, June 27, 1766, *WJP* 12:116–17; Johnson to Gage, July 4, 1766, and Gage to Johnson, August 18, 1766, *WJP* 5:303, 346.

5. Proceedings, July 23–July 31, 1766, *NYCD* 7:854–56; a draft of the proceedings from the Canadian Archives and the formal copy from the British Public Record Office (Kew, England) are photo-reproduced in Francis Jennings, William N. Fenton, Mary A. Druke, and David R. Miller, *Iroquois Indians: A Documentary History*, 50 microfilm reels (Woodbridge, Conn., 1984), reel 28, Newberry Library, Chicago.

6. Over a beer at McCormick and Schmick, Chestnut and Rush Streets, Chicago, Helen Hornbeck Tanner suggested to me in 1999 that the Anishinabeg accorded Wyandots a sense of honor and precedence, though not leadership. For Johnson's dependence on the Six Nations and for a slightly different interpretation of Teata's role, see Michael J. Mullin, "Sir William Johnson's Reliance on the Six Nations at the Conclusion of the Anglo-Indian War of 1763–65," *American Indian Culture and Research Journal* 17 (1993): 79–82.

7. *NYCD* 7:857–58, 860–61.

8. Ibid., 861–67.

9. Ibid., 858, 861, 866–67.

10. Johnson to Gage, August 8, 1766, *WJP* 12:152; abstract of a dispatch from Sir William Johnson to Lords of Trade, August 20, 1766, Shelburne Papers, WCL.

11. Norman MacLeod to Johnson, August 4, 1766, *WJP* 12:150.

12. George Turnbull, examination of John Maiet, August 4, 1767, Gage Papers; Jehu Hay to George Croghan, August 28, 1767, Norman MacLeod to Johnson, October 8, 1767, *WJP* 5:644, 723.

13. Peckham calls him "Maiet"; White calls him "Maret." My reading of the difficult documents suggests Maiet, but one "Jean Morad" was reported to have wintered with the St. Joseph Potatwatomis in the winter of 1767–68, the same time this man was said to have gone among them. Thus Richard White's "Maret" may be correct. White, *Middle Ground*, 299 n. 58; Peckham, *Pontiac and the Indian Uprising*, 301–2.

14. George Turnbull, examination of John Maiet, Frenchman, August 4, 1767, Gage Papers.

15. Ibid; Jehu Hay to George Croghan, August 28, 1767, *WJP* 5:644.

16. Jehu Hay to George Croghan, August 22, 1767, *WJP* 5:637–38.

17. Jehu Hay's Journal of Indian Transactions, September 3, September 13, 1767, *WJP* 5:671–72; deposition of Elleopolle Chesne, September 4, 1767, *WJP* 5:652–53.

18. Jehu Hay to Croghan, August 28, 1765; Jehu Hay's Journal of Indian Transactions, September 13, 1767, *WJP* 5:644, 673.

19. Jehu Hay's Journal of Indian Transactions, September 1, 1767; Jehu Hay to Croghan, Detroit, September 21, 1767; and Hay to Croghan, October 15, 1767, *WJP* 5:675, 688, 730; Turnbull to Gage, Detroit, May 12, 1768, and Turnbull to Gage, Detroit, April 25, 1768, Gage Papers.

20. Benjamin Roberts to Johnson, June 23, 1766, *WJP* 5:279; Norman MacLeod to Johnson, August 4, 1766, *WJP* 12:150. Monsieur Philip Dejean's loyalty to the British at Detroit was not questioned. He served as a justice of the peace by 1767, and he joined

with several British and French traders in signing two petitions to have trade restrictions loosened. Oddly enough, the second petition was in French; see *WJP* 5:653, 656, 813.

21. Johnson to John Johnson, January 26, 1767, *WJP* 5:475; Johnson, "Review of Indian Affairs in the Northern District," September, 1767, *NYCD* 7:966; Frederick Christopher Spiesmacher to Johnson, February 25, 1768, *WJP* 12:450.

22. "Reponse de Pondiac a une Parole et un Collier envoyé par Mons. Hay . . . le 10 May, 1768," enclosed in Turnbull to Gage, June 14, 1768, Gage Papers; a complete English translation is in Peckham, *Pontiac and the Indian Uprising*, 306–7.

23. "Mr. Charles Gouin's Account [1824]," *Michigan Pioneer*, vol. 8 (1907), 350; "Mr. Pettier's Account [1825]," *Michigan Pioneer*, vol. 8 (1907), 364; "Mr. Jacques Parent's Account," *Michigan Pioneer*, vol. 8 (1907), 358–59; Peckham, *Pontiac and the Indian Uprising*, 311–16. Peckham comes as close as we probably ever will to correcting earlier accounts and establishing the knowable circumstances of Pontiac's death. But I do suggest a slightly different location.

24. Daniel Bloüin and William Clajon, "Recueil de Pièces . . . contenant ce qui s'est passe de plus intéressant, dans la Colonie Anglais de sa Majesté au pais des Illinois . . . ," certified by Whitehead Hicks, New York, July 8, 1771, 156, 166–67, and "Memoire du Sieur Daniel Bloüin," July 9, 1771, 17, Gage Papers (this item is uncataloged; see volume 138); S. L. Maurin, S.J., to Briand, June 14, 1769, and Gibault to Briand, June 15, 1769, CISHL 16:556; Lt. Col. John Wilkins to Gage, Fort de Chartres, November 12, 1770, and John Wilkins to Gage, June 1, 1772, Gage Papers; *Pennsylvania Gazette*, fol. 3, item 7932, August 17, 1769; Gage to Johnson, August 6, 1769, *WJP* 7:76. The map is in Father Pierre de Charlevoix, *Histoire et description général de la Nouvelle France* (Paris, 1744).

25. Bloüin and Clajon, "Recueil de Pièces," 156, 166–67; S. L. Maurin, S.J., to Briand, June 14, 1769, and Gibault to Briand, June 15, 1769, CISHL 16:556.

26. Lt. Col. John Wilkins to Gage, Fort de Chartres, November 12, 1770, and John Wilkins to Gage, June 1, 1772, 9, 11, 15, 16–17, 29, Gage Papers; Memoire du Sieur Daniel Bloüin, July 9, 1771, 18–19, Gage Papers.

27. Gage to Johnson, July 15, 1768 [but internal evidence says 1769], *WJP* 12:547.

28. Copy of a letter from John Stuart to Lt. Gov. Bull, Charleston, June 1, 1766, CO 5/67, fol. 13.

29. John Stuart to Lt. Gov. Bull, June 1, 1766, and John Stuart to Board of Trade, July 10, 1766, CO 5/67, fols. 13, 45; Alexander Cameron to John Stuart (copy), May 10, 1766, CO 5/66, fol. 398, also extracted in Native American Collection, WCL.

30. Johnson to Gage, March 22, 1766, Gage Papers.

31. Johnson to Gage, February 20, 1766, and Francis Fauquier to Johnson, April 11, 1766, *WJP* 12:21, 68; Gage to Johnson, May 11, 1767, and Stuart to Johnson, November 28, 1767, *WJP* 5:548, 832; Johnson to earl of Shelburne, May 30, 1767, *NYCD* 7:928–30; Johnson to Croghan, March 16, 1768, and Johnson to Gage, January 5, 1770, *WJP* 12:472, 769–70.

32. Gage to Johnson, December 25, 1769, *WJP* 7:319; Memoire du Sieur Daniel Bloüin, July 9, 1771, Gage Papers.

33. Croghan to Gage, Fort Pitt, June 17, 1766, Ayer MSS, Newberry Library, Chicago.

34. Jehu Hay's Journal of Indian Transactions, August to September 1767; Alexander McKee to George Croghan, September 20, 1767; Croghan to Johnson, September 25, 1767; and Croghan to Johnson, October 18, 1767, *WJP* 5:670, 686–87, 701, 737; Croghan to Gage, September 27, 1757; Croghan to Benamin Franklin, October 2, 1767; and journal entry for October 17, 1767, in Howard Peckham, ed., *George Croghan's Journal of His Trip to Detroit in 1767* (Ann Arbor, Mich., 1939), 20–21, 24, 32; Gage to Shelburne, January 22, 1768, CO 5/86, fol. 9.

35. Croghan to Gage, Fort Pitt, May 9, 1768, Gage Papers; Croghan to Gage, September 27, 1767, and Croghan's Journal, entries for November 22 and November 23, 1767, all in Peckham, *Croghan's Journal*, 22, 43–44; Jehu Hay to Croghan, August 28, 1767; Alexander McKee to Croghan, September 20, 1767; and Edward Cole to Johnson, October 25, 1767, *WJP* 5:643–64, 686, 755.

36. Gage to Shelburne, April 7, 1767, CO 5/85, fol. 91; Gage to Shelburne, January 22, 1768, CO 5/86, fol. 9.

37. Gage to Shelburne, January 22, 1768, CO 5/86, fol. 9.

38. For the Stanwix proceedings, see *NYCD* 8:111–34; for the deed, see *NYCD* 8:135–37; Congress at Fort Stanwix, September 15–October 30, 1769, and November 6, 1769, *WJP*12:617–29, provides additional information, especially for the first six weeks of the meeting. For an early critical examination, see Alvord, *Mississippi Valley in British Politics*, 2:69–71. More critical are Randolph C. Downes, *Council Fires on the Upper Ohio: A Narrative of Indian Affairs in the Upper Ohio Valley until 1795* (Pittsburgh, 1940), 143–44, and Jack Sosin, *Whitehall and the Wilderness: The Middle West in British Colonial Policy, 1760–1775* (Lincoln, Nebr., 1961), 181–94, who include Shawnee and other complaints. For Genesee Senecas, see David Zeisberger, "1769 Diary," translated typescript in Miscellaneous File, Ethnohistory Archive, 67; John Armstrong to Joseph Shippen, August 8, 1769, CO 5/87, fol. 161; Croghan to Gage, December 22, 1769, *WJP* 7:315–17.

39. Croghan to Johnson, September 18, 1769, and Journal of Alexander McKee, May 1769, *WJP* 7:182–83, 184–85; Norman MacLeod to Johnson, May 10, 1769, *WJP* 6:750–52.

40. Croghan to Johnson, March 26, 1766, *WJP* 5:109–10; Farmar to Gage, April 24, 1766, Gage Papers.

41. Gage to earl of Hillsborough, February 4, 1769, CO 5/87, fol. 70; Gage to earl of Shelburne, August 24, 1767, CO 5/85, fol. 155; Gage to Shelburne, August 24, 1767, CO 5/85, fol. 155; Gage to Shelburne, January 22, 1768, CO 5/86, fol. 9; Croghan to Gage, Fort Pitt, June 17, 1766, Ayer MSS, Newberry Library, Chicago; Croghan to Johnson, March 26, 1766, and Norman McLeod to Johnson, October 8, 1767, *WJP* 5:109–10, 723; Guy Johnson to Gage, July 5, 1768, *WJP* 12:543–45; Journal of Alexander McKee, enclosed in Croghan to Johnson, September 18, 1769, *WJP* 7:182; Farmar to Gage, April 24, 1766, Gage Papers.

42. David Zeisberger, Diary, July 7, 1775 (translated transcript), *Records of the Moravian Mission among the Indians of North America*, microfilm at the American Philosophi-

cal Society, Philadelphia, reel 8, file 141, 15:3; James Wood, "Journal," in *Revolution on the Upper Ohio*, ed. Rueben Gold Thwaites and Louise Phelps Kellogg (Madison, Wisc., 1908), 44.

43. Henry Stuart to John Stuart, August 25, 1776, in K. G. Davies, ed., *Documents of the American Revolution* (Shannon, Ireland, 1976), 12:202–3; Gregory Evans Dowd, *A Spirited Resistance: The North American Indian Struggle for Unity, 1745–1815* (Baltimore, 1992), 47–48.

44. George Morgan to the Delawares, Philadelphia, July 12, 1778, in Louise Phelps Kellogg, ed., *Frontier Advance on the Upper Ohio, 1778–1779*, State Historical Society of Wisconsin Publications 23 (Madison, 1916), 110–11; see also Kellogg, introduction to *Frontier Advance*, 14–15.

45. Washington to Chevalier de Failly, Lieutenant Colonel, Headquarters, June 13, 1778, in Kellogg, *Frontier Advance*, 90. Six months earlier, the marquis de Lafayette had recommended de Failly to Horatio Gates and Henry Laurens. See Stanley J. Idzerda, *Lafayette in the Age of Revolution: Selected Letters and Papers, 1776–1790* (Ithaca, N.Y., 1977), 1:182–83.

46. Henry Hamilton to Haldimand, Detroit, October 6, 1778, in Michael Shoemaker et al., eds., "Haldimand Papers," *Michigan Pioneer*, vols. 9–11, 19–20 (1886), 9:486.

47. On these expeditions see Downes, *Council Fires on the Upper Ohio*, 228–47; James P. Pate, "The Chickamauga: A Forgotten Segment of Indian Resistance on the Southern Frontier" (Ph.D. diss., University of Mississippi, 1969), 91–102; and Barbara Graymont, *The Iroquois in the American Revolution* (Syracuse, N.Y., 1972), 191–222. McKee to Lernoult, Shawnee village, May 26, 1779; D. Brehan to Haldimand, Detroit, May 28, 1779; Bennett to De Peyster, St. Joseph's, August 9, 1779; and Bennett to De Peyster, September 1, 1779, in "Haldimand Papers," 9:423, 410, 392–93, 395.

48. Haldimand to Henry Clinton, Quebec, January 1780, in Louise Phelps Kellogg, ed., *Frontier Retreat on the Upper Ohio: 1779–1781*, State Historical Society of Wisconsin Publications 24 (Madison, 1917): 122–23; De Peyster to Haldimand, Michilmackinac, August 15, 1778, in "Haldimand Papers," 9:368. In the spring of 1780 a large party of British-allied Potawatomis from the St. Joseph River headed south on a raiding expedition, but most of the warriors turned back on hearing the falsehood that four thousand French troops had garrisoned Vincennes, the Indians' objective. R. David Edmunds, *The Potawatomis: Keepers of the Fire* (Norman, Okla., 1978), 109.

49. Colonel La Balme to M. Chevalier de la Luzerne, Fort Pitt, June 27, 1780, CISHL 5:163–68; Clarence W. Alvord, introduction, CISHL 2:lxxxvix–xcii; "Inhabitants of Cahokia to De La Balme, Sept 21, 1780," CISHL 2:535–53.

50. McKee to Haldimand, Swan Creek, Miami River, November 18, 1794, in "Haldimand Papers," 20: 385; intelligence communicated to Joseph Chew, in ibid., 515.

51. Quoted in and translated by Charles E. A. Gayarré, *History of Louisiana* (1885; New York, 1972), 3:422. Gayarré includes most of the document in his thiry-five-page quotation. A photostat of the document is housed by the Library of Congress, Washington, D.C., with photostats from the Archives of France: Affaires Etrangères, Memoires et Documents, vol. 10, pt. 3, 309–40.

52. James E. Seaver, *A Narrative of the Life of Mrs. Mary Jemison*, fwd. George Abrams (1824; Syracuse, N.Y., 1990), 43–44, 47–48; Dowd, *Spirited Resistance*, 23–46.

53. "Substance of a Talk delivered at La Maiouitinong," May 4, 1807, National Archives Microfilm M222, reel 2: L-1807, National Archives Branch, Philadelphia. Dowd, *Spirited Resistance*, 127–44.

54. Peckham, *Pontiac and the Indian Uprising*, 239; *Pennsylvania Gazette*, fol. 2, item 18772, August 4, 1763; item 18769, August 4, 1763; item 22434, January 17, 1765.

Index

Benevissica, 168

Bernard, Francis, 143

Blackbird, Andrew J., 12

Black Boys. *See* Brave Fellows

Black Dog (Makachinga), 249, 250, 260–61

Black Fly, 221

Bloüin, Daniel, 260, 262

Blyth, William, 201

Board of Trade, 177, 182–83, 234, 239, 240, 241, 247

Bon, James, 215

Bonnair, 238

Bougainville, Louis-Antoine de, 48, 66, 92, 186–87

Bouquet, Henry, 3, 49, 51–52, 65, 69, 71, 76, 78, 79–80, 85, 86, 87, 95, 108, 179, 204; Pontiac's War, 128, 145–46, 155, 156, 157, 158, 162–68, 183, 189, 190, 196, 205, 216, 241

Bowman, John, 268

Braddock, Edward, 29, 43, 45, 46, 50

Braddock's Road, 115, 143

Bradstreet, John, 68, 69, 112, 180, 181, 242, 247; in Pontiac's War, 153–62

Brainerd, David, 39, 99

Brainerd, John, 39–40, 99, 191

Brant, Joseph, 143

Brant, Mary, 149

Brave Fellows (Black Boys, Loyal Volunteers), 203–10; confused with Paxtonians, 209–11

British forces: advantages of in warfare, 117–18, 139–40; and Brave Fellows, 203–13; captives of, 83–88, 165–67; and the Delawares, 33–37, 51–53, 84, 90–91, 186–87; at Detroit, 58–63; discipline among, 66; expansionism of, 78–83; French surrender to, 54–55; gifts to Indians as issue for, 70–75; Indians insulted by, 63–70; Indians serving as agents for, 148; Indian suspicions of, 58–59; and intertribal warfare, 262–64; leaders of, 3; murders of

and by, 191–203; and the Ottawas, 55–56; supplies cut off from, 132–34, 145; and trade with Indians, 27–28, 59, 75–78, 87, 239–41; in wars with French, 44–53. *See also* Covenant Chain, Iroquois-British; Great Britain; Pontiac's War

Brodhead, Daniel, 268

Brown, Enoch, 204–5, 274

Bull, Captain, 82, 152

Bunyan, John, 99

Burd, Fort, 130

Burd, James, 194

Burton, Ralph, 112

Bushy Run, battle of, 145–46

Byrne, Michael, 68

Cadillac, Antoine de La Mothe, Sieur de, 28

Cahokias, 221, 260

Calhoun, Thomas, 129

Callender and Company, 206

Campbell, Donald, 55, 56, 59, 60, 61, 62, 64, 75, 77, 103, 105–6, 120, 121, 123, 132, 135

Campbell, James, 237

Campbell, John, 167, 180, 229, 230–31

Campbell, Robert, 141

Canasatego, 37, 102

canoes, 131–32

Capitulation of Montreal, 54–56, 177

Carden, John, 230

Catawbas, 29

Catholic Indians, unwillingness of to support Pontiac's War, 3, 105, 109–11, 112, 147

Catholicism: introduced to Ottawas, 19–21

Cavendish, Fort. *See* Chartres, Fort de

Cayugas, 153, 194

Céloron de Blainville, Pierre-Joseph, 42–43

Charles II, King, 34

Charlesvoix, Pierre François Xavier de, 16

Rackman, 132

Radin, Paul, 12–13

Raudot, Antoine Denis, 19

Ray, David/Robert, 203

Read, Charles, 197, 199, 203

Riddle, William, 141

Robertson, Archibald, 171

Robertson, Lieutenant, 132

Rockingham, marquis of, 234–35

Roger, 184, 185

Rogers, Robert, 3, 4, 6, 7, 55–56, 59, 63–
    64, 75–76, 100, 138, 237–38, 250

Roman Catholic church. *See* Catholic
    Indians; Catholicism

Ross, John, 221

Royal Proclamation of 1763, 177–79, 190,
    193, 233–34, 235

Rutherford, John, 92

Sagard, Father Gabriel, 16, 19

St. Ange de Bellerive, Louis, 171–72, 218,
    221, 222, 228, 232, 250

Saint-Frédéric, Fort, 43, 44

St. Joseph, Fort, 124, 125, 127, 128, 131

St. Regis Indians, 63

St. Vincent, 159

Sandusky, Fort, 77, 79, 124, 125, 126, 128,
    131, 133

Sauks, 93, 126

Schlosser, Fort, 124, 154, 242

Schlosser, J., 195–96

Schoolcraft, Henry Rowe, 16, 18

Seamor, Robert, 201, 202

Seneca George, 200–201

Senecas, 66, 89, 137; divisions among,
    149, 153–54; and Seneca-Mingo plot,
    105–7. *See also* Genesees

Seven Years' War, 43–53, 76

shamans, 17, 19, 93, 94

Shawnees, 38, 40, 41, 64, 76, 80, 84–85,
    86, 91, 263, 264; Bouquet's campaign
    against, 162–68; Bradstreet's peace
    with, 155–58; British dealings with,
    215–16; and Delawares, 92; French

assistance sought by, 217–19; and the
    Iroquois League, 186; Johnson's offen-
    sive against, 149–53; in Pontiac's War,
    143–44; uniting with other tribes
    against the English, 264–66

Shelburne, Lord, 235, 242, 244

Shelby, Evan, 268

Shickellamy, John, 191

Shingas, 91, 129, 130

Shippen, Edward, 191

Simons, Trent, and Franks, 243

Sinnott, Pierce Acton, 225

Six Nations Iroquois. *See* Iroquois
    League

Slaughter, Samuel, 191

slavery, feared by Indians, 65–66, 78, 82–
    83

smallpox, 23, 35, 94, 190, 211

Smith, James ("Black Boy Jimmy"), 204–
    5, 207, 208–9, 210–11

Smith, Matthew, 196

Smith, William, 205, 207–8

Society of Jesus. *See* Jesuits

sovereignty, as issue between Indians and
    British, 3, 178–79, 185, 216

Spain, French cessions to, 170–71, 173

Squash Cutter, 213

Stamp Act crisis, 233, 235

Standing Turkey, 200

Sterling, James, 70–71, 103, 104, 136

Sterling, Thomas, 231, 232

Stuart, John, 169, 181–82, 200, 226, 245–
    46, 263–64

Stump, Frederick, 201, 204, 210

Sullivan, John, 268

Susquehanna Company, 81, 82

Susquehanna Delawares, 38, 39–41, 47,
    81–82, 144

Susquehannocks, 35, 38, 192

Tahaiadoris, 105, 106–7

Taitt, David, 246

Takay, 118

Tamaqua, 51–52, 82, 129, 164, 165